THE CHURCH, DICTATORSHIPS, AND DEMOCRACY IN LATIN AMERICA

◆

Jeffrey Klaiber, S.J.

ORBIS BOOKS

Maryknoll, New York 10545

The Catholic Foreign Mission Society of America (Maryknoll) recruits and trains people for overseas missionary service. Through Orbis Books, Maryknoll aims to foster the international dialogue that is essential to mission. The books published, however, reflect the opinions of their authors and are not meant to represent the official position of the society.

Copyright © 1998 by Jeffrey Klaiber, S.J.

English translation by the author of the work originally published as *Iglesia, dictaduras y democracia en América Latina* (Lima: Pontifical Catholic University, 1997).

This edition published by Orbis Books, Maryknoll, NY 10545-0308.

Manufactured in the United States of America
Manuscript editing and typesetting by Joan Weber Laflamme

Library of Congress Cataloging-in-Publication Data

Klaiber, Jeffrey L.
    [Iglesia, dictaduras y democracia en América Latina.   English]
    The church, dictatorships, and democracy in Latin America /
Jeffrey Klaiber.
      p. cm.
    Translated by the author.
    Includes bibliographical references (p.   ) and index.
    ISBN 1-57075-199-4 (pbk.)
    1. Latin America—Politics and government—1948-
2. Authoritarianism—Latin America—History.   3. Government,
Resistance to—Latin America—History.   4. Catholic Church—Latin
America—Clergy—Political activity—History.   I. Title.
F1414.2.K5313   1998
322'.1'0980904—dc21   98-34451
                                                 CIP

Contents

INTRODUCTION   1

1. CHURCH, POWER, AND POPULAR LEGITIMACY   3

The Colonial Legacy   3
The Church: Between Tradition and Change   5
The Church: Defender of Democracy   6
The Church: Source of Religious Legitimacy   7
The Power of Symbols   8
Defense of Human Rights   8
Legitimizing the Opposition   9
The Church as Mediator   9
Participatory Spaces   10
Conditions and Limitations   11

2. BRAZIL (1964-1985)   20
The First National Security State

Background: An Independent Church   20
The Brazilian Military Regime   23
The Church (1964-1970): Cautious Legitimization   25
The Church: Target of Repression   27
The Church (1970-1978): Protest and Persecution   29
Arns in São Paulo   30
The Commission of Peace and Justice   31
The Northeast and the Amazon   32
The Native Missionary Council   33
Two Martyrs: Lunkenbein and Burnier   33
The CNBB Confronts the Government   34
The "Abertura" (1978-1985)   36
The Base Communities and Redemocratization   36
The Labor Strikes   38
The Final Stretch   39
The Conservative Shift   39

3. CHILE (1973-1990)   42
The Vicariate of Solidarity and the National Accord

Profile of the Church   43

The Social Christians   44
Silva and Frei   45
Allende (1970-1973)   47
Pinochet's Regime   48
The Church and Pinochet: Four Stages   49
First Stage (1973-1976): Prudence and Caution   50
Second Stage (1976-1982): Persecution and Defense
    of Human Rights   53
The Vicariate of Solidarity   54
Third Stage (1982-1985): Leadership and Democracy   57
Fourth Stage (1985-1990): The National Accord
    and the Legitimization of Democracy   60

4. ARGENTINA (1976-1983)   **66**
The "Dirty War"

The Liberal Oligarchy and Yrigoyen (1880-1930)   67
Catholicism Integralism   67
The Eucharistic Congress of 1934   69
Perón and Peronismo   70
Onganía and Catholic Corporatism   71
Catholic Radicalism   72
Perón and the End of Illusions   73
Military Messianism and Christianity   75
Profile of the Church (1976)   76
The Roots of Conservativism   77
The Official Church: Actions and Omissions   79
The Church Persecuted   81
Angelelli and the Bishops Who Protested   82
Pérez Esquivel and Human Rights   83
The Mothers of Plaza de Mayo   84
The Protestants   85
The Transition: Church and National Community (1981)   86
From the Malvinas/Falklands to Alfonsín   87
Alfonsín and the Trials   88
The Church (1983-1990): Ambiguities   89
Conclusion: Two Churches   90

5. PARAGUAY (1954-1989)   **92**
The Longest Dictatorship

The Church: General Characteristics   94
First Tensions (1954-1970)   95
Confrontation and Hardening of Relations (1970-1976)   96
The Christian Agrarian Leagues   97
Repression and Retreat (1976-1983)   99

Recouping and Prophetic Leadership (1983-1989)   100
The Fall of Stroessner   107

6. URUGUAY (1973-1990)   110
A Long Silence and a Moral Referendum

From Welfare to Repression   110
Bordaberry and the Civilian-Military Regime   111
The Repression   112
The Church: A Profile   112
The Church vis-à-vis the Regime   114
The Transition to Democracy   115
The Church in the Transition   116
SERPAJ and Human Rights   116
The National Referendum   118
The Church: A New Image   119

7. BOLIVIA (1952-1989)   121
Strikes, Coups, and Elections

The Changes in the Church   122
Church, Miners, and Barrientos   123
Banzer (1971-1978)   126
The Justice and Peace Commission   127
The Hunger Strike of 1977-1978   129
Instability on the Way to Democracy (1978-1982)   130
The Return to Democracy and the National Dialogue   134
Paz Estenssoro and the Strikes of 1986 and 1987   136
The Church as Mediator: A General Assessment   139

8. PERU (1980-1995)   141
The Shining Path

From Velasco to Fujimori   143
The Shining Path: Origins and Trajectory   145
The Protestants   148
The Catholic Church: Background   150
Ayacucho (1980-1992)   151
The Jesuits, OAASA, and IPAZ   153
The Attacks against the Church   153
Cajamarca   155
Puno   157
The Jungle   160
The Episcopal Conference, CEAS, and CAAAP   162
Human Rights and the Peace Movement   163
Lima: María Elena Moyano and Michel Azcueta   165
The End of a Long Night   167

9. EL SALVADOR (1980-1992)   168
The Bloodiest Civil War

The Role of the United States   170
The Chronology of the War   171
The Church of Oscar Romero   173
Arturo Rivera y Damas: Mediator   175
The Ambiguities of Dialogue   178
The Kidnapping of Inés Guadalupe de Duarte   181
Humanizing the War   182
From Sesori to the Nunciature (1987)   183
The Church and the National Debate (1988)   184
ARENA and the FMLN   186
The Massacre of the Six Jesuits   187
The Road to Peace   189
Chapultepec: The Final Celebration   191
The Truth Commission and the Amnesty Law   191
The Church and the Peace   192

10. NICARAGUA (1979-1990)   193
Christians and Sandinistas

Background: Liberals, Conservatives, and Marines   194
The Church: Background   196
Two Worlds in Collision   200
First Stage: The Hardening of Positions (1979-1982)   201
Second Stage: The Sharpening of Tensions (1982-1986)   205
Third Stage: The Search for a Modus Vivendi (1986-1990)   208
A Looking Back   215

11. GUATEMALA (1954-1996)   216
The Longest Civil War

Political Background   217
The Church: From Persecution to Reconstruction (1871-1964)   222
Toward an Indian Church   223
The Church Awakens   227
The Dialogue for Peace   229
The Government and the URNG: A Forced March   236

12. MEXICO   239
The PRI and Chiapas

The PRI: A Bureaucratic-Authoritarian Party   240
The Church: From Persecution to Mutual Toleration   242
The Big Debate: Who Legitimates Whom?   246
The New Law   249

Chiapas: The Background of an Uprising   250
The EZLN and the Church   252
The Church in Chiapas and Samuel Ruiz   253
The Church and the Popular Struggle   255
"In This Hour of Grace"   256
Samuel Ruiz as Mediator   257
A Controversial Dialogue   258
The Dialogue Falters   261
The Church and Democracy   262

CONCLUSIONS   **263**
Utopias and Topias   269

NOTES   **271**

BIBLIOGRAPHY   **297**

INDEX   **319**

Introduction

The efforts of the Catholic church to defend human rights and promote democracy, especially during the recent military regimes in Latin America, have been widely recognized, at least in academic and church circles. Furthermore, there are several recent works which deal with specific cases—Brian Smith on the Pinochet regime, Emilio Mignone on the "dirty war" in Argentina, Michael Carter on Paraguay, and Phillip Berryman on Central America, among others. These and other studies have been important for writing this book.

Nevertheless, in the midst of these studies something was lacking: an overall composite view. The purpose of this book is, therefore, to present a panoramic view of the role that the church played in the defense of human rights and in promoting democracy from Mexico to Chile during the period of the military dictatorships that ruled a good part of Latin America from the sixties on and which gave way to democratic governments in the eighties and nineties. Furthermore, within this same time frame we will include the different internal wars—whether caused by "traditional" guerrillas or by terrorists—that did not always occur under military dictatorships. In these cases the time frame is established by the dates of each internal war, from the beginning to the end of the peace process, which in some cases took place in the nineties. Each chapter will deal with two fundamental themes: first, the role of the church during the dictatorships or the internal wars; and second, the contribution the church made to the peace process and the return to democracy.

By means of a comparative analysis of eleven different countries we hope to highlight what was common and what was peculiar to each of the countries selected. Among the eleven, we have included those that were under the national security regimes: Brazil, Argentina, Chile, and Uruguay. We will also cover Paraguay under Stroessner and Bolivia since the 1952 revolution up until the 1989 elections. We will then compare three Central American countries that experienced internal wars: Nicaragua, El Salvador, and Guatemala. Not all countries in this book—Mexico and Peru, for example—represent cases of military dictatorships. Mexico is an example of an authoritarian civilian state, and Peru during this period was a democracy that was seriously challenged by terrorist violence in the form of the Shining Path. In the case of Mexico we will examine the role of the church in contributing to the creation of a real democracy from below, with reference to Chiapas. In both cases, Peru and Mexico, the church had an important role in the peace process.

We will not include Ecuador, in part because the church apparently did not play an important role in the redemocratization process. Colombia and Venezuela had already returned to democracy (in 1958 and in 1959, respectively) when the last cycle of military dictatorships swept over Latin America. Given the limitations of time we did not include the Caribbean area. Nevertheless, we will include references to Cuba and Haiti in the bibliography.

In general, the picture is very positive. Even in the case of Argentina, where the hierarchy took a very timid stance during the "dirty war," there was a valiant minority of bishops, priests, religious women, and laypersons who raised the banner of human rights. In this sense this book is not limited to the role of the official church; we will also include the "people of God," that is, base Christians who contributed to this theme. Finally, even though the central theme is the Catholic church, we will mention the role of the different Protestant churches and groups that also contributed to the defense of human rights.

I have visited all the countries that appear in this work. Furthermore, I have had the opportunity to meet personally with some of the protagonists in this history: Arturo Rivera y Damas (El Salvador), Jorge Manrique (Bolivia), Raúl Silva Henríquez (Chile), Ismael Rolón (Paraguay), Juan Landázuri Ricketts (Peru), Paulo Evaristo Arns (São Paulo), Adolfo Pérez Esquivel (Buenos Aires), Luis Pérez Aguirre (Uruguay), among others. In each country I received the help and cooperation of a great number of committed Christians who very often were the primary witnesses of the events narrated in this history.

The members of my own religious order were especially helpful. I wish to thank especially Father Jesús Vergara, S.J., the director of the Tata Vasco Center in Mexico City; Ricardo Bendaña, S.J., in Guatemala; Joe Mulligan, S.J., in Nicaragua; the Jesuits in the Antonio Guasch Center of Paraguayan Studies (CEPAG); the CIAS (Center for Research and Social Action) community in Buenos Aires; and the Jesuit community in the Bellarmine Center in Santiago, Chile. I also wish to express my gratitude to the Jesuits of Georgetown University, who offered me the Jesuit Chair for 1990-91. It was during that year that I conceived the idea of writing this book. In Peru, the country where I have resided for the greater part of the time since 1963, I was a witness to the entire period of terrorism from the beginning until the end, minus my year at Georgetown. Of course I want to thank my many friends in Peru—Jesuits, colleagues at the Catholic University of Peru, students, committed Christians—who have all become my family here.

I hope that this book helps the reader to appreciate, perhaps with greater clarity than before, the fact that the church fulfilled a vital role in the struggle for human rights and the restoration of democracy in Latin America. Indeed, the contemporary political history of Latin America simply could not be written without taking this fact into account.

1.

Church, Power, and Popular Legitimacy

In order to appreciate the role the church played in the process of redemocratizing Latin America and in strengthening the new emergent popular democracy, it would be helpful to refer to Max Weber's concept of "legitimacy." According to Weber, three types of authority have appeared in history, each one based on its own type of legitimacy: traditional, charismatic, and rational authority.[1] It is not necessary to accept all of Weber's ideas to agree with him that all authority is based on some kind of *legitimacy,* which we might define as "the popular consent that undergirds power." It is interesting to note that Weber did not limit the concept of legitimacy to the rational or the legal. This is especially important for studying governments in Latin America that may be legal but lack popular "legitimacy," or, most typical, de facto governments that function outside the normal legal framework.

As historian Peter Smith pointed out, in Latin America two different concepts of legitimacy have co-existed.[2] The last-century caudillos and many twentieth-century dictators incarnated values the "people" considered important or essential for the good of the nation: order, efficiency, and respect for tradition. In Weber's thinking, the caudillos represented both traditional and charismatic authority; with their uniforms, medals, and high-sounding titles they incarnated the paternalistic authoritarianism that was the outstanding note of the colonial period. For their part, the liberals, who wrote the constitutions and the laws, represented a new type of legitimacy: that of modern democracy based on the concept of equality before the law. A good deal of modern Latin American history can be understood as a clash between these two concepts of legitimacy.

THE COLONIAL LEGACY

In the middle of all of this, however, neither the caudillos nor the liberals enjoyed the legitimacy the Catholic church possessed. The church was the

3

only colonial institution that touched the lives of all persons on all levels of society—from the viceroy right down to the Indians in the most remote villages. It is often said that the church legitimated the colonial order. That statement is true, but it is also incomplete. The church also legitimated concepts and persons that escaped political control. To begin with, by not recognizing political power as an absolute end in itself, and certainly not above itself, the church in fact constituted a potentially dangerous civil corporation out of the state's control. Under the concept of royal patronage the church and the state worked together in relative harmony; together they reflected the medieval ideal of Christendom. But even in times of harmony there were abundant conflicts between the two powers: the religious defended the neophyte Indians against the demands of the secular clergy, who, for their part, were generally supported by the secular authorities, while missionary bishops like Toribio de Mogrovejo in Lima and Vasco de Quiroga in Mexico stood out as defenders of the Indians against civilian rulers.

In the eighteenth century the Spanish Bourbons imposed new rules on the game; they replaced benevolent paternalism with absolutism. But it was precisely at that moment in history when the church ceased to be a guaranteed supporter of royal power. Among the ideological leaders who questioned and delegitimized the underpinnings of royal power were many mestizo and creole priests: Miguel Hidalgo and José María Morelos in Mexico, Tomás Ruiz in Central America, Mariano José de Arce in Peru, and Ildefonso Muñecas in Bolivia, among others. In short, although the official church legitimized colonial power, it never identified itself totally with that power, and finally, important groups within the church openly challenged civil authority.

In essence, the church's legitimacy did not come from the state but from religion. This point needs to be stressed in order to avoid any kind of reductionism which would view the church as just another social group. The church was the *only* colonial corporation that could confer religious legitimacy on persons and institutions, and that legitimacy in turn gave those persons and institutions a privileged status. Religion, and the legitimacy that it conferred, gave a special status to Indians, blacks, and the poor, who otherwise would have lived on the margin of society and without any special protection. One small example is sufficient: Martin of Porres, the illegitimate mulatto (his father finally recognized him, but not in the beginning) who entered the Dominican order in Lima toward the end of the sixteenth century. Given his humble origins, colonial society would never have allowed him to advance much up the ecclesiastical ladder, and so it was. He remained all his life a doorkeeper and an infirmarian. Nevertheless, he enjoyed a special legitimacy that only the church could grant: he was held to be saintly, and he was also a member of a prestigious religious order. When he died, the viceroy himself helped carry the coffin of this mulatto religious, no doubt in recognition of his popularity. With this example we can make a generalization: even within a nondemocratic and paternalistic order, the church, and religion in general, offered "spaces" (in religious life, the missions, the lay confraternities, and so on) in which the popular classes could find protection and enjoy a certain social status.

THE CHURCH: BETWEEN TRADITION AND CHANGE

In the eighteenth and nineteenth centuries liberalism emerged as a new and powerful political force, and it constituted a new source of legitimacy. The church, which did not learn to change with the times, lost a measure of its own legitimacy in the eyes of liberals, positivists, and other reformers of advanced thinking. The church symbolized the old colonial order, while liberalism represented modernity and progress. This tension also involved economic interests: the liberals favored the new capitalistic order that competed with the older colonial system. On the other hand, this battle between liberalism and Catholicism was only carried out on the level of the upper and middle classes. As Claudio Véliz observed, the popular classes, immersed as they were in the world of popular religiosity, which combined elements of Catholicism with pre-Columbian beliefs, were unaffected by this ideological confrontation.[3] The caudillos, astute observers of these realities, rose up as spokesmen for the popular classes. In the twentieth century many political leaders also recognized the power of popular symbols and especially those taken from popular religiosity. Zapata in Mexico, Haya de la Torre in Peru, and Eva Perón in Argentina all used religious symbols to legitimize themselves in the eyes of their followers.[4]

Throughout the nineteenth century the church steadily lost influence among the upper classes, and in the twentieth it began losing influence among the popular classes as well. With industrialization, migrations from the country to the city, and an increased level of political consciousness among both peasants and workers, the popular classes soon fell under the influence of the new populist and marxist doctrines. The church came seriously close to finding itself marginalized in the wake of these great changes, which were sweeping over Latin America.

Nevertheless, against all predictions to the contrary, including those of Max Weber himself, the Catholic church changed: it ceased to be a bulwark of the established order and turned into a force for social change.[5] This internal change did not occur overnight. For years, beginning in the twenties, different Catholic Action groups dedicated themselves to the mission of raising the consciousness of the rest of the church on the social doctrine of the popes. The Second Vatican Council gave a great impetus to this process of change and, finally, in the episcopal conference of Medellín (1968) the church broke away from its historical alliances. In Medellín the bishops made a dramatic call to create a new social order based on justice and human rights. With this change the church legitimized many of the ideals of the old liberals—democracy and human rights. At the same time the church also legitimized the war cry of the old populist leaders (Haya de la Torre, Perón, Lázaro Cárdenas) in support of social rights. Most of all, the church legitimized an entire popular movement that had been emerging since the end of the Second World War among the peasants, workers, inhabitants of *barriadas* or *favelas*, and so on. As Charles Reilly put it, through liberation theology and its social and educational pastoral activities, the church in effect legitimized the new popular democracy of Latin America.[6]

But this process was a two-way street: the church legitimized popular democracy, and it in turn received a new legitimacy from the popular classes. As a result, the two concepts of legitimacy became fused together: the older one based on tradition and order, and the new one inspired by the ideas of democracy and human rights. With the support of the renewed church of Medellín the popular classes forged a new identity as Christians, an identity that was an amalgam of values drawn from popular religiosity and the mystique of the popular struggle.

THE CHURCH: DEFENDER OF DEMOCRACY

As a consequence of these changes, the church necessarily realigned itself vis-à-vis political power. During the last cycle of military dictatorships the absence of one of the traditional bastions of the established order—the church—was most striking. The church not only did not support the established order, but it even took a leading role in delegitimizing that order. This change in roles was so striking that in most of Latin America, including Argentina, where the hierarchy supported the dictatorship, the church was openly persecuted. Thanks in large part to this historic change in the church, the military regimes which based themselves on the doctrine of "national security" were not able to convert themselves into authentic totalitarian states, as in Germany under Hitler or the Soviet Union under Stalin. In fact, in many cases, the church was the principal obstacle to the dictatorships.[7]

A few observations need to be made in order to avoid presumptuous generalizations. In the first place, in not a single situation did the church represent the entire nation. This is obvious in the case of Uruguay, where Catholics constitute only half or less than half of the population. In the majority of the rest of Latin America the percentage of Catholics oscillates between 87 percent (Bolivia) of the population and 94 percent (Nicaragua). Furthermore, these statistics are mere guides, which at times say very little. It is well known, for example, that in many Latin American countries only about 10 percent of the Catholic population fulfills the Sunday mass obligation. Between this 10 percent, which practices its religion regularly, and the other 90 percent, which claims to be Catholic, there are many different degrees of belonging to the church. Furthermore, it is logical to presume that most rightwing Catholics were in agreement with the dictatorships and did not agree with the denunciations of the dictatorships made by their own bishops. As a general rule, when the bishops took up the banner of human rights, they enjoyed considerable support; but when they touched social themes, that support diminished. Finally, it should be noted that ecumenical-minded Protestants supported the denunciations of human-rights violations made by the Catholic church as well as the demand to return to democracy.

However, beyond all statistics, the important fact remains that in the midst of all the political crises which divided the civilians, the Catholic church became the only national institution which the great majority, whether of the left, the center, or the right, could accept as a common meeting ground. In fact, the church became a sort of tribunal of final judgment, above the state itself. Before this tribunal all social groups aired their differences, entered into dialogue, or, putting aside their ideological differences, forged multi-class alliances. In essence, the church enjoyed a moral and historical legitimacy which no other national institution enjoyed. Let us now review the different ways the church contributed to democracy and the redemocratization of Latin America.

THE CHURCH: SOURCE OF RELIGIOUS LEGITIMACY

The church contributed to democracy in many ways. In the first place, when it denounced the dictatorships, it deprived them of legitimacy, which in previous times the church had almost always guaranteed them. This delegitimization by the religious power was especially important in the case of certain regimes—Argentina, Chile, and Brazil—that specifically justified themselves as defenders of Western Christian civilization. Obviously, to be disqualified by the Catholic church, which was a living symbol of Western Christianity, represented a serious drawback. Given that situation, some dictators had to seek legitimization elsewhere. Some sought out ultraconservative bishops, and others went to Protestant fundamentalists. Pinochet, without ceasing to identify himself as a Catholic, had recourse to the Pentecostals. Ríos Montt in Guatemala surrounded himself with all the symbols of his new evangelical religion. In Argentina it was not necessary to break with tradition: the official church, in spite of numerous denunciations made in private, supported the military regime in public. In reality, with the exception of Ríos Montt, there never was a total break between the dictatorships and Catholicism, or better put, Catholic symbols. Even when the official church condemned them, the military everywhere continued to have masses celebrated in honor of the patron saint of the armed forces and to hold other religious-military ceremonies. There were many cases of tensions over the use of symbols. In Nicaragua, while Cardinal Obando celebrated official masses without the Sandinista leaders, the latter attended masses in popular neighborhoods of Managua.

THE POWER OF SYMBOLS

The act of legitimizing or delegitimizing governments was not done only by words but by symbols and symbolic gestures as well. This was particularly important in the case of the Catholic church, so rich in liturgical traditions, devotions, and popular religious manifestations. The cry of the Cristeros— "Long live Christ the king!"—contained a message of protest not evident in the literal meaning of the phrase. It represented a denunciation of Mexican liberalism and its disdain for popular religious beliefs.

There are abundant examples of the use of symbols and symbolic gestures to condemn or to approve political actions. When General Manuel Noriega canceled the May 1989 elections, the archbishop of Panama, Marcos MacGrath, celebrated a mass surrounded by the leaders of the opposition. In that situation words were superfluous.[8] In Paraguay on various occasions the bishops reproached General Stroessner and other authorities by the simple gesture of not inviting them to attend certain traditional processions. In the final stages of Stroessner's dictatorship Archbishop Rolón organized processions of silence to protest repressive measures. In this situation the liturgical silence of thousands of Paraguayans, each carrying a lighted candle, made a far greater impact than any verbal discourse could have.

Besides the power of symbols, it is important to emphasize the role of religion as a source of consolation and inner peace. For practicing Christians, the symbols of religion and participation in the liturgy positively helped them to overcome their fear. As several authors have observed, one of the most important contributions of the church in the fight against state terrorism or terrorism from below consisted in offering the faithful a place of refuge where they could regather their interior spiritual forces and recuperate their sense of dignity as human beings.[9]

DEFENSE OF HUMAN RIGHTS

At the same time, the church extended its mantle of protection to victims of repression. Throughout Latin America the church founded offices or centers for the protection of human rights.[10] In many cases these offices or centers were the only places where thousands of persons in danger of losing their liberty or their lives could seek refuge. Some of these centers became famous: the Vicariate of Solidarity in Chile, Tutela Legal in El Salvador, the Commission of Peace and Justice in São Paulo, among others. In these centers ordinary citizens, whether they were Christians or not, could seek advice and help to find a "disappeared" relative. These centers, armed with teams of lawyers and social workers, visited prisons and detention centers to follow up on the whereabouts of political prisoners. In this way the church became one of the principal defenders of the victims of state terrorism. Even in those countries where there were no dictators, these centers offered an important service to persons caught between two lines of fire: the forces of order, on the one hand, and on the other, the armed subversives. In Peru the Episcopal Commission of Social Action (CEAS) listened to denunciations of violations of human rights or to requests for aid from thousands of refugees who had been displaced from the emergency zones.

LEGITIMIZING THE OPPOSITION

The church did not limit its role to denouncing dictators or protecting the persecuted. It positively sought out ways to help the civilian opposition to return to democracy. In this sense, at the same time that the church delegitimized de facto regimes, it legitimized the democratic opposition and its agenda for reconstructing democracy. In Chile, Cardinal Fresno encouraged the opposition parties to form a common front in order to offer an alternative to Pinochet. The result of this effort was the National Accord, which was the product of a multiparty dialogue that was publicly supported by the church. In Brazil this was the principal role of the church: to support the efforts of the parties and popular organizations to unite together as a common front. In his visit to Paraguay, Pope John Paul II, after being received by Stroessner, and much to the chagrin of the dictator, addressed the "constructors of peace," who happened to constitute the political opposition to the government.

Besides legitimizing civilian opposition, the church frequently took the initiative to strengthen unity among the opposition and to influence the alternative agenda. In several countries—El Salvador, Paraguay, Guatemala, Bolivia—the church called upon the principal social and political groups, and that included the military, to participate in a national dialogue. As a result, the civilians representing different parties and different ideologies were able to do what they could not do on their own: arrive at a national consensus that could serve as a common ground for the transition to democracy.

THE CHURCH AS MEDIATOR

Another important role the church assumed was that of mediator. In several countries, especially those caught up in a civil war, the church offered its services to mediate between the government and the armed groups in opposition: El Salvador, Nicaragua, Guatemala, and Mexico (Chiapas). In these cases the church's mediating role was key for diminishing tensions and reaching a negotiated peace. But the church did not limit its mediating role to war situations. In Bolivia, for example, it frequently mediated between the government and the miners' unions, and on other occasions between the political parties in situations of electoral disputes.

PARTICIPATORY SPACES

Finally, the church promoted democracy by creating spaces of participation, either for explicitly religious groups or for groups associated in some way with the church. Churches have always served as refuges and meeting places in times of crisis, and that was the role the Catholic church assumed under the national security regimes and in other places where violence reigned. The base ecclesial communities *(Comunidades eclesiales de base)* grew and expanded, especially during the military regime in Brazil. But the base ecclesial communities were not the only "free spaces" for the popular classes. Many other groups associated with the church arose in that period: mothers' clubs, youth clubs, popular kitchens, student organizations, cooperatives, and peasant leagues. In countries where political or union activities were forbidden, the base communities and these other organizations provided a secure place in which ordinary Christians could communicate with each other.

Furthermore, with the aid of biblical courses, literacy programs, and in the liturgy itself, the church carried out an important conscientization mission. In general, however, most priests, religious women, and catechists were careful to avoid direct political references in the liturgy. Conscientization was carried out on the deeper level of affirming the dignity of the faithful, who were also encouraged to fight for their rights and fulfill their civic obligations. In fact, under the influence of the Second Vatican Council, Medellín, and liberation theology the ideal that was constantly placed before the faithful was that of service to the community.

In this sense the church's work among the poor was a model of the application of the ideas of Paulo Freire on education as a tool of liberation, or those of John Dewey on the school as a preparation to live in democracy. In the popular parish, in the base communities, and in other popular Christian associations, the poor learned to dialogue among themselves and to act in solidarity. The typical popular parish not only encouraged the faithful to participate in the civic concerns of the neighborhood, but it also provided them with the capacity to do so: the ability to speak in public and to assume leadership roles. In her autobiography Rigoberta Menchú recalls the importance of her formation as a catechist in Catholic Action for becoming a union organizer (see chapter 11). In Nicaragua many popular leaders in the revolution against Somoza were delegates of the Word, and in Peru many of the leaders of the peasant vigilantes who fought against the Shining Path were simultaneously rural catechists.

For women of the popular classes, especially, the church provided a vital space in which they could affirm their dignity as persons. In all Latin America, with the backing of the church, women founded mothers' clubs, popular kitchens, and educational centers.[11] In these clubs and kitchens the women discussed topics of common interest such as how to raise their children, *machismo*, light and water service in the neighborhood, and so forth. This theme—the social and political impact of the church on the popular classes—has been widely commented on by other authors and there is no need to develop it at length here.[12] Naturally, the Protestant churches also fulfilled many of these same functions, although, in the case of the fundamentalists, within an intellectually narrower and more conservative framework.[13]

Keeping in mind this general view of the ways in which the church contributed to democracy, let us now consider the different factors that conditioned or limited the church during the period we are examining.

CONDITIONS AND LIMITATIONS

In theory—that is, to say what the church proposed in its own documents—the post-conciliar and post-Medellín church should have been a forthright proponent of democracy and human rights. In practice, however, there were a great number of external and internal pressures, human limitations, and ideological and psychological factors that influenced the conduct of the human beings who directed or who belonged to the church. Among these many factors or conditions, six in particular stand out: the papacy, church unity, internal tensions, personal charism and strategic location, the concrete political context, and foreign church influence. The order in which we present these factors does not necessarily represent their hierarchical weight; in each individual case it would be necessary to determine which were, in fact, the decisive factors.

THE PAPACY

In any discussion about the Catholic church the preponderant role of the papacy must necessarily be included. The pope names the bishops and the nuncios, and ratifies elections that take place in the episcopal conferences; he also approves the elections of the superiors of religious orders and congregations. He is the central figure who in the final instance approves or rejects candidates for all important appointments or elections in the church. Naturally, the spiritual leader of one billion Catholics (according to the 1990 census) does not govern the church alone. He works through a hierarchical bureaucracy that has many steps leading to the top. On the first level there is the curia (made up of congregations and general offices). Second are the tribunals and special commissions that constitute the Vatican bureaucracy. On a third level is each country's episcopal conference, which represents local ecclesial power. Finally, the bishop of each diocese is the person immediately responsible for that jurisdiction.

To all of this one should add the religious orders and congregations, which are independent of the bishops but in the final instance derive their right to exist from the pope. There are, therefore, many people and many levels of power within the church. But it is the pope who ultimately confers upon the church his own vision of where the church should direct its efforts. Although there is a vast distance between the pope and the local churches, sooner or later papal policy will make itself felt even in the most remote regions of the Catholic world.

In the colonial period, however, the pope was a rather distant figure who did not intervene directly in the daily routine of the Latin American church. In fact, he was not well informed about the reality of that continent. In practice, by means of royal patronage (or the *padroado* for the Brazilians), the king named all the bishops and controlled the church's bureaucracy. Nevertheless, as a symbol the pope enjoyed a special status in the world of popular religiosity. In the frontispiece of his chronicle, sixteenth-century Indian Felipe Guamán Poma de Ayala depicts the pope sitting on his throne, and a bit lower, the king, on his knees with his crown on the floor, as signs of deference to the Holy Father.[14]

After the wars of independence the Holy See struggled to take control over the church. After a period of tension the new governments and the Holy See signed concordats relative to the naming of bishops and other topics of mutual interest.[15] This period, which corresponds to almost all of the nineteenth century for most of Latin America, and the beginning of the twentieth century for Brazil and Cuba, was characterized by the phenomenon of *Romanization.* The popes of that period took measures to ensure their influence over the church in the New World, and one of those measures was to inculcate in the bishops, priests, and militant Catholics the Vatican's hostility toward liberalism and other forces which threatened the church in Europe. In 1858 Pius IX created the South American Pontifical College for Latin American clergy. In 1934 the Colegio Pio Brasileiro was founded exclusively for the Brazilian clergy. Also, in 1889 Leo XIII invited the Latin American bishops to attend the Latin American Plenary Conference, the first formal meeting between the pope and the Latin American episcopate. The contrast between the beginning of the nineteenth century and the end is quite striking. In the wars of independence numerous creole clergy disobeyed the pope's exhortations to remain loyal to the king. But at century's end the Latin American church marched step in step at Rome's beck and call.

The outcome of this process was ambiguous. On the positive side, the affection and loyalty the faithful felt for the pope strengthened the different local churches in their battles against anticlerical liberalism. On the negative side, the church became excessively dependent on Rome and lost contact with modern culture. In general, instead of trying to understand the modern world and to establish points of dialogue, militant Catholics, inspired by the example of the popes who made themselves "prisoners" of the Vatican (1870-1929), attempted to reconquer society and to restore colonial Christendom.

Nevertheless, Rome was capable of changing, and in fact did change its antimodern mentality. In the twenties and thirties both Pius XI and Pius XII encouraged the Latin American church to modernize itself and to leave behind its integralist mentality. In a famous response in 1934, Eugenio Pacelli, then the secretary of state, advised the Chilean bishops to maintain their independence with respect to political parties, even those that claimed to be Catholic (see chapter 3).

In the postwar period Pius XII (Pacelli) and John XXIII accelerated this process of adaptation to the modern world. In 1955 Pius XII called upon the Latin American church to organize local episcopal conferences, and in that same year he approved the creation of CELAM (the Latin American Episcopal Conference). In 1958 he also recognized the founding of CLAR (the Latin American Conference of Religious). Both the episcopal conferences and the religious conference represented the "modern" tendency to establish supra-regional ties of solidarity among bishops and religious. These new organizations also constituted an important step toward the forging of a common Latin American identity for the church. In 1958 Pius XII also created the Pontifical Commission for Latin America (CAL), an office in Rome that aims to strengthen ties among the Holy See, CELAM, and the local episcopal conferences.[16]

Finally, the Second Vatican Council (1962-65) constituted another important step in the formation of the Latin American church. With its emphasis on collegiality (the conferring of greater autonomy and responsibility on the episcopal conferences), lay participation, and the recognition of the distinct cultural values of each local church, the Council in effect put an end to the process of Romanization. Furthermore, the experience of being in the Council motivated certain progressive bishops to dream of having their own council for Latin America. The result was the second episcopal conference of Medellín (1968). Paul VI not only approved that initiative, but he also went to Medellín to preside over the eucharistic congress that preceded the general conference. Amid praise and a few vacillations, Paul VI encouraged the church to follow the general orientations of the Council.

During this period the three popes—Pius XII, John XXIII, and Paul VI—named bishops who represented the new orientation of openness to the modern world. In fact, the great majority of bishops who had to face the dictatorships of the sixties and later were named by these popes. It is important to note that the great change in the church occurred at the outset of the new cycle of dictatorships in Latin America. Some parts of Latin America—Paraguay, Cuba, and Haiti—were already under dictatorships when the Council began. In spite of that fact, the changes also came to be felt in those countries.

With the election of John Paul II (1978) very soon a conservative change with respect to his predecessors was felt. The change was most noticeable in the naming of new bishops, who tended to be less progressive and in some cases very conservative. For different reasons—the situation of the church in communist countries, certain signs of lack of control in Western countries—the pope believed that it was necessary to strengthen the lines of authority in the church and to fortify internal unity.[17] On the other hand, the papacy of John Paul II coincided with the redemocratization of Latin America. Given this temporal coincidence, the new orientation in Rome did not affect most of the local processes, which followed their own preestablished agenda. In those countries in which the episcopal conferences had a clear vision of what they wanted—Brazil, Chile, and Paraguay—the pope simply supported the bishops. Even in a few cases where new episcopal appointments gave an immediate conservative orientation to the local church, this did not affect the church's role as defender of human rights and democracy. A case in point is Chile. In the middle of the long Pinochet dictatorship (1973-90) a conservative archbishop, Juan Francisco Fresno, was named to succeed Silva Henríquez, the progressive archbishop of Santiago. But Fresno, even given a more conservative bent, supported the general lines of his predecessor in defending human rights and, as we shall see, made his own positive contribution to the redemocratization of Chile.

Other cases are more ambiguous. In their public addresses Paul VI and John Paul II condemned the repression and violation of human rights in Argentina during the "dirty war," but they did not reproach the Argentinean episcopal conference for its silence during the war. Whatever criticisms they made were made in private.[18] Nevertheless, it is interesting to note that when the Argentinean bishops finally distanced themselves from the military regime, they cited John Paul II to condemn the suppression of human rights.

Equally problematic was the situation in Nicaragua. In general the pope supported Cardinal Obando when he criticized the Sandinista regime. However, at the same time, when it became evident that Obando himself was an obstacle to putting an end to the internal war in Nicaragua, the Holy See, through its nuncio, encouraged the cardinal to be more open to dialogue with the Sandinistas (see chapter 10).

Another related factor is the special role that the papal nuncios play and which certain members of the Latin American hierarchy have played. Papal nuncios not only represent the Holy See before local governments, but they also inform Rome about the local church. The nuncio's opinion on the proposed candidates to become bishops has a special weight in the Congregation of Bishops. Furthermore, three ex-nuncios during this period came to occupy powerful posts in Rome: Sebastiano Baggio, nuncio in Brazil (1964-69); Angelo Sodano, nuncio in Chile (1977-88); and Pío Laghi, nuncio in Argentina (1974-80). Baggio was named prefect of the Congregation of Bishops (1973-84) and president of CAL (the Pontifical Commission for Latin America). In general, Baggio supported the conservative swing placed into motion by Archbishop Alfonso López Trujillo, secretary general and later president of CELAM.[19] In 1991 Sodano was named secretary of state of the Vatican, and Pío Laghi was named prefect of the Congregration for Catholic Education.

Besides these Italians, two Latin Americans came to occupy important posts in Rome: Eduardo Pironio, bishop of Mar de la Plata and president of CELAM (1972-75); and Alfonso López Trujillo, archbishop of Medellín and Pironio's successor as president of CELAM (1979-83). In 1975 Pironio, a progressive, was named prefect of the Congregation of Religious; and in

1990, López Trujillo, the main architect of the anti–liberation theology campaign in Latin America, was named president of the Pontifical Commission on the Family. López Trujillo in particular influenced papal views on Central America.

ECCLESIAL UNITY VERSUS INTERNAL DIVISIONS

In all institutions unity is esteemed as a positive value. But this is especially true in the Catholic church because, according to its own teachings, the church should be a sign of unity for all people. Therefore, to undermine or to question unity is seen as a grave fault. All episcopal conferences attempt to present themselves to the public as a united group. As we mentioned in the case of Argentina, in general the Holy See respects this unity and supports the decisions of the bishops. If the pope entertained doubts about some decisions, he kept them in reserve for internal dialogue. Nevertheless, for obvious reasons, internal unity was not and is not easy to secure. Especially during the period we are covering, bishops, priests, religious women, and the laity were submitted to great political and social pressures that were already creating divisions among the general populace.

Furthermore, priests and bishops are strongly influenced by their own religious and theological formation. The two central events in recent Latin American church history were Vatican II and Medellín. Put somewhat simplistically, ecclesiastical leaders were guided by two different ecclesiologies or views of the church. Many bishops and priests in Latin America may be considered conservatives, because they still follow a pre–Vatican II ecclesiology. For them, the church is essentially a spiritual monarchy that functions along hierarchical and paternalistic lines, from top to bottom. According to this model the bishops, who represent the magisterium (the teaching power) of the church, see themselves as teaching authorities commissioned to teach the truth to the faithful. The duty of the faithful is to listen to these teachings. Generally, conservative bishops and priests work closely with tradition-minded cultural elites. By way of contrast, the Vatican Council proposed the model of the church as community, which, without ceasing to be hierarchical, aims to encourage intercommunication, spontaneous participation, and fraternal dialogue. Bishops, priests, religious, and laity who opt for this model see themselves more as pastors called to help the faithful to grow in maturity and to assume leadership roles. To use a comparison taken from the world of education, the conservative is the old-fashioned teacher who demands attention and respect from the students. The progressive bishop, priest, or lay leader aims to be the teacher who nurtures the students and helps them to grow in liberty and responsibility.

These two models also differ with regard to the way Catholics see non-Catholics. For conservatives, unity and religious uniformity are positive values, whereas religious and cultural pluralism are negative factors. For post-conciliar progressives, religious unity continues to be an ideal, but religious and cultural pluralism are also esteemed as values. These two ecclesial models are, of course, stereotypes; in between there may be many variations and nuances. The important point is that differing theological orientations must be taken into account in order to understand the divisions that existed and exist in many episcopal conferences.[20]

CHARISM AND STRATEGIC LOCATION

The majority of bishops who were called upon to take a leadership role under the dictatorships were progressives possessed of exceptional human qualities. Raúl Silva Henríquez in Chile, Oscar Romero in El Salvador, and Ismael Rolón in Paraguay were recognized and acclaimed by thousands of persons of all social classes as the spokesmen for the conscience of their respective countries. In Brazil, Paulo Evaristo Arns, Aloísio Lorscheider, Hélder Câmara, and Pedro Casaldáliga stood out as natural leaders with striking and forceful personalities. Not all administered key dioceses: Hélder Câmara was named archbishop of Olinda and Recife, one of the poorest archdioceses in Brazil; and Casaldáliga is a bishop in Mato Grosso. Nevertheless, their voices were heard throughout all Brazil and, indeed, throughout the entire Catholic world. Some prelates possessed and possess special qualities as mediators: Arturo Rivera y Damas in El Salvador, Rodolfo Quesada in Guatemala, and Samuel Ruiz in Chiapas.

Besides charism, being strategically located is also important. For example, in Brazil the most important archdiocese after independence was Río de Janeiro. The archbishop there during the military regime was Cardinal Eugênio Sales, a conservative. For this reason the church in Río did not stand out as a center of Christian protest under the military. But in 1970 Paulo Evaristo Arns, a progressive, was named archbishop of São Paulo. Given the enormous demographic and economic weight of São Paulo, the archbishop of that archdiocese, who is usually a cardinal, is automatically a person of considerable influence in the Brazilian church. Very soon Arns, with his vigorous personal style, filled the vacuum left by Sales and assumed a role as national leader, along with other progressive bishops, and defender of human rights.

In two other cases—Nicaragua and El Salvador—the importance of being the ordinary (the ecclesiastical term for the titular bishop of a diocese) of the capital of the country became quite evident. Miguel Obando y Bravo, archbishop of Managua, became the visible head of the Nicaraguan church; Arturo Rivera y Damas, the archbishop of San Salvador, fulfilled the same role in El Salvador. But Rivera y Damas, like his predecessor, Oscar Romero, was not the president of the episcopal conference, at least for most of his reign. In fact, the episcopal conference was dominated by conservatives. Nevertheless, the fact that he was the archbishop of the most important ecclesiastical jurisdiction in the country, plus his own personal moral authority, made him a natural candidate to be the principal mediator during the civil war. Only toward the end of his administration, when he had already fulfilled his mission as mediator, was he elected president of the episcopal conference.

THE CONCRETE POLITICAL CONTEXT

The church reflects the historical and cultural context in which it functions, and in turn it is influenced by that context. In certain countries of Latin America—Mexico, Argentina, and Colombia—one can discern unmistakable integralist tendencies in the church. In each case there are different factors to explain this phenomenon. In Mexico, in the face of violent anticlerical liberalism, and especially after the Cristero revolt, the church turned in upon itself. At the same time popular religiosity in Mexico was particularly strong. In this case one can speak of a nationalistic and popular integralism. In Colombia the liberals and conservatives divided into clearly discernible bands, and the church aligned itself with the latter. In Argentina the church also sided with conservative groups, but the peculiar note in the Argentinean case is the especially strong alliance between the church and the military. One can find similar alliances in the rest of Latin America, but in Argentina this alliance went to an extreme. In this case one can speak of a nationalistic and elitist integralism.

At the other end of the spectrum one finds Cuba, Haiti, and Uruguay. In these three countries the church historically has been very weak, wielding little influence on politics and society. In Cuba and Haiti, in spite of the existence of a popular black religiosity, the church did not have strong roots in the rural areas and chose instead to strengthen its presence among the urban middle and upper classes. In Uruguay there emerged a markedly European society, which was also liberal and laicist.

The three "ABC" countries—Argentina, Brazil, and Chile—represented different models of the national security state. Even though there were evident similarities among the three, there were also notable differences. For example, for different historical reasons, in Argentina and Brazil the Christian Democratic Party did not flourish. In both of these countries the bishops did not trust lay groups that were not fully under their control; instead, they preferred dealing directly with the political authorities. By way of contrast, the Chilean Christian Democratic Party, although not officially tied to the church, nevertheless functioned as a sort of bridge between the church and society. This fact explains partially why the Chilean church was so progressive: progressive lay leaders could influence the church and at the same time maintain a certain autonomy with respect to the bishops. In Brazil there was a dynamic lay movement, which did influence the bishops, but that movement existed only within the structures of the official church. Returning to the Chilean example, the existence of a large centrist party like the Christian Democrats turned out to be an advantage for the church. Both Cardinal Silva Henríquez and Cardinal Fresno had recourse to the party as an instrument to reconstruct democracy in Chile. When the civilians, united around the Christian Democrats, were able to walk on their own, the church gradually stepped aside. By way of contrast, in Argentina, given the absence of a significant Christian Democratic Party—that space had been preempted by *peronismo*—the bishops prescinded from the civilians and dealt directly with the military.

In other latitudes, where civil war and terrorist violence were the order of the day, the church intervened as mediator according to the circumstances of each country. In Nicaragua, Guatemala, and El Salvador the church was able to mediate between the government and guerrilla forces because the two sides recognized the church as a valid and trustworthy institution. The leaders of the FSLM (the Sandinistas), the FMLN (the Farabundo Martí National Liberation Front), and the URNG (the National Revolutionary Union of Guatemala) in Guatemala emerged from the ranks of the new Latin American left, which had come to appreciate the importance of religion, and, in particular, the conscienticizing efforts of the Catholic church. The contras in Nicaragua who, of course, represented the opposite political extreme, looked to Archbishop Obando y Bravo as one of their defenders. In Bolivia the church was the principal mediator from the sixties until the eighties between the government and the miners, and at times, between the political parties. By way of contrast, such mediation was impossible in Peru: the Shining Path's dogmatism eliminated that possibility. Nevertheless, even in that situation religion was important as a spiritual arm that inspired the popular classes in their fight against terrorism.

FOREIGN INFLUENCE

Normally the only "foreign" influence in the local church is the Vatican. But given the special ties between North and South America, the North American church has maintained a very close connection with the church in many parts of Latin America, especially in Central America. To a lesser extent Europe, especially Spain, which historically sent over the greatest number of missionaries, is also vitally interested in Latin America. In the case of the United States, the North American episcopal conference condemned without ambiguities the military intervention of its own country in El Salvador and Nicaragua. Archbishop Rivera y Damas counted on the moral support of the North American bishops, a fact which gave him considerable leverage in dealing with the other bishops in his own episcopal conference. In the case of Nicaragua the North American episcopal conference did not support the attitude of Cardinal Obando with regards to the Sandinista government and the contras; on the contrary, it condemned President Reagan's policy of aggression in that country.

When the six Jesuits at the Central American University of San Salvador were assassinated, the University of Georgetown mobilized its considerable resources to get that crime investigated and to pressure the American Congress to suspend military aid to El Salvador. At the same time, given the fact that five of the six Jesuits were Spanish by origin, the Spanish government also applied pressure on the government of El Salvador to investigate the crime. Needless to say, the Society of Jesus in the United States, Spain, and the rest of Europe used the occasion to do some consciousness-raising as regards the political realities of El Salvador.

Beyond the official church, there were and are numerous Christian groups—Catholic and Protestant—in the United States, Canada, and Europe that organized themselves in order to express their solidarity with the Latin American church, especially to help refugees in war zones.[21] At the same time different human-rights groups also took a very active role in condemning the dictatorships, repression, the use of torture, and so on. The great majority of these groups maintain close ties with the different human-rights offices and centers run by the church, such as Tutela Legal in El Salvador, the Vicariate of Solidarity in Chile (no longer in existence), and the Episcopal Commission for Social Action in Peru, among others. By way of contrast, the human-rights groups had little influence on the Argentinean episcopal conference during the "dirty war."

With this general introduction we can now proceed to examine concrete cases. The order we will follow responds in part to chronological as well as regional criteria. We will begin with Brazil and the southern cone countries—Argentina, Chile, Paraguay, and Uruguay. Besides their obvious regional links, each one of these countries was an example of the national security state. The "bureaucratic-authoritarian" state that was installed in Brazil and in the other southern cone countries was created by military and civilian technocrats who aimed to secure development at the cost of democracy and human rights. In these cases the state repressed the opposition and had recourse to terrorism in order to impose order.[22] We will then examine two Andean countries, Peru and Bolivia. In reality, Bolivia under Hugo Bánzer and García Meza came close to the profile of a national security state and, in this sense, could be considered along with the southern cone countries. On the other hand, the church in Bolivia stood out for its mediating role in labor and political conflicts. Thus the Bolivian situation seems closer to that of Nicaragua, El Salvador, and Guatemala, where the church also fulfilled an important mediating role. Peru constitutes a unique case. Although there was no formal dictatorship during the period we are covering, there definitely existed a state of terror that threatened its democratic stability. In this situation the church was important for its role in the struggle against the Shining Path and in defending human rights.

We will then move on to examine three cases in Central America: El Salvador, Nicaragua, and Guatemala. In each one of these countries the church played an important role in the campaign against the dictatorships and in the redemocratization process. Finally, we will look at the church's effort in Mexico to contribute to the construction of a real democracy in a country dominated by a bureaucratic-authoritarian party, and within that context we will pay particular interest to the church's mediating role in Chiapas.

2.

Brazil (1964-1985)

The First National Security State

During the long reign of the Brazilian military (1964-85) the church played a key—some would say decisive—role in the process of returning to democracy. At the outset the majority of the bishops supported the military; but when the military government gave clear signs of converting itself into an authoritarian regime based on the concept of national security, which resulted in the systematic repression of civil society and the church itself, the bishops and the progressive sectors of the church became the "voice of the voiceless." During this period Hélder Câmara, Paulo Evaristo Arns, Aloísio Lorscheider, and Pedro Casaldáliga—to mention but a few leading figures—became famous not only in Brazil but in the entire Catholic world. Finally, when the military did decide to return to democracy, the church assumed the role of legitimizer of democracy and shield of protection for opposition groups of all social classes. The church encouraged the parties, labor unions, students, and numerous popular organizations in their efforts to organize themselves, and supported the common front that finally managed to dislodge the military from power in the 1985 elections.

The church also became the target of many attacks; priests, religious men and women, and laypersons became victims of the terrorism unleashed by the death squads and the brutality of state security forces. The Brazilian church was a model of ecclesial unity, which in turn inspired the laity and civil society in general. Although there were conservative bishops and priests—without mentioning certain ultra-rightwing Catholic lay groups—who opposed the process to redemocratize, these did not stop the rest of the church.

BACKGROUND: AN INDEPENDENT CHURCH

Brazil is the biggest Catholic country in the world. This fact is reflected in the Brazilian episcopal conference (CNBB), which is numerically the largest one after Italy (472) and the United States (418). In 1991 it had 382 member bishops, among them six cardinals.[1] Furthermore, Brazil has 13,836 priests. This means about one priest for every 10,439 inhabitants.[2] However, the most striking feature of the Brazilian church is its lay movement, perhaps one of the most active and dynamic in Latin America. Furthermore, from the period of Catholic Action up to the period of the base ecclesical communities, this lay movement has generally been fostered by the bishops themselves.

With the end of the Old Empire (1889) the church was freed from the tutelage of royal patronage, and in 1891 the constitution formally separated church from state. Although the Brazilian church went through its own Romanization phase, like the rest of the Latin American church, it nevertheless managed to retain its own sense of identity, thanks in part to the need to reorganize itself after separating from the state. The initial relations between the church and the new liberal state were characterized by tension and mutual distrust. Anti-liberal Catholic political parties proliferated. Finally, under the leadership of Dom Sebastião Leme, the bishop of Recife and Olinda, and later the archbishop of Río de Janeiro (1930-42), the church not only reorganized itself but even came out of the process fortified. Under Leme, the church managed to forge a new sense of identity and a clear sense of what mission it was to fulfill in Brazilian society. Most of all, Leme encouraged the creation of a well formed and militant laity. In 1922 Jackson de Figueiredo, a leading Catholic integralist, founded the Dom Vital Center. His successor, Dom Alceu Amoroso Lima, with ideas closer to those of Jacques Maritain than to Jackson de Figueiredo, until his death in 1983 came to symbolize an entire generation of committed Catholics. He was proud to be the "right hand" of Leme and was one of the principal founders of Brazilian Catholic Action. The integralist orientation of Jackson de Figueiredo resurfaced in the movement Acção Integralista Brasileira, founded by Plínio Salgado in 1932.[3] The latest manifestation of this tendency was Tradition, Family, and Property, founded in 1960 by Plínio Correa de Oliveira. Nevertheless, thanks largely to the leadership of Leme, Alceu Amoroso Lima, Hélder Câmara, and other founders of Catholic Action, these integralist groups never came to dominate the Brazilian church as they did in Argentina.

But Dom Sebastião was no sympathizer with popular democracy, least of all democracy forged by the left. He favored the neo-Christendom model, which called for the reconquest of society by an elite corps of Catholics. With this mindset he had no difficulty in joining hands with the paternalistic and authoritarian regime of Getulio Vargas, whom he considered a personal friend. The neo-Christendom model of Leme complemented perfectly the Estado Nõvo of Vargas. During the postwar years the number of alternatives increased somewhat for Catholics. As Scott Mainwaring pointed out, one can detect three different tendencies in the Brazilian church during this period: one that favored returning to the neo-Christendom model; another one that favored modernization, but within a conservative and paternalistic mold; and finally, a reformist and pluralistic tendency.[4] It was this third tendency that actually prevailed at least for a while. In the fifties and the beginning of the sixties the specialized groups of Catholic Action—Catholic University Youth (JUC) and Young Catholic Workers (JOC)—displayed intensive energy and were enthusiastically supported by the progressive bishops, especially Dom Hélder Câmara, who became the prototype of the modern and pluralistic bishop. The precise place of Hélder Câmara in the contemporary history of Brazil and the church is difficult to measure, but there is no doubt that it is a very important place. He played a key role in founding the Brazilian episcopal conference (CNBB), of which he served as the first secretary general. He also served as auxiliary bishop of Río de Janeiro (1952-64) and later as archbishop of Olinda and Recife. Thanks to him and other progressive bishops, although a minority, the bishops' conference was born with a modern and reformist orientation.

At the same time, the laity in Catholic Action displayed an intense dynamism and creativity. During this period, which corresponds to the developmentalist era of Kubitschek and the populism of Jãnio Quadros, the peasants organized themselves under the leadership of Francisco Julião while the workers began creating the first unions independent of the state. These new and exciting changes influenced lay Catholics. In the Northeast the Natal Movement, which combined social action with the gospel message, got underway. The Natal Movement gave rise to a series of radio schools (schools in which peasants gather to learn by listening to special radio programs) and medical posts; it also contributed notably to the creation of a regional bishops' conference.[5] For its part, the Catholic student movement (JUC), especially in the wake of the Cuban revolution, underwent a radicalization process. Some of the Catholic militants of this period channeled their concerns into direct political action. In 1961 they founded Popular Action (Acção Popular), a political group independent of the church. Other militants collaborated with the Base Educational Movement (*Movimiento de Educação de Base*), a literacy project inspired by the ideas of Paulo Freire on education as an instrument to conscienticize peasants. In this case the movement was founded as the fruit of an agreement made between the church and the state. In 1963 the movement had seven thousand radio schools, many of them run by parishes. One of the directors was Marina Bandeira, a veteran Catholic militant.

Soon, however, some of these progressive groups, feeling the weight of the social and political pressures of the times, found themselves in opposition to the hierarchy. The coming to power of João Goulart in 1961 accelerated this internal radicalization in the church. And Goulart's coming to power also set off the alarm that eventually ended in the military takeover of 1964.

The absence of a large Christian Democratic party was especially noticeable in this period. The Christian Democratic Party of Brazil was founded in 1945, with its principal base in São Paulo. Jãnio Quadros was elected mayor of São Paulo as a Christian Democratic, but later he abandoned the party. Nevertheless, the party supported him in the presidential elections of 1960 and won a few seats in several state assemblies. Finally, however, Goulart's election produced severe divisions in the party. In 1965 General Castelo Branco eliminated all political parties, and, with that, the Brazilian Christian Democratic Party disappeared. Besides these political factors, Christian Democracy in Brazil did not enjoy the same close relationship with Catholic Action that existed in other countries—in Chile for example—nor did it have the automatic support of the bishops. In Brazil, as in Argentina, the bishops preferred to deal with lay movements they could control instead of legitimizing movements or parties, no matter how Catholic they were, which they did not control.

THE BRAZILIAN MILITARY REGIME

The military *golpe de estado* of March 31, 1964, signaled the beginning of a new military cycle in all Latin America. Furthermore, the Brazilian military was the first to try out the model of the national security state, which was subsequently copied by other military governments, especially in the southern cone. Nevertheless, unlike Argentina, Chile, Uruguay, and Bolivia, but somewhat like Paraguay, the Brazilian military maintained the forms of constitutional democracy, including political parties and elections. On the other hand, their control over society and the daily lives of citizens was no less repressive than in the other cases. With control of the police, the army, and intelligence services, and especially certain specialized groups like the Department of Political and Social Order (DOPS) and the Center of Operations of Internal Defense (CODI), the Brazilian military managed to set up a spy network capable of taking note of all the actions, publications, and movements of millions of Brazilians.

The military regime went through three distinct periods. The first one (1964-67) was characterized by relative moderation. During the second period (1967-78), which was marked by notable repression, the national security state was firmly installed. During the third period (1978-85) the military returned to a moderate line, eliminated many of the more repressive measures of the national security state, and allowed the political parties and other civilian organizations to function once again. During Castelo Branco's government (1964-67) Institutional Act Number 2 (1965) suppressed all political parties and created two new ones: one to represent the government (ARENA, National Renovating Alliance), and the other to represent the opposition (MDB, the Brazilian Democratic Movement). Given this system of two parties, the military managed to marginalize the left and control elections. For a while the president of the Republic was chosen directly by the military; later an electoral college was created for that purpose. At the same time direct election of state governors was eliminated in favor of indirect elections in the state assemblies. Within the framework of this restricted democracy the opposition could maintain certain limited channels of expression. The press and other means of communication continued to function, but under state censure.

The full installation of the national security state occurred under the governments of General Arthur da Costa e Silva (1967-69) and General Emilio Garrastazú Médici (1969-74). Under the Law of National Security (promulgated in 1967 and modified in 1969) the government gave itself the right to detain any person suspected of being a subversive. The most important measure, however, was Institutional Act Number 5 (AI-5) of December 1968, by which the government suppressed the right of habeas corpus and other basic liberties. The most repressive years under the military occurred during these two governments. The increase in repression was due in part to the efforts of the civilians to recoup their democracy. In 1967 several different political groups merged to form the United Front (*Frente Amplio*), which was able to organize many demonstrations throughout the entire country. Also, in 1968 the students organized their own demonstrations. Ironically, by creating only one party of opposition, the military facilitated the task of the opposition. In the elections for congress in November 1974, in spite of all the government's careful planning, the opposition party (MDB) dramatically increased its presence in the national congress, although it fell short of an absolute majority. Finally, between 1969 and 1973, a guerrilla movement appeared but was quickly put down by the army.

Under General Ernesto Geisel (1974-79) the military government, recognizing the inevitable, announced its formal decision to return to multiparty democracy without restrictions. In 1978 Geisel eliminated Institutional Act Number 5 and granted amnesty to a small number of exiles. This opening occurred in spite of an outbreak of terrorist violence from the right that resulted in several assassinations and bombings between 1975 and 1978. From that moment on civil society began to give new signs of life. The workers organized strikes and the Organization of Brazilian Lawyers promoted a campaign in favor of direct elections, first for the state assemblies and later for the presidency of the Republic. The popular organizations grew considerably during these years. The last of the military presidents—João Baptista Figueiredo (1979-85)—accepted the challenge of organizing the transition from an authoritarian state to a civilian democracy. In the final stage, between the municipal elections of 1982 and the presidential elections of 1985, the parties, workers, and students organized demonstrations and marches demanding the right to vote directly for the president of the Republic. Finally, in 1984 a group of dissidents in the government's party went over to the opposition and formed the Democratic Alliance. The Alliance was able to elect Tancredo Neves as president. Although it was still indirect, Tancredo Neves's election was perceived as a victory because the civilians managed to defeat the military using the very system that the latter had created.

For each one of these periods in political history there is a corresponding period for church-state relations. In the first period—1964-70—the church approved and legitimized the military regime. In the second period—1970-78—the church, under persecution, became the principal voice of protest against the regime. In the third period—1978-85—the church supported and legitimized the opposition that led the country back to democratic rule.

THE CHURCH (1964-1970): CAUTIOUS LEGITIMIZATION

The great majority of Brazilians received the news of the military over-throw with relief; only a minority was alarmed. In the month preceding the overthrow President Goulart had taken a radical turn: he nationalized several oil refineries and announced his intention of carrying out an agrarian reform. In light of these actions thousands of Brazilians organized protest marches in all the principal cities of the Republic. Many religious groups, particularly Tradition, Family, and Property, participated with the slogan "With God and the Family for Liberty." Shortly after taking power the new military govern-ment published a message in which it claimed to share entirely the church's desire for greater justice in Brazil:

The social doctrine of the revolution coincides with the social doctrine of the Church. The revolution shares the desires to secure social justice for the people.[6]

In reply, the hierarchy expressed its thanks to the armed forces for saving the country from communism:

A short time ago Brazil was the stage for grave events which profoundly modified normal situations. Attending to the generalized and anxious expectations of the Brazilian people, which witnessed the accelerated march of Communism to take power, the armed forces acted on time, avoiding the installation of a bolshevique regime in our land.[7]

However, the same document also warned against the use of arbitrary methods to extirpate communism. Furthermore, with evident reference to groups like Tradition, Family, and Property, the bishops condemned calum-nies and irresponsible accusations against church-connected persons.

This formal pronouncement of the CNBB signaled the end of the progres-sive springtime in the Brazilian church. That same month Hélder Câmara was transferred to the archdiocese of Olinda and Recife. The dominating figure in the CNBB from that moment until 1970 was Agnelo Rossi, the cardinal of São Paulo, of center-right tendencies. He was supported by the secretary general who replaced Hélder Câmara, Dom José Gonçálvez, an integralist. Dom Hélder's new assignment did not necessarily mean that he had been "exiled"; in reality it is quite normal for an auxiliary bishop with a bureaucratic position to be sent out at some point in his career to take charge of his own diocese. Nevertheless, his leaving the CNBB did, in fact, open the way for the conservatives to consolidate their position. It also ensured that the episcopal conference would not become a tribunal of protest against the military regime. Once in his new archdiocese, Dom Hélder and the other sixteen bishops of the Northeast region published their own message, which was much more critical in tone than that of the CNBB.[8] Thus arose two poles of tension in the church: the national bishops' conference (the CBNN), based in Río de Janeiro (and later on in Brasilia), and the bishops of the Northeast region. In February 1974 Dom Hélder Câmara won the Nobel Peace Prize, an international recognition that consecrated him in his prophetic role as spokesman for the poor and the marginalized.

Under Marshall Castelo Branco church-state relations were relatively tension-free. The government avoided all situations of potential conflict, and Cardinal Rossi and other bishops never failed to show up to celebrate anniversary masses in thanksgiving for the military takeover of 1964. Nevertheless, as time went on, two factors combined to create new tensions. In the first place, the civilians organized themselves to protest military rule, and the government responded with repression. In the second place, Vatican II (1962-65) began to have an impact on the church in Brazil, as elsewhere. It was quite evident that the conciliar reforms favored progressives such as Hélder Câmara. These mounting internal tensions reached a climax in two crises: the confrontation between Catholic Action university students and the bishops; and a clash between the bishops of the Northeast and the military government.

Since the sixties the conservative—and some moderate—bishops had expressed their concern over the increasingly radical stands of the laity in the Base Educational Movement, and especially in the JUC and other groups of Catholic Youth. Finally, after many internal debates the JUC declared in July, 1966, that it no longer considered itself an "extension of the hierarchical apostolate."[9] The bishops faced this challenge by recognizing that the youth organization they themselves had created could no longer belong to the official church. That same year the bishops of the Northeast issued a declaration, which in reality was inspired by documents of Workers' Catholic Action of Recife and Rural Catholic Action. In it the bishops supported many of the demands of the workers and called for an agrarian reform.[10] This episcopal document provoked an immediate reaction from the military government. The rightwing press turned Hélder Câmara into its favorite target. In an excess of bad taste the sociologist Gilberto Freyre compared Dom Hélder to Goebbels(!). In the same article he also described the archbishop of Recife as "Brazil's Kerenski."[11]

It was in this context—with the progressives in retreat and under sharp criticism—that the military of the hard line, Costa e Silva (1967-69) and Médici (1969-74), came to power.

THE CHURCH: TARGET OF REPRESSION

Marshall Costa e Silva began his mandate with the prospect of governing a relatively prosperous and stable country. Everything indicated that Brazil was about to emerge as a new economic power: the yearly growth rate was 11 percent, and many development projects were underway, such as highways being built into the Amazon region.[12] Politically, the parliamentary system of two official parties seemed to be functioning smoothly. Relations with the church were harmonious. In fact, on the occasion of the publication of *Populorum Progressio*, the president sent a message of congratulations to the pope. Soon, however, the military regime found itself directly challenged by large groups in both society and church. In 1967 several leading politicians, among them ex-presidents Juscelino Kubitschek, Jãnio Quadros, and João Goulart (in exile) formed a "United Front," which managed to galvanize thousands of Brazilians to participate in huge demonstrations in the streets of São Paulo, Río, and other cities. In April 1968 the government outlawed the Front. The university students, motivated in part by the repression in their own country and inspired by the student movement in France, took up the torch of protest. In March, in Río de Janeiro, a student, Edson Luis Lima Souto, was killed when the police attacked a group of students. During the mass celebrated for him a week later the cathedral was full. After the mass mounted cavalry attacked some of the participants, which included a good number of priests. Soon protest demonstrations spread all over Brazil. The largest march—100,000 students—took place on June 26 in Río. Many priests and religious women participated. Finally, in response to the repression against the student movement, an urban guerrilla movement sprang up. By 1973 it had been thoroughly repressed; nevertheless, its existence served to justify even harsher security measures by the military.

In the middle of these protest marches and the emergence of a guerrilla group the government decreed Institutional Act Number 5 on December 13, 1968. This act, which eliminated habeas corpus and other basic liberties, formally inaugurated the national security state in Brazil. The military government also suspended congress for a year. In 1969 Costa e Silva died unexpectedly of a heart attack and a military junta named General Emilio Garrastazú Médici as his successor. Médici, a former director of military intelligence, represented the victory of hardliners over moderates in the military. His administration (1969-74) was the most repressive and authoritarian of the entire military regime.

Without having planned for it, the church became a special target of repression. The agents of the DOPS and other national security organizations carefully observed all actions of Catholics associated with the left: students, middle-class professionals, bishops, priests, and religious sisters and brothers. One of the first clashes between the new national security state and the church occurred in the diocese of Volta Redonda, in the state of Río de Janeiro. The bishop, Dom Waldyr Calheiros, was known as a progressive, and the movement for youth (JUDICA) in his diocese fell under suspicion. In November 1967 the police detained a group of youth belonging to JUDICA when they were distributing anti-government leaflets. A short time later soldiers broke into the bishop's residence. In response the CNBB registered a protest note—for the first time. In spite of the protest a French deacon who worked as a moderator to the youth in the diocese was expelled from the country.[13]

Other incidents soon followed. In August 1968 the police expelled another foreign priest, Father Pierre Wauthier, of French origin, who worked in São Paulo as a worker-priest.[14] This particular incident prompted Cardinal Rossi to distance himself from the government. Finally, in January 1969 the government promulgated a law that threatened to expel any foreigner who acted against "national security."[15]

In practically all of these cases the accusations had no foundations. But there were situations in which certain clergy and religious did, in fact, have ties with guerrilla groups. In November 1969, in São Paulo, a group of Dominicans (including Frei Betto) and ex-Dominicans, two secular priests, and a Jesuit were accused of having contacts with a group known as Action for National Liberation, founded by Carlos Marighella.[16] In 1971 a military tribunal condemned three of the group to four years of prison. In another case a religious woman who was superior of her community in Ribeirão Preto, was arrested in October of that year under the same accusation. Although she protested her innocence, she was expelled from the country and condemned in absentia.[17]

Catholic conservative groups, especially Tradition, Family, and Property, applauded these repressive measures against progressive Catholics. TFP never ceased in denouncing Hélder Câmara and other progressives as subversives and Communists. In 1968 TFP organized a campaign to collect signatures—they collected 1,600,000—to denounce leftists in the church. Among the signatories were the wife of the president, several ministers, and high-ranking military.[18] Two prelates, Dom Gerald Sigaud, the archbishop of Diamentina, and Dom Antonio de Castro Mayer, the bishop of Campos, lent their encouragement to the campaign. Furthermore, twelve bishops and archbishops sent a letter to the president of the Republic in which they assured him that they were not in agreement with the statements of the other bishops of the CNBB.[19] One of the favorite targets for these critics was the Belgium priest Joseph Comblin, who taught at the Theological Institute of Recife. Comblin, an important adviser to many bishops and the author of many works sympathetic to liberation theology, was expelled from the country in 1972. The CNBB, tired of these defamation campaigns, declared that TFP was not a movement recognized by the hierarchy and could not be considered officially a Catholic association.[20]

Finally, faced with these hostile acts and the increased limitations placed on democracy, the bishops began to take a more critical attitude toward the regime. Cardinal Rossi represents a typical case. At first he approved the military takeover. But when the government began to break into homes and expel priests and religious he began to place greater distance between himself and the government. In July 1968 eleven North American priests were detained by agents of the DOPs in São Paulo. In response, several members of other congregations organized a demonstration right in front of the central office of the DOPs. Several of the protesters were detained but subsequently released. However, harassment of churchpersons did not cease. In August security agents broke into the home of some Dominicans and carried off one of them, Frei Chico. This time Rossi sent a letter of protest to the governor of the state asking for him to intercede before the federal government. During this incident the newspaper *Estado de São Paulo* published an editorial that supported the government. Rossi sent his own letter of protest to the newspaper, which in turn accused the cardinal of "losing his serenity."[21] Later, in October, Rossi declined to receive the Order of National Merit, a medal given out by the president himself. He excused himself by pointing out that he did not want to give the impression of desiring to "strengthen the ties between the government and the church." Finally, he canceled the anniversary mass commemorating the president's assumption of power. A journalist for *Jornal da Tarde* caught the dramatic significance of these symbolic gestures; they constituted, he wrote, "the beginning of hostilities between the church and the state."[22]

In 1969 new incidents and hostile acts aggravated the tension. In January, Geraldo Bonfim, a Capuchin friar, was detained because of a sermon he gave in a fishing village in the state of Ceará.[23] Purportedly, the sermon contained "concepts which went against national security."[24] In May he was sentenced to a year in prison.[25] Of a more serious nature, a young priest, Antônio Henrique Pereira, a close collaborator with Dom Hélder Câmara, was murdered. Father Pereira, who worked with the youth in the archdiocese, was tortured and shot to death, apparently by a death squad. His murder was evidently a warning to the archbishop. Thousands of people attended the funeral.[26] Nevertheless, these demonstrations of public protest had little effect on the government, especially after General Médici came to power. According to one author, between 1968 and 1973 "around 100 priests were detained and processed for political reasons."[27]

THE CHURCH (1970-1978): PROTEST AND PERSECUTION

It was precisely during this, the worst period of repression, that the church emerged as the principal voice of protest in Brazil. The military of the hard line prevailed until 1974, when the government's party suffered a significant electoral defeat and was forced to cede to the moderates. The new president, General Ernesto Geisel, announced a new policy of relaxation and at the same time formally declared that the country would return gradually to democracy. Nevertheless, the general atmosphere of repression and persecution did not change substantially. In reality, this anomalous situation reflected an internal struggle between hardliners and moderates. Geisel himself did not have complete control over the security forces, which continued to act on their own. Between 1974 and 1978 the security forces and different paramilitary groups practiced rightwing terrorism, which resulted in numerous assassinations, disappearances, and violations of human rights. Between 1964 and the end of Geisel's regime approximately 10,000 Brazilians were exiled, 4,682 lost their civil rights, 245 students were expelled from universities, and close to 300 persons were murdered or disappeared.[28]

Although the church under Cardinal Rossi's leadership as president of the CNBB had already distanced itself from the military government, it still projected the image of a conservative and timid institution. But between 1968 and 1971 a new generation of progressive bishops emerged and began filling in important posts in the hierarchy. The new bishops—Paulo Arns, Aloísio Lorscheider, Ivo Lorscheiter, Luciano Mendes de Almeida, and others—joined the grand old leader of the "old guard," Hélder Câmara, and gave a radically new orientation to the church. Vatican II and the episcopal conference of Medellín encouraged this new orientation, while internal repression helped push the church to take a more decisive stand with respect to the military regime. Four focal points of this new ecclesial leadership stood out: the Northeast (Hélder Câmara); the Amazon region (Pedro Casaldáliga); São Paulo (Paulo Arns), and finally, the national bishops' conference (Aloísio Lorscheider and his successors). Although at the time it was not too evident, this transition to a progressive era began during the conservative period. The 1968 elections in the CNBB ratified the conservative hegemony. Rossi was reelected president and Dom Eugênio de Araujo Sales—the future conservative cardinal-archbishop of Río de Janeiro—replaced Hélder Câmara as the one responsible for the social question. However, Gonçálvez was replaced by Dom Aloísio Lorscheider as secretary general. This last change was decisive: in 1971 Lorscheider, one of the architects of the progressive church, was elected president of the CNBB. In 1970 Cardinal Rossi had been called to Rome to head the Congregation for the Evangelization of Peoples. His successor was Paulo Evaristo Arns, one of his auxiliary bishops. With Arns in São Paulo and Lorscheider in the presidency of the CNBB the church in Brazil took on an entirely new orientation.

ARNS IN SÃO PAULO

Paulo Evaristo Arns, a Franciscan, is the son of one of the many immigrant German families that settled in southern Brazil (Santa Catarina). He did special studies at the Sorbonne and taught as a professor at the Franciscan seminary in São Paulo, and later on at the Catholic University of Petrópolis. As head of the church in the archdiocese of São Paulo he became known worldwide for his energetic defense of human rights and his stand on social justice. He was named a cardinal in 1973. It is sufficient to witness his Sunday afternoon mass in the "Praça da Sé," in the center of São Paulo, in order to understand how he became the "voice for those who have no voice." Small in stature, he nevertheless vibrates with energy and dynamism. He establishes an immediate and spontaneous rapport with the faithful who fill the cathedral, many of whom live in the *favelas*. He exudes a spontaneous goodness but also projects an image of firmness. He was one of the many bishops who supported the military coup of 1964, but within time he became one of the strongest voices of protest against human-rights violations under the military. The principal organ by which he channeled his denouncements of those violations was the Archdiocesan Commission of Peace and Justice.

THE COMMISSION OF PEACE AND JUSTICE

The commission was first founded in 1968 in Río de Janeiro, but under the leadership of Cardinal Eugênio Sales its orientation was very cautious and nonassertive. By way of contrast, Arns in São Paulo took an aggressive role. He personally visited political prisoners, many of whom belonged to the Catholic left, and witnessed the signs of torture. In January 1972, when a Catholic union leader, Luis Hirata, died as a result of being tortured, Arns decided to found his own chapter of the Commission of Peace and Justice, which in 1974 acquired legal recognition. By so doing, the São Paulo chapter also won independence from the central commission in Río. The Commission of Peace and Justice in São Paulo fulfilled many of the same functions as the Vicariate of Solidarity in Chile.[29] It investigated cases of torture, missing persons, and human-rights violations in general. The most dramatic case, which highlighted the church's struggle in favor of human rights, occurred in 1975 when a well-known journalist, Wladimir Herzog, died as a result of torture. Herzog, a Jew of Yugoslav ancestry, was also a Marxist. He learned that the security forces were looking for him and freely turned himself in. But he was not to leave the confines of the DOI-CODI building in São Paulo alive. His death provoked a student demonstration, and the forty-two bishops of the state of São Paulo published a public letter of protest. Arns personally initiated a letter-writing campaign denouncing the death of the journalist to all Brazil. Finally, he organized an ecumenical service in the cathedral with the family of the victim, a rabbi, and several Protestant ministers present. The government tried to dissuade him from holding the service, and on the day of the service the police attempted to block access to the cathedral. Nevertheless, in the midst of a tense silence, eight thousand people managed to get through the police blockades to attend. By this dramatic gesture of human solidarity with a non-Catholic Arns put on the mantle of defender of human rights for all Brazilians. From that moment on the majority of middle-class Brazilians ceased to support the military regime.[30]

At first the Commission of Peace and Justice concentrated specifically on human-rights violations, but after a while Arns widened its functions to include the victims of social injustice. For that purpose he founded the Archdiocesan Commission of Pastoral Care for the Marginalized and the Street Children. Along with this new commission he also established a center to take in victims of domestic violence and abandoned children. In recognition of his work in favor of human rights Arns has received many prizes from different groups all over the world. In 1987, in São Paulo, the First Lady of France, Danielle Mitterand, conferred upon him the Legion of Honor.[31] In the last year of the military regime he and Presbyterian minister Jaime Wright sponsored the report *Brasil: Nunca Mais* (published in English under the title *Torture in Brazil*). Following the model of *Nunca más* of Argentina, the Brazilian report summarizes the many cases of tortures, illegal detentions, and missing persons. It declares that there were 125 undeniable cases of missing persons, but adds that the number could be as high as 300.[32] In August 1995 President Cardoso offered to give the families of 136 political prisoners who had disappeared death certificates and compensation.[33]

THE NORTHEAST AND THE AMAZON

Much before this change of direction in the CNBB, the Northeast and the Amazon regions had already become focal points of protest. In May 1973 the bishops of the Northeast published one of most radical documents in all of Brazilian history: "I Have Heard the Cry of My People." This document analyzed the harsh social and political reality of the Northeast, highlighted the poverty, the lack of nutrition, the low educational level, and so on. It also questioned the kind of development the government was promoting. While the government spoke of "development," it simultaneously allowed the existence of "conditions of oppression" and state terrorism. This declaration, which was condemned by the government, was widely acclaimed outside of Brazil, including by the BBC of London. Encouraged by this stand the bishops of the Central-Western region also published a statement that month—"The Marginalization of a People"—which followed the same lines as those taken by the bishops of the Northeast. A third statement, *Y Juca Pirama* ("The Indian: The One Who Must Die"), issued by the bishops of several states with an Indian population, formed a trilogy with the first two.

These letters vividly captured the harsh social conditions in which thousands of Brazilians lived. They also reflected the state of tension that existed between the church and the military along with the power elites that supported the military. In the Amazon basin the government fostered colonization and development projects. But the type of "development" involved usually meant giving a green light to large landowners and companies that pushed the natives and poor settlers out. Very often the Indians, who numbered around 190,000, and the *posseiros* (poor immigrants) did not have legal titles, even though they had lived and worked on the land for years.[34] In the midst of this unequal fight the church intervened to defend the Indians and immigrants. Among the bishops who stood out were Pedro Casaldáliga of São Feliz de Araguaia, Estevão Cardoso in the southern part of Pará, and Moacyr Grechi of Acre-Purus. Casaldáliga in particular was singled out for harassment on account of his protests and proposals for an agrarian reform. In 1971 he was detained by the police and in 1972 his house was searched.

One of the most dramatic examples of official persecution occurred in his diocese. In 1973 Father François Jentel, a French-born Franciscan, was condemned to ten years of prison after being accused of inciting the peasants to violence. Father Jentel had, in fact, defended the members of his parish in Santa Teresinha against the incursions of CODEARA, the Company for the Development of Araguaia, which forcibly attempted to move the people out of the area. In May 1972, in defense of their town, the inhabitants of Santa Teresinha resisted with arms. Even though at that precise moment Father Jentel was absent, he was nevertheless condemned as the "intellectual author" of the confrontation.[35] When he finished one year of his sentence he was retried and absolved. He left Brazil, attempted to return in 1975, but was then formally expelled. This particular case typifies the relations between the church in the Amazon, the police, and the military.

THE NATIVE MISSIONARY COUNCIL

These tensions were especially evident in the conflicts between two organizations: CIMI and FUNAI. CIMI (Consejo Indigenista Misionero, or Native Missionary Council) was founded in 1972 by the bishops and religious superiors in order to foster pastoral work among the natives and to defend them and their culture against the encroachments of the companies and white colonizers. FUNAI (National Foundation for the Indian), on the other hand, was the government's organization; under pretext of "civilizing" the Indians, it in reality aimed to organize the natives in a way that would be compatible with the demands of the companies. In 1973 President Médici attempted to abolish CIMI and place the Indians totally under FUNAI's control.[36] The bishops protested and managed to save CIMI, but the criticisms and harassment continued. In March 1978 General Euclydes Figueiredo, the president's brother, denounced the priests and religious who worked in the Amazon as "cowards" and "traitors" who "incite the poor against the rich."[37]

TWO MARTYRS: LUNKENBEIN AND BURNIER

This resentment against the church reached such a level of hostility that it resulted in the murder of two priests—Rodolfo Lunkenbein and João Bosco Penido Burnier. Their murders sent shockwaves throughout the entire

Brazilian church. Rodolfo Lunkenbein was a German-born Salesian priest who arrived in Brazil in 1958. He was in his third year as director of the Indian Colony of Meruri of the Bororos Indians in Mato Grosso, which had been entrusted to the care of his religious congregation. On July 15, 1976, sixty-two armed persons, incited by local landowners, arrived in cars with the evident aim of intimidating the missionaries and the Indians. The immediate pretext of their incursion was the attempt—authorized by FUNAI—to draw clearer lines around the colony in order to protect the Indians from further encroachments. The invading force killed Father Lunkenbein and Simão Cristino, an Indian, and wounded four others.[38]

The other murder took place on October 11 that same year. João Bosco Penido Burnier was a Jesuit priest who had served as vice-provincial of his order in Minas, Goiás, and Espíritu Santo. At the time of his death he was the regional coordinator of CIMI in the Northeast part of Mato Grosso. He and Bishop Casaldáliga were en route to a pro–native rights meeting when they learned that two women were being subjected to torture in the nearby town of Ribeirão Bonito. They went to the town and straight to the local jail. There, in the presence of Casaldáliga, a soldier hit Father Burnier and then shot him to death.[39]

These two murders produced indignation and gave rise to many protest marches. On both occasions the government expressed its regrets and ordered those responsible to be taken into custody. But problems with the government hardly ended with these tragedies. In September of that year the bishop of Nova Iguaçú, Dom Adriano Hipólito, known for his criticisms of the death squads, was kidnapped and humiliated in public by one of those death squads.[40] The year 1976 was without doubt one of the worst for the church in Brazil.

THE CNBB CONFRONTS THE GOVERNMENT

Of great importance for the bishops, priests, religious, and laypersons who raised their voice in protest during that period was the support they received from the national bishop's conference. Under Dom Aloísio Lorscheider the CNBB once again became a progressive tribunal as it had been in Hélder Câmara's time. Lorscheider, like Arns, comes from German stock in the south; he is also a Franciscan and a theologian. He was elected secretary general of the CNBB in 1968 and president in 1971. He was named archbishop of Fortaleza in the Northeast in 1973 and hence is also a member of that regional block. He was elevated to the rank of cardinal in 1976. Given his exceptional personal qualities—spontaneous warmth and an even temperament—he was elected president of CELAM and was considered a papal candidate in 1978. He has a gift for conciliating parties in conflict, an asset that helped him to create a new consensus in the CNBB. Under his leadership the church in Brazil came to be one of the most progressive in the world, and during the period of extreme repression it projected an image of firm internal unity. The secretary general, Dom Ivo Lorscheiter, who was subsequently elected Lorscheider's successor in 1979, kept that same orientation.

With Lorscheider in charge the CNBB condemned state repression and the death squads without any ambiguities.[41] As a result, the CNBB and its regional offices became targets for attacks.[42] In November 1976, in response to the murders of Lunkenbein and Burnier and the kidnapping of the bishop of Nova Iguaçú, the CNBB published one of its most important statements, "Pastoral Message to the People of God." The statement takes the government severely to task for allowing the death squads to operate without sanction. In reference to the doctrine of national security it declares that the state is not the nation, and human rights are not granted by the state. It then goes on to establish a parallel between the national security state and the totalitarian regimes in the communist world. Finally, the bishops call for protection of the rights of the poor, especially the Indians in the Amazon basin.[43] In March 1977 the CNBB issued another letter, "The Obligations of a Christian in the Political Order," which repeated many of the concepts developed in the first letter. The two documents give witness to Cardinal Lorscheider's conciliatory powers. The letter "The Obligations of a Christian in the Political Order," which is highly critical of the government, was approved by 210 votes against 3.[44] One of the three dissidents was Dom Vicente Scherer, the cardinal-archbishop of Porto Alegre. He criticized the CNBB's statement, affirming that "the government of Brazil is not fighting against the church."[45]

Nevertheless, the immense majority of bishops, progressives and conservatives believed that the church was a victim of a systematic persecution by paramilitary groups and death squads, which in turn represented an illegal branch of the government. In 1978 and 1979 there were new outbreaks of rightwing terrorism that affected the church. In September 1978, in Belo Horizonte, a powerful bomb exploded near a Catholic school where a group of students was holding a meeting on human rights in Brazil.[46] During this same period many university students and seminarians were kidnapped. The bishop of Nova Iguaçú received new threats. For its part the government downplayed these actions or placed the blame on the church for having gotten involved in politics. While still a candidate for the presidency, General Figueirido publicly criticized the church's documents and ridiculed the bishop's statements on political topics: "It's as though the Supreme Command of the Army were to publish a document on theology."[47]

During the preparatory stage for the third episcopal conference at Puebla, Cardinal Arns and the bishop of Goías, Dom Tomás Balduíno, requested the Ecumenical Center of Documentation and Information to prepare a document on church persecution in Brazil. The document, which was approved by the majority of the bishops, states that between 1968 and 1978 122 members of the church were imprisoned. This number includes 9 bishops, 84 priests, 13 seminarians, and 6 religious women. Another 273 pastoral agents were also detained.[48]

THE "ABERTURA" (1978-1985)

Between 1978 and 1979 the regime took important measures to dismantle the national security state and accelerate the process of redemocratization. During this period, popularly known as the *Abertura* (the "opening"), the more moderate among the military replaced the hardliners and supported the efforts of President Geisel and his successor, General Figueiredo, to open up spaces for the political parties, the unions, and other democratic associations. During the presidential campaign of 1978 Geisel took the first and most symbolic step: on October 13 he revoked Institutional Act Number 5. Later he suspended the censure that hung over radio and television, and in December he authorized the return of several dozen political exiles. Finally, in August of the following year, Figueiredo—the new president—offered amnesty to all exiles.

For its part the church put aside its highly critical stance and came out in full support of this change of attitude and called for dialogue with the government. In September 1977 the president of the Senate, Petronio Portela, with the aim of reforming the constitution, sought dialogue with important groups such as the OAB (Order of Brazilian Lawyers) and the CNBB. Cardinal Lorscheider, along with other representatives, received the senator in the central office of the episcopal conference "with a long embrace."[49] Portela visited all the cardinals, with the notable exception of Paulo Arns, who apparently did not measure up to the senator's standards for dialogue.[50] The cardinal of São Paulo replied that he was always open to dialogue, although he also expressed his disagreement with reforms that were hatched "between four walls."[51]

With its eyes on the November 1978 elections, the church published several pamphlets on "political education" and organized short seminars to help awaken the faithful with regards to their civic duties. The titles of the pamphlets varied from diocese to diocese: "Vote and Participate" (Belo Horizonte); "Faith in God and Peace on Earth" (Acre-Purus); "The ABC of Elections" (Río de Janeiro); "Everybody to the Election Tables on the 15th" (São Paulo); and so forth.[52] Many of the pamphlets were written especially for the base ecclesial communities and other groups of Christians on the popular level. By means of these activities the church was now assuming, discreetly but quite visibly, the role of legitimizer of the transition to participatory democracy. Although Figueiredo himself had criticized the church for its statements on politics, he now recognized the church as an important stabilizing force. On March 8, 1979, the president-elect visited Cardinal Lorscheider in the main office of the CNBB in Brasilia. Lorscheider described the visit as a "good sign" for future church-state relations.[53]

THE BASE COMMUNITIES AND REDEMOCRATIZATION

On the popular level the church made an important contribution to the process of returning to democracy by means of its pastoral work in different church-connected organizations such as CIMI (Native Missionary Council), the MEB (Base Educational Movement), the CTP (Pastoral Commission on Land), and the Brazilian Peace and Justice Commission, all of which depended on the CNBB. However, the feature that most distinguished the church in Brazil in the seventies and eighties was the growth and expansion of the base ecclesial communities. Following the crisis of Catholic Action, which was largely a middle-class association, a vacuum was immediately felt in the church. Although of a very different character, in some ways the base ecclesial communities filled that vacuum. Created around 1963 and 1964 in response to the priest shortage in popular neighborhoods, the base communities soon went far beyond their initial design and acquired their own unique identity. Among other important differences from Catholic Action, the base communities never lost their direct link to the hierarchy, in spite of the fact that at times and in some parts of the rest of Latin America they seemed to constitute a "parallel church." At first their existence did not draw much attention. But they soon spread throughout the countryside and in the *periferías* of the big cities. In 1975 they held their first national meeting in Vítoria, in the state of Espírito Santo. Friars Leonardo Boff and Carlos Mesters, two intellectuals who made major contributions to the theology underlining the communities, were both present. According to Boff, with the emergence of the base communities the church was practically "reinventing" itself from below.[54] By the time of the third national meeting in 1978 in João Pessoa, Paraíba, there were around fifty thousand base ecclesial communities in all of Brazil. By the nineties the number of communities was estimated to be around a hundred thousand, with two million participants.[55] The presence of bishops at these national encounters underlines the ecclesial character of the communities. At the seventh meeting, in Duque de Caxias in August 1989, some eighteen hundred delegates attended, along with eighty-five bishops, practically a fourth of the entire hierarchy.[56]

This rapid growth of the base communities coincided with the repression of the unions and parties. Thus the communities constituted one of the few free spaces in Brazil. It is tempting to see in them a sort of "safety valve" for civilian society. No doubt the communities, strongly influenced by liberation theology and the new biblical consciousness fostered by Vatican II, were seedbeds of political and social consciousness-raising. During the elections of 1978 they studied and discussed the pamphlets on political education distributed by the bishops.

Furthermore, the base communities were especially important for women, who normally had no special place to ventilate common topics.[57] Within time there emerged many other popular organizations with more specific ends: mothers' clubs, the Movement for Baby Care Centers, and so on. The communities constituted the first national web that interconnected thousands of poor women during the military dictatorship. Even after the new popular organizations appeared, the communities continued to maintain ties with them.

Nevertheless, in the midst of all their social and political consciousness-raising, the base ecclesial communities never lost their essentially religious character. When the newer and more explicitly social and political organizations arose, the base communities did not attempt to compete with them. At times, for lack of experience and carried away by naive enthusiasm, some base community leaders publicly supported certain leftist candidates, such as Lula in the 1982 elections. Nevertheless, in spite of the many pressures to turn into political-action groups, the communities survived the transition period without losing their original religious character.

THE LABOR STRIKES

In 1978, 1979, and 1980 Brazil's workers carried out nationwide strikes, which gave testimony to the fact that the civilians were coming back to life. The 1978 strike—the first since 1968—began with the metal workers of São Bernardo (São Paulo). It soon spread to many other regions in the country. Its principal spokesman was the young and charismatic union leader Luis Inacio Lula da Silva, popularly known as Lula.[58] In the 1979 strike it was estimated that some three million workers participated. During the strikes the church expressed public sympathy for the workers. When the government closed down the strikers' headquarters, the archdiocese of São Paulo opened up parish halls and other church facilities for the strikers. At the same time, Frei Betto appeared in public assemblies with Lula. In the 1979 strike the church offered its good offices as mediator and even asked Lula to suspend the strike in order to create a more tranquil climate. Lula acceded to the request and managed to negotiate a salary raise for the workers.[59] The 1980 strike, however, turned out to be a failure. Nevertheless, the general result of the three strikes was positive: the workers left behind their fear and regained confidence in themselves.

Soon the workers made use of a new law passed by Figueiredo's government that allowed for the existence of more than two parties. Buoyed by the new strength they had demonstrated in the strikes, the workers created their own political party: the Party of the Workers (PT). Lula—the party's leader—was surrounded by leftist intellectuals, Trotskyites, and Catholic militants from the popular class. In the 1982 elections for state and municipal posts the PT demonstrated considerable electoral strength, but not as much as Lula's admirers had hoped for. The mutual sympathy between the base ecclesial communities and the PT lasted well after the return to democracy. In 1989 Luiza Erundina de Sousa, the PT candidate for mayor of São Paulo, was elected with the enthusiastic support of the base communities. For its part, the official party of opposition, the MDB, transformed itself into the PMDB: the Party of the Brazilian Democratic Movement.

The bishops, of course, did not officially approve of any one party. Their position was to support any party which represented real democracy, and this included both the PMDB and the PT.

THE FINAL STRETCH

Between 1982 and 1985 civil society came alive again with even more vitality than before the military takeover: new political parties emerged, some of which were much more representative of the popular class; and the unions and the many other popular organizations displayed signs of considerable dynamism. In this new context the church put aside its mantle of lonely prophet and handed over the torch to the newly organized civilian groups. Church leaders decided that their role now consisted in supporting the redemocratization process. The civilians reconquered power through multi-class alliances. After each victory the allied parties and associations set new and more ambitious goals. Between 1980 and 1981 the parties, the popular organizations, the Organization of Brazilain Lawyers, and the press united in a common front, with full support from the church. In the November 1982 elections the opposition forces won a majority in the lower house, and they also won in the ten most important states in the country. In 1983 a new goal was set: to demand direct elections for the presidency of the Republic. Throughout 1984 mass demonstrations were held in favor of the campaign, with the presence of artists and athletes in all the main cities: Curitiba, São Paulo, Belo Horizonte, Porto Alegre, Río de Janeiro, and others.[60] Finally, several groups in the government's party broke away and formed an alliance with the opposition. In January 1985 Tancredo Neves, the governor of Minas Gerais, who had become a symbol of the country's desire to return to democracy, was elected president by the electoral college, 480 votes to 180.[61] With the aim of thanking the church, Neves visited the CNBB twice: once as a candidate, in August 1984, and then, in February 1985, as president-elect. He was received by Dom Ivo Lorscheiter, since 1979 the president of the CNBB.

Although the church in general no longer maintained a high profile in politics, it continued to influence the political agenda with proposals to favor the situation of the Indians and the peasants. In fact, even though the country returned to democracy, violence in the countryside was still the order of the day. Between 1985 and 1986 in different parts of the jungle and the Northeast an Italian missionary, a Brazilian priest, and two religious women were murdered as a result of land conflicts.[62]

THE CONSERVATIVE SHIFT

The church in Brazil, which was considered one of the most progressive in the world, went through an internal crisis right in the middle of the process of returning to democracy. The conservative shift, which began during the pontificate of John Paul II, coincided with the last years of the military regime. Given that chronological coincidence, the shift did not substantially affect the church's role in the redemocratizing of Brazil. Furthermore, the progressive bishops continued to prevail in the church long after the new Roman orientation had begun to affect other episcopal conferences that were smaller and less united. Dom Aloísio Lorscheider's successors—Dom Ivo Lorscheiter (1979-87) and Dom Luciano Mendes de Almeida (1987-95)—presided over the CNBB during the transition to democracy without changing the basic progressive orientation of the Brazilian church, although new conservative appointments increasingly narrowed the progressives' margin. Without doubt the polemic over liberation theology and the strong pressures Rome exerted on the progressives also served to slow down and limit the church's social leadership.

The pope's twelve-day visit in 1980 revitalized the faith of thousands of Brazilians. The pope's social message, clearer and more energetic than that of the conservative bishops, encouraged progressives. Nevertheless, papal policy (and that of Cardinal Ratzinger) consisted in strengthening certain key figures who represented the new Roman orientation, such as Cardinal Eugênio Sales of Río de Janeiro and Bishop Kloppenburg of Novo Hamburgo. On the other hand, although they still continue to have much weight in Brazil, the leading progressives—Arns, Lorscheider, Casaldáliga, and others—were marginalized in Roman circles. The man who found himself in the middle of this shifting power balance was Leonardo Boff, the author of many works on liberation theology, which the Congregation for the Doctrine of the Holy Faith had questioned for a long time. In 1984 Boff was called to Rome to defend his ideas, and in May 1985 he was formally silenced. Finally, after many new meetings in Brazil and exchanges of letters, a summit meeting was held in Rome between March 13 and 15, 1986. With the pope presiding, Cardinal Ratzinger, the heads of the principal Roman offices, and on the other side, the president of the CNBB, five cardinals, and several bishops representing the fourteen ecclesiastical regions in Brazil, all gathered together. The encounter served to create a new climate of trust between Rome and the progressive wing of the Brazilian church. One concrete result was the lifting of the ecclesiastical sanction on Boff. Also, a prohibition on publishing the fifty-four volumes in the collection *Theology and Liberation,* a project of the Editorial Vozes, was also lifted.[63]

Nevertheless, this climate of good will turned out to be only the euphoria of the moment. As time went on Cardinal Ratzinger and the conservative bishops in Brazil continued to apply pressure to diminish the influence of the progressive groups and to marginalize their most visible spokesmen. Unlike what occurred in Nicaragua, however, this internal crisis did not become acute enough to break episcopal unity, or at least the appearance of unity, during the more critical years of military rule. With more conservative changes it is doubtful if the Brazilian church can maintain the same unity and orientation that characterized it during the military period.[64] What is unquestionable is the fact that during the long military regime, when the parties, the press, and other normal associations of civil society could not act, the church in Brazil, by defending human rights and speaking out in the name of the persecuted and marginalized poor, fulfilled a historical mission of singular importance.

3.

Chile (1973-1990)

The Vicariate of Solidarity and the National Accord

The church in Chile stood out for its social concern long before many other parts of Latin America. During the Pinochet regime it distinguished itself for its defense of human rights and its forceful protest against an inflexible dictatorship. The church also played an important role as mediator between the different political opposition groups in their quest for a national consensus; by so doing it also conferred upon them moral legitimacy in the struggle to restore democracy. The two cardinal archbishops of Santiago, Raúl Silva Henríquez and his successor, Juan Francisco Fresno, distinguished themselves for the different but complementary roles they played during this long process: the former as a national symbol of protest against the regime, and the latter as a symbol of national reconciliation among the opposition groups.

In order to understand the Chilean church it is helpful to place it in the context of the country in general. In many ways Chile seems like a Mediterranean country—Spain or Italy—and its political evolution reflects that similarity. Chile enjoyed a long period of social stability and democratic rule following its independence. Racially homogeneous (the Mapuche population was less than half a million in a general population of thirteen million inhabitants in 1992), the country managed to forge a common national identity long before many other Latin American nations. On the other hand, toward the end of the nineteenth century Chile began experiencing several social and political crises, the product in part of urbanization and industrialization. Until the 1930s it was still a predominantly agricultural country. But from that period on the urban population, especially in the central valley where Santiago is located, grew rapidly. By 1991, 39.9 percent of the population lived in urban areas, while only 17.8 percent in rural areas.[1] Politically, the liberal-conservative axis turned into a tri-party system when the Socialist Party emerged in 1901. The democratic tradition of the country was aborted twice in the first decades of the twentieth century when the military took power: in 1924 a junta removed President Arturo Alessandri, and in 1925 Carlos Ibáñez, who had participated in the *golpe* of 1924, seized power, but with the aim of turning it back over to Alessandri. Later Ibáñez was elected and served as president from 1927 to 1931. These takeovers reflected the growing polarization of the different social forces in the face of increased demands by the workers.

In 1938 Pedro Aguirre's Popular Front, made up of the Radical, the Socialist, and the Communist parties, came to power. Politics regained a bit of stability in the fifties with the emergence of the Christian Democratic Party, which represented a new center between the nationalist right and the growing left. But this precarious stability collapsed in the Allende years when the center fractured into warring factions and once again politics became polarized between the right and the left. Pinochet's seizure of power was but the final step in a long process that involved many internal divisions and tensions that had been accumulating for a half century.

PROFILE OF THE CHURCH

The Chilean church has long characterized itself by the relatively high level of culture and formation of its clergy and laity. In addition to the many schools run by religious, in 1888 the Catholic University of Santiago was founded, and another one in Valparaíso was founded in 1928. The church was not a great landowner, as in Mexico and other countries, and the clergy in general came from the middle classes. Nevertheless, the church did suffer from certain other defects characteristic of the rest of Latin America. Partially due to the priest shortage, it tended to concentrate its efforts in the cities and to ignore the rural areas. In 1941 Father Alberto Hurtado, S.J., published a book that provoked many comments: *¿Es Chile un país católico?* (*Is Chile a Catholic Country?*). Father Hurtado pointed out that there was only one priest for each three thousand inhabitants and that, according to the national census, only 3.5 percent of the men regularly fulfilled their Sunday obligation.[2] A survey carried out in 1965 revealed that those statistics had not changed substantially. According to the survey, only 12.9 percent of the Catholic population of Santiago regularly attended Sunday services.[3] Furthermore, for that year there was one priest for every 3,245 inhabitants in the entire country.[4] The proportion of foreign clergy among the religious orders is more or less 50 percent of the total, and about 30 percent of the secular clergy is foreign. In 1992 there were 680 foreign priests in Chile.[5]

Partially due to the efforts of the liberals to curb its influence, in the nineteenth century the church sought support in the Conservative Party, which for years was considered the party of the church. Furthermore, as Father Hurtado noted in his book, the church steadily lost influence among the workers and the peasants. Given this situation, different groups within the church saw the need to face the church's declining presence in Chilean society with greater realism. These groups also were conscious of the need for the church to win greater independence with respect to the Conservative Party. In 1922 Archbishop Crescente Errázuriz issued a pastoral letter in which he declared that "the church does not answer for the actions of any political party." And in 1934, in response to a letter of the bishops requesting clarification on that theme, the Vatican secretary of state, Eugenio Pacelli—the future Pope Pius XII—answered without ambiguity that the church should maintain strict independence from all parties.[6] In 1925, during the presidency of Arturo Alessandri of the Liberal Party, the government promulgated a new constitution that separated the church from the state. For many Catholics, and particularly the bishops, this was a lamentable decision. Others, however, realized that it signified the beginning of a new era of independence for the church with respect to the state, and most of all, to the Conservative Party.

THE SOCIAL CHRISTIANS

The movement called *Social Christianity* had a special importance for the future orientation of the Chilean church, perhaps more so than in any other country in Latin America. The founders of that movement in Chile were a group of young lay leaders formed in Catholic Action, who joined the Conservative Party in 1934: Bernardo Leighton, Eduardo Frei, Manuel Garretón, Radomiro Tomic, and Rafael Agustín Gumucio. By 1937 this small group founded their own association, the National Phalanx, within the Conservative Party. In 1938 the National Phalanx, or the *Falange*, decided not to support the conservative candidate for the presidency and separated from the party. Although the *Falange* was small—it won 4 percent of the national vote—it was important because for the first time it offered an alternative for Catholics: it opposed liberal anticlericalism and communism, like the Conservative Party, but unlike the latter, it also called for social justice. Another group under the leadership of Eduardo Cruz Coke, representing more conservative social Christians, approached the *Falange* and in 1957 all social Christians joined together to found the Chilean Christian Democratic Party.[7] From the moment of its creation the new party established itself as the center of gravity in Chilean politics.[8] The star figure in the party was, of course, Eduardo Frei. In 1949 he was elected to the senate and reelected in 1957.

The *Falange* did not initially enjoy the favor of many bishops, especially when it dared to criticize some of the conservative stands of the hierarchy. Nevertheless, there were priests and bishops who did sympathize with the idea of taking a stronger stand on the social question. In his memoirs Cardinal Raúl Silva Henríquez describes Alberto Hurtado, S.J., and Manuel Larraín as "the two most influential figures in the Chilean church."[9] Alberto Hurtado (1901-52), who suffered the consequences of poverty in his youth, was possessed of a special charism that left an indelible impression on youth and workers. He entered the Society of Jesus and displayed a remarkable apostolic zeal. Besides being the moderator to Catholic Action, he also founded a Christian workers' union (1948), a refuge for the poor (*el Hogar de Cristo*, "the Home of Christ"), and the magazine *Mensaje* (1951). He considerably influenced the lives of many priests and politicians, especially in their social orientation.[10] He was beatified in 1994. Manuel Larraín, the bishop of Talca from 1938 to 1966, identified himself with the cause of the workers and stood out in the Second Vatican Council as one of the principal progressive voices in Latin America. Pope Paul VI entrusted him with the task of preparing the way for the episcopal conference of Medellín. While preparing for the conference he was killed in an automobile accident.

SILVA AND FREI

Two figures symbolize the changes in Chile in the sixties: Raúl Silva Henríquez and Eduardo Frei Montalva. Silva, born into a middle-class Christian family in Talca, joined the Salesians and was ordained a priest in 1938, having completed the last four years of his studies in Italy. He held several posts in his own congregation and was named national director of Cáritas of Chile. In 1959 he was consecrated bishop of Valparaíso and in 1961 was named archbishop of Santiago. His naming clearly responded to the desires of the departing nuncio, Sebastiano Baggio, and obviously to those of Pope John XXIII, who lifted him up over a long list of other candidates. In 1962 he was named a cardinal, the second one in Chilean history. He stood out as a progressive in the Second Vatican Council, along with Manuel Larraín. He injected new life into the archdiocese and, among other measures, set into motion a reform of the church's properties. In appearance somewhat severe and austere, in reality he is a very warm man and, as archbishop, was also very efficient and dynamic.[11]

Eduardo Frei's "Revolution within Liberty"—the theme of his presidency (1964-70)—created a climate of great expectations that affected the church as well. Frei (1911-82), the son of a Swiss immigrant, stood out as a leader of Catholic Action. He influenced many others in the church, priests and laypersons, who shared his views on the need to carry out radical changes in Chile. He was elected with the support of the political right, which voted for him not out of a desire for change but rather out of fear of communism. Once in power Frei pushed forward an agrarian reform and "Chileanized" the big American-owned copper companies; that is, he turned over 51 percent of the ownership into the hands of the state. His objective was to secure greater social justice without destroying the capitalist system. He was conscious of the fact that his attempt to carry out reforms within the democratic system was being closely observed as a contrast to the Cuban revolution, on the one hand, and, on the other, the different military regimes that had come to power in much of the rest of Latin America.

During this period new research centers, almost all created by the Jesuits, were founded to promote social change. The most important of these centers were ILADES (Latin American Institute of Doctrine and Social Studies), the Bellarmine Center, and DESAL (Center for Latin American Social Development). The most prominent person behind the creation of all these centers was the Belgian Jesuit Roger Vekemans, who arrived in Latin America with the express mission of putting into practice a plan of the Society of Jesus for founding centers of reflection and social action. Other important Jesuits who cooperated in this undertaking were Manuel Ossa, Hernán Larraín, Gonzalo Arroyo, José Aldunate, Mario Zañartu, and Patricio Cariola. Almost all were trained in the social sciences in American or European universities. Also, Pierre Bigó, a French Jesuit, had considerable influence as an exponent of the church's social doctrine. These centers, notably DESAL, maintained direct but informal ties with Frei's government and influenced many of his reforms. When Salvador Allende came to power in 1970, Vekemans, who had been accused of receiving aid from the Central Intelligence Agency to contribute to Frei's campaign, left Chile and established his residence in Colombia, where he became an adviser to Cardinal López Trujillo and different conservative groups within the Latin American church.

The obvious sympathy the progressive sectors in the church felt for Frei, as well as the harmony between the Jesuit-run centers and the government, led many people to consider the Christian Democratic Party as the church's party. Although this was never officially true, and Cardinal Silva carefully kept a prudent distance from the government, nevertheless, the approximation of the church to the party and vice versa was too evident to deny. Statistics confirm the fact that the majority of Catholics voted, first for Jorge Alessandri, the conservative president who governed between 1958 and 1964, and then for Frei. A survey in 1958 revealed that the majority of practicing Catholics voted for Frei (37.0 percent) or for Alessandri (43.0 percent). By way of contrast, only 11.1 percent of Catholics voted for Allende.[12]

Toward the end of the sixties the Chilean church experienced the same internal divisions and the same extremes that affected the rest of the Latin American church. In August 1968 a group of eight priests and two hundred laypersons took over the cathedral of Santiago in order to protest the wealth and power of the church. Greatly displeased, Cardinal Silva suspended the eight from the priesthood. However, after a reconciliation dialogue, he forgave them.[13] At the other extreme, in 1967 the Chilean Society for the Defense of Tradition, Family, and Property, clearly inspired by the original Brazilian model, was founded. The society's magazine, *Fiducia*, denounced progressive sectors in the church, especially the centers run by the Jesuits, for the alleged aid they gave to the growth of communism.[14] The same group also managed to establish its presence at the Catholic University. However, this and other integralist groups did not have much influence in the church in general, and many members left Chile when Allende came to power. Chilean-style integralism was reborn with the advent of Augusto Pinochet.

ALLENDE (1970-1973)

The election of Salvador Allende as president in September 1970 opened the doors to a new period of tensions and uncertainties. Allende won with only 36.2 percent of the vote (compared to Rodomiro Tomic's 27.8 percent, and Alessandri's 34.9 percent). Given the fact that none had an absolute majority, the election had to be decided in the national congress. In October, after arduous negotiations between the Christian Democrats and representatives of Popular Unity (the coalition of leftist parties that supported Allende), Allende was formally elected president. Two days before his election General René Schneider, commander in chief of the army, who had taken a stand in favor of the constitution and democracy in the face of other military who wanted to abort the process, was assassinated in the streets of the capital. An assassination like this, done by the ultra right with the evident aim of impeding Allende from coming to power, was a warning signal of the violence to come. Nevertheless, President Frei and the Chilean congress went out of their way to respect the democratic process and to transfer power to the first Marxist in the world to be freely elected to the presidency of a country.

Much to the contrary of what one would have expected—a Marxist president vis-à-vis a Catholic prelate who sympathized with Christian Democracy—in fact, the relations between Allende and Cardinal Silva were quite cordial. Allende had already visited Silva once before, during the elections of 1964 in order to assure him that his political movement was not going to hurt the church. Before the 1970 elections the socialist leader made a similar visit and promise. Finally, after his election as president he visited the cardinal again. On this occasion Silva gave him a bible as a gift. These gestures of courtesy notwithstanding, the Popular Unity's coming to power produced new tensions in the country and even within the church.

The most notorious case of polarization within the church involved the Christians for Socialism. In April 1971 a group of priests under the leadership of the Jesuit Gonzalo Arroyo founded the Group of Eighty. By 1972 the group, now considerably bigger and more plural, adopted the name Christians for Socialism. The movement expressed its approval for the socialist system and criticized the church for its conservative stands. The priest-founders met with Fidel Castro when he visited Chile in November 1971, and a few of them went to Cuba to join in the sugarcane harvest and to have a first look at socialism. The cardinal attempted to open the door to dialogue with the group and even attended one of their meetings. Finally, however, the group grew so intransigent that it came to constitute a "parallel church." In April 1973 the bishops prohibited clergy and religious from belonging to the movement.

In the meantime, Allende's government had a brief run-in with the church. In February 1973 the minister of Education announced a plan to create the Unified National School system, which in practice would consist of a program to disseminate socialist doctrines in both state and private schools. However, after a meeting with Silva, Allende, who was more flexible and pragmatic than others in his government, canceled the program. Indeed, the church was called upon to act as mediator on a number of occasions as the political situation worsened throughout 1973. The specter of a civil war loomed over the country. Ultra-leftwing groups incited workers and peasants to take over factories or to seize land. At the other extreme, in June a group of military organized a strike that was quickly put down by their commanders. In the middle of these crises Allende had recourse to the cardinal to organize meetings between himself and leaders of the Christian Democrats, who constituted the most important of the opposition parties. In mid-August Allende met with Patricio Aylwin in the cardinal's home. Nevertheless, the meetings failed to produce results, in part because Allende failed to convince the opposition that he had control over the ultra leftwing. Finally the high command in the army concluded that a civil war was imminent if the government did not restore order in the country. On August 23 Allende named General Augusto Pinochet as head of the army, unaware that he had also named his own successor. On September 11, in the midst of black smoke, the military assaulted the Palace of the Moneda and installed a junta. President Allende died during the assault.

PINOCHET'S REGIME

Pinochet's military regime had all the characteristics of a national security state. It was authoritarian, repressive, aggressively anti-Marxist, and hostile toward traditional multiparty democracy. From an institutional and legal viewpoint it went through two stages. First, from 1973 until 1980 it was a military government under the command of a junta presided over by Pinochet. In 1977 the government, which had already repressed the leftist political parties, dissolved all the parties. In 1980, in an effort to legitimize the regime and also to institutionalize it, Pinochet promulgated a new constitution, which in turn proclaimed him to be the "constitutional" president. According to the new rules, in 1988 the government bound itself to convoke a plebiscite to ratify the candidate designated by the commanders of the armed forces for the period 1990-98. If this candidate (who turned out to be Pinochet) were rejected, then general, multiparty elections would have to be held. In the beginning the military regime in Chile did not differ greatly from those in Brazil and Argentina. But within time Pinochet came to be more than just a representative of the armed forces; in fact, he became a caudillo who used the armed forces as his personal power base.

From an economic point of view a slightly different chronology for the stages in the regime's lifespan can be perceived. Between 1973 and 1982 orthodox Milton Friedman neo-liberalism was applied, so much so that Pinochet's advisers were known as the "Chicago boys." But between 1982 and 1983, in response to popular protests and the apparent failure of the neo-liberal model, the government decided to adopt a policy of state protectionism. During those years the civilians began to reorganize themselves, and the politicians began to search for alternatives to Pinochet's project.

Within an authoritarian and corporatist framework, Pinochet and the military were determined not only to eliminate leftist parties but *all* political parties and any other group which, in the military's mind, caused divisions among Chileans. In 1977 Pinochet announced the installation of a new political order, which was defined as an "authoritarian, protected, integrating, and technical democracy of authentic social participation."[15] But Pinochet was no mere military technocrat. He felt called by a messianic mission which, according to the tradition of the Chilean army, fused religious symbols with military mission and ideology. The patroness of the Chilean army is Our Lady of Carmel, who is acclaimed as the Virgin General. Pinochet and other officers never ceased to justify the takeover of 1973 in terms of a religious crusade. In 1986 the vice–commander in chief of the army, Santiago Sinclair, declared: "The eleventh of September of 1973 happened in order to repel the oppressive aggression of Marxism which was snatching God from our minds and replacing the legitimate owners of the country." With reference to Pinochet, he added: "He is fighting without rest against that materialist heresy and its causes."[16] Pinochet himself practiced this type of rhetoric and frequently took the church to task for being an accomplice of the general disorder:

> "The grade of confusion noticeable in certain important sectors and spiritual institutions which have abandoned and traitored their transcendental mission leads them to depart from the true path of unity and the healthy good-neighborliness of the Chilean people, and pushes them onward toward the turbulent waters of political pragmatism and even toward atheist and materialist positions."[17]

In 1974 the military created the Superior Academy of National Security in order to treat the relation between ideologies and national defense.[18] In Chile the armed forces did not experience the same openness toward civilians and the church that occurred in Peru in the case of the Center of Higher Military Studies. On the contrary, all new ideas were circulated among themselves or shared with like-minded civilians. Indeed, the concern over the changes in the Catholic church led the military to approach the fundamentalist Protestants, because they stood for order, respect for authority, and anticommunism—values that at one time the Catholics stood for.

THE CHURCH AND PINOCHET: FOUR STAGES

Four different stages in the relations between the church and Pinochet may be distinguished. During the first stage (1973-76) the church oscillated between cautious support and growing concern about human-rights violations. In the second stage (1976-82) the church itself became the object of systematic persecution and began to react with a firmer and more well-defined stand toward the military regime. During this and the following stages the Vicariate of Solidarity stood out for its efforts in defense of victims of the regime. During the third stage (1982-85) the church assumed the role of moral leadership against a government that aimed to institutionalize itself in power. At the same time the church devoted its energies to fostering unity among the opposition groups. During these years Cardinal Silva retired and his successor, Juan Francisco Fresno, continued his policies. In the fourth and last stage (1985-90) the church took the initiative and called upon the civilians to unite and present an alternative political program before the country. The result of that effort was the National Accord, which represented the first step toward the reinstallation of civilian democracy and which eventually led to the defeat of Pinochet in the 1988 plebiscite.

FIRST STAGE (1973-1976): PRUDENCE AND CAUTION

The first reaction of the bishops toward the military takeover was one of caution. A small minority thoroughly approved the military's move. The hierarchy, then, reflected the same tendencies found among the general population. According to one estimate, among the thirty members of the hierarchy at that moment, six could be classified as conservatives, eleven as centrists, and twelve as progressives. *Centrists* were defined as those who sympathized with the Christian Democrats, while *progressives* were more inclined to view the left or leftist Christian Democrats with sympathy.[19] Six of the bishops openly approved of the takeover and the military junta. The archbishop of Valparaíso, Emilio Tagle Covarrubias, declared in 1974 that "the life of Chile as a free and sovereign nation has been saved."[20] Given these differences among themselves, the bishops tended to act as individuals before the government. Also, there were no signs of a systematic persecution against the church itself. In the light of the magnitude of the repression unleashed by the military and the police in the wake of the takeover—the Central Intelligence Agency claimed that close to eleven thousand persons died or disappeared in October and November—the church suffered relatively little.[21] Nearly seventy priests, almost all tied to the Christians for Socialism movement, had to leave the country. Two priests, Juan Alsina and Michael Woodward, were detained, tortured, and killed, and another one disappeared.[22]

Cardinal Silva himself visited the military junta on September 16 and agreed to preside over a prayer service on the eighteenth, Chile's independence day. On the same day as the prayer service, the auxiliary bishop of Santiago, Fernando Aristía, sent a letter to Pinochet denouncing human-rights violations, and on September 24 Silva visited the national stadium where the army had rounded up all persons whom it considered to be subversives. The majority belonged to leftist parties. In his memoirs Silva relates how the experience of finding himself in the presence of hundreds of prisoners who saw in him their one hope of leaving alive moved him to tears.[23]

The most important initiative of Silva, one month after the takeover, was to create the Committee of Cooperation for Peace. Under Cristián Precht, a young diocesan priest, the committee sought out the support of ecumenical Protestants and Jews. The three hundred lawyers who worked for the committee helped the persecuted leave the country, visited prisons, and gave legal counsel to more than seven thousand detainees who had been condemned or who were in danger of disappearing.[24] The committee was the forerunner of the Vicariate of Solidarity.

After several months of uncertainty, the episcopal conference decided to issue a collective statement on the situation in the country. The statement, "Reconciliation in Chile" (April 24, 1974) signaled the end of the period of unconditional approval of the government. However, even then, at least three bishops—Juan Francisco Fresno of La Serena, Emilio Tagle of Valparaíso, and the Vicar Castrense, Francisco Gilmore—disagreed with the document.[25] In their statement the bishops treated the junta with considerable benevolence: "We do not doubt the good intentions of our rulers."[26] But the bishops also expressed their concern for the "lack of efficient judicial safeguards for personal security which results in arbitrary and excessively long detentions . . . interrogations under physical and moral duress."[27] This same ambiguous mixture of deference toward the military and criticism can be observed in other documents produced during 1974.

Notwithstanding the fact that he did not have the full support of all the bishops, Cardinal Silva gradually took upon himself the responsibility of questioning and censoring the government, which in turn singled him out as the principal source of opposition in the hierarchy. In the same month as the letter on reconciliation, on the occasion of his Easter message, Silva surprised the faithful with the statement that he "bore a death sentence over himself."[28] On the first anniversary of the takeover he rejected the idea of commemorating that event with a religious celebration. Rather, the only religious service held was to commemorate Chile's day of independence, September 18.

In October another conflict arose when the junta fired all university rectors (presidents) and named others in their place. Silva resigned as grand chancellor of the Catholic University because the rector named by the military changed the vice-rector without consulting him. He stated that he would not consent to being reduced to a mere ceremonial figurehead. At the same time he announced the creation of the Academy of Humanism, a center of studies that would function under his personal protection and therefore independently of military control.[29] During 1975 the number of incidents increased. One of the most dramatic cases occurred in November when the DINA (Directorate of National Intelligence) attacked the residence of the Columban fathers and arrested Sheila Cassidy, an English medical doctor, on the pretext that she had aided a subversive.[30]

THE PEACE COMMITTEE IS DISSOLVED

The principal bone of contention between the government and the cardinal was the Peace Committee. In September 1975 the secretary of the episcopal conference, Carlos Camus, held a conference for the foreign press in which he declared, with sincerity but imprudently, that some of the members of the committee had "Marxist ideas."[31] This declaration confirmed Pinochet's opinion of the committee. In November Pinochet requested the cardinal to dissolve the committee, because it was "an instrument which the Marxists-Leninists are using to create problems which disturb our peace and tranquility."[32] Furthermore, the government used every opportunity to display hostility toward the committee. On one occasion it refused to allow the committee's vice president, Helmut Frenz, a Lutheran bishop, to reenter the country. Under this kind of pressure Silva decided to send a message of good will to the government: in December he dissolved the committee.

Very slowly the episcopate came to realize that General Pinochet did not represent a transitory junta—and therefore something that would be tolerable—but rather a military government that planned to institutionalize itself in power with the aim of eradicating Marxism and carrying out many other important changes in Chilean society. This awakening is reflected in the collective episcopal letter "Gospel and Peace," published in September 1975. In it, the bishops denounced the irrational anti-Marxism of many persons who fail to analyze the fundamental causes that give rise to Marxism, such as poverty and social injustice. They also censure chauvinistic nationalism, which, unlike genuine Christian nationalism, acts blindly without real love of country.[33] This letter and the dissolution of the Peace Committee signaled the end of the first stage of church-state relations. Increasingly, the bishops recognized the fact that isolated reactions were not sufficient to respond to a regime seriously committed to the transforming of society without any reference to the civilian population, human rights, and other achievements of humanity and Christianity.

PINOCHET AND THE PROTESTANTS

The percentage of Protestants in Chile is one of the highest in Latin America. In 1985 it was close to 22 percent of the total population, and 80 percent of those Protestants belonged to Pentecostal churches.[34] Mainline or historical Protestants rejected Pinochet's authoritarian rule and established ties of solidarity with the Catholic church. The Lutheran bishop, Helmut Frenz, whom we mentioned above, was the vice president of the Peace Committee and ended up being expelled from the country by Pinochet in 1975. But a good number of Pentecostals, more conservative and anti-Catholic, openly embraced the military regime. Pinochet, of course, accepted this support with pleasure because it constituted a type of legitimization of his government that he could not secure from the Catholic church. On December

13, 1974, in the Diego Portales Building, he received twenty-five hundred Protestants with their pastors. The visitors also published a declaration of support of the military government.[35] In July of 1975 a group of thirty-one pastors (from among the four hundred different Protestant churches in the country) formed a Council of Pastors with the aim of institutionalizing their support for the government.

Few things caught the attention of observers more than Pinochet's "Te Deums" with the Protestants. In the light of the fact that the Catholic church did not plan to commemorate the anniversary of the military takeover with any religious services, Pinochet accepted the invitation of the Council of Pastors to attend a religious service in the principal cathedral of Pentecostalism in Santiago. On September 14, 1975, accompanied by several members of his cabinet, he was received in the Pentecostal church of Jotabeche (the name of the avenue where it is located). Pastor Francisco Anabalón gave thanks for the country's rulers and asked the Almighty to protect "his servant, Augusto, the Head of State. . . . "[36] Pinochet returned to that church in 1976 and again in 1977.

Furthermore, on several occasions he received important representatives of fundamentalist Protestantism, such as Jimmy Swaggart in 1987.

The majority of Protestant churches disapproved of this kind of overt legitimization, which came close to being obsequious. Nevertheless, with his visits to the Pentecostals, Pinochet gained one of his objectives. In 1981, when he asked the cardinal to celebrate a Te Deum in thanksgiving for his installation as constitutional president, Silva accepted, but under one condition: that he not attend a similar ceremony with the Pentecostals.[37]

SECOND STAGE (1976-1982):
PERSECUTION AND DEFENSE OF HUMAN RIGHTS

In March of 1977 Pinochet formally decreed the dissolution of all political parties in Chile. With this act the government underlined its will to institutionalize the military regime and reconstruct the country according to its own design. Furthermore, in 1978 Pinochet expelled General Gustavo Leigh, who represented a more conciliatory tendency, from the junta and thus consolidated his own personal position. That year he also composed a new constitution, which was submitted to a national plebiscite in March 1980. By so doing, he converted himself into a constitutional president for a term of eight years, which ended with the plebiscite of 1988.

This process was accompanied by a systematic repression of civil society and persecution of anyone suspected by the state. The DINA, reinforced by paramilitary groups that acted with impunity, continued to detain all persons who voiced their opposition to the regime, some of whom simply disappeared. In November 1976 twelve communist leaders were detained and later all disappeared. In November 1978 the public received a new shock when a common grave with fifteen cadavers was discovered in Lonquén, outside of Santiago—clearly the work of a paramilitary group.[38] Earlier, in August, the bishops of Santiago, Copiapó, Linares, Talca, Temuco, and Arica had denounced a total of 273 cases of disappearances, 216 from the archdiocese of Santiago.[39] In October 1976, in the streets of Washington, D.C., Orlando Letelier, ex-minister of Defense and former ambassador to the United States, and his secretary, Ronnie Moffit, were killed by a bomb that exploded in Letelier's automobile. The United States government harbored no doubts that the DINA or agents in its employ were behind that act of terrorism. (In March 1995 General Manuel Contreras, ex-chief of the DINA, was condemned by the Supreme Court of Chile and sentenced to seven years in prison for that crime. Another military, Pedro Espinoza, received a six-year sentence.)

The church did not escape this selective and systematic persecution. The most notorious example occurred in Pudahuel Airport in August 1976, when three bishops returned from the ill-fated meeting in Riobamba, Ecuador, which ended with the detention of all the visiting prelates. The three—Enrique Alvear, Fernando Ariztía, and Carlos González—known for their progressive stands, were assaulted by agents of the DINA, who threw rocks at the bishops and yelled insults. In this case there appeared to be collusion between Ecuadorians and Chileans, because the bishops in Ecuador received the same treatment. The Permanent Committee of the Episcopate issued a communiqué the next day protesting the attack at the airport as well as the verbal aggression against the church in the media.[40]

THE VICARIATE OF SOLIDARITY

Undoubtedly the most important institutional response of the church to the repression of the military regime was the creation of the Vicariate of Solidarity. The Peace Committee had barely been dismantled at the end of 1975 when the cardinal announced in January 1976 the foundation of the Vicariate of Solidarity. In many ways it represented a continuation of the Peace Committee: it watched out for human-rights violations, especially those of persons who were detained. But there were two important differences. In the first place, the Vicariate of Solidarity was an institution created by the cardinal and run directly under his personal protection. As a consequence, it was not subject to the close scrutiny of all the other bishops, some of whom would not have approved of its activities. Second, it did not have the same ecumenical character. The reason for this change was to reinforce its ties to the Catholic church. The battle lines were now clearly drawn: the Catholic church as an institution had now formally taken up the cause of human rights in Chile in direct defiance of the wishes of Pinochet. If the government had "declared war," the church, in the person of Cardinal Silva Henríquez, responded by declaring war as well, although in this case using only legal and moral arms.

In its long history (1976-92) the Vicariate of Solidarity became the principal bone of contention in the church's relations with the government. It also came to be the only institutional space in which Chileans could find refuge from the regime and have their rights protected. Finally, it became the voice of Chile before the outside world. Silva designated Cristián Precht, who had been director of the Peace Committee, as the first vicar. The thirty-four-year-old Precht worked closely with the cardinal and gave a dynamic impetus to the new foundation. The Vicariate of Solidarity, which functioned in the offices of the archdiocese right next to the cathedral, had a team of between 150 and 200 priests, lawyers, and consultants working for it. Among their many activities they gave the highest priority to cases of detainees to make sure that they did not disappear. The Vicariate also organized seminars and conferences, and published books and pamphlets with the aim of conscienticizing the public about human rights. In 1978—the Year of Human Rights—it intensified its work of conscientization by organizing multiple panel discussions and conferences. Although it requested that its members not engage in partisan activities, in fact a good number were associated with the left.[41]

The Vicariate investigated hundreds of cases each year, which were all brought before the courts. By way of example, in 1978 it offered legal counsel to 224 persons accused of subversion or detained by the government. By 1983 the number of persons who received aid from the Vicariate dramatically increased to 5,123.[42] Furthermore, the Vicariate kept careful records of all cases of arrests, detentions, and the judicial processing of those cases. In recognition for its efforts in defense of the civil rights of Chileans, the Vicariate received numerous distinctions and prizes. In 1978, in the name of the Vicariate, Cardinal Silva received the United Nations' Prize for the Defense of Human Rights. In 1986 the Vicariate was also awarded the Prince of Asturias Prize for Freedom; and, in 1987, the prize for human rights from the Carter-Menil Foundation in Houston, Texas. Furthermore, the Vicariate received financial assistance from forty-one different religious and humanitarian organizations around the world, including Amnesty International, the Ford Foundation, and Lutheran World Relief. These institutions and foundations recognized and supported the Vicariate precisely in order to give it the greatest visibility possible and to channel world opinion through it to all of Chile. For very good reasons the Vicariate became the major thorn in the side of the government.

Pinochet's relationship with Silva and the Vicariate oscillated between cold indifference and open hostility. On several occasions the lawyers and consultants who worked for the Vicariate were detained and harassed. On the very day of the Pudahuel incident two of its lawyers were expelled from the country.[43] In 1985 José Manuel Parada, a former communist leader who worked as the head of the documentation center in the Vicariate, was murdered in mysterious circumstances. The following year a doctor and a lawyer from the Vicariate were arrested and jailed for nearly a year, accused of "covering over terrorist activities."[44] And in 1988, in an attempt to silence the Vicariate and besmirch its image, the military prosecutors, hoping to show direct links between the Vicariate and terrorism, demanded to examine the Vicariate's medical records. The vicar at that time, Santiago Tapia, and his successor, Sergio Valech, resisted those demands and refused to hand over the records.[45]

The Vicariate, like the Peace Committee, served as the most important forum during the military regime in which Christians and believers in democracy and human rights of different political backgrounds could come together and discover their common ties. President Patricio Aylwin expressly recognized this fact in a speech commemorating the Vicariate's sixteenth anniversary:

"In those years when political parties were forbidden and all such activity was repressed, it was difficult and even dangerous to get together to discuss common desires and projects for the good of Chile. . . . The Church in the Vicariate of Solidarity organized meetings, seminars, round tables, and discussions which served to gather together those of us who opposed the regime. Through these activities we could discuss our common plans and engender a climate of solidarity among Chileans of different ideological positions, all united by a common desire to reestablish democracy and free association in our country."[46]

In his speech Aylwin specifically cited two groups created within the Vicariate: the Chilean Commission on Human Rights and the Group of Twenty-Four to Study the Constitution. This latter group, of which Aylwin was a co-founder, aimed to design an alternative constitution to the one written by Pinochet. In essence, the Vicariate was the seed from which democracy was born once again in Chile.

OTHER PRIVILEGED SPACES

In 1977 Cardinal Silva created the Vicariate of Pastoral Work among Workers and named Father Alfonso Baeza as moderator. This new vicariate was specifically aimed to establish the church's presence in the working world. Like the Vicariate of Solidarity, it offered a safe place where workers could organize and express themselves freely.

Also, the Academy of Christian Humanism drew together intellectuals of different political tendencies, although most were from the ranks of Christian Democracy, MAPU (United Movement of Popular Action), and the Christian left.

The Jesuit magazine *Mensaje* remained one of the few publications critical toward the government that was not closed down. Its circulation rose from 5,000 in 1974 to 11,400 in 1976.[47]

CLASHES AND INTEGRALISTS

The Third Latin American Episcopal Conference of Puebla, which revealed the sharp differences that existed among the bishops of all Latin America, reflected similar differences among the Chilean bishops. A few Jesuits, such as Pierre Bigó and Renato Poblete, as well as Roger Vekemans in Colombia, participated in the consultation document, which was later rejected by the progressives because of its European focus. In 1980 a eucharistic congress was held in Santiago, to which Christian intellectuals of different tendencies were invited. Those of a leftist persuasion, however, did not attend. The deep divisions that existed before Allende still persisted. Joseph Comblin, the Belgian theologian, was invited to the congress, but the government denied him permission to enter the country.[48]

Integralist groups such as Tradition, Family, and Property reorganized themselves after the military takeover, but they did not come to exercise significant influence in the church. In 1976 TFP published a book entitled *La Iglesia del Silencio en Chile (The Church of Silence in Chile)*, which denounced the Marxist infiltration in the church. In 1977 Bishop Marcel Lefebvre was invited to Chile by his sympathizers. Except for his brief encounter with the Protestants, Pinochet himself, who justified his authoritarianism in religious terms, would have been the perfect representative of Catholic integralism.

THIRD STAGE (1982-1985): LEADERSHIP AND DEMOCRACY

After converting his regime into a constitutional one in 1980, Pinochet should have been able to enjoy certain internal peace, most of all because he had the support of powerful groups on the political right. Furthermore, with the coming of Ronald Reagan to power the pressure from Washington to amend his policies with respect to human rights was greatly lessened. And in fact, the level of state repression diminished between 1980 and 1982, but the peace that was felt in those years was but the calm before the storm. Between 1982 and 1983 Pinochet was forced to recognize the failure of his neo-liberal program. In 1982 alone national production fell 14 percent and unemployment was six times more than it had been in 1972.[49] The next year, 1983, was characterized by huge demonstrations. Pinochet drastically changed his economic policies and established a new policy of "directed state supervision," which included protecting Chilean products. For the first time since he took power he made a gesture of reconciliation: in June 1983 he permitted 185 exiles to return.[50]

But the protests against the regime were not a mere expression of discontent over hunger and unemployment; they symbolized psychologically the loss of fear on the part of the civilian population. As a consequence, after

1983 Pinochet was forced to resort to repression once again, but this time he did it in the face of a country that did not fear him as much and that had overcome the paralysis that had immobilized it for the first few years after the takeover. It was in this context that the church assumed the role of the voice of the nation in favor of returning to democracy.

"The Rebirth of Chile"

In the second stage (1976-82) the bishops had emphasized human rights. In their collective statement "The Rebirth of Chile" (December 17, 1982), they announced the beginning of a new stage by insisting on the return to democracy as an urgent priority for establishing peace. For the first time the church spoke clearly about a political alternative to the constitution imposed by Pinochet. In their letter the bishops analyzed four crises: the economic, the social, the institutional, and the moral. They criticized the 1980 constitution because "it does not fulfill what is required for the integral respect of human rights."[51] They went on to lay down three conditions for a Christian solution to the crisis in which the country found itself: respect for human dignity, recognition of the value of work, and "return to full democracy."[52] The bishops also criticized the neo-liberal program, which had produced only more misery, violence, and insecurity. The call for a return to a "full democracy" became the leitmotif of all future episcopal statements. Furthermore, the episcopal letters captured the public sentiment that expressed itself in the demonstrations. In their letter of August 12, 1983, "A New Call," the bishops literally turned a church document into an exceptional eyewitness report. The letter describes a clash between the police and protesters in Santiago that the bishops witnessed during their meeting: "We saw the helicopters and heard the noise caused by the protesters and the bullets."[53] In their letter "For a Real Democracy," October 14, 1983, they exhort the government to enter into dialogue with the civilians in order to restore democracy.

From Silva to Fresno

In May 1983 Cardinal Silva announced his retirement as archbishop of Santiago, and in June Juan Francisco Fresno, the archbishop of La Serena, succeeded him. For conservative groups this produced great satisfaction because the sixty-eight-year-old Fresno was known for his conservative stands; he was one of the bishops who openly supported the military takeover. Pinochet's wife, Lucía, made a widely known comment: "God has heard us."[54]

As if to confirm this appreciation, the new archbishop (created a cardinal in 1985) sent signals of reconciliation toward the government. However, at the same time he also assured the director and staff of the Vicariate of Solidarity that they could continue with their work. In reality, Fresno was named just at a moment when the government promised to be more flexible and to enter into dialogue with the opposition. Fresno's conciliatory gestures hit the right note for that moment. In fact, church-state relations were about to undergo another crisis, just as in Silva's time.

Hope for a real dialogue in 1983 was motivated in part by two events. First, in August, following the initiative of Gabriel Valdés of the Christian Democratic Party, five centrist parties formed the Democratic Alliance with the aim of dialoguing with the government. Second, Sergio Jarpa, the minister of the Interior and founder of the National Party, accepted that challenge to enter into dialogue. Furthermore, Jarpa created a very favorable atmosphere for dialogue by allowing twelve hundred exiles to return.[55] This move to dialogue was nearly jeopardized by the assassination of the governor of Metropolitan Santiago on August 30. Nevertheless, the two sides went ahead and met in the cardinal's residence: Jarpa with representatives of the Alliance.

Soon, however, this small effort dissipated into thin air. In September, in response to new protest demonstrations, the government arrested many leaders of the Christian Democrats and other groups. Worse still, in 1984, in response to intensified marches and the appearance of a terrorist group called the Manuel Rodríguez Patriotic Front, Pinochet imposed a state of siege on the country. The CNI (National Center of Information, created in 1978 to replace the DINA, which had been disbanded) applied the same drastic and repressive measures as the DINA had before. Church-state relations deteriorated, and many incidents affecting that relationship aggravated the situation. In January 1983 four armed persons who had been involved in the assassination of the governor of Metropolitan Santiago sought refuge in the papal nunciature. Throughout 1983 and 1984 the situation of the four asylum seekers produced great friction between the government and the Vatican, which through its nuncio, Angel Sodano, defended their right to asylum.[56] In September 1984, during another protest march, a stray bullet killed a French missionary, Father Andrés Jarlan. His funeral was the occasion for another anti-government demonstration. In November a crisis in Pinochet's cabinet was, strangely enough, attributed to the church. Jarpa, the Interior minister, accused the Chilean bishops of having had an encounter with Marxist leaders in Rome. According to the minister, such an encounter made dialogue between the government and the church impossible and, as a consequence, his own effort to promote dialogue had been in vain. In reality, the bishops, who were in Rome to fulfill their *ad limina* visit, had a meeting with exiled Chileans, among whom were to be found several Marxists. Although Pinochet did not accept Jarpa's resignation, the minister's accusations about a "conspiracy" between bishops and Marxists served to heighten church-state tensions. Furthermore, the government denied permission to enter the country to the vicar of the Vicariate of Solidarity, Monsignor Ignacio Gutiérrez, of Spanish nationality, because he had participated in the meeting in Rome.[57] Furthermore, the government published a decree that obliged all foreign residents to swear an oath of obedience to the laws of Chile. The intent of the decree was to control the participation of foreign religious in protest demonstrations. Finally, the government imposed a strict censure on the church's radio programs.

The bishops responded to this systematic aggression in a message on November 16, "Letter to the Catholics of Chile." In their letter they criticized Minister Jarpa for his irresponsible accusations; denounced the suppression of the church's activities, specifically a social week that was canceled under pressure; and, with respect to the radio transmitters, announced that in the future they would have recourse to "internal channels of communication of the church."[58] Finally, they added that the fight against terrorism and delinquency did not "authorize anyone to humiliate, terrorize, or mistreat other persons." This letter, and indeed all those published by Fresno during this period, were expressed in the same energetic tone that characterized the episcopal messages in Cardinal Silva's time. The merit of Fresno consisted in the fact that he continued the same mission begun by his predecessor in maintaining internal unity in the church against the dictator's evident intent to divide it. The picture at the end of 1984 was quite disillusioning: in spite of their good intentions the civilians had not been able to forge a common front or present to the country a plan to return to democracy. Fresno decided to take the initiative and convoke the civilians himself. This decision turned out to be decisive for the return to democracy.

FOURTH STAGE (1985-1990): THE NATIONAL ACCORD AND THE LEGITIMIZATION OF DEMOCRACY

At the end of 1984 Cardinal Fresno initiated a personal and private dialogue in his residence with different political leaders. On July 22, 1985, he invited the same leaders to meet jointly. The leaders represented eleven different parties, from the right to the left. The rightwing closest to Pinochet was not present, nor was the Communist Party or any other leftist groups that espoused anti-democratic or violent means to achieve power. The eleven included the far-right National Party; the Christian Democratic Party, located in the center; and two opposing groups from the Socialist Party. All together, these parties represented about 80 percent of the electorate of the country.[59] In recognition of its electoral weight and centrist position, the other parties acknowledged the Christian Democratic Party as the principal architect of the Accord.[60] The group ratified three men who enjoyed the confidence of the cardinal to act as coordinators: Fernando Léniz, who had been a minister under Pinochet; José Zabala, a Catholic businessman; and Sergio Molina, the vice president of the Christian Democratic Party, who had served as a minister under Frei. The three redacted the first draft of the Accord. Finally, on August 25 the whole group approved the final document, which was presented to the cardinal the next day.

The "National Accord for the Transition to Full Democracy" was a statement of basic principles that laid down the fundamental legal and economic guidelines for the return to democracy. Naturally, it called for general elections by direct vote for congress and the presidency. But it also called for the need to establish priority goals for "eliminating extreme poverty and marginalization."[61] Noticeably absent is any reference to trials for the military or punishments to be meted out, a topic that was debated among the eleven parties but was not incorporated in the final document.[62] The text of the Accord was widely distributed, and even the Communist Party, which did not sign it, agreed to support some of the basic ideas. Cardinal Fresno had achieved what been lacking since the beginning of the dictatorship: a multiparty consensus that united the vast majority of the civilians.

Pinochet, of course, did everything possible to ignore this dramatic change. The cardinal sent him a copy of the document, while representatives of the Accord tried to approach leading representatives of the government to explain its significance. As if to highlight how little importance the Accord had for the regime, in December Molina and Zabala were received by the subsecretary of the minister of the Interior. Finally, on December 24, Pinochet received Cardinal Fresno, but he avoided talking about the Accord and even treated his visitor with discourtesy.[63] In the face of this new unity among the civilians who refused to recognize his constitution, Pinochet felt threatened; but instead of opening himself up to dialogue, he became even more intransigent. Fresno, on the other hand, did everything possible to make dialogue easier. He sent clear signs of reconciliation to the military, warned priests about participating in protest demonstrations, and condemned the use of violence in any form. On one occasion he expressed his displeasure over the fact that the Vicariate of Solidarity had allowed Senator Edward Kennedy, on a visit to Chile in January 1986, to be interviewed on its premises.[64] For Fresno, that particular action, which identified North American political criticism of the regime with the church, constituted a provocation for the Chilean military. Finally, Fresno captured public sentiment when he declared, "Chile has a vocation to encounter, not confront."[65]

From a short-term view the Accord was not particularly successful. The government did not accept the invitation to dialogue, and the opposition had no choice but to follow the government's preset schedule. But from a long-term view the Accord was of great importance: it gave new impetus to the parties in their quest for unity and consensus. With the backing of the cardinal the Accord became a new national banner under which all democratic parties could march together.

In August 1992, in the Círculo Español of Santiago—the very place where it had been signed—the principal founders met for the seventh anniversary of the Accord: Cardinal Fresno, now retired as archbishop; Sergio Molina, minister of Planning; and President Aylwin. Aylwin pointed out the principal achievement of the Accord:

"The country lived in an atmosphere of divisions between friends and enemies, and people of different tendencies were able to overcome their differences and look for a new basis for consensus. I believe that the climate of reconciliation which the country is still experiencing under my government was born at that moment."[66]

The massive mobilizations and frequent clashes between the *carabineros* (the Chilean police) and the rest of the population only tended to harden the government vis-à-vis the opposition. Pinochet himself provoked a wave of protests when he declared in July 1986 that he had a "legitimate right" to prolong his mandate beyond 1989.[67] On September 7, 1986, the Manuel Rodríguez Patriotic Front attempted to assassinate Pinochet, and several of his body guards were killed. Although the great majority of opposition leaders, and the church of course, condemned the attack, Pinochet pointed to it as proof that Marxism was still conspiring against the country with violent means, just as in the days of Allende. In fact, Pinochet was not totally wrong, because since 1980 the Communist Party had approved of a policy that justified revolution and the use of terrorism against the dictatorship. In response to the attempt on the president's life the government unleashed a new wave of repression that ended in the death of many leftist leaders and the imprisonment of many thousands in concentration camps.[68]

THE PAPAL VISIT (1987)

The pope visited Chile between April 1 and April 6. As in the case of other countries under authoritarian regimes, the government attempted to manipulate the visit for its own benefit. Naturally, Pinochet exploited to the maximum a photo of himself and John Paul II as they stood together in a balcony of the Moneda (the presidential palace). But the pope carefully sought out his own photo opportunities to project a different image to the rest of the world. For example, he was photographed conversing with a woman who had been a victim of an assault by the army during a demonstration in Santiago.[69] In general, an atmosphere of peace and concord reigned during the visit. Except for one noisy outburst during an open-air mass, there were no notable confrontations between the police and the people. But this fact was a victory for the opposition, not Pinochet. In the words of Cristian Precht, the first vicar of the Vicariate of Solidarity, "The visit helped the country to mobilize itself, and we were able to encounter ourselves as a people."[70] According to Precht, the most applauded word when the pope spoke was "reconciliation."[71] But that word was associated with the National Accord and the democratic opposition, not with the regime in power.

THE 1989 PLEBISCITE

On October 5 Chileans turned out en masse to vote yes or no: yes, in favor of Pinochet continuing eight more years in power; or no, in favor of holding new elections and returning to direct, multiparty democracy. The government held the plebiscite because the 1980 constitution called for it. Also, international pressure demanded that the government fulfill its word. Finally, Pinochet, after fifteen years in power, suffered from the blindness caused by arrogance: in spite of warnings to the contrary he believed that he was going to win.[72] Earlier, in February, sixteen parties had banded around the Christian Democratic Party to constitute a united front to support the no vote. The main spokesman was Patricio Aylwin. The experience gained in the National Accord helped greatly to win a new multiparty consensus. After months of indecision the Communist Party also came out to support the no vote. A key agreement, which the Communists accepted, was the need not to jeopardize the plebiscite by demonstrations or acts of violence, which the government would use as a pretext to call off the election, especially if the results were not favorable.

Once the civilians organized themselves, the church increasingly played a background role. Nevertheless, it continued to influence events, especially by pressuring the government to hold honest and truly democratic elections. In April 1988 the episcopate published a message that stipulated the necessary conditions for the election results to have "moral authority," that is, for them to be acceptable to the country and to world opinion. Among those conditions the letter observed that the election would have to be the result of wide participation; the votes would have to be scrupulously counted; and they must be verifiable by everybody.[73] Finally, even before it was known that Pinochet was going to be the candidate (he was officially named by the armed forces on August 30), on August 10 the bishops expressed their opinion in favor of a consensus candidate who would be capable of presiding "impartially over the process of returning to democracy."[74] Indirectly, the bishops implied that they did not want the candidate to be Pinochet, who had never distinguished himself for his impartiality.

During the campaign itself the bishops in general maintained a discreet silence. Nevertheless, a couple of them, Carlos Camus of Linares and Jorge Hourton, an auxiliary bishop of Santiago, took a public stand in favor of the no vote. Furthermore, a pamphlet in favor of the no vote, which was widely circulated throughout lower-class neighborhoods, bore the signature of a hundred priests, religious women, and lay leaders.[75] The official church, which did not approve of that kind of political activity among priests and religious, played a different but equally important role by sponsoring two campaigns, "Bethlehem" and "Participate," to encourage the people to register and vote. Although the church's aim was simply to promote civic consciousness, many groups on the right perceived the campaigns to be an indirect way to mobilize the people against the regime. This suspicion was confirmed when Carlos González, the president of the episcopal conference, declared: "What is at play in this plebiscite is not the candidate Don Augusto Pinochet or another, but rather a presidential government or a military government."[76]

The plebiscite was conducted in an orderly and peaceful way. On the night of the election, when it became evident that it was not going to favor the government, Pinochet considered denying the results, but under pressure from other generals, he gave in. The no vote won by 54.7 percent, while the yes vote garnered 43 percent. Pinochet accepted the defeat with bad grace, and in the days following the election he placed partial blame on the church. In a speech he delivered on October 26 he declared with a threat, "We were set back but not defeated." He also compared the plebiscite with that "other plebiscite in which the people chose between Christ and Barrabas, and the people voted for Barrabas."[77] The bishops noted that the comparison was not very appropriate. In another speech Pinochet blamed his defeat on the United States, the Soviet Union, and "liberation theology"![78]

Notwithstanding the dictator's self-pity, the church once again took the initiative to help bring about a smoother transition to democracy. On October 27 Archbishop Bernardino Piñera, the vice president of the episcopal conference, organized a luncheon to which he invited Patricio Aylwin and Sergio Molina of the Christian Democrats; Jovino Novoa, a former leader of the Independent Democratic Union; and Sergio Jarpa, the former minister of the Interior who was currently the president of the National Renovation Party.[79] From that moment until the presidential elections of 1989, life in Chile followed its normal rhythm under democracy. The group of sixteen for the no vote turned into the Parties for Democracy, with one single candidate, Patricio Aylwin. The right fielded two candidates: Hernán Büchi, closely identified with the government; and Francisco Javier Errázuriz, of a more populist tendency. The results of the 1989 presidential elections were practically a repetition of the plebiscite: Aylwin won with 55.2 percent of the vote, Büchi received 29.4 percent, and Errázuriz, 15.4 percent. On March 11, 1980, Aylwin assumed the presidency of the country.

Notwithstanding the general jubilation over returning to democracy, there were many deep wounds still to be healed, and many important leaders in the Pinochet regime still remained in positions of power. Pinochet himself continued as head of the army, and many authorities in the judicial branches and in the municipal governments who had been named by the military regime remained in place. The persistence of these "authoritarian enclaves" meant that the country still had a way to go before becoming a full democracy.[80] And the country still had to face the trauma of having lived for seventeen years under repression. According to the Chilean Commission of Human Rights, between 1973 and the year of the plebiscite, 15,405 persons were killed, 2,206 disappeared, 164,000 were exiled, and 155,000 were detained in camps or in prison.[81]

Of all the traditional institutions in Chile that emerged from that long captivity, the Catholic church enjoyed the greatest prestige and credibility.[82] The church and the bishops had managed to present an image of unity and internal cohesion that inspired Christians and Chileans in general. Even the political right, which did not share the social orientation of the church, admitted that the latter acted impartially and in a spirit of genuine reconciliation when it dealt with the military and Catholics on the right. On the evening of August 18, 1992, in the Catholic cathedral of Santiago, the church celebrated the fortieth anniversary of the death of Jesuit Alberto Hurtado. In the midst of a crowd of young and old, President Aylwin showed up for the occasion, along with many other political notables. The two former archbishops of Santiago, Cardinals Raúl Silva Henríquez and Juan Francisco Fresno, walked up the aisle together. Carlos Oviedo, who succeeded Fresno in 1990, presided over the mass. This festive occasion also brought to light the line of continuity in the Chilean church: from the generation of the social Christians in the time of Alberto Hurtado up to the generation of Silva, Fresno, and Aylwin. There are few countries in Latin America where the church is so closely identified with democratic continuity as Chile.

4.

Argentina (1976-1983)

The "Dirty War"

The military regime that governed Argentina between 1976 and 1983 was one of the most repressive in all Latin America. In the name of "Western Christian civilization" the Argentinean military imposed a state of terror that led to the disappearance of 8,960 Argentineans, according to the official report of the commission designated by President Raúl Alfonsín.[1] Other sources put the numbers much higher: between 10,000 to 20,000.[2] At the end of 1977 Argentina, with 18,000 political prisoners, topped the list of countries with "innocent persons imprisoned."[3] During this period the official church denounced flagrant violations of human rights, but in general it did not take clear and decisive steps to back up those denunciations, as the church in Chile and Brazil did. And this in spite of the fact that many of the victims of this state terror were committed Christians, among them one or two bishops and several priests and religious women.

What saves the image of the Argentinean church is the courageous effort on the part of a minority within the official church—some bishops and priests—and a great number of laypersons beyond the circle of the official church who did take a clear and determined stand in defense of the rights and lives of their fellow Argentineans. Adolfo Pérez Esquivel, the winner of the Nobel Peace Prize, the Mothers of Plaza de Mayo—the immense majority of whom were practicing Catholics—and other groups that defended human rights, fulfilled the role in Argentina that the Vicariate of Solidarity did in Chile and the episcopal conference did in Brazil. In one sense, however, the Christians in Argentina were more valiant precisely because they did not have the support of the hierarchy. The timidity of the official church with regard to the defense of human rights, and in some cases, the outright approval some bishops and priests expressed for the military regime, was not a momentary lapse but rather the consequence of certain factors deeply rooted in Argentinean history. A brief examination of that history will help to shed light on the church's role during the "dirty war."

THE LIBERAL OLIGARCHY AND YRIGOYEN (1880-1930)

In the second part of the nineteenth century Argentina experienced an unprecedented economic boom. It emerged as one of the principal suppliers of beef, wheat, and wool to the world market. So close were the ties to Europe, and England in particular, that the oligarchy that established its dominance during this period—landowners, managers of meat processing plants, and bankers—adopted English ways, although Buenos Aires resembled Paris more than London. Buenos Aires, which was both the political and financial capital of the country, acquired the cosmopolitan airs of a great European city. At the same time waves of immigrants, principally Italians and Spaniards, poured into the country in search of new opportunities. Certain intellectuals, such as José Ingenieros and Carlos Bunge, enthusiastic over this material progress, preached the virtues of scientific discipline and pragmatism. In the interior provinces, in Córdoba, Salta, Jujuy, Santiago de Estero, the rhythm of life was much slower and the weight of colonial traditions was more evident. In reality, two different cultures had emerged: that of the *porteños*, characterized by European pretensions and liberal attitudes, and that of the interior provinces, more colonial and conservative, and resistant to the preponderant weight of Buenos Aires.

The waves of immigrants gave rise to a new popular and middle class, both of which demanded a greater participation in the general prosperity. Toward the end of the century anarchists and socialists began influencing the working class. The man who emerged as a spokesman for this rising discontent was Hipólito Yrigoyen, who belonged to the Civic Union, also known as the Radical Party. He was elected president of the country in 1916 with the aid of the Sáenz Peña Law (1910), which established universal suffrage for men. In fact, once in power Yrigoyen did not propose any radical changes. Nevertheless, his election served as a weather vane which announced that times had changed: the middle and lower classes were emerging as key political actors. Yrigoyen left power in 1922 but returned in 1928, only to be overthrown in 1930 in the wake of the worldwide depression.

CATHOLICISM INTEGRALISM

In the midst of this prosperous and materialistic society the tradition-laden church did not find a comfortable niche, and, indeed, it was marginalized by the liberal governments. In 1884 the government of President Julio Roca prohibited religious instruction in state schools. Not only liberals but also the great mass of immigrants ignored the church. Although most were Catholics, they did not look to the church as a necessary halfway house to become part of Argentinean society. Many of them joined the ranks of the new working movement and became anarchists or socialists. On the other hand, the church brought over many new religious orders and congregations, which staffed hospitals, orphanages, and other social services for the poor. But the church lacked a social message.

In the light of this loss of influence, certain priests took the initiative to change the church's mentality and build a bridge to these new social classes. Of note in this regard was Father Federico Grote, who founded the Workers' Circles in 1892, and in 1902 the League of Christian Democracy. But other Catholics, frightened by the changes in society, chose to close the doors to new currents. This was the mentality of the Catholics who gave rise to Argentinean Catholic Action in the twenties and who founded the magazine *Criterio* in 1928. The founder of this new channel of Catholic thought was Monsignor Gustavo Franceschi, who, even though he cited Jacques Maritain, was in fact much closer to Catholic integralism. The magazine supported the overthrow of Yrigoyen in 1930.

This Catholic intellectual revival coincided with the rising discontent with democratic institutions and concern over the advance of socialism. The year 1919 witnessed the "Tragic Week," during which the police clashed with strikers in Buenos Aires. During that week, which resembled the "Red Scare" in the United States, several hundred demonstrators were killed. Furthermore, Yrigoyen's last years were characterized by corruption and inefficiency. The world depression constituted the final blow to public confidence in the government. The first military man who took charge, General José Féliz Uriburu, lacked charism and was soon replaced by General Agustín Justo, who presented himself as a candidate in the presidential elections of 1931, which the military manipulated to its advantage. Justo's election represented the return of the oligarchy, but this time under military control.

In the midst of these social and political traumas Argentina's identity crisis became even more acute. Many important sectors in the upper and middle classes, in the army, and in the church, attracted by fascism, rejected liberalism, which they associated with English influence, as well as socialism and leftist populism, which were considered to be the basic causes of social disorder. At the same time a new nationalistic sentiment took hold of the middle and lower classes, the result, in part, of the efforts of the descendants of the immigrants to identify with their new country. In this case, being Argentinean was a quality associated with the port city or with a romanticized notion of the world of the gauchos in the interior provinces. In this context Catholicism was perceived to be an integral part of the new nationalism: to be an authentic Argentinean meant to be a Catholic (whether one practiced or not), because Catholicism was one of the traditional elements of Argentinean culture. This new national Catholicism became the ideological banner of many Argentineans of the upper and the lower classes, but it was especially so in the church and the military, both of which sought to strengthen national unity in the turbulent thirties. From that moment on this new ideological banner became the connecting link between generations of the military right up to and including the military regime presided over by General Videla. The formal consecration of this new ideology took place in the International Eucharistic Congress held in Buenos Aires in 1934.

THE EUCHARISTIC CONGRESS OF 1934

After two years of planning the thirty-second International Eucharistic Congress was held from October 10 to October 14, 1934. This was the time and the place for the debut of the newly refurbished Catholicism, now more confident of itself. The country had witnessed the collapse of the liberal social order, and in the face of an uncertain future the church presented itself as an anchor of security and a bulwark of traditional values, which many Argentineans now yearned to possess. The congress's organizer was Archbishop Santiago Luis Copello, created a cardinal in 1936. But the man who attracted the most attention was the special visitor from Rome, Eugenio Pacelli, the future Pius XII. President Justo himself assumed the role of patron of the event. From the very first moment the congress was in the hands of integralist Catholics who saw that moment as the occasion to weld together even more tightly the concepts of church and country, Catholicism and national identity.[4] The man in charge of publicity was the novelist Gustavo Martínez Zuviría, better known by his pseudonym, Hugo Wast. In the keynote address, which he delivered on October 12, a date known in Spain and Latin America as the Day of the *Raza* (Race), Zuviría exalted the values of hispanism and placed the blame for most of Argentina's evils on liberalism. Zuviría, also known for his anti-semitism, later became minister of Education. During the ceremonies, which brought together some 200,000 Catholics, the armed forces solemnly consecrated themselves to the Virgin of Luján. In another solemn act President Justo consecrated the nation to the Blessed Sacrament. The congress was, without doubt, the biggest event in Argentina that year.

The congress also gave rise to an alliance of a more directly political nature: between the church and the armed forces, and certain groups of civilians who rejected liberalism and socialism. This alliance gave birth to something that had not existed before in Argentina: the model of a Catholic corporate society. From then on all political leaders in the country—the military, Perón, and even the weak democratic governments that followed Perón—felt obliged to have recourse to the church to legitimate themselves. The church, of course, used this new social power to influence the march of government and society. In 1939 Monsignor Franceschi, the director of *Criterio*, quite satisfied with this new role of the church in society, declared: "We are now about to experience a new Middle Ages."[5] The perduring strength of this Catholic corporatist model explains to a large extent why the church in Argentina did not make great efforts to promote the creation of a Catholic party, or a party linked to the church, such as the Christian Democratic Party in Chile. In Argentina a party like that was not necessary because the church could deal directly with the political establishment, without intermediaries. Furthermore, the church had no particular reason to deal with a political party when it could deal directly with the other great national corporation that subscribed to the same ideals as the church: the armed forces. Both believed in order, hierarchy, social harmony, and both rejected communism and liberalism.

In fact, a Christian Democratic Party did arise in Argentina, but its history and final failure only served to confirm the intuitions of the Catholic integralists. There were Catholics who looked to Jacques Maritain as their source of inspiration, but they were few in number. They did not have the support of Catholics who were more to the right, and Perón carried the masses with him. The party was formally founded in 1955, and in the 1961 national elections it won 5.2 percent of the entire vote. Later, the government of General Onganía (1966-70) provoked an internal crisis: the party split over the issue of remaining faithful to its democratic creed or supporting Onganía's Catholic corporate regime.[6] In 1981 the party was just barely able to pull the splintered factions back into one fold.

Therefore, there did exist a democratic current among Argentinean Catholics, but that current did not have the support of many bishops, nor was it supported by rightwing Catholics of the upper and the middle classes, and certainly not by the military. As historian Fortunato Mallimaci points out, that lack of confidence in democracy became a salient note of Catholic integralism in Argentina:

> Their lack of confidence in popular participation and their antidemocratic doctrines led them to share the same authoritarian and messianic visions as certain other social actors: businessmen, union leaders, bishops, military officials. They mutually reinforced each other.[7]

PERÓN AND PERONISMO

The church's new confidence in itself, as expressed in Franceschi's words, soon dissipated in the face of a new phenomenon: *peronismo*. In 1943 the military took power once again, and under General Pedro Ramírez and his successor, General Edilmiro Farrell, many army officers who sympathized with fascism closed the doors even more to the country's liberal traditions. But the new regime was not particularly popular, most of all because the leaders did not know how to deal with rising social discontent. One man among them did, however. The vice president and minister of Labor, Juan Domingo Perón, saw quite clearly the importance of gaining the support of the working class. Deposed and jailed in October 1945 by other officials, he walked free thanks to the popular support he received from the *descamisados*, or "shirtless ones," whom he promptly galvanized into a well-organized machine. His mistress, Eva Duarte, an actress and radio star, lent the new movement the charism of her attractive personality. On October 17 Perón was welcomed back by the *descamisados* in the Plaza de Mayo, and in February of the following year he was elected president. The popular classes had not had a spokesperson in the Casa Rosada since Yrigoyen. But Perón proved to be quite a bit more than another populist leader; his personal charism also incarnated both the new nationalistic sentiment as well as social concern.

Once in power he used his popularity to silence voices of opposition, many of which belonged to the upper classes. He also nationalized foreign-owned properties, attempted to break the bounds of economic dependency, and, with his wife, Eva, created a national welfare state. Initially many Catholics saw in Perón the fulfillment of their integralist dreams: he created a strong nationalistic state and showed social concern without being either socialist or liberal. His doctrine, *Justicialismo*, proposed to follow a third way: neither communist nor capitalist, something like the social doctrine of the church. Furthermore, Perón, an astute politician, sought the favor of the church by establishing religion courses in state schools.

Finally, however, the church distanced itself from Perón and Perón from the church. A highly personalistic and authoritarian leader, he did not admit of any control over himself or his movement. Furthermore, the church, the army, and other "corporations" that pretended to represent the nation viewed with concern the near messianic sentiment Perón and Eva awoke in the lower classes. Clearly, the two partners in the pact celebrated at the 1934 eucharistic congress had no control over Peron's ecstatic followers. But Peron's star began to decline in the latter years of his first administration: bad government, corruption, and the increasingly arbitrary use of power finally led to his downfall. The death of Eva Perón in 1952 left him without the charismatic glow of the first years. His relations with the church deteriorated when he legalized divorce and suppressed the obligatory teaching of religion in state schools. In 1954, stung by the church's criticisms, he denounced the "infiltration" of the clergy in unions and politics. The following year he permitted his followers to retaliate, which in some cases meant burning churches. In September of 1955 the army forces rose up and forced him into exile.

ONGANÍA AND CATHOLIC CORPORATISM

During the Perón years many youth formed in Catholic Action began entering the military and government service with the hope of bringing Catholic values to the public forum. It is somewhat symptomatic of this new strategy that the planes which dropped bombs on the Plaza de Mayo in 1955 in order to overthrow Perón bore the slogan "Christ Conquers."[8] The governments that succeeded Perón were both conservative and liberal. Following the weak liberal civilian governments of Arturo Frondizi (1958-62) and Arturo Illia (1963-66), both of whom were overthrown, General Juan Carlos Onganía installed a Catholic corporate regime. He claimed to represent the "Argentine Revolution," which meant fostering national capitalism while at the same time opening the doors to transnationals. It also meant suppressing unions and political parties.

Under Onganía many Catholics formed in Catholic Action and the cursillos de Cristiandad held important posts in the government. On November 30, 1969, President Onganía consecrated the nation to the "protection and intercession of the Immaculate Heart of Mary."[9] But this new authoritarian developmentalism did not placate the popular classes. Strikes and student unrest spread everywhere. The high point came between May 13 and May 30 when the workers in Córdoba initiated a strike. They were soon followed by workers in La Plata, Resistencia, San Juan, Salta, and Rosario, while university students came out in support. Dozens of persons were killed in the subsequent clashes between police and protesters. This chapter in violence, known as the *Cordobazo,* sealed the end of Onganía's regime. In 1970 Onganía was overthrown by General Roberto Levingston, who in turn was replaced in 1971 by General Alejandro Lanusse.

CATHOLIC RADICALISM

Toward the end of the sixties another symptom of discontent appeared: guerrilla and terrorist movements. Several different groups emerged— Trotskyites, communists, leftist *peronistas,* and rightwing *peronistas.* The group that most captured the public's attention was the *Montoneros*—leftwing *peronistas.* They carried out their first action in May 1970, when they kidnapped and later killed General Pedro Aramburu, one of the officials who had overthrown Perón and who had governed the country from 1955 to 1958. The *Montoneros* were inspired by their romanticized version of the gauchos and a much idealized view of Perón, then living in exile. They imagined themselves to be "Perón's soldiers," at the service of his movement. The core group of founders had been formed in Catholic Action. Later, some of them founded the Tacuara, an extreme rightwing group. The Tacuara, which used the Maltese cross for its insignia, distinguished itself for its anticommunism and anti-semitism.[10] In the *Montoneros* the extreme right and the extreme left came together under the banner of *peronismo,* which somehow covered all kinds of tendencies. What the leaders had in common, apart from their Catholic conservative origins, was their authoritarianism and elitism. In reality, they transferred their integralist Catholic concepts to the guerrilla movement. These strange ties also explain why there was a certain attraction between the *Montoneros* and the organization called Priests for the Third World.

In December 1967 a group of Argentine priests published a document in support of the "Manifest of Eighteen Bishops of the Third World." With that document the organization Priests for the Third World was born. With time the organization came to have slightly more than five hundred members, that is, approximately 9 percent of the entire Argentinean clergy.[11] Many of these priests worked in the "misery villages" around Buenos Aires, a fact which accounted for their attraction to socialism. But in their internal debates they came to embrace *peronismo* because, in the words of one of their founders, the "people are *peronistas*."[12] The priest who most stood out as the movement's spokesman was Carlos Mugica. Born into a conservative Catholic family, his father was a minister in the Frondizi government. A charismatic idealist, Mugica admired Che Guevara, visited Cuba, but finally arrived at the conviction that the people's heart was with Perón. Armed by this realization he twice visited the leader himself in Spain and at the same time established links with the *Montoneros*. Previously, in 1964, he had taken a few of their future leaders with him to work in the "misery villages." But he personally rejected the *Montoneros'* violence. Nevertheless, when two of their leaders were killed in a shootout in 1970, he presided over their funeral and presented them as an "example for youth." Hundreds of Catholic Action youth were also present. As a consequence of his sermon and his known sympathy for the *Montoneros*, in May 1974 Mugica was shot down in front of his parish by a rightwing paramilitary group, probably the Triple A (Argentinean Anti-Communist Alliance). The popular priest's funeral was attended by an endless crowd.

Increasingly, the priests in the movement became objects of a systematic persecution. At the same time the movement underwent internal divisions and from 1974 on it practically ceased to function. During the first year after the 1976 takeover, several priests of the movement were murdered and others fled the country.[13]

It is important to emphasize the Catholic origins of some of the *Montoneros*, as well as their sympathy for the Priests for the Third World, in order to understand, in part, the military's obsession with persecuting Catholic "radicals." But this same relationship also explains the aversion conservative bishops felt for Catholic progressives, even for those who believed in democracy and rejected violence. From the point of view of the integralist bishops, the progressives seemed to lend support to Marxism and subversion.

PERÓN AND THE END OF ILLUSIONS

There were few myths more widely spread and deeply entrenched than the one built around the figure of Juan Domingo Perón and his companion, Eva. During the seventeen years that he spent in exile, while the political situation in Argentina became more unstable, popular expectations that only he could save the country acquired messianic dimensions. Naturally Perón himself encouraged these expectations and very astutely presented himself as the solution for all problems. Hence, there arose a *peronismo* of the right, made up of the old "shirtless" ones, and a *peronismo* of the left, made up of a new generation which, perhaps ignorant of the corruption and mismanagement of Perón's last years, built their illusions around the first reformist years of Perón. More to the point, they hoped to capitalize on those reforms and turn them into a socialist project.

Once again the relations between Perón and the church turned ambiguous, in part because after the Council and Medellín the church had acquired a new social sensibility. Several Catholic authors published books to show the remarkable affinity between *Justicialismo* and the social doctrine of the church. One of those authors was Carlos Mugica, the previously mentioned charismatic leader of the Priests for the Third World.[14] In a congress that took place in Santa Fe, the priests of that association publicly approved of *peronismo* because, they declared, it was the expression of the people in their search for social justice.[15] On November 11, 1972, Perón returned to Argentina for the first time after a long absence, and on December 6 he played host to a group of sixty priests belonging to the movement Priests for the Third World in his home in Buenos Aires. This encounter—between an experienced politician and a group of idealistic priests—seemed very much like the other famous encounter between Fidel Castro and the priests of the Group of Eighty in Santiago, Chile, almost a year before. However, after the meeting some of the priests left disillusioned when they realized that the Argentinean leader did not promise to carry out a socialist revolution, as they had hoped.

The great and final return took place the following year. In March 1973 the military government allowed free elections, although they vetoed Perón himself. But Perón's party put up Héctor Cámpora with the slogan, "Cámpora in the government, Perón in power." Cámpora won the elections and dedicated himself to preparing the way for Perón to become the president legally. In June, Perón returned to the country for the second time and was received triumphantly at the airport by a mass of his faithful followers and other spectators. In September new elections were held, and at the age of 77 the old caudillo became president of Argentina for the third time. His companion on the ticket was his new wife, María Estela (Isabel) Martínez. The euphoria of his return, however, soon dissipated. It became apparent that Perón did not plan to make radical changes, and his honeymoon with the left ended abruptly. The *Montoneros,* quite disenchanted, announced that from then on they would fight for "*peronismo* without Perón." With that they took up arms and returned to guerrilla warfare and the use of violence.

Perón's death in July 1974 created a climate of uncertainty and confusion. His wife, Isabel Perón, became president but was incapable of controlling a situation that became increasingly more violent. The leftist guerrilla groups— the *Montoneros,* the Revolutionary Army of the People, and others—committed robberies, kidnappings, and assassinations. In response, the rightwing paramilitary groups set out to hunt down and kill the guerrillas and their sympathizers. The most notorious of these groups was the Triple A, directed by José López Rega, a former secretary of Perón who was then serving as minister of Welfare under Isabel Perón. The number of deaths provoked by both sides rose dramatically: 47 in 1973, 180 in 1974, and, finally, 894 in 1975.[16] The military pressured Isabel Perón to exercise more control over the situation, and in July 1975 they themselves expelled López Rega from the country. Finally, in November, they took over the reins of the fight against subversion. When they finally seized power—on March 24, 1976—few were surprised.

MILITARY MESSIANISM AND CHRISTIANITY

Many Argentineans, tired of disorder and violence, welcomed the military takeover. But very few imagined that the violence the military was about to unleash would be much worse than that which existed before. Furthermore, General Jorge Videla, head of the first junta, was considered a moderate. Nevertheless, the Argentinean military regime soon exhibited all the characteristics of the bureaucratic-authoritarian national security state. As in the cases of Chile and Brazil, religion was also mixed in with militarism. But the messianism of the Argentinean military seemed to be even more pronounced than in those other cases. Almost all of the top officials, beginning with Videla, were nearly perfect examples of Catholic integralism; all were nationalistic, anticommunist, anti-liberal, and in some cases, anti-semitic. In Argentina, with its large Jewish population (there were 400,000 Jews in Buenos Aires), this last characteristic acquired a special significance.[17] The architects of the military takeover were guided by the notion of the just war against the enemies of the nation. In their defense of "Western Christian civilization" they were motivated by a totalizing vision that absolutized good and evil and did not leave room for neutrality, compromise, or dialogue.

What the military called a "dirty war" was in reality the practice of state terrorism. In the "Final Report," which they published before leaving power and with the evident aim of justifying themselves before public opinion, the authors refer to twenty-five thousand subversives, of whom fifteen thousand were allegedly armed. Yet the majority of observers believe that the number of subversives was really around two thousand, of whom perhaps only 20 percent were armed.[18] To be sure, the *Montoneros* committed reprehensible crimes. Nevertheless, the military responded by going far beyond the reasonable use of force. Thousands of Argentineans were kidnapped and tortured without any judicial process. Sometimes torture was applied to persons even when it was known that they probably did not have any direct connection to the subversives.[19] In different interviews Videla shed light on the military mind. According to him, terrorism did not consist only in actions but in ideas as well:

"Terrorism is not defined only by killing with an arm or placing a bomb; it is also defined by inciting others to act by the force of ideas contrary to our western Christian civilization."[20]

In an earlier interview (1975) he declared without ambiguities:

"If it is necessary in Argentina that all the people who threaten the security of the country die, then they should die."[21]

Finally, another depressing note in the Argentinean case was the existence of a mindset and the use of methods that made it look like Nazi Germany. The report made by Alfonsín's government points to the crude anti-semitism practiced by lower class officials. At times these officials would greet Jewish prisoners with cries of "Heil, Hitler!" and "Long live Christ the King!"[22] The journalist Jacobo Timerman, who was kidnapped in 1977 and held for two years, was liberated thanks to the pressure of friends outside the country. His testimony on the anti-semitism of his persecutors is especially revealing.[23] Furthermore, the method used to exterminate the selected victims seemed very much like that of Hitler's Germany. During the seven-year dictatorship close to 8,960 (the official figure) Argentineans were pulled out of their homes or taken prisoner in public. Then they were sent to one of 340 different detention centers without notifying their families or others. Later, they simply "disappeared." The government systematically denied that it was an accomplice of the kidnappings, and it even denied the existence of the centers. The policy of the Argentine military, unlike that of Pinochet who rounded up the "subversives" in the national stadium and in other known centers, consisted in denying any knowledge whatsoever of the facts. Just as in Nazi Germany, the victims disappeared without any judicial process at all, like night and fog.

PROFILE OF THE CHURCH (1976)

In order to understand the church's reaction to the military regime, it is helpful to keep in mind a few of its facets and characteristics. Numerically, there were more than 80 bishops in full activity for more than sixty dioceses.[24] In 1988 there were 5,378 priests, almost equally divided between the secular clergy and the religious.[25] It is not easy to pin down the exact number of foreigners among the clergy. A source for 1961 put the number at one-fourth of the diocesan clergy.[26] There are no official figures for the religious clergy, but given the fact that many religious are missionaries, obviously there were and are more foreigners among them. However, given the fact that many of the foreigners happen to be Spaniards or Italians, their presence does not attract attention in a society with so many immigrants of those nationalities.

In many parts of Latin America during that period the progressives prevailed in the hierarchy. By way of contrast, in Argentina the bishops who predominated were conservatives and integralists. One author classified ten bishops in the category of "integralists" or "ultraconservatives," followed by a block of "conservatives," then in fewer numbers, "moderates," and finally, "progressives."[27] Certain bishops—like Adolfo Tortolo, president of the episcopal conference at the time of the military takeover; Victorio Manuel Bonamín, the military chaplain; and Antonio J. Plaza, the archbishop of La Plata—clearly belonged to the ultraconservatives. They openly supported the military coup and justified the suppression of the guerrillas, even with the use of torture.

The next block, made up of some forty conservatives, objected to the brutality of the regime, but not to the extent of criticizing it in public or breaking relations with it; they were basically in agreement with the general objectives. The two cardinals, Raúl Primatesta, the archbishop of Córdoba who succeeded Tortolo in 1976 as president of the episcopal conference, and Juan Carlos Aramburu, the archbishop of Buenos Aires from 1975 to 1990, fall into this category. Antonio Quarracino, the bishop of Avellaneda and later archbishop of La Plata and finally of Buenos Aires, also belonged to this group. He also served as secretary general of CELAM between 1978 and 1982. The nuncio during this period, Pío Laghi (1974-80), generally sided with the conservative block, in spite of the fact that he had the power to speak up as an independent voice. The moderate block was made up of the bishops who supported the reforms of Vatican II, but who, out of timidity or fear of breaking episcopal unity, did not stand out for their protests. Such would be the case of Eduardo Pironio, the third Argentine cardinal. Pironio was auxiliary bishop of La Plata, later bishop of Mar de Plata, and in 1975 he was named pro-Prefect of the Congregation for Religious in Rome. In spite of his progressive positions in favor of the Council, he did not take a very clear public position with respect to human-rights violations in his own country. Furthermore, the absence of Pironio during the military years facilitated the dominance of the conservatives.

The progressive bishops who did take a clear and positive stand were in the minority. Among them were Enrique Angelelli, the bishop of Rioja; Carlos Ponce de León, of San Nicolás; Jorge Novak, of Quilmes; Miguel Heseyne, of Viedma; Jaime Nevares, of Neuquén; and Alberto Devoto, of Goya.

THE ROOTS OF CONSERVATIVISM

The bad Argentineans who leave the country organize themselves against their country, and with the support of dark forces, spread news and carry out a campaign in combination with those who work in the shadows within our territory. Let us pray for the happy outcome of the arduous mission of those who govern us temporally and spiritually. We are sons of a nation in which the church enjoys a level of respect unknown in all countries which have been condemned as Marxist.
    —Antonio Plaza, Archbishop of La Plata, 1977[28]

The conservative orientation of the Argentine hierarchy is especially re-markable if one compares it to the Chilean church. Both countries were recipients of a large European immigration and both have a long democratic tradition, at least until 1930 in the case of Argentina. But in Argentina there was no Raúl Silva Henríquez, nor a Vicariate of Solidarity, nor did the church distance itself from the state.

In order to understand this conservativism it is well to underline, in the first place, the influence that national Catholicism had on many clergy, who reacted against liberalism and the populism of Yrigoyen and Perón. Many bishops frankly shared the same mentality as that of the military as regards the identification of Catholicism with country. For both, communism repre-sented a virus that had infected the national body, and the elimination of that virus constituted a step toward health for the church and for society. Further-more, as a consequence of national patronage (which ended in 1966), the bishops were accustomed to defer to the state, which in turn helped support the church economically.[29] The bishops looked upon the church as a corpora-tion that had a mission to cooperate with the other corporation, the state, to help create peace and order.

Another factor should be taken into account: the social origins and the for-mation of the Argentine clergy. Very much to the contrary of simplistic Marxist stereotypes, which pointed to the union of the church with an oligarchic state, in fact the most representative figures among the conservatives—Tortolo, Aramburu, Primatesta, Quarracino—were almost all descendants of lower-class immigrants. The immigrant lower class esteemed hard work, but it also envied the aristocratic upper classes. For bishops like Tortolo, Plaza, and others, to mix with the rich and powerful, and to find themselves looked upon with re-spect by the upper class, meant a step up in life. Furthermore, Argentine seminaries have usually been very conservative. The model that they set for their seminarians was that of the priest who stands for order and tradition. In general, Vatican II had very little impact in the Argentinean church. The typical Argentinean bishop knew little theology, especially post–Vatican II theology. Tortolo, who was president of the episcopal conference at the time of the military takeover, kept his diocese of Paraná like a fortress that pro-tected itself against the changes emanating out of the Council. In fact, he invited Marcel Lefebvre to visit his diocese before the latter went into open rebellion with Rome.

Another factor that weighed heavily in the episcopal conference was in-stitutional unity. In order to maintain that unity the bishops preferred to speak out in terms of general principles but to avoid concrete applications, espe-cially in the area of human-rights violations. To refer to concrete cases, or to publicly denounce the government, would have provoked even greater divi-sions among the bishops. For that reason the moderate bishops limited their role to that of signing the documents prepared by the conservative majority. At the same time, however, the progressive minority felt obliged to speak out and make its protest known outside the episcopal conference. Finally, another factor led even moderates to fear criticizing the government too openly, and that was the presence of Catholics or persons of Catholic upbringing in the subversive groups. As Bishop Bonamín put it, "The churches have also given birth to guerrillas."[30] In order to clearly distance themselves from the Catholic radicals, the bishops went to the other extreme of confusing subversion with legitimate protest against the government.

Finally, there is a lesson to be learned from the absence of a Catholic party or a Christian Democratic Party of a national scale. In Chile that party fulfilled many social functions: as a respectable forum where a Christian could ventilate his or her social concern, and as a counterweight to conservative bishops. In Argentina the conservative bishops reserved for themselves the right to define the limits and the norms governing the political conduct of Catholics. But in Argentina there was no large party identified with Catholicism that could offer an alternative to the "official" line. Those Catholics who represented progressive social Christianity were simply marginalized by the conservative bishops. As we saw earlier, the Christian Democratic Party of Argentina was very small and therefore very limited in its capacity to have any impact on a nationwide basis.

THE OFFICIAL CHURCH: ACTIONS AND OMISSIONS

The most conservative group within the hierarchy justified the military takeover and defended, without ambiguities, the actions of the military. In September 1975, during the funeral of a military officer who had been killed by terrorists, and in the presence of General Roberto Viola, chief of operations of the Army, the military vicar, Victorio Bonamín, declared: "The army is expiating the impurities of this country. Would not Christ want the armed forces one day to go beyond their normal functions?"[31] As though this coincidence of opinions were not enough, on the day of the takeover—March 24—General Videla and Admiral Massera met in a long session with Tortolo, then the military chaplain and the president of the episcopal conference. As a general rule Bonamín and Tortolo never lost an opportunity to praise the army and the military government.

But at year's end Tortolo was replaced as president of the episcopal conference, and Raúl Primatesta, the cardinal-archbishop of Córdoba, was elected his successor. Without doubt the outright integralism of Tortolo, as well as his rejection of Vatican II, turned out to be a source of embarrassment to the other bishops, who saw the convenience of electing someone else, a conservative to be sure, but one who would be more prudent and cautious in his dealings with the government. From that moment on the episcopal conference began to express its concern over the acts of violence committed by the forces of order. But the conference also adopted the policy, which perhaps at that moment seemed prudent and productive, of limiting public criticism to general principles while in private pressuring the government to resolve particular cases.

Toward the end of 1982 the episcopate published a volume containing a selection of documents—previously published between 1970 and 1972—that referred to violence, human rights, and the disappearances. Unpublished documents were also included. These included messages the episcopal conference had sent to the military junta or to the minister of the Interior. The bishops explained this course of action:

> For the Argentinean hierarchy it would have been easy to take the attitude of condemning outright the government of the armed forces; nevertheless, it chose not to do so, not because it desired to support the government, but for the good of the community, and in that way avoiding the introduction of an additional element of confusion.[32]

In their messages to the military the bishops revealed that they were fully aware that something terrible was happening in the country: "We bishops frequently received the anguished complaints of the families of persons who had disappeared, or been kidnapped or detained."[33] In other letters the bishops refer to the systematic use of torture and the common practice of robbing the victims of their belongings.[34] The bishops did not just send messages. The executive committee of the episcopal conference paid at least twenty different visits to the military junta between 1976 and 1983 to discuss the question of human rights. In fact, in a summary of one of those meetings, held on September 28, 1978, the bishops expressed their frustration over not receiving a satisfactory answer to their concerns: "We demanded to be informed of the situation of human rights and we expressed our unhappiness at the inefficiency of the meetings."[35] In another meeting, between several bishops and General Videla, held on June 25, 1980, the prelates pointed out the discrepancies between the national security doctrine and the teachings of the church.[36]

From all this it clearly can be affirmed that the bishops did try to call the attention of the military, both in writing and in person, to its acts. Furthermore, there were cases in which the opportune intervention of the bishops probably saved some lives. But the criticism leveled at the hierarchy resides in the fact that it did not take a clear and decisive *public* stand in the defense of human rights. Furthermore, at times their words contradicted their actions. In his work on this topic Emilio Mignone—a lawyer, educator, and militant Catholic, whose daughter, Mónica, a catechist who worked in a "misery village," had been kidnapped and never seen again—relates how he sought aid from the church but found the door of the military vicariate closed. When he tried to investigate the situation of other families that had suffered disappearances, he discovered that the office of the military vicariate listened to their complaints but in practice did little to pressure the military to be accountable for its actions. Furthermore, on several occasions certain bishops and priests practically stood with the military in justifying the repression. On one occasion the Mothers of the Plaza de Mayo attended a mass to pray for their disappeared sons and daughters. But the priest who gave the sermon spoke of young people who, under the influence of drugs, easily ended up as subversives. The Mothers abandoned the church as a sign of protest.[37] In 1982 Cardinal Aramburu and in 1983 Quarracino as well made statements to the foreign press in which they denied that there were "disappearances" in Argentina. According to Quarracino, the persons who had disappeared were, in reality, living outside the country.[38] Later he claimed that he never made such a statement. In general, in spite of their messages to the military, the most important figures in the hierarchy did not hide their lack of sympathy for human-rights groups that applied pressure to find out the truth about the victims of state terror.

THE CHURCH PERSECUTED

This lack of a decisive and energetic commitment to the defense of human rights is all the more telling considering the fact that some of the victims were members of the official church. Of course, in those cases the bishops did call for the attention of the military, but in general they limited their action to that of listening to the official explanations.

Even before the military takeover the murder of Carlos Mugica by paramilitary groups showed that the military had no moral limit and that the church, especially the progressive sectors, was a valid target. Yet the first act of violence directed against the church after the takeover was of such magnitude that it leads one to suspect that it was probably done by a paramilitary group "out of control." On the morning of July 4, 1976, in St. Patrick's parish in the fashionable neighborhood of Belgrano (Buenos Aires)—the very parish of President Videla—three priests and two seminarians were shot to death in cold blood. These religious belonged to the Pallottines, a congregation that came over in the nineteenth century to attend to the immigrants, especially the Irish. In fact, the popular pastor of the parish, Father Alfredo Kelly, was an Argentinean of Irish ancestry. The murderers painted slogans on the walls of the room where they left their victims in a crude attempt to throw the blame on subversive groups.

But the evidence pointed strongly in another direction. The United States embassy, using its own sources, informed the papal nuncio, Pío Laghi, that the authors of the crime were paramilitary.[39] In this case the reaction of the church was typical. The nuncio and Cardinal Aramburu visited the military junta to express their indignation. The junta denied any knowledge of who might be responsible and promised to rectify the repression that the government had unleashed. A public mass was celebrated for the religious and the nuncio expressed his sorrow for the tragedy. But in his message he made no reference to an independent investigation into the crime.[40] The matter ended there, and the case was only reopened after the military left power.

This first crime was followed by many others. On July 18, 1976, two priests who belonged to Priests for the Third World were kidnapped and killed in Chamical, near Rioja, a diocese about four hundred miles from the Chilean frontier. The bishop of the diocese, Enrique Angelelli, who had previously denounced the government for its human-rights violations, died in a car accident on August 4. He carried with him documents that allegedly proved the complicity of the military in the death of the two priests. A year later another bishop, Carlos Ponce de León of the diocese of San Nicolás, a friend of Angelelli who had likewise denounced the military, also died in a car accident, the cause of which was never determined. In December 1977 two French religious women who belonged to the Institute of Foreign Missions and who worked with the Mothers of the Plaza de Mayo were kidnapped and "disappeared." President Valéry Giscard d'Estaing himself sent a special emissary to ask for explanations, but once again the Argentinean authorities claimed ignorance of who was responsible.

Finally, there were many committed laypersons, like Mónica, Emilio Mignone's daughter, who also disappeared. In a few very exceptional cases, thanks to the intervention of bishops, religious superiors, and the foreign press, some of the kidnapping victims returned to the light of day. Two Jesuits were captured in May 1976 and held in the Mechanical School of the Army—the detention center for hundreds of the disappeared. In October of that year both were dumped into a vacant lot, alive.[41]

ANGELELLI AND THE BISHOPS WHO PROTESTED

Enrique Angelelli was born in 1923 in Córdoba and studied for the priesthood in Rome, where he was ordained in 1949. He was ordained a bishop in 1960 and was appointed head of the diocese of Rioja in 1968. He was an eminently pastoral man who had a very close relationship with the people in his diocese. One of his favorite hobbies was to write poetry. Even before the military takeover he had problems with the military commander of that region, General Luciano Benjamín Menéndez, who later served as the commander in chief of the army during the War of the Malvinas. In February 1976 the vicar general of the diocese was detained and subjected to an interrogation. In June the two priests, Gabriel Longueville and Carlos de Dios Murias, were kidnapped and killed. Angelelli made a report on the crime for the nuncio, who then spoke with President Videla about the case. Finally, however, the efforts of Angelelli to investigate the death of the two priests led to his own death. On August 4 Angelelli and another priest visited Chamical, where the two French priests had worked. He celebrated a mass and in his sermon denounced the military for their crimes. From Chamical he headed toward the provincial capital with documents relating to the case. Suddenly two other vehicles closed in on his van and drove him off the road. The bishop's body was found about 25 yards from his van, but the documents and the other vehicles were, of course, gone. The official report closed the case on the grounds that there was no reason to continue the investigation.[42] But in 1984 (after the military regime) another judge ordered the case to be reopened and in 1986 he arrived at quite a different conclusion:

> I deem to be thoroughly credible the belief that what cost the life of Enrique Angelelli, the bishop of La Rioja, was homicide; which homicide occurred in a place previously chosen.[43]

The silence of the majority of Angelelli's fellow bishops about his death was scandalous. By way of exception, Carlos Ponce de León, the bishop of San Nicolás, attended Angelelli's funeral and denounced his death as another example of violations of human rights. Ponce de León died a year later, also in a car accident.[44] The death of these two bishops without doubt had the intended effect of creating a climate of fear in the church. In spite of that, four bishops continued to raise their voices in protest. From the very beginning Jaime de Nevares, bishop of Neuquén, in the southeastern part of the country, denounced human-rights violations. In large part for that reason he was called upon by President Alfonsín to be a member of the Permanent Assembly of Human Rights, created in 1975; later, in 1983, he was also appointed a member of the National Commission on the Disappearance of Persons. Also deserving of honorable mention is Jorge Novak, the bishop of Quilmes, who joined the Ecumenical Movement for Human Rights, founded in 1976. Finally, Miguel Heseyne of Viedma became a thorn in the side of the government. In 1977, when President Videla visited his diocese, Heseyne personally pleaded with the president for the lives of the innocent and the poor.[45] Later he wrote a series of public letters to the president and the minister of the Interior in which he accused them of covering up crimes. In a letter to Videla, dated December 16, 1979, he declared:

> We know there were tortures and attacks on human dignity, even in the most elementary and anti-Christian ways, both done by the subversives and the armed forces.[46]

Videla answered the letter, justifying the repression as a necessity in time of "war," and praised the "abnegation and heroism" of the armed forces.

PÉREZ ESQUIVEL AND HUMAN RIGHTS

In the decade of the seventies several human-rights groups emerged in Argentina: the Permanent Assembly of Human Rights (1975), the Commission of Relatives of the Disappeared and Those Detained for Political and Labor Reasons (1976), the Ecumenical Movement for Human Rights (1976), the Center of Legal and Social Studies (CELS) (1979), and finally, the most famous of them all, the Mothers of Plaza de Mayo (1977). Although each one of these groups pursued a different specific objective, all worked in close coordination. This was due in large part to the work of Adolfo Pérez Esquivel, who won the Nobel Peace Prize in 1980 for his campaign in favor of human rights.

Pérez Esquivel was the Latin American coordinator of SERPAJ, the Justice and Peace Service, founded in the sixties. Pérez Esquivel himself had been influenced by such figures as Thomas Merton, Martin Luther King Jr., and Mahatma Gandhi. Furthermore, as a committed Catholic he followed very closely the changes in the church after Medellín. For a while, when he was unable to return to Argentina, he worked in Riombamba, Ecuador, as a lay missionary with his family at the invitation of Leonidas Proaño.[47] He played a key role in founding the other human-rights groups that were close to SERPAJ. In each Latin American country the church promoted the creation of peace and justice commissions. But in Argentina the man in charge of that commission was Archbishop Quarracino, who was more sympathetic to the military than to human-rights causes. As a result, that commission was totally ineffective. SERPAJ and the other groups filled that vacuum.

Pérez Esquivel suffered the same fate as many other human-rights activists. He was held in prison for fourteen months, and then spent the next fourteen months under surveillance in his home. When the news arrived that he had been chosen as the recipient of the Nobel Peace Prize, he was immediately thrust into the limelight of world attention. But he was not congratulated by the Argentine government or by the episcopal conference of his own country. For them, the prize was seen as a reproach to their own conduct.

THE MOTHERS OF PLAZA DE MAYO

The most famous protest group during the military regime was the Mothers of Plaza de Mayo. Inspired by Pérez Esquivel, who assumed the role of spiritual guide for the group, mothers whose sons and daughters had been kidnapped decided to undertake a positive and daring initiative. On a Thursday in April 1977 a group of fourteen mothers appeared suddenly in the historic Plaza de Mayo, in front of the Casa Rosada, the seat of Argentina's executive branch.[48] In an orderly way and in silence they walked around the Plaza in procession. Within time, other mothers lost their fear and joined the first group. Every Thursday during the entire dictatorship, and long afterward, the mothers paraded around the plaza, converting their action into a consecrated ritual. In September 1979 the Interamerican Commission of Human Rights, a dependency of the Organization of American States, visited Argentina and was profoundly impressed by the spectacle of two thousand mothers of sons and daughters who had disappeared. The weekly ritual of the mothers moved national and world opinion and turned out to be the most convincing proof that there were massive violations of human rights in Argentina. The government tried to ignore the mothers and finally turned to harassment. In December 1977 six mothers were kidnapped along with the two French religious women. They were never seen again.

Toward the end of 1977 another group emerged: the Grandmothers of Plaza de Mayo. Among the disappeared were mothers who had given birth while in prison. But their sons and daughters also disappeared. Later investigations revealed that at least 217 babies had been born in detention centers. These babies were turned over for adoption, and they were frequently adopted by families of the police or the military. The Grandmothers demanded information not only about their sons and daughters but about their grandchildren as well. Within time fifty-one of those babies were located, all living with families that were not their own biologically.[49]

The Mothers and the Grandmothers of Plaza de Mayo were and are laywomen; they do not represent the official church. Nevertheless, their movement had an explicit religious motivation. The vast majority were practicing Catholics and they frequently met in churches. They also attended masses together to pray for their missing children, and at times they used religious symbols to express their sorrow. On one occasion they carried nails in a procession to symbolize the fact that Christ was once again being crucified.[50] The official church did not distinguish itself for prophetic gestures. Rather, it was the people of God, represented by the Mothers and Grandmothers of Plaza de Mayo and many laypersons like Pérez Esquivel, who fulfilled that mission.

THE PROTESTANTS

The Protestant community of Argentina is relatively small (perhaps 5.5 percent of the population) and mainly descended from European immigrants. Most Argentine Protestants belonged to the urban middle classes and in general were not overly involved in politics.[51] Nevertheless, during the military dictatorship an important minority among them actively promoted the cause of human rights and supported the protest against the regime. The most notable example was the Ecumenical Movement for Human Rights, which was made up of Protestants of the mainline churches: Methodists, Lutherans, Presbyterians, Disciples of Christ, and others. The Methodist bishop Federico Pagura and the emeritus Methodist bishop Carlos Gattinoni both participated in the movement, along with Jorge Novak, the Catholic bishop of Quilmes. Theologians like José Míguez Bonino supported the criticism leveled against the government from a liberationist perspective. There were also victims among the Protestants. In its report CONADEP referred to the case of Mauricio Amílcar López, a pastor, who was also the executive delegate of the World Council of Churches as well as the president of the University of Luján. He was kidnapped in 1977 and never seen again.[52] Also, the Jewish community was represented by Rabbi Marshall Meyer and the journalist Jacobo Timerman, whom we mentioned before. Meyer also formed part of CONADEP, along with Jaime Nevares and Carlos Gattinoni.

THE TRANSITION: CHURCH AND NATIONAL COMMUNITY (1981)

From 1979 on the moderate sector among the bishops began to assert itself in the hierarchy. The international ill-fame of the military government, plus criticisms from Catholics around the world, prompted the bishops to distance themselves from the regime and to take a more energetic attitude in favor of human rights. The third general conference of the Latin American bishops held in Puebla (1979) condemned the doctrine of national security, a fact that forced the Argentine bishops to take a clearer stand with respect to their own government, which was a model of the national security state. Also, the papal mediation conducted by Cardinal Samoré in the conflict with Chile over the Beagle Canal served to strengthen the prestige of the papacy and the church in general. In addition, the international censure that hung over the military government helped to speed up its internal collapse. Finally, given the fact that the government had fairly well wiped out the subversive groups, it no longer had a reason to be. In the absence of well-organized political parties—and *peronismo* had been thoroughly discredited—only the church could fill the vacuum and propose generally acceptable rules for returning to democracy.

The most important ecclesial document of that period, and perhaps one of the best in the history of the Argentine church, was "Church and National Community," published by the episcopal conference in May 1981. It was clearly intended to be a clarion call to begin the process of returning to democracy. The first part includes a historical section in which the bishops emphasize the Latin and Catholic roots of the nation. The bishops go on to criticize the bad tendencies of liberalism, but they also praise democracy as a historic aspiration of the Argentine people. The document attempts to find an equilibrium between the evil of subversion and the evil of state terrorism. The bishops cite John Paul II in order to condemn the suppression of human rights in the name of the common good.[53] They criticize the prolonged state of emergency, which was used to justify the suppressing of basic civil liberties.[54] At the same time they tie democracy and social justice together, the latter being a condition for the former.[55] In the most positive part of the document they call upon Argentineans to reconstruct their nation so that it can become a "national community." And, as the bishops point out, that community can be achieved only through dialogue and reconciliation.

Finally, the bishops call for a general pardon and condemn the attitude of an "eye for an eye."[56] Although the call to pardon is worthy of praise, an important omission is immediately noticeable: there is no call for justice for the innocent victims of state terrorism. With this letter the church defined what would be its basic pastoral orientation: reconciliation, dialogue, and participation. The military itself, in search for a way out of power, had recourse to the church's concepts. In this case, however, it did so out of expediency. It understood "reconciliation" to mean total amnesty for its own crimes.

FROM THE MALVINAS/FALKLANDS TO ALFONSÍN

In 1981 General Videla finished his mandate as chief of the junta and was replaced by General Roberto Viola, who in turn was followed by General Leopoldo Galtieri in 1982. It was Galtieri who made the fatal decision to capture the Malvinas (Falkland, for the English) Islands, which were a British colony. John Paul II's visit during the conflict, aimed at fostering an atmosphere favorable to peace, somewhat assuaged national wounds following the military debacle and the loss of many lives. The defeat over the Malvinas precipitated an internal crisis that soon led to the collapse of the military regime. For this very special reason, unlike the Chilean or the Brazilian military, the Argentine military was not able to make a pact with the civilians, which forced the military to accept certain conditions after the transition to democracy was made. In light of the generalized repudiation over its incompetence in the war and its gross violations of human rights, the military had no choice but to convoke elections and turn the country back over to the civilians. Under General Reynaldo Bignone—Galtieri's successor—elections were held in October 1983. In December, Raúl Alfonsín, the candidate of the Radical Civic Union Party (Yrigoyen's party) became president of the republic.

But the military did not simply leave. A few months before relinquishing power it published a document known as the "Final Report." The report turned out to be a justification for its actions in power and at the same time a call for national unity. The report invited all Argentineans to look for reconciliation with a "Christian spirit." But the most dramatic section of the document, and the most chilling, was the frank statement that the disappeared were probably all dead: "All those persons who appear on lists of the disappeared and are not among the exiled or living in the underground may be considered dead."[57] For the first time the military admitted that it knew what had happened to the missing persons, at least the majority of them. Finally, three weeks before the elections, the military government promulgated a "Law of National Pacification," by which the military granted its members full amnesty and pardon for the means they used to combat subversion while in power.

ALFONSÍN AND THE TRIALS

Within three days after taking office President Alfonsín declared null and void the Law of National Pacification and ordered the chiefs of the first three juntas arrested. Thus began the long, dramatic process by which Argentinean society judged those responsible for the crimes committed during the military regime. At the same time Alfonsín created CONADEP, the National Commission on the Disappearance of Persons. Under the presidency of the novelist Ernesto Sábato, the commission devoted itself to investigating all known cases of missing persons, as well as bringing to light the hidden side of repression: the location of the detention centers and the jails where the people disappeared; the methods of torture used to extract confessions; and so forth. Although the commission was not created to judge the accused, in fact its abundant findings did serve as material for the trials of the military.

At first Alfonsín charged the Supreme Council of the Armed Forces to carry out the investigation into the accusations against its own members. But finally, in October 1984, in the face of the "unjustified delays" of the Council, the Federal Court of Appeals of Buenos Aires was charged with the duty of processing and judging the military, police, and civilians accused of human-rights violations. The accused military were turned over from military jurisdiction to the civilians. During the trials, which were witnessed by the entire nation, the highest commanders of the first juntas were brought as prisoners to the court and forced to face eight hundred different witnesses. On December 30, 1986, the Supreme Court of Justice ratified the sentences meted out by the Federal Court of Appeals. Former General Jorge Videla and former Admiral Massera were sentenced to life imprisonment. Former Brigadier General Orlando Agosti was condemned to three years and six months. Among the members of the second junta, General Viola received a sentence of sixteen years and six months, and Admiral Armando Lambruschini received eight years. General Ramón Camps, the chief of police of the Province of Buenos Aires, was sentenced to twenty-five years in prison. At a later date former president Galtieri received a twelve-year sentence, but in his case the reason given was "failures and omissions" during the Malvinas war. Several vice-ministers in his government also received varying sentences.

The spectacle of a Latin American nation judging the principal members of a former military government for crimes against the people astonished world opinion. Alfonsín and the government counted on popular support to carry out the trials. But he also felt the pressure of the armed forces, many conservative groups, and the official church not to go too far. In 1986, in the face of the sheer accumulation of cases against the military, the Argentine congress passed the Law of Final Termination, which established expiration dates for initiating new cases. In April 1987 the first of several military uprisings during Alfonsín's administration broke out. Under pressure from the military and other groups, congress passed the Law of Due Obedience, by which lower officials were exonerated from being brought to trial because they had acted out of obedience to their superiors. In the opinion of many, these laws constituted a sort of de facto amnesty.[58] Nevertheless, the final blow against the triumph of justice came under Alfonsín's successor, Carlos Menem, who assumed office in July 1989. In October Menem gave a general pardon to 277 military and civilians who had been condemned for human-rights violations, for ineptitude in the Malvinas war, or for participating in the uprisings of the *carapintadas* (the "painted faces," a reference to the military who rebelled against Alfonsín). At the end of December 1990 Menem granted a second general pardon—in spite of popular protests—which affected the leaders of the first juntas, including Videla and Viola.

THE CHURCH (1983-1990): AMBIGUITIES

The church had already prepared the way for returning to democracy in "Church and National Community." But the experience of actually finding itself once again in democracy gave rise to ambiguous and ambivalent reactions. On the one hand, the progressive groups came out in support of the popular demonstrations that called for the return to democracy.[59] But the integralists and conservatives continued to dominate in the episcopal conference. Each group had quite a different view of the role the church ought to play in post-military Argentina. Among a host of sensitive topics there were two that especially created a wedge between the church and large numbers of Argentineans: divorce and the military trials.

In 1984 several different proposals were made to legalize divorce in Argentina. Many bishops carried out campaigns against the proposals and organized a great demonstration in July 1986 in the Plaza de Mayo. Many leading figures of the political right were present. All the slogans of the old integralism were repeated: Catholic family and Catholic nation. The progressive bishops were quite uncomfortable at this spectacle of the church becoming another "pressure group."[60]

Of a graver nature was the question of the trials and the pardons. In its public statements the church called for reconciliation and pardon, but it did not call for bringing the guilty to trial. Indeed, on one occasion Cardinal Quarracino proposed the idea of passing a "law of forgetting."[61] In this context the hierarchical church received the news that the military chiefs were to be tried with little enthusiasm. But they did applaud the decision of President Menem to grant a pardon for those who had been tried and condemned. By way of exception, the progressive minority—Heseyne, Novak, and Nevares—along with two Methodist bishops and other leaders connected with the human-rights groups or CONADEP, such as Ernesto Sábato, lamented the decision.[62] The papal visit in 1987 reflected this ecclesial ambiguity. During his meeting with youth on April 11, the pope spoke extemporaneously when he made this following exhortation:

"Let brothers cease to confront brothers; let there be no more kidnappings or disappearances; let there be no place for hatred and violence, and may the dignity of persons be always respected."[63]

But the following day, in his address to the bishops, he praised their conduct during the dictatorship:

"I know of your selfless efforts to save lives, thus giving witness to the demands of the Gospel. Silenced and forgotten: God knows of your faithfulness!"[64]

CONCLUSION: TWO CHURCHES

As a consequence of the extraordinary influence that the tradition of national Catholicism, forged in the eucharistic congress of 1934, had over it, the Argentine church lost vital contact with large sectors of the population. This was most poignant in the case of *peronismo*. That same tradition impeded the church from becoming a symbol of national unity under Videla and the other military, much less a symbol of democracy and human rights. Although the bishops, through discreet diplomacy, saved many lives, they preferred to function as a corporation vis-à-vis the military and thus contribute to peace and order in society. They did not opt to speak as a single voice in the name of the people in general or at least in the name of the poor or the victims of oppression. For that reason, their call to reconciliation did not have the same moral force as it did in the case of other episcopal hierarchies in Latin America: Chile, Brazil, Paraguay, and so on. And for that reason the church did not fit in well in the new democratic and pluralistic Argentina after the dictatorship.

On the other hand, for quite some time a new church, identified with Vatican II and Medellín and nourished by the tradition of social Christianity, had also been emerging. The bishops, priests, religious women, and laypersons who protested in favor of human rights, and who frequently suffered the consequences of their protest, represented a small but valiant minority. And that progressive minority has steadily grown. Beginning in 1986 a group of laypersons connected with the Center Nueva Tierra (New Earth) in Buenos Aires, with the support of several bishops and priests, has organized theological seminars for the popular classes. The group modeled its seminars on the summer course in theology run by the Catholic University in Lima, Peru. By way of example, at the fourth seminar, held in the diocese of San Justo in 1989, there were 450 participants. For the fifth seminar, held in 1990 in the diocese of Morón, there were 760 participants, the majority of whom were laypersons.[65] In many ways the internal divisions in the church reflected the same division between modern, pluralistic Argentina, on the one hand, and on the other, conservative and traditionalist Argentina. It can be foreseen that, given the bitter memories of the military regime that still linger on, these two churches will continue to coexist side by side for some time.

In April 1995, moved by the desire to foster a real national reconciliation, General Martín Balza, the head of the army, admitted publicly that the armed forces had followed "immoral orders" during the "dirty war." This was the first time that a high army official had assumed moral responsibility for the actions of members of the army. The veteran leader of the *Montoneros,* Mario Eduardo Firmenich, also spoke in public, not to ask for pardon but rather to justify his actions.[66] After these statements, many other confessions followed.[67] For its part, the church took an agonizingly long time to make its own statement on the subject. Finally, in a document entitled, *Walking toward the Third Millennium*, the final product of an ad hoc committee designated by the episcopal conference in December 1995, the bishops collectively asked "humbly for forgiveness from God for guilt we can be accused of." The bishops go on to state:

> We are deeply sorry for not having been able to mitigate even more the pain produced by this drama. We express our solidarity with those who were wounded by it, and we sincerely lament the participation of sons of the church in the violation of human rights.[68]

Although the document stops short of admitting guilt, it does suggest that the official church had dared to glance, at last, albeit timidly, into the mirror of a dark past.

5.

Paraguay (1954-1989)

The Longest Dictatorship

Peace had been officially decreed, and it was forbidden to place the
official peace in doubt; We were fed up with peace. All the stores sold
the same kind of peace, and nothing grew in the country, not even
tapioca.[1]
—Bartomeu Melià, S.J.

The dictatorship of Alfredo Stroessner was one of the longest in the contemporary history of Latin America: thirty-five years. But, within the
authoritarian tradition of Paraguay, it was not so exceptional. In the last century José Gapsar Rodríguez de Francia (the "Supreme One") ruled for
twenty-five years; Carlos Antonio López and Francisco Solano López, both
for eighteen years. Paraguay, a country poor in natural resources and with
access to the ocean only through the La Plata River, suffered grave losses as
a consequence of two wars in its post-independence history. In the War of
the Triple Alliance (1865-70), against Argentina and Brazil, Paraguay lost
more than half of its 500,000 inhabitants.[2] In the War of the Chaco (1932-
35), although this time Paraguay was the winner, many thousands of young
men died. That war—with Bolivia—also put an end to a long period of rule
by the liberals, to be followed by a period of great instability, military takeovers, a civil war (1947), palace intrigues, and constantly shifting alliances
between the military and civilians. During this period the Colorado Party
emerged as the single most important political force. In this sense Stroessner
did not really overthrow a democratic government but rather one dominated
by a single party, which was also characterized by corruption and conspira-
cies.

Alfredo Stroessner (1912–), son of a German father and a Paraguayan
mother, was a career military man. He was known for his discipline, capacity
for work, and his ability as an administrator. He came to be head of the army,
and in 1954 he allied himself with the head of the police—a rival whom he

later exiled—and took power. The merit of Stroessner did not consist in the fact of his taking power but in his ability to retain it for such a long time. Unlike other dictators of Latin America, he did not base his power only in the army but in civilian society as well, and concretely in the Colorado Party. That party, founded in 1887 with the official name, National Republican Association, was a model of a corporative party based on clientalism. Through its "sectionals" the party had bases everywhere in the country, and once in power it always favored party members. Stroessner had barely seized power when he was named the party's candidate for presidential elections. Thus, during the dictatorship, there were elections and there was a parliament. But the party controlled two-thirds of the parliament, and Stroessner tolerated the presence of certain opposition parties as long as they respected the perimeters that he established. The other parties and even some leaders within the Colorado Party were simply silenced or exiled. In the presidential elections, in which Stroessner was usually the only candidate, he normally won between 80 percent and 90 percent of the vote. The appearance of democracy, plus the prosperity the country enjoyed in the sixties and seventies, created the impression that Paraguay's dictatorship was relatively bland. Furthermore, Stroessner and his party never ceased to announce to the world that in Paraguay there reigned an atmosphere of "peace, work, and welfare."

In reality, Stroessner was just as capable of using violence as a Somoza or a Pinochet. In the sixties the army put down several guerrilla movements and rarely took prisoners. In the seventies thousands of peasants who belonged to the Christian Agrarian Leagues were rounded up in concentration camps. Police brutality, kidnappings, torture, and violent deportations also formed part of normal life under Stroessner. In spite of that, the dictator allowed certain parties and opposition newspapers to exist, precisely to create the appearance of democracy. In practice, however, Paraguay became a totalitarian state, or in the description of historian Paul Lewis, a "praetorian state."[3] Stroessner was the head of the government, head of the armed forces, and head of the dominant party in the country.

The Antonio Guasch Center of Paraguayan Studies (CEPAG), run by the Jesuits, did a study on the Stroessner era; the study reports that four different stages can be discerned. In the first stage (1954-59) Stroessner consolidated the alliance between the Colorado Party and the military, and marginalized the opposition. In the second stage (1959-67) the dictator sought to legitimate his government by holding elections, but at the same time he drastically repressed all guerrilla movements and strikes. In the third stage (1967-78), the government permitted a controlled pluralism but put down all social movements with a heavy hand. It was during this period especially that the government openly attacked the church. Finally, between 1978 and 1989, the dictatorship showed signs of internal decay, and civil society began coming back to life.[4] During this last stage the church encouraged and legitimated the opposition groups.

THE CHURCH: GENERAL CHARACTERISTICS

The Paraguayan church suffered much during the long dictatorships of the nineteenth century. Francia (1814-40) suppressed all religious convents, closed down the seminary, and virtually governed the church himself. His successor, Carlos Antonio López, without losing control of the reins over the church, normalized relations with the Holy See and allowed the seminary to reopen. But the dictatorship of his son, Francisco Solano López, as well as the War of the Triple Alliance, constituted a disaster for the church. In 1868 Solano, who had led the country into the war, ordered the only bishop in the country, Manuel Antonio Palacios, to be shot, and twenty-four priests along with him, for having allegedly conspired against him. At the end of the war a total of thirty-three priests survived in all Paraguay.[5]

The great savior of the church was Juan Sinforiano Bogarín, first as bishop and later as archbishop of Asunción (1894-1949). He managed to get the church back on its feet and to establish certain autonomy with respect to the government. Under his energetic leadership many religious orders and congregations came to the country: the Vincentians, the Salesians, the Franciscans, the Divine Word Society, the Oblates, the Jesuits (who returned in 1927), and others. Bogarín also fostered the creation of Catholic Action in 1932, and in 1937 he held a eucharistic congress, which gave witness to the new vitality of the church. His moral authority was so widely recognized that when he died in 1949 his funeral turned out to be a major national event. A government newspaper declared: "Archbishop Bogarín was the greatest Paraguayan of our times."[6]

His successor, Juan José Mena Portal (1949-70), the national moderator of Catholic Action, worked to modernize the church. While he was archbishop he founded the national episcopal conference (1956), the Federation of Religious (1959), and the Catholic University of Asunción (1960). He also invited many feminine congregations to the country. In spite of these signs of progress, the Paraguayan church suffers from many of the limitations typical of the rest of Latin America. Although the great majority of Paraguayans are Catholics (around 90 percent), only about 30 percent regularly attend mass.[7] This state of affairs is due in part to the influence of liberal anticlericalism, but also to the fact that the church has a very limited presence in the rural areas where the majority of the people live. In the middle of the sixties, for example, there was one priest for every 4,516 inhabitants.[8] In 1990 one-half of all priests (of a total of 425) were foreign-born, and most of them belonged to religious orders and congregations. Finally, there were 1,141 religious women, and 14 bishops in the hierarchy.[9] Among non-Catholics, the Mennonites, who began arriving from Canada in 1927, founded colonies in the Chaco region.

The relations between the church and the Stroessner regime went through four different stages: (1) initial tensions, 1954-70; (2) open confrontation and hardening of relations, 1970-76; (3) repression and the search for a new modus vivendi, 1976-83; and (4) national leadership and legitimization of the opposition, 1983-89.

FIRST TENSIONS (1954-1970)

During the first years of Stroessner, Archbishop Mena Portal sought to establish a harmonious relationship with the government. There were other bishops, especially the two auxiliaries of Asunción, Ramón Bogarín and Aníbal Maricevich, and Ismael Rolón, the prelate in charge of the national shrine of Caacupé, who wanted to take a harder line. The first clash with the state was precipitated by a Paraguayan priest, Ramón Talavera, the pastor of a poor neighborhood in Asunción. In 1958 Talavera criticized the dictator from his pulpit, and very soon a movement formed to support his denunciations. The government pressured the archbishop to quiet the priest, but in vain. Finally, after threatening Talavera, certain persons connected to the Colorado Party and the government kidnapped and brutally beat him. The archbishop sent Talavera to Uruguay for his safety, and the government denied him permission to reenter Paraguay. In his exile Talavera continued to denounce the regime, but when he also criticized the church for its alleged complicity, he was suspended from the priesthood.[10]

Talavera acted as an individual, even when he had the support of other persons. In the sixties new centers of protest emerged and new voices of opposition were heard. The new Catholic University became one of those centers. Since it was private and run by the church, it could function more freely than the state universities. Among early Stroessner critics were a group of Jesuits who had come from Spain to collaborate in the university. At the same time other Jesuits were busy creating the Christian Agrarian Leagues, which came to constitute a considerable force in the rural areas. In the period right before and after Medellín tensions between the government and the university reached a critical point. In 1968 the police attacked a march that had been organized to protest over a medical student whose exemption from the army had been canceled because of his involvement in certain Catholic activist groups. The government placed the blame for the march on the university professors and expelled four Jesuits and closed down the newspaper (*Comunidad*) run by members of that religious order. The episcopal conference and the papal nuncio registered their protest over these expulsions, but the government responded by applying pressure to expel even more religious. As a precautionary measure, the archbishop sent one of the Jesuits at the university, Father Luis Ramallo, to Chile, but the government was not satisfied with that gesture, and in October 1969 arrested and deported Father Francisco de Paula Oliva, another Jesuit at the university. His deportation provoked another protest march, which was violently repressed by the police. This time Mena reacted with unusual energy and excommunicated the minister of the Interior and the chief of police. The minister in question decided to make his peace with the church, among other reasons because he wanted to be present for the religious wedding of his daughter(!). The archbishop accepted his apologies and those of the chief of police. This was but the first of many encounters that were to take place between Christian militants and the Stroessner regime.

The decision of the archbishop to respond to the government's aggressive actions went beyond a mere spontaneous and individual impulse. In fact, it signaled the beginning of a collective stand by the bishops. Earlier, in 1967, the episcopal conference criticized the constitution that had been promulgated that year because it allowed Stroessner to be reelected for a fourth term. In January 1969 the bishops sent a letter to the president urging him to free political prisoners and to respect human rights. In April they published a collective letter in which they condemned a proposed law that bore the ironical title, Defense of Democracy. The proposed law would suppress freedom of the press and give the government the power to detain arbitrarily its critics. In words that did not allow for misunderstanding the bishops stated: "The proposed law would legitimate totalitarian absolutism."[11] As a further gesture of protest the bishops decided to suppress the yearly pilgrimage (December 8) to the shrine of Our Lady of Caacupé, in which government officials traditionally participated; instead, they organized a procession of silence and penance in Asunción. The exclusion of representatives of the government, and particularly the president of the republic, from participating in the most important Catholic ritual in the country provoked Stroessner's anger, and he ordered an attack on the participants in the silent procession. Mena in turn ordered masses to be suspended, at least for a short period. Although both sides had more or less made their declaration of war, neither wanted to make a formal break. In 1970 Mena, quite advanced in years and not up to this kind of confrontation, resigned.

CONFRONTATION AND HARDENING OF RELATIONS (1970-1976)

Mena's successor was Ismael Rolón, who soon became a living symbol of resistance to the Stroessner regime, right up to the very end. Tall and stately in appearance, the new archbishop looked somewhat like a patriarch of the Old Testament, although his sense of humor did not fit with the Old Testament stereotype. A Salesian priest, in 1960 he was named the prelate in charge of Caacupé, the site of Paraguay's most popular devotion, and in 1966 he was ordained a bishop. He was also known as a progressive who identified himself with the church's message at Medellín. His first action as archbishop was to send conciliatory signals to the government, and he made a visit to President Stroessner as required by protocol. Nevertheless, by way of two symbolic gestures he also broke with tradition. First, he ceased to observe the practice of giving his Christmas message from the presidential palace, which former archbishops had traditionally done, and instead, delivered the message in the cathedral. Second, and more important, in February 1971 he renounced his right to belong to the state council. The constitution of the republic assigned a seat in the council to the archbishop of the capital city. In his letter announcing his decision, Rolón explained that given the state of tension between the state and the church, it was no longer appropriate for him to sit on the state council. In his words: "Given the situation of growing abuses and evident violations of human rights, the church finds itself impeded from collaborating with the government."[12] He added that he did not want the people to interpret his presence on the council as a sign of "approval of the current state of affairs."[13]

Very soon incidents occurred that aggravated the tensions. In February 1971 a Uruguayan priest, Uberfil Monzón, was invited by Bishop Ramón Bogarín to collaborate with his social-pastoral planning. Using the pretext that Monzón allegedly had ties with the Tupamaros of Uruguay, the police arrested the visiting priest, subjected him to torture, and then deported him. In the meantime an auxiliary bishop of Montevideo, Andrés Rubio García, arrived in Asunción in search of the missing priest. But when he arrived at the airport he was subjected to insults from women police. In response, Rolón excommunicated the minister of the Interior and the chief of police, the second time for both of them. Soon both sides backed down, but Stroessner had made his point: for every protest or criticism he would retaliate with force. Later, in the name of all the bishops, Rolón demanded that exiled priests be allowed back into the country. The dictator ignored the demand. In September 1972 the police put down another protest march of the Catholic University, which had by then been targeted as a focal point of opposition.

THE CHRISTIAN AGRARIAN LEAGUES

In 1960 a group of peasants who lived in the area of the old Jesuit missions requested aid from the church to defend themselves against local landowners who exploited them. With the support of several union leaders who were committed Christians, members of the third order of St. Francis, and several priests, notably a group of Jesuits, the peasants gave birth to the Christian Agrarian Leagues. Within time the leagues grew to have close to ten thousand members, almost all in the eastern part of Paraguay.[14] The leagues combined elements of cooperativism, trade unionism, and primitive Christianity, at least according to their idealized version of the Bible. Their basic philosophy was taken from the Paraguayan concept of *yopoi* ("from all for all"). The leagues created common warehouses which sold goods at low prices for the benefit of the peasants. They also founded free schools inspired by the ideas of the Brazilian educator Paulo Freire on education as a tool for conscienticizing. In the department called Missions, twenty-eight of these little schools were set up, staffed with fifty teachers from the people themselves.[15] In 1969 in Jejuí, to the north of Asunción, a community was founded in a very poor area that was to be part of the government's agrarian reform. The community, which took as its model the early Christians, owned everything in common. Although its population was small, Jejuí became the coordinating center for sixty peasant communities.[16] By 1970 the government had begun to accuse this novel experiment of being communist inspired, and soon the leagues became targets of state persecution.

But the leagues also became a problem for the church. From the very beginning several bishops and priests had lent encouragement to the leagues. But the leagues were autonomous and did not depend upon the church. As they grew in number and enjoyed a measure of success, some of the peasant leaders were carried away by messianic expectations and began criticizing the hierarchy as a privileged elite.[17] Some of the league peasants invaded private property and seized churches, actions that aggravated tensions between the hierarchy and the leagues. In 1973 a meeting was held in Caacupé between bishops, priests, and leaders of the leagues. The bishops hoped that the priest advisers would give a clearer orientation to the leagues, but the peasant leaders resented what they considered to be clerical interference. From that point on the church and the leagues began going their separate ways. One consideration in the mind of the bishops was their desire not to complicate their relationship with the government by giving the appearance of legitimating a movement the government viewed as a threat.

The full repression of the leagues occurred between 1975 and 1976. In February 1975 the army attacked the community of Jejuí, and the little peasant schools were closed down. Many peasants were interned in concentration camps.[18] By the end of 1976 the leagues had practically ceased to exist. At the same time the government turned its attention to the activities of certain Jesuits considered to be instigators of this and other movements. Earlier, in 1972, two Jesuits connected with the leagues had been deported. In January 1976 the police took by assault the Jesuits' principal school in Asunción, Cristo Rey. As a result, more Jesuits were expelled from the country. In the midst of all this a new subversive movement, which purportedly planned to overthrow the government, was discovered. The government attempted to tie this group, known by its initials, OPM (Political Military Organization), to the Jesuits. In April, Cristo Rey was assaulted for a second time. Ten more Jesuits were expelled from the country. Bartomeu Melià (one of the expelled Jesuits) named this the "seventh expulsion of the Society of Jesus" in the history of Paraguay.[19] Also, many seminaries throughout the country were placed under surveillance.

During this period close to three thousand people were detained in concentration camps.[20] One of the most notorious of these was the camp of Emboscada, where hundreds of peasants were held as common prisoners. Different Christian groups responded by founding the Church Committee for Emergency Help. The committee was made up of the German Lutheran church, the Disciples of Christ, and the Catholic church.[21]

REPRESSION AND RETREAT (1976-1983)

The elimination of the leagues, the assaults on Cristo Rey, the expulsion of the Jesuits, the massive detention of peasants and other persons, as well as many other repressive acts, convinced the bishops that it was impossible to confront the government by direct action. By 1973 the episcopal conference had already begun to follow a more moderate line. Another factor was the radicalization of certain church groups. The bishops decided that the best course of action was to fortify the spiritual formation of the laity, especially the youth. They fostered the creation of base ecclesial communities, which, unlike the peasant leagues, had an ecclesial and spiritual character. The church had to face another problem as well: the growing lack of priests as a result of the post-conciliar crisis. Between 1967 and 1977 approximately eighty priests—about 20 percent of all the clergy—left the priesthood.[22]

The increased emphasis on spiritual formation did not mean that the bishops now approved of the government. It represented, rather, a tactical retreat in order to regroup, recuperate strength, and return to the battle at a more opportune time. That the church had not given in can be seen in the collective episcopal letter published in June 1976 and titled "Between Persecution in the World and the Consolation of God." In it the bishops condemned the repression, the torture, the breaking into homes, and the expulsion of priests. On the other hand, they also admitted there were extremists in the church, who should not be confused with other Christians who were motivated by healthy idealism.[23]

Also in 1976 Bishop Ramón Bogarín, a key member of the progressive church, died. His successor was Angel N. Acha Duarte, a conservative. That same year the military seized power in Argentina, a fact that strengthened Stroessner in his own country. Furthermore, the country enjoyed unprecedented prosperity thanks to the gigantic hydroelectric project of Itaipú, which Paraguay shared with Brazil, and similar shared projects with Argentina. The only note off key was Jimmy Carter's new administration in Washington and the American president's insistence on respecting human rights. In fact, during the Carter years members of the political opposition met with some frequency in the American embassy. But with two military dictatorships flanking him—Brazil and Argentina—Stroessner felt secure in the face of foreign criticism.

Faced with an apparently all-powerful regime, which exercised control over society on all levels, the church accentuated its role as representative of the religious and moral sentiments of the people. Given the state of repression, the bishops saw the importance of protecting that special role that constituted the church's strength. In June 1979 the bishops published another collective letter, "The Moral Cleansing of the Nation." In it they noted that relations between church and state had improved a bit.[24] They then directed their attention to public corruption, which manifested itself in the form of the idols of wealth (a veiled reference to the prosperity generated by Itaipú), pleasure, and power. They limited their criticism of the regime to the vague observation that "for reasons of national security intermediate bodies have been eliminated." But they did add: "We have the impression that the objective is to terrorize the people."[25] Still, the letter carefully avoided a generalized critique of the regime.

On the other hand, the church attended pastorally to the victims of persecution. Rolón personally visited the detention center of Emboscada and talked with the prisoners. As a result he was able to improve their situation somewhat.[26] Meanwhile the people continued to attend the processions to Caacupé and other religious demonstrations in great numbers, a sign that they found consolation and strength in their religious faith.

RECOUPING AND PROPHETIC LEADERSHIP (1983-1989)

In its study of the Stroessner years the CEPAG team of Jesuits terms the last stage of the dictatorship "The Eroding of the Dictatorship's Legitimacy (1978-1989)."[27] One of the causes of Stroessner's decline was the growing isolation of Paraguay in the midst of the redemocratization of the rest of Latin America, especially that of its neighbors, Argentina in 1983, and Brazil and Uruguay in 1985. Furthermore, Jimmy Carter's government had severely condemned the Stroessner regime, and Ronald Reagan, in spite of his rightwing tendencies, continued to single out the Paraguayan regime as a black sheep for its violation of human rights. Stroessner, censured by the United States and without support from his powerful neighbors, was forced to draw support exclusively from within.

But that support was also eroding. In contrast to the boom years of the seventies, in the eighties Paraguay experienced a recession. Construction on the great hydroelectric projects of Itaipú and Yacyreta fell behind, and unemployment rose from 2.1 percent in 1980 to 15 percent in 1983.[28] Furthermore, income from these projects and the country's exportations only benefited the upper and middle classes, not the majority of Paraguayans. Economist Aníbal Miranda concluded in a study on the period from 1974 to 1980 that the 20 percent of the people lowest on the economic scale received about 5 percent of the total national income, while the top 5 percent received about 70 percent of the wealth.[29] Along with the recession and the lopsided distribution of wealth there were other more immediate factors, such as a fall in the price of soybeans, torrential floods in 1983 that seriously affected agricultural production, and foreign debt.

Finally, the government and the party suffered from the internal decay produced by a long dictatorship and official public corruption. In 1984 the Colorado Party divided into two groups: the militants and the traditionalists. The militants wanted at all costs to maintain the system, with or without

Stroessner. But if it meant without Stroessner, the militants expressed their preference for the dictator's son, Gustavo, or another military leader. The traditionalists were made up of *colorados* who pointed out that the party existed before Stroessner and that opening up to democracy would be good for all. In 1987 the struggle between the two factions was so overt that Stroessner purged the party and the government of the traditionalists. In the February 1988 elections, in which Stroessner was reelected for the seventh straight time, the traditionalists campaigned in favor of voting in blank. This internal division in the party drew the attention of higher echelon officers in the army, who had also begun questioning the prolongation of a dictatorship that divided the Paraguayans and kept the country isolated internationally. Furthermore, since the seventies the legal opposition had withdrawn from parliament. They joined with the groups of opposition that were "illegal but tolerated" to form a National Accord. At the same time an entirely new popular movement began emerging: unions, peasants, women, all claiming their rights. Bit by bit civil society was beginning to come alive after decades of passivity and fear. This was the most important phenomenon in the last years of Stroessner's rule: the people lost their fear. In the midst of these new events, the church took on the role of legitimator of the opposition.

THE CHURCH AND THE NATIONAL DIALOGUE

On different occasions the church offered its good offices as mediator to foster some kind of dialogue between the government and the rest of society, or at times between the political parties and other organizations that did not form part of the government. The episcopal conference declared 1973 the year of "fraternal dialogue," and in its pastoral letter "The Moral Cleansing of the Nation" the bishops offered to cooperate in the "search for concrete solutions" to the nation's problems.[30] But these were also years of harsh repression, which did not permit real dialogue to take place.

In 1979 the National Accord was born. The four founding parties had in common the fact that all were excluded from parliament: the Revolutionary Party of February, the Authentic Radical Liberal Party, the Christian Democratic Party, and the Popular Colorado Movement. The last of these four was a dissident group that had been expelled in 1959 from the Colorado Party. In December 1983 the Accord requested the episcopal conference to cooperate in the task of creating a national dialogue, and the bishop replied affirmatively.[31] But the process of achieving that dialogue proved to be very slow. In March 1984 the government interrupted the process when it closed down the daily newspaper, *ABC Color*, which represented practically the only voice of opposition in the country, outside of the church. The international press joined in the unanimous condemnation of the government's action. In the presence of the newspaper's director, Aldo Zuccolillo, and the newspaper employees, Archbishop Rolón celebrated a mass in the cathedral in which he prayed for liberty.[32] This symbolic gesture reinforced the church's image as the legitimator of the opposition and therefore the natural forum in which to discuss national reconciliation.

Finally, in January 1986 the episcopal conference formally designated three bishops—Jorge Livieres Banks, Felipe Santiago Benítez, and Oscar Páez Garcete—to organize the national dialogue. Livieres, an auxiliary bishop of Asunción, was in charge of relations with the media and, in effect, was the principal architect of the dialogue. In April, speaking for the episcopal conference, Livieres announced the ground rules for the dialogue and the schedule to be followed. During the first stage the church would play host to the political parties, unions, and student organizations. In the second stage a debate would be held to discuss the proposals presented in the first stage. The reactions to the announcement were generally very favorable, except in the government and the Colorado Party. In its answer to the church's invitation to participate in the dialogue the Colorado Party replied that there was no need for a special dialogue in Paraguay because the parliament was the normal place for national dialogue. Furthermore, the Colorado Party declared that it wished to dialogue only with "legal" representatives and not with "minorities."[33]

In May and June delegates from the political parties arrived at the episcopal conference to hand in their proposals. The declarations of the parties and the interviews they conducted with the bishops captured the attention of the public. The new dialogue was turning into a sort of popular national assembly—exactly what the Colorado Party feared. Finally, under pressure, the official party sent a representative—Juan Ramón Chávez—to have an interview with the bishops. In order not to create the impression that it had ceded to public opinion, a party spokesman explained that the interview with the bishops was purely for the purpose of conveying information.[34]

After the meetings between the parties and the bishops the church invited the media (and, of course, *ABC Color*, which was still closed down), businessmen, and labor unions not dominated by the Colorado Party to express their views freely to the bishops. The idea of participating in a national dialogue turned out to be quite popular. The Paraguayan Peasant Movement proposed holding a Popular National Dialogue. The government, of course, reacted with hostility toward this movement for dialogue, as it was obviously threatening the foundations on which the government rested. In April a group of militants of the Colorado Party attacked Radio Ñanduti, which frequently denounced government abuses. Elsewhere political parties and their leaders were subjected to harassment. On May 30 twenty-five hundred religious and laypersons paraded in silence through the streets of Asunción, and on June 12 thirty-five hundred youth from the interior arrived in the capital to join a march commemorating the War of the Chaco. The youth march, which included several veterans of the war, ended in a mass celebrated by Archbishop Rolón. Also, reflection days were organized in the parishes. Of special importance was a debate organized by the Catholic University in which three hundred members of all the opposition parties and other groups gave their opinions on the political changes that Paraguay needed. These marches, debates, and meetings provoked the minister of Health, Adán Godoy Jiménez, who was also one of the vice presidents of the country, to declare:

> "Once and for all this attempt at dialogue has got to stop, and the Colorado Party should be allowed to continue governing with its wise leadership in order to achieve more prosperity and development. . . . We do not believe in the dialogue that they want to implement. We are the promoters of national dialogue, which can only be done in the national parliament and on other officially recognized levels."[35]

For the second stage of the dialogue the episcopal conference extended an invitation to a wide spectrum in society. Between July 30 and August 30, 1987, in the local minor seminary, seven political parties, five social and human rights organizations, five newspapers, and two radio stations participated in the dialogue, as well as twelve distinct lay movements and three Protestant groups. Not all who were invited came. By far the most important absentee was the Colorado Party, although it maintained informal contact with the bishops. The parties naturally broached themes such as democratic participation, constitutional reform, agrarian reform, health, and education. In fact, the proposals of the parties virtually constituted plans for reforming the government and the country. The ecclesial groups emphasized topics relating to the family and public morality.

The final document was published in December. The conclusions contain an unambiguous and explicit condemnation of the dictatorship as well as a call to restore democracy:

> The identification of government-party-armed forces and the concentration of absolute power in the chief of the executive branch have served to deform republican and democratic institutions by erecting in their place a dictatorial, autocratic, and totalitarian regime—an authentic democratic regime will not be possible as long as General Alfredo Stroessner continues in power. His leaving the presidency is a basic condition for a transition to democracy.[36]

The effort to create a national dialogue did not fulfill all the expectations of the organizers. As Michael Carter notes, the dialogue organized by the church did not "convert itself into the driving force behind the transition to democracy." One reason for that shortcoming was that the most important political party in the country and the armed forces did not participate.[37] Nevertheless, the outcome was in general very positive. Under the protection of the church the political parties and social movements not only lost their fear to express themselves, but they even went on to constitute a united front with multiple local support groups, all bound together under the banner of a new national consensus.

THE PROCESSION OF SILENCE, 1987

During 1986 and 1987 many public demonstrations of a religious nature were held in which ordinary believers could express their disapproval of the government in a symbolic and peaceful way. These religious demonstrations also served to fortify the new confidence the people felt, and at the same time to delegitimize the regime. Government authorities, frustrated over not being able to control the power of symbols, frequently sent agents to harass those who participated in masses or processions. The most notable of those symbolic expressions was the procession of silence held on October 30, 1987. The procession was organized by several women who belonged to the Archdiocesan Committee of the Laity. In preparation for the big event, one month before all the parishes began the practice of having a minute of silence during mass, and the church bells rang every Friday at the same hour.[38] In order to emphasize the purely religious character of the procession, the participants were exhorted not to sing or pray aloud, nor—obviously—to bring signs or any other symbol relating to politics. Notwithstanding the absence of slogans or chants, there was no doubt about the purpose of the procession. In the official newspaper of the archdiocese, *Sendero*, the faithful were exhorted to participate with this petition in mind: "for a more just, fraternal, and God-oriented society."[39]

The procession was impressive. On the night of October 30 close to thirty-five thousand persons carrying torches walked through the downtown area of the capital in total silence. The participants were greeted by Archbishop Rolón in the park in front of the cathedral with these words: "Our Lord is pleased that you were able to overcome your fear and shame."[40] Two hundred priests concelebrated the mass. In Rolón's opinion the procession of silence represented the precise moment when most Paraguayans, and especially practicing Christians, lost their fear of Stroessner and his regime.[41] The silence of the marchers disconcerted the police, who did not know how to respond in the face of a demonstration that was so clearly of a peaceful, religious nature. Similar processions were held in the towns and cities in the rest of the country.

THE PAPAL VISIT, 1988

The biggest event in Paraguay in 1988 was the papal visit, set for May. Following a custom that the pope had established in other countries, the visit to Paraguay was also the occasion to canonize a saint, in this case Blessed Roque González, the Jesuit martyr in the Reductions. From the beginning, the government, aware of the pitfalls and advantages of a papal visit, tried to control the preparations. But the bishops resisted all attempts at manipulation, and as a result, once again tensions surfaced between church and state. For example, the government tried to eliminate from the planned itinerary a visit to the diocese of Concepción, purportedly for reasons of security. But it was evident to most that the real reason was that the bishop of that diocese was Aníbal Maricevich, one of the harshest critics of the regime. The biggest bone of contention, however, was the meeting that was planned between the pope and the "builders of society." The Archdiocesan Committee of the Laity invited thirty-eight hundred persons to attend. Among the invited were professionals, writers, intellectuals, teachers, political and union leaders, as well as lay leaders of church groups. The government feared that the meeting would turn into an anti-government demonstration, and worse, that it would occur before the eyes of the entire world. One week before the pope's arrival the government announced the suspension of the meeting. Government officials explained that they could not tolerate the presence of persons who "resist participation and peaceful living-together because they carry on their political battles outside the law."[42]

After communicating these facts to the Holy See, the bishops responded with the threat to reduce the papal visit to the single act of canonizing the new saint.[43] In the face of that threat, which would have been a public humiliation for the regime, the government backed down and the pope visited Concepción and attended the meeting with the builders of society. John Paul II arrived in the middle of torrential rains, which forced some of the planned activities to be suspended. Nevertheless, the people turned out en masse in the rain, a display of faith that touched the pope. John Paul II visited Encarnación, the Sanctuary of Caacupé, Villarrica, and met with the indigenous groups of the Chaco. But all attention was focused on the meeting with the builders of society, held in the sports stadium of Asunción.

The stadium filled up with those who had been invited, but government authorities were conspicuous by their absence: three rows of seats reserved for them remained vacant. The organizers of the event chose as the theme "The Truth Will Make You Free."[44] The meeting began with a small dramatic performance, which focused on a tree without leaves that represented Paraguay. Through symbolic gestures the dancers and the chorus that accompanied them communicated the message that without freedom there can be no life. The pope's message, as though it had been planned to coincide with the dramatic presentation, caught the sentiment of the moment. John Paul called for creating a "society founded in truth."[45] During the entire visit, out of diplomatic courtesy, the pope avoided any direct reference to the regime that had invited him. Nevertheless, his audience made its own application every time he made references to "freedom," "truth," "corruption," and so forth.

Naturally the government did everything possible to control the media and to project an image of complete harmony between the church and the government. Shortly before the pope arrived, a propaganda poster appeared everywhere in the capital bearing the image of the pope and Stroessner together, with the following inscription: "Blessed are they who sow peace in the name of the Lord."[46] Unfortunately for Stroessner, although the pope did not verbally criticize his regime, he did so by nonverbal expressions. At the airport and other places John Paul listened to Stroessner's praise of his government with an unsmiling face and a frown. One woman captured the feeling of many when she commented the following day, "The pope doesn't like hearing lies."[47] Furthermore, by attending the meeting with the builders of society, whom he energetically encouraged to carry out their mission, the pope symbolically legitimized the opposition. Also, the meeting with the Indians of the Chaco allowed the spokesman of the indigenous groups to highlight the sufferings and the abuses to which they had been subjected. The pope's visit certainly reinforced the new collective self-awareness, born in the procession of silence, which helped thousands to lose their fear and to grow in courage.

The Expulsion of Father De la Vega

The papal visit had barely ended when the government returned to its tactics of harassing churchpeople, as if to send the message that the visit had been nothing but an insignificant interruption in the normal life of Paraguay. The first of those incidents was the expulsion of the Jesuit Juan Antonio de la Vega, which in turn led to a new confrontation between church and state. The immediate cause of the expulsion was a talk on liberation theology which Father De la Vega gave in a meeting with students. Liberation theology was very much discussed before and during the papal visit. In July the Assembly of the Federation of Religious, which drew together some one thousand priests and religious men and women, focused on the theme of the "New Evangelization." At the end of the assembly a resolution was made to continue the analysis of liberation theology.[48] The same day the students at the national university organized a panel on that theological current and invited Father De la Vega to participate in the panel. De la Vega, a Spaniard, had worked for years in Latin America, first in Peru and later in Paraguay. Besides being a priest, he was also a lawyer and a university professor. He was known for his defense of the rights of prisoners and was widely respected. In the panel he pointed out the positive elements of liberation theology. The next day he was apprehended by agents of the government and charged with "making propaganda in favor of violence."[49] His arrest provoked many protests and he was set free. But on July 17 he was detained again, and this time expelled to Argentina. Archbishop Rolón immediately suspended the traditional Te Deum sung in the cathedral on August 15, the day on which Stroessner was to begin his eighth term. The suspension of the Te Deum was seen as a direct affront to Stroessner, who would be the principal authority present. But Rolón did not act precipitously; he consulted with the other bishops and the priests of his archdiocese before acting. Only the nuncio, Bishop Jorge Zur, objected.[50] In Rolón's opinion, De la Vega's expulsion was not an isolated incident but a premeditated attack on the whole church.

In order to express their protest and to support Rolón, the laity of the archdiocese decided to organize another silent procession, which was scheduled for August 6. The second silent procession was as impressive as the first. This time close to forty thousand people, spanning fourteen blocks, marched toward the cathedral. Unlike the first procession, however, some of the political groups and union wards infiltrated the procession with the aim of making explicit political propaganda. During the mass they distributed fliers and sang "Patria Querida" ("Dear Homeland"), which had become the standard protest song during the dictatorship. In reprisal, the police attacked the protesters, who included women and children. In spite of this momentary lapse in discipline, the second procession was successful because it demonstrated the church's power to call the people out to take a stand, whether during a papal visit or afterward.

In October the bishops published a pastoral letter on liberation theology. The intent of the letter was to make the church's stand on that theological current clear in the light of Father De la Vega's expulsion. The bishops not only defended the expelled Jesuit, but all priests, religious women, and laypersons against the charge of being "Marxists" or "subversives":

> With satisfaction we can affirm that the theological positions currently taught in this country faithfully follow liberation theology. We are not aware of anyone charged by the church to teach in its name—bishops, theologians, priests—who use the Marxist method or who ground themselves in that ideology.[51]

Other clashes and incidents followed. In November in a meeting of the Colorado Party, one of the leaders publicly insulted Bishop Maricevich, in whose diocese the meeting was held.[52] In December, on the occasion of the fortieth anniversary of the Universal Declaration of Human Rights, a march for life was organized and ended with a mass in the cathedral. Thirty different social and political organizations participated. Once again the police attacked the marchers and carried off several leaders of the Archdiocesan Lay Committee to jail. In spite of these shows of force, the real weakness of the regime was increasingly evident. It no longer had the power to inspire terror. Paraguayans sensed that they were witnessing the last days of the dictator. After the silent processions, the papal visit, and other religious demonstrations, the people had lost their fear. Symbols had more power than arms. The church had acted as a vanguard for the rest of society, which was beginning to come alive once again.

THE FALL OF STROESSNER

But Stroessner did not fall as the result of a popular civil protest movement or as a result of internal decay, but rather as a consequence of a traditional military *golpe de estado*. On the night of February 2, 1989, army forces under General Andrés Rodríguez, father-in-law of Stroessner's son and the number two man in the army, attacked military headquarters considered bastions of loyalty to the regime. After a battle that cost many lives, General Alfredo Stroessner resigned and was sent into exile. The new provisional president sought to legitimize his action by declaring that he acted to defend democracy, human rights, and "our Christian, Catholic, apostolic, and Roman faith."[53] During the next few days he consolidated his position by expelling the most notorious followers of Stroessner from the government and by removing many officials from the army who were loyal to the ex-dictator. He called for elections in May, but for that he was criticized by the anti-Stroessner opposition groups because they were given very little time to prepare. Quite obviously, holding elections so close to the overthrow of the dictator favored the man who had done it, and General Rodríguez was a candidate.

Stroessner's successor made an effort at rapprochement with the church. On several occasions he expressed words of sorrow for the bad treatment the church had received. On February 5 he and his wife attended a mass for those who had been killed during the takeover. In the midst of the applause, directed mainly at Archbishop Rolón and the clergy, the general joined in the general jubilation.[54] He also participated in a "chain of hope" organized by Radio Cáritas in the front of the cathedral. Archbishop Rolón invoked the thousands who participated—politicians, students, workers, Indians, handicapped, representatives of different Christian confessions—to work together to construct a new Paraguay. All prayed the Our Father together and sang with fervor the erstwhile forbidden song, "Patria Querida."

The beginning of a new era also coincided with the end of another: that of Archbishop Ismael Rolón. His last major act was to offer his blessing for General Rodríguez on May 15, when he took his oath as president after winning what was probably the first really free election in Paraguay's history. Rolón had already presented his resignation for reason of age several months earlier, and on July 2 he celebrated his farewell mass.

Some observers noted that in the case of Paraguay, unlike other Latin America nations that returned to democratic rule, there was no question of "returning" to democracy; rather, it was being created for the first time.[55] Before Stroessner, politics were dominated by small groups of civilians or the military. But during the long Stroessner dictatorship the sentiment for democracy spread to all social classes. In the post-Stroessner era the Colorado Party continues to dominate, and many of the old ways continue to determine political conduct.[56] Nevertheless, the changes that occurred were deep and there will be no going back, at least in the near future.

Given its high profile in defense of democracy and human rights, the church enjoys considerable esteem. But the church has also made its adjustments to the new democratic order. For example, it did not reclaim its seat on the state council, and in view of the fact that civil society is once again functioning normally, it has also greatly reduced its presence in the public arena. Nevertheless, in 1990 the episcopal conference published a collective pastoral message, "The Process of Transition to Democracy," in which the bish-ops point out the profound changes that still must be carried out before a lasting democracy can exist in Paraguay.[57] In retrospect, it can be seen that the Paraguayan church, which is much smaller than that of other Latin Ameri-can countries, enjoyed certain advantages in the long struggle against the Stroessner regime. The bishops were strongly united, and there were no ma-jor integralist groups. Conservative religious sentiment was expressed by Stroessner himself and his followers. Nor were there any important dog-matic progressive groups, except in the case of the Christian Agrarian Leagues. It was a relatively open and flexible church, and therefore capable of con-verting itself into a channel of expression of the majority of the people. Certainly when the Paraguayan church celebrated the end of Stroessner's dictatorship, it did not seem at all like the submissive and weak church that it had been under Francia in the last century, or even like the conservative church that it was at the beginning of Stroessner's regime.

6.

Uruguay (1973-1990)

A Long Silence and a Moral Referendum

During the civilian-military dictatorship that governed Uruguay from 1973 to 1985, the church played a modest and at times ambiguous role regarding the promotion of human rights. Uruguay has a strong laicist tradition, and the church's influence is very limited compared to the considerable influence it wields in Argentina, Chile, and Brazil. Furthermore, the hierarchy was divided and did not present a united front before the government. Nevertheless, the archbishop of Montevideo, Carlos Parteli, a progressive, lent moral support, although not always publicly, to the Christians who fought for human rights.

However, the most interesting aspect of this history was not so much the church's role during the dictatorship itself, but rather its direct participation in the campaign to return to democracy and in the movement to bring human-rights violators to justice. In Chile and Brazil the military left power on the condition that they would not be tried and judged. In Argentina, where the military leaders were brought to trial, the hierarchical church disapproved of that process, although there were some bishops and many rank-and-file Christians who did support it. In Uruguay the Christians who belonged to the Justice and Peace Service (SERPAJ) played an even more decisive role than in Argentina in mobilizing the people to rectify past injustices. Although they did not achieve their objective, at least on the legal level, they did win a moral victory because they turned the question of human rights into the number one national issue.

FROM WELFARE TO REPRESSION

For years Uruguay seemed to be one of the big exceptions with respect to the rest of Latin America. It is a small country with a population predominately of European ancestry, and for most of its history since independence it has been blessed with prosperity and apparently solid democratic institutions. Indeed, it was a model for the rest of the continent. It is also a highly urbanized country: in the sixties a little over half of the population lived in Montevideo. Since the days of José Battle y Ordóñez (president, 1903-07; 1911-15) an equilibrium was established between the two traditional parties, the Blanco (White) and the Colorado (Red), a fact that contributed notably to internal stability. On two occasions, 1933 and 1942, this stability was interrupted by military takeovers. Nevertheless, the two parties resolved their differences and restored their traditional pact. Most important, Battle and his successors forged a national welfare state that controlled the economy and satisfied the basic needs of its citizens. The role of the state was so large that at one time it employed 30 percent of the labor force.[1]

But this idyllic state of affairs came to an abrupt close in the sixties. First, the economy suffered a recession, and society entered a state of paralysis. As one observer noted, there was no room for social or economic mobility.[2] The absence of opportunities, combined with the recession, produced resentment among workers, university students, and young professionals. In 1967, amid growing social tension and following the death of President Oscar D. Gestido (elected in 1966), the vice president, Jorge Pacheco Areco, assumed the presidency. Pacheco decreed several harsh measures ("immediate security measures") to repress expressions of social discontent. During his administration Uruguay's famed welfare state turned into a police state. Pacheco was particularly worried about an outbreak of guerrilla activity, a phenomenon that had never occurred before in Uruguay.

The Tupamaro Movement for National Liberation, founded in the early sixties, reflected the frustration of the radicalized middle classes. It was made up principally of students and young professionals, with a smaller percentage of blue-collar employees and workers. Numbering around a thousand, they were carried away by romantic visions of copying the Cuban revolution and applying the guerrilla tactics of Che Guevara to Uruguay.[3] In the beginning they limited their activities to robbing banks and offices of transnational companies, but increasingly they turned to terrorist violence. In 1970 they carried out their most spectacular action: they kidnapped several diplomats and murdered one of them, Dan Mitrione, an American adviser to the Uruguayan police. As a result of these kinds of actions, they lost whatever initial popular sympathy they might have had. In 1972 the government dramatically escalated its counterinsurgency measures and managed to wipe out the Tupamaros.

BORDABERRY AND THE CIVILIAN-MILITARY REGIME

Pacheco's successor, Juan María Bordaberry, took the final steps to institutionalize the new police state. Elected president in 1971 with the support of the Colorado Party, Bordaberry, a conservative Catholic, was the president of the Federal League of Rural Action. In June 1973, with the support of the armed forces and under pressure from them, he closed down parliament and began ruling by decree. He widened the nets to capture not just Tupamaros but all persons suspected of having ties with the left. In June, 1976, after a run-in with the military, he resigned, and the military designated another civilian to be president—Aparicio Méndez. Uruguay was now virtually a bureaucratic and authoritarian military dictatorship with a civilian as a figurehead. The Uruguayan military, although less experienced in the art of governing than the Argentine military, followed the same doctrine of national security as their counterparts in the rest of the southern cone. They scheduled elections with the objective of legitimizing their hold over the country, calling for a plebiscite in 1980 to ratify their permanence in power. What they did not plan on, however, was to be defeated, which is exactly what happened. That surprise defeat signaled the beginning of the end of the military, who were finally obliged to call for free elections in 1984.

THE REPRESSION

In its study *Nunca más* ("Never Again"), SERPAJ observed that the repression in Uruguay was not as spectacular as in Chile, where the presidential palace went up in smoke, or as in Argentina, where thousands were murdered.[4] Uruguay's repression was characterized instead by the high degree of sophistication in the means used to control the population and by the length of the detentions. The number of persons who died as a result of state terrorism was relatively small compared to the other cases. According to SERPAJ, there were around 160 detainees who disappeared, and most of them were Uruguayans who lived in Argentina: another proof of the complicity between the national security regimes.[5] On the other hand, according to the People's Permanent Tribunal, between 1968 and 1978 "approximately 55,000 persons were detained in jails and military headquarters, which is to say one in every 50 inhabitants."[6] A report published by the Organization of American States refers to 80,000 persons "detained, abused, or tortured."[7] Furthermore, given Uruguay's small size, it was relatively easy to impose nearly total control over the country. Fortunately, Uruguay's long liberal-democratic tradition, which did not include the death penalty, served as a buffer and prevented it from going through Argentina's "dirty war" experience, which included thousands of extra-legal executions.

THE CHURCH: A PROFILE

It is a commonplace to note that Uruguay is the most secularized society in Latin America. For several historical reasons—Uruguay was colonized when Europe itself began going through a secularization process—the Catholic church found itself in a society that was at times hostile toward it, although the principal attitude was one of indifference. According to a study done in the sixties, less than half the population professed to be Catholic.[8] The church in Uruguay was never rich or a great landowner. It did, and does, have sufficient spiritual authority to convoke a considerable number of the faithful on the occasion of certain processions. In 1934, for example, some 100,000 Catholics attended the Corpus Christi procession.[9] Given the small population of Montevideo, that turnout was more than respectable. In 1981 there were 12 bishops (the Uruguayan episcopal conference was founded in 1965), 599 priests of the secular clergy and 394 priests belonging to religious orders and congregations. Furthermore, 61 percent of the religious clergy were foreign born, compared to 15 percent of the diocesan clergy.[10] Compared with Brazil and Argentina, the church in Uruguay is very small.

The Uruguayan church entered the modern world very gradually. The first winds of change were felt when Carlos Parteli, who had been coadjutor archbishop since 1966, had been named archbishop of Montevideo in 1976. Parteli, who had studied in the South American College in Rome, was named bishop of Tacuarembó in 1960. As new archbishop of the capital city he put into motion a pastoral plan that emphasized the importance of the laity, especially the youth. During his administration (he resigned in 1985) he came to be a much beloved pastor and was, without doubt, the key churchman during the dictatorship. There was another progressive bishop, Marcelo Mendiharat of Salto (1968-85), but Mendiharat was expelled by the military in 1972, depriving Parteli of much needed support among the largely conservative hierarchy. Among the leaders of the conservative wing were the Jesuit bishop Carlos Mullin, of Minas, and Antonio Corzo, of Maldonado and Punta del Este. Corzo became the main spokesman in the church against communism. Overall it was a divided hierarchy and hence very limited in what it could do.

Nevertheless, many Catholics began to take progressive stands in politics. The first Catholic political party in the country was the Civic Union, founded in 1912. Although small, it was esteemed by many because of the intellectual and moral quality of its main representatives. In the sixties a new generation of professionals and university students pushed to modernize the party, and in 1962 the Civic Union changed its name to the Christian Democratic Party of Uruguay. Two years later a conservative group in the party broke off to form the Civic Christian Movement. The Christian Democratic Party began taking increasingly progressive positions and finally ended up as the driving force behind the United Front, which was founded in 1971. The United Front was a populist coalition of all the leftist parties, which included the communists and socialists. Its candidate was Líber Seregni, a retired general. The Tupamaros supported the United Front, although numerically the Tupamaro sympathizers may have represented only 5 percent of the total electorate.[11] The Front won 18.3 percent of the vote in the election.[12] The fact that the Tupamaros supported it tended to polarize the elections and to provoke much hostility toward the Front. Many Catholics in the Christian Democratic Party, as well as most leftists, among whom were to be found many priests and religious women, sympathized with the Front. What surprised many was the attitude of the official church toward the Front. In its declaration on the elections the episcopal conference warned Christians not to support either Marxist or liberal ideologies. But in the same document the bishops stated: "We did not find sufficient reason to recommend nor to exclude any of the current parties as a legitimate choice."[13] The influence of Parteli was clearly observable in this declaration, which tacitly approved of the presence of Catholics in the Front.

THE CHURCH VIS-À-VIS THE REGIME

Between 1968 and 1974 the hierarchy, following Parteli's leadership as head of the episcopal conference, assumed a cautious but critical position before the civil-military regime. In June 1972 the conference emitted a declaration that pointed to the atmosphere of violence in the country. The bishops condemned the violence caused by the subversives, but they also censured the government's arbitrary reactions, which did not distinguish between subversives and others who wanted change without violence. In their words: "To give in to the temptation to treat as subversives those who have merely wanted renovation will only serve to multiply the number of people tempted to resort to violence."[14] In a public response Bordaberry himself rejected the bishops' statement as simplistic, and then went on to justify the use of drastic means by pointing to the "intransigent and intolerant" nature of the country's subversives.[15]

However, this initial critical attitude soon dissipated and the hierarchy began looking more and more like their Argentinean counterparts. This step backward was most noticeable from 1974 on. One factor to explain this change in the bishops' attitude was the near total control the security forces exercised over society and even over the church. On several occasions priests and religious women were arrested and submitted to interrogations. In August 1972 Román Lezama, a Jesuit, was arrested and imprisoned because he was believed to have contact with the Tupamaros. Although he was freed in December, he was obliged to present himself every ten days at a military base to give an account of his activities.[16] But the most notorious case was that of Bishop Marcelo Mendiharat. That same year Mendiharat, the bishop of Salto since 1968, was forced to submit to an interrogation. As it turned out, his niece's husband had been accused of giving diocesan funds to the Tupamaros. Although Mendiharat stated that he had no knowledge of any such activity, he was known for his progressive views. On the occasion of a trip he took outside the country, the other bishops advised him not to return in order to avoid being arrested. He remained in exile from 1972 to 1985.

Parteli himself was forced to support acts of hostility. The most dramatic occurred on the occasion of the Corpus Christi procession in November of 1973. On the very day of the procession, the biggest in the country, the government suspended permission for the procession on the grounds that earlier in the morning anti-government leaflets had been distributed in the churches. Parteli protested the government's arbitrary decision and noted that the leaflets had been thrown out of the windows of passing cars, clearly the work of the government itself.[17] Even more destructive than government harassment were the efforts of rightwing Catholics and the conservative bishops to undermine Parteli's leadership. During his *ad limina* visit to Rome in 1974 he was surprised when Pope Paul VI himself chastised him for bad leadership of the church in Montevideo. Later the pope apologized to Parteli in a letter, noting that he had not taken sufficiently into account Parteli's own report of the state of the archdiocese.[18] But the damage was done, and Parteli was deeply hurt by the pope's criticism. From that point on he softened his criticism of the government and did his best to search for consensus among his fellow bishops. But in this case consensus meant giving in to the conservatives, such as Corzo and Mullin. Corzo was a militant anticommunist, and Mullin was a personal friend of Bordaberry, whom he frequently visited.[19] As a consequence of this change in orientation, after a promising beginning the bishops limited their actions to sending private messages to the government.[20] It was not until the 1980 national plebiscite that the hierarchy once again began to take more energetic and positive stands.

THE TRANSITION TO DEMOCRACY

In November 1980, 57 percent of the Uruguayan electorate voted against a new constitution that would have legitimated the armed forces as permanent guardians of the government.[21] Given this unexpected rejection, the military worked up another plan. In 1981 they designated Gregorio Alvarez, a retired general, president of the country. In November 1982, according to the new plan, elections were held within each political party. In calling for these elections the government in fact recognized the parties as legitimate. In all the parties the groups most opposed to the government won.

With these elections the demand to return to democracy grew. Street demonstrations, held with or without permission, grew in frequency and in size. On May 1, 1983, an enormous crowd showed up to celebrate Worker's Day, and in November the parties summoned the whole population to show up for another civic act in front of the obelisk in the park named after Battle y Ordóñez. It was, according to all accounts, the largest gathering in the history of the country. In the meantime, the politicians entered into dialogue with the military. In the Park Hotel seven high-level meetings were held during 1983. The civilians continued to organize marches and demonstrations in order to persuade the military that it could not stop the transition to democracy. In spite of this public pressure, the military held firmly to the decision to exclude from the dialogue all leftist parties and certain politicians on the right whom it considered intransigent. Among the latter was Wilson Ferreira Aldunate, the leader of the National Party. On the other hand, the military freed Líber Seregni, the head of the United Front. The most acceptable broker for both sides turned out to be Julio María Sanguinetti, of the Colorado Party, a fact that favored his candidacy to succeed the military as president. In August 1984 the military and the politicians solemnly signed the Naval Club Pact, by which they agreed upon the final details for the transition, which included presidential elections in November. As foreseen, Sanguinetti became a candidate, won the election, and assumed the presidency in February of the following year. Nevertheless, just as in the case of Chile, the military left power only after binding the civilians to accept certain terms, which included conducting their own military affairs without civilian interference.

THE CHURCH IN THE TRANSITION

On the occasion of the 1980 plebiscite the bishops published a declaration criticizing the government's proposed constitution. In it they affirmed: "There is no real dialogue, nor legitimate social consensus, without a scrupulous respect for the will of the majority."[22] Most of all, they rejected the attempt to suppress basic liberties in the name of "national security." The episcopal conference also distributed to the parishes pamphlets intended to orient the laity regarding the plebiscite. In one of the points the bishops expressly condemned the doctrine of national security. Discussion groups were formed and the general consensus generated among Catholics was one of opposition to the military's constitution.[23] During the electoral process the bishop's conference made other public statements that motivated discussion in the parishes and in lay groups.

SERPAJ AND HUMAN RIGHTS

More important than the bishops' statements, however, was the role played by SERPAJ. In April 1981 a small group of militant Christians decided to carry out the first public act denouncing human-rights violations since the beginning of the dictatorship. They were encouraged and advised by Adolfo Pérez Esquivel, the Nobel Peace Prize winner in 1980. Until 1984 SERPAJ was the only human-rights organization in the entire country. The founder and driving force was a young Jesuit priest, Luis Pérez Aguirre, whose personal charism served to attract many idealists to the cause. Since 1975 Pérez Aguirre had worked in defense of abandoned or abused children. He founded a home on a farm for the children, which he called La Huella. At the end of

1979 he founded the magazine *La Plaza*, which aimed to stimulate dialogue among Uruguayans on the country's social and political problems from a Christian perspective. In 1982 the magazine was suppressed. That notwithstanding, the young Jesuit managed to get his campaign off the ground.[24] Soon SERPAJ became a model for other human-rights groups with more specific objectives. In 1977 the Mothers and Relatives of Uruguayans Disappeared in Argentina was founded. With the aid of SERPAJ other groups were founded: The Movement of Mothers and Relatives of Those Accused by Military Justice (1982), and The Mothers and Relatives of the Disappeared in Uruguay (1983), which worked closely with the former group. In 1984 SERPAJ collaborated in founding the Institute of Legal and Social Studies of Uruguay, which aimed to offer legal counsel to the victims of human-rights violations.[25]

In 1983, as a consequence of two dramatic events, SERPAJ became the focus of national attention. In June SERPAJ denounced the torture of twenty-five youths who had been detained. This was the first time in Uruguay that the victims and their families dared to denounce publicly, and with proof, human-rights violations committed by the forces of order. The scandal created was so great that the military broke off dialogue with the civilians on the transition to democracy and on August 2 the government decreed the suspension of all political activity. At once SERPAJ responded with a measure totally unknown in a country so secular and European as Uruguay: it called upon the citizens to participate in a hunger strike. Pérez Aguirre, along with another priest and a Methodist minister, fortified themselves inside a former convent and began their fifteen-day fast, scheduled to end on August 25, the day of national independence. Many other activities accompanied this central event: marches, which included the clanging of pots and pans, and blackouts, in which people voluntarily left their homes in darkness. Archbishop Parteli tried to visit the hunger strikers but was stopped by a military cordon. Finally SERPAJ was declared outside the law. But by that time the hunger strikers had achieved their objective: they prodded the political parties, unions, and popular organizations to mobilize themselves. Concretely, SERPAJ organized the Multi-Sector Commission, which summoned all important civic groups to come together to forge one great campaign for returning to democracy. Among other activities the Multi-Sector Commission helped to mobilize the thousands of Uruguayans who turned out for the November meeting before the obelisk in Battle Park. Later, in 1984, as a result of SERPAJ's initiative, the National Coordination of Human Rights, which pulled together all human-rights groups in Uruguay, was founded.[26] All during 1984 and 1985 SERPAJ organized many demonstrations and marches to bring attention to the cause of the families of the disappeared and imprisoned. By means of these activities SERPAJ managed to turn the human-rights issue into a topic of national debate. All the political parties felt obliged to take up the banner of human rights and to pressure the military to moderate its conduct. Later, as Father Aguirre observed, it became evident that the parties were more interested in promoting their image than in promoting the cause of human rights.[27] Once in power, the parties backed away from their promise to try those responsible for gross violations of human rights.

THE NATIONAL REFERENDUM

In March 1985 Uruguay's parliament approved the Law of National Pacification, which granted amnesty to political prisoners and all those who had been exiled for political reasons. The law expressly excluded from the amnesty all those who had been responsible for meting out inhuman treatment or detaining persons who later disappeared.[28] The law represented a great victory for the civilians and especially for the human-rights groups. It seemed as though Uruguay was about to follow the example of Argentina when it returned to democracy. However, in the course of the year the politicians went back on their word. As the official investigation proceeded, the military proved to be very uncooperative, and in private conversations with political leaders military leaders let it be known that they considered the Pacification Law an act of pure vengeance. In December parliament produced the Law of Limitations on State Punishment, which extended the original amnesty to include all military and police involved in acts of repression or torture during the dictatorship. The new law annulled all the exceptions that had been made regarding human-rights violators in the Law of National Pacification.

On the same day that parliament voted for the new law, the human-rights groups organized a demonstration that included the mothers of the disappeared. Afterward, three women, Elisa Delle Piane, Matilde Rodríguez, and María Ester Gatti, organized a campaign to have a national referendum to annul the general pardon granted by the government. In January 1987 the National Commission Pro-Referendum was created. Most politicians and observers were skeptical about the possibility of the referendum getting off the ground, and the government used tactics to intimidate the organizers. Nevertheless, the campaign soon turned into a veritable national crusade. SERPAJ and the other human-rights groups collected signatures throughout the country. Finally, in December 1988, the National Commission Pro-Referendum handed over to the Court of Elections a list of 630,000 signatures: a number far above that required by law. Indeed, it was a very respectable number, considering Uruguay's small population. The Elections Court examined the signatures and announced that the referendum would take place in April. For the first time in the entire history of Uruguay the people in general, as opposed to the traditional political parties, had imposed their will. Morality had won over pragmatic politics.

The referendum engendered impassioned debates over human rights everywhere in Uruguay. It also provoked, for the first time, an honest and frank assessment of the country's recent history, including the role of the armed forces. On April 16, 57 percent of the country voted in favor of a full amnesty and 42.5 percent voted against.[29] This was without doubt a defeat for the human-rights groups, the mothers and relatives of the disappeared, and other victims of repression. Nevertheless, it is interesting to note that the vote against the amnesty won in Montevideo by 56.4 percent. This meant that the vote in favor of the pardon won in the interior, where tradition prevailed and where there was considerably less repression. Although the defeat discouraged the human-rights groups, nonetheless many saw the campaign to hold the referendum as a moral victory. As a result of that campaign many more Uruguayans were made aware of human-rights issues. In particular, SERPAJ used the slogan made popular in the years after Medellín—There is no peace without justice—as its principal argument. In spite of the defeat SERPAJ intensified its efforts to assure that some justice would be done. Following the example of Argentina and Brazil it produced its own *Uruguay: Nunca más* ("Uruguay: Never Again"), published in 1989, with abundant collected testimonies on tortures, detentions, and disappearances during the dictatorship. Unlike similar reports in Argentina and Chile, however, SERPAJ's investigation was not the fruit of an official commission, but rather the work of a private group with the aid of volunteers and the cooperation of witnesses and victims who had suffered during the process.

THE CHURCH: A NEW IMAGE

Many things changed in Uruguay during the long civil-military dictatorship. One thing that changed was the naive belief that long dictatorships, typical of the rest of Latin America, could never occur in Uruguay. Another change was the general perception many Uruguayans had of the church. For many, raised in a secular atmosphere, the church's role in defending human rights and promoting democracy was a surprise. In general, the church gained a new respectability as a result of the role played by Parteli and other progressive churchpeople, and especially by SERPAJ. For conservative Catholics the new activist role of the church was highly inconvenient.

This change in roles can be perceived in certain incidents and gestures. One somewhat humorous indication of how times had changed was a visit the leading Masons of Uruguay paid to Archbishop Parteli during the tense days of the transition to democracy. The Masons proposed issuing a joint statement with the Catholic church calling for the military to continue its dialogue with the civilians. Parteli politely declined the invitation but proposed that each make a separate statement.[30] Another example occurred as a result of John Paul II's visit in May 1988. President Sanguinetti was so impressed by the pope and the popular response to the pontiff's visit that he fully approved the proposal to keep a great white cross that had been raised in the center of the capital as a permanent remembrance of the visit. Finally, when Sanguinetti's successor, Luis Alberto Lacalle, a practicing Catholic, took his oath of office in 1990, he participated in an ecumenical service presided over by the Catholic archbishop of Montevideo. This was the first time since 1894 that a Uruguayan president had participated in a public and official religious service.[31] Although Uruguay continues to be a highly secular society, the church now enjoys status as an important social force that it never enjoyed before.

7.

Bolivia (1952-1989)

Strikes, Coups, and Elections

In 1952 the National Revolutionary Movement (MNR), led by Víctor Paz Estenssoro, carried out one of the most important political and social revolutions in contemporary Latin America. The Bolivian national revolution overthrew the nearly feudal oligarchic regime associated with certain powerful families—the Patiños, the Hochschilds, and the Aramayos—who were the principal owners of Bolivia's mines. Middle-class civilians, workers, and peasants participated in the revolution, which was to constitute the basis of a new political legitimacy. Nevertheless, the revolution and the major changes that it produced, as well as many populist experiments—often carried out with short-term vision—also brought about great social and economic instability, which in turn led to many *golpes de estados* from the right and the left.

The complicated process that Bolivia went through since the revolution until the elections of 1989 may be broken down into the following periods: (1) state populism (1952-64) under the democratic civilian governments of Paz Estenssoro and Hernán Siles Zuazo, who ruled with the help of an alliance with Juan Lechín, the all-powerful boss of the COB (*Central Obrera Boliviana*), the general worker's confederation of Bolivia; (2) the populist government of René Barrientos (1964-69), which represented the beginning of a new militarism, although in this case still within the social definitions of the revolution; (3) more militarism, characterized by great instability and zigzags from the nationalistic right, represented by General Alfredo Ovando (1969-70), to the leftist populism of General Juan José Torres (1970-71); (4) the national security state under General Hugo Banzer (1971-78), which promoted a state capitalism favorable to the business class; (5) the return to democracy (1978-82), characterized by great instability (there were eight different governments during this period, including the brutal dictatorship of General García Meza); and (6) the reestablishment of democracy under Siles Zuazo (1982-85) and the final consolidation of the process under Paz Estenssoro (1985-89) and Jaime Paz Zamora, elected president in 1989.[1]

Political scientists had devoted much attention to this complicated political process, but few have recognized the key role played by the church, which intervened at certain decisive moments and helped deal with many impasses. During this period the church in Bolivia went from being a typically conservative and traditional church to one of the most progressive in Latin America. During the Banzer and García Meza regimes it became a leading voice for human rights and the popular demand to return to democracy. It also played an important role as mediator: at times it mediated between the miners and the government; at other times between the different political parties; and finally, between the military and the civilians. In the midst of the new social forces that emerged after the revolution—and given the weakness of political democratic institutions—the church constituted the only institution that enjoyed the necessary legitimacy to serve as a forum for a national dialogue among the new forces unaccustomed to moderation and the art of seeking consensus.

THE CHANGES IN THE CHURCH

Before the sixties the church in Bolivia was typical of the church in the entire Andean region: small, conservative, fearful of communism and Protestantism, and little concerned about social or political questions. The Bolivian church was protected by the government for most of the nineteenth century, but in the beginning of the twentieth century it felt the impact of liberal anticlerical legislation. In 1906 the government declared freedom of religion for non-Catholics, although the Catholic church continued to be protected by national patronage until 1961. The number of vocations went steadily downhill, and more and more foreign missionaries came to fill the gap. In the nineteenth century the Jesuits, the Salesians, and the Vincentians arrived, and in the twentieth, the Augustinians, the Society of Maryknoll, the Josephines, the Oblates of Mary Inmaculate, the Dominicans, and others.[2] In 1988 there were 727 priests in the entire country, of whom only 221 were Bolivians by birth.[3] Almost all the rest belonged to religious orders or foreign mission societies. Of the approximately 1,523 religious women, about half were foreigners. Of the 29 bishops, 12 were foreign born.[4] The missionaries took charge of the apostolic vicariates and *prelaturas nullius* (that is, areas on the way to becoming dioceses), which were created in the jungle and the altiplano. It is very telling that for years the most representative figure in the hierarchy was a German missionary—also Bolivia's first cardinal—Clement Maurer, archbishop of Sucre (1951-83). Maurer also served as president of the episcopal conference on a few occasions.

The 1952 revolution took the church by surprise, and it contributed little to that process. Nevertheless, the social changes that began taking place, as well as the presence of missionaries from the First World, helped to forge a new social mentality in the church. Especially after Vatican II the church in

Bolivia began to speak out on social and political themes. Of special interest were the efforts of the Canadian Oblates who worked in the mining camps. With the support of Jorge Manrique, Jesús López de Lama, and other progressive bishops, the Oblates became priest-miners and expressed their solidarity with the miners in their public statements. In 1965 the archbishop of La Paz, Abel Atezana, along with 126 priests, signed a document supporting the demands of the miners.[5] Other priests influenced university students. They also founded reflection centers, which gave an intellectual impetus to their social activity. In 1966 a group of American Dominicans founded the Bolivian Institute of Study and Social Action (IBEAS), and in 1969 the Oblates founded the Center of Integral Development for their pastoral agents. In Cochabamba in 1966 and 1968 short courses were offered for the continuing formation of priests, religious women, and laity, especially catechists and deacons. Of special importance was the program for Aymara deacons organized by the Maryknoll Fathers and the auxiliary bishop of La Paz, Adhemar Esquivel. The Jesuits founded CIPCA (Center of Research and Social Promotion) and ACLO (Loyola Cultural Action), with centers in Chuquisaca, Potosí, and Tarija. The Jesuits and Oblates also founded several radio stations: Radio Fides, in La Paz; Radio Loyola, in Sucre; and Radio Pius XII, in Potosí. On the level of popular education, in 1966 the Jesuits founded the *Fe y Alegría* (Faith and Joy) schools, which by 1985 had more than eighty-five thousand students.[6] In Cochabamba and Sucre the Spanish missionaries of the Work of Hispanic-American Priestly Cooperation took charge of the seminaries.

Ecumenical Protestants also changed with the times, especially the Methodist church, which on several occasions expressed its solidarity with the miners. The most representative ecumenical group was ISAL (Church and Society in Latin America), founded in Bolivia in 1968. Ecumenical Protestants, however, constituted a very small percentage of the population. In 1988 it was estimated that about 87 percent of all Bolivians were Catholic. On the other hand, the great majority of the remaining 13 percent of non-Catholics belonged to the more fundamentalist groups.[7]

CHURCH, MINERS, AND BARRIENTOS

The first important mediating action conducted by the church took place in 1968 when the bishops, President Barrientos, and the COB (the national worker's federation) signed an agreement after four months of negotiations. General René Barrientos, who had seized power in 1964, represented a new generation of young military who had been formed by the ideals of the revolution. His decision to overthrow Paz Estenssoro, who had been elected for the third time, was a reaction to a general crisis of corruption in the National Revolutionary Movement. But Barrientos also acted because many civilians—and the army—were afraid of the radicalization of the miners. Once in power,

Barrientos emerged as a charismatic caudillo; he won the favor of the peasants, many civilians who depended on state patronage, and the business class. He also managed to win support from the United States, a most important achievement considering the fact that one-third of the national budget came from American aid.[8] But Barrientos did not give in to the demands of Juan Lechín, the all-powerful union chief of the COB. As a result, clashes between the government and the miners (who made up the majority of the workers in the COB) become more and more frequent. The church was an acceptable mediator to both sides: to the miners, in part because of the strength of popular religiosity among them, and in part due to the new solidarity the church expressed for their demands; and to the government, because Barrientos sympathized with the social ideals of the revolution but also saw in the church a stabilizing social force. The agreement, signed in the presence of Cardinal Maurer, Jorge Manrique, the archbishop of La Paz, the papal nuncio, and the bishops of Cochabamba, Santa Cruz, and Corocoro, promised to be the basis of a new social peace. In the document Barrientos expressed his approval of the church's role in promoting the health and education of the miners. A committee made up of representatives of COMIBOL (the State Mining Corporation of Bolivia), the COB, and the church was created on the spot. Its purpose was to make sure that the agreements were kept.[9]

INTER-ECCLESIAL TENSIONS

Within a few months the miners and their priest friends complained that the agreements were not being kept.[10] Nonetheless, the church had already established its credentials as a mediator and would be called upon to fulfill that function many more times. Furthermore, the death of Barrientos, whose helicopter crashed in April 1969, put an end to the era of good will among the state, the church, and the workers. After a short period of civilian rule under Luis Adolfo Siles Salinas, who had been Barrientos's vice president, General Alfredo Ovando took power in September 1969. Of a rightwing nationalistic tendency, Ovando expropriated Bolivian Gulf, an American petroleum company. But in October 1970 Ovando himself was overthrown by General Juan José Torres, who ushered in a brief period of leftist populism. In the meantime the church experienced its own tensions between avant-garde groups and the hierarchy. As elsewhere, the tensions were produced largely as a result of differing interpretations of Vatican II and Medellín. Furthermore, Che Guevara's guerrilla movement (1967), followed by a local guerrilla outbreak in Teoponte (1969-70), as well as a radicalization of the university students, also served to heighten tensions.

Jorge Manrique, archbishop of La Paz between 1967 and 1987, came to symbolize the progressive church in Bolivia. His antecessor, Abel Atezana, like the majority of the other bishops, and probably the majority of Bolivians, condemned Che Guevara's guerrilla movement (Che was killed after his capture in 1967). But in July 1970 another group, inspired by Che's movement, and composed largely of university students, made its debut. Unlike the guerrillas of Ñancahuazú (Che's group), the guerrillas of Teoponte (the region where they operated) included several Christian idealists, in particular, Néstor Paz, an ex-seminarian. After eighty-seven days the army managed to wipe them out. Later, a Jesuit, José Pratts, paid homage to the dead by calling them "martyrs of the church today."[11] In September, Archbishop Manrique himself led the funeral procession for the slain combatants. That month Pratts, three other priests, and a Protestant pastor were expelled from the country by Ovando, who believed that they had ties with the guerrillas and that they espoused socialist ideas. But popular protest over the expulsion was so great that it contributed to Ovando's overthrow that year. The miners and workers, including Juan Lechín himself, expressed solidarity with the expelled religious.[12]

Faced with the socialist tendencies of many Christians, and perhaps anticipating the leftist government of Juan José Torres, Archbishop Manrique published a pastoral letter in October 1970 in which he expressed his views on socialism. He criticized Marxism but declared that "there is no conflict between Christianity and neo-socialism."[13] Shortly afterward the priests in the mining areas published a statement supporting Manrique.[14] Also, in 1971 Cardinal Maurer issued a message on the church's properties and called for a return to evangelical simplicity.[15] But these advanced positions of the bishops stood in contrast to some of their actions. In 1969 the bishops, worried over the possible influence of these progressive ideas on future priests, decided not to renew the contract of the priests of OCSHA—the Spanish missionary society for cooperation with Latin America—to run the seminaries in Sucre and Cochabamba. In 1970 they closed the seminary in Cochabamba and in 1971 went so far as to forbid the OCSHA priests to return to the country. Another crisis arose over ISAL, the avant-garde ecumenical group, which was the Bolivian equivalent of ONIS in Peru or the Priests for the Third World in Argentina. ISAL had its offices in the archdiocesan offices of the Catholic church in La Paz, and the Jesuit José Pratts was one of its principal leaders. ISAL supported the miners and openly approved of socialism, but it went a step too far by criticizing the church for its conservative positions and its properties. In November 1970 a group of Christians connected with ISAL published a letter in which they criticized the ambiguous role played by the papal nuncio in Bolivia. At the end of the year ISAL was asked to leave the offices of the archdiocese. The bishops, quite annoyed by ISAL's criticisms, wanted to make it clear that ISAL was not an organ of the church. Following Banzer's takeover, ISAL left the country.

Much less clear is the case of IBEAS, the research center of the American Dominicans. In April 1970 a group of students assaulted IBEAS's center in La Paz, and later the government expropriated it on the pretext that it was a center for American espionage. Progressive church groups supported the government's move, while the bishops protested it. In the midst of these ambiguous gestures—public sympathy for Christian guerrillas and disapproval of ISAL—the bishops displayed a general ambivalence toward the changes in both society and the church. This ambivalence reflected divisions within the hierarchy itself. On one side was the old guard: Maurer and majority of the bishops. And on the other, the new guard: Manrique in La Paz, Adhemar Esquivel, who promoted the Aymara deacons; and Jesús López de Lama in Corocoro.

BANZER (1971-1978)

In August 1971 Colonel Hugo Banzer overthrew the leftist populist regime of Juan José Torres. The new regime was supported by the majority of the military, the business class—especially those with economic interests in Santa Cruz—certain sectors of the MNR, and the pro-fascist Bolivian Socialist *Falange*. Banzer fostered state capitalism and made good use of the state's monopoly over the basic mineral and oil resources to favor the expansion of private capitalism and national development. Thanks to the high price of oil, which in 1974 represented 25 percent of Bolivia's exports, Banzer was able to execute many public works, construct new buildings, and pave many highways. Also, the cocaine traffic, concentrated in the region of Chapare, injected an important number of dollars into the national economy. Banzer's power, and the relative stability of this regime, depended to a great extent on state clientalism. In fact, the number of state functionaries rose considerably during those years. Politically the Banzer period can be divided into two periods: from 1971 to 1974, when he governed with the civilians who supported him; from November 1974 until 1978, when he governed without either civilians or parties, giving rise to an openly authoritarian state.

Banzer drastically repressed all social groups opposed to the regime, especially workers and peasants. Between 1971 and 1978 around 19,140 Bolivians were exiled, including Juan Lechín and four ex-presidents.[16] Thousands were detained at different times, and there were numerous cases of torture. However, the number of persons killed by the state was relatively low. The universities were frequently closed and all union activity was forbidden. One particular case gained special notoriety: the so-called massacre in the Cochabamba Valley in January 1975. In protest against the prices fixed by the government, the peasants in that central region blocked the roads. In retaliation the military harshly repressed them. Many died or disappeared.[17]

In the beginning relations between the government and the church were somewhat ambiguous. In the wake of the leftist government of Torres the hierarchy came out in support of the newly installed regime. Also, Banzer presented himself as the spokesman for the "Christian and patriotic people of Bolivia," who were opposed to atheism and communism. He participated in numerous religious processions and received a papal blessing from Cardinal Maurer during the Te Deum of 1975. Nevertheless, Banzer did not hesitate to treat progressive priests and religious women harshly and forcibly to enter parish homes and convents. Toward the end of 1972 eighteen priests, four religious women, and three Protestant pastors were forced to leave the country.[18] That year security forces forcibly entered fifteen homes of religious. By the end of Banzer's regime more than a hundred priests had been expelled. Furthermore, at different moments priests and nuns were detained in police stations, and the church's radios were taken over. In April 1972 the police searched the residence of the bishop of Corocoro.

Finally, faced with these aggressive actions, the bishops began taking a harder line toward the regime, some more than others. In January 1973 a group of ninety-nine priests, religious women, and Protestant pastors signed a manifesto entitled "Gospel and Violence." The document, which was widely circulated, served as a call to arms for progressive Christians. It denounced the government for suppressing democracy, for murder, for violations of human rights, and for using the courts to persecute people for their political ideas.[19] The Interior minister, Mario Adett, noting that the majority of those who signed the document were foreigners, suggested that they all return to their home countries. He went on to recommend as a model of conduct the fundamentalist pastor Julio César Ruibal, who, instead of getting involved in politics, preached "peace, love, and the Gospel."[20]

THE JUSTICE AND PEACE COMMISSION

That same month the bishops announced the creation of a Justice and Peace Commission. The commission, headed by former president Luis Adolfo Siles Salinas, proposed to raise the consciousness of Christians in the area of social justice and human rights. More specifically, it aimed to investigate cases of violations of human rights, disappearances, detentions, and torture.

The commission had barely begun its work when it carried out one of its first public initiatives. Siles Salinas and the Dominican priest Arturo Sist offered themselves to the minister of the Interior as hostages in exchange for five women who had been arrested illegally. This dramatic gesture had its effect, and the women were released.[21] From that moment on the commission became the focal point for the defense of human rights in Bolivia. In another dramatic case it investigated the death of a former Interior minister, Andrés Selich, who was murdered in the very residence of the current minister of the Interior.

By means of numerous letters sent to the president of the Republic and other government officials, fasts and prayer vigils, and visits to jails, the commission was able to channel the cry in favor of human rights and transform it into concrete actions. For that reason the government singled out the commission as a special target to harass. In March 1975 two priests, Eric de Wasseige, a Dominican and president of the commission, and Jorge Wavreille, an Oblate who collaborated with it, were expelled from the country. The church, the miners, and other human-rights groups protested this arbitrary action. Nevertheless, the bishops, feeling the weight of the government's pressure, backed down and in 1975 declared the commission in "recess."

For a while a specialized section of the commission—the Committee to Help Detainees—continued its work of visiting prisoners and watching out for their rights. Father Alejandro Mestre, S.J., and later several religious of different congregations, assumed that task. In October 1977 another and rather different entity was created: the Permanent Assembly on Human Rights. The Assembly, presided over by former president Siles Salinas and Father Julio Tumiri, was supported by the hierarchy but was independent of the official church. Furthermore, the assembly was an organism directly tied to the United Nations. Also, it had an ecumenical character: the Methodist, Lutheran, and Episcopalian churches of Bolivia supported it. The assembly sought to maintain close ties with international human-rights groups to avoid being isolated. Although it was different in many aspects from the Commission on Justice and Peace, the assembly filled the vacuum created when the latter was dissolved. It played a major role during the hunger strikes of 1977 and 1978. Finally, in July 1977 the Commission of Justice and Peace was reorganized and began to function again, along with the assembly.

INTEGRALIST GROUPS

During this period the Bolivian church, and specifically the hierarchy, was in general very progressive. Cardinal Maurer and the majority of the other bishops opted for maintaining cordial relations with the Banzer regime, but they never approved of its repressive actions. On the other extreme, small groups of priests and laypersons emerged who did not hesitate to support the regime and to condemn the progressive groups within the church. One example was the Conference of Diocesan Clergy, organized under the leadership of Father Luis Rojas Caballero, in Santa Cruz. At the annual meeting in 1975 some 130 priests attended, all diocesan clergy and all Bolivians. The group expressed its rejection of the "foreign interference in the internal affairs of the country" as well as the "Marxist infiltration in the church."[22] The archbishop of Santa Cruz denied having granted authorization to the group to meet in his archdiocese. Also, the American Dominicans who founded the Mansion in Santa Cruz—the principal meeting place for Catholic charismatics—were criticized by progressive Catholics for their silence on social questions. In Cochabamba the Bolivian National Social Legion frequently attacked progressive church groups. In 1976 in La Paz another group appeared: Bolivian Youth Pro-Christian Civilization, replete with red berets and images of Our Lady of Fatima.[23]

Banzer himself frequently used religious images to reinforce his claim to be a defender of Christian values. When he was no longer in power, he turned up in 1979 as a civilian candidate with his own political party, National Democratic Action. During the campaign his party gave out flyers bearing the images of the Lord of Great Power and the pope. The words on the flyers condemned atheistic communism and exhorted the readers not to vote for the MNR and the United Democratic Front, Hernán Siles Zuazo's party.[24] Archbishop Manrique stepped in and condemned such overt political use of religious images.

THE HUNGER STRIKE OF 1977-1978

Toward the end the Banzer regime showed signs of a generalized break-down. Under international pressure, particularly from the American government under Jimmy Carter, Banzer announced elections for 1978, two years before the officially scheduled date. Also, many restrictions were removed and some of the political parties were allowed to function once again. But a general amnesty was not conceded to all exiles or political prisoners. The church took on a more aggressive role and criticized the government more openly. Toward the end of 1976 Cardinal Maurer handed over to Banzer a list of proofs that, contrary to what the government claimed, it did foster birth control. This incident, which could have occurred under a democratic government, had a more sinister significance because the birth-control program was linked to a program to foster immigration, in this case, white settlers from South Africa. The image of the regime as quasi fascist and racist was not helped when it was discovered that the government was knowingly sheltering Klaus Altmann ("Barbie"), the former Gestapo commander in Lyons, France, who in 1977 still occupied an important post in the ministry of the Interior. Furthermore, in 1976 the Mining Confederation asked the bishops to help the miners in their efforts to establish a dialogue with the government. The government did not listen to the miners nor did it accept the church's mediation.[25] In December, 1976, in response to a regime that showed signs of corruption and that governed purely by force, the bishops published a new letter, "Peace and Fraternity." The letter analyzed the social situation of the country and pointed out that there still existed an enormous gulf between a "privileged minority" and the great majority of citizens who lived in extreme poverty. The bishops also censured the government for having suspended the political parties, the unions, and other representative associations. Finally, they condemned the "tendency to control the church's actions with regards to its social teachings."[26]

But the most serious confrontation between church and state, one which practically pushed the regime over the brink into the abyss, was a major hunger strike that began in December 1977 and soon turned into a national protest movement against the government. On December 28 four women initiated a lonely hunger strike on the premises of the archdiocesan offices in La Paz. The women called for a general amnesty for all political prisoners and their return from exile. They also called for the right of unions to exist and for the army to cease its occupation of the mining camps. Archbishop

Manrique not only allowed the women to have their strike on his premises, but he even gave them comfort and support. Soon others joined the strike, among them two priests, a Salesian and a Jesuit. Finally the valiant action of the four women turned into a national crusade. Twenty-eight different groups, totalling twelve hundred people, joined them. The strike spread to Potosí, Oruro, Tarija, Sucre, and Santa Cruz.

The strikers used hospitals, union headquarters, and the premises of the archdiocesan newspaper, *Presencia*. But mainly they used churches, which added a religious dimension to the cause. The principal mediators between the strikers and the government were Siles Salinas, the former president, and other members of the Permanent Assembly of Human Rights. The international press gave the strike important coverage. On January 17, 1978, the police stormed the different centers where the strikers gathered. In response, Manrique threatened to place the city of La Paz under interdict. Apparently that threat was taken seriously because the archbishop's threat was read in a cabinet meeting.[27]

The church made a false move when Cardinal Maurer, without consulting the strikers, designated himself their mediator and signed with the government a document that purported to put an end to the strike. Naturally the strikers disowned the document. Later Maurer recognized his error and came out in support of the strike, which lent it new legitimacy. On the evening of January 17 Banzer announced a general amnesty on television. However, before the amnesty actually took place, many complicated negotiations had to be carried out. Although the strike was supported by workers, students, and housewives, there is no doubt that the presence of priests, religious women, and friends from the Methodist church gave the strike a powerful legitimacy. In spite of the lack of enthusiasm on the part of several of the bishops—notably Maurer, Prata, and Mestre—Manrique's energetic action in La Paz in support of the strike served to rally most of the bishops and ordinary Christians around the banner.[28]

INSTABILITY ON THE WAY TO DEMOCRACY (1978-1982)

FRUSTRATED ELECTIONS AND NATUSCH'S COUP

After announcing that he would not be a candidate, Banzer designated General Juan Pereda Asbún as the official candidate for the elections to be held in July 1978. When it became evident that the opposition candidate, Hernán Siles Zuazo, was going to win, Pereda simply committed massive electoral fraud. When that provoked cries of protest, he overthrew his own patron—Banzer—and seized power. However, in November General David Padilla, with the support of the armed forces, overthrew Pereda and promised new and free elections. For the new elections, scheduled for 1979, three candidates presented themselves: Paz Estenssoro, Siles Zuazo, and Banzer. Banzer, the former dictator, had formed his own political party, National

Democratic Action, on the right. This time Paz Estenssoro came out number one, but by such a small percentage that it was not sufficient to win the presidency. Archbishop Manrique offered his good offices as mediator to resolve that impasse, and he interviewed each of the candidates. As a result of Manrique's intervention, Paz Estenssoro agreed to "converse" with the other candidates.[29] The discussions led to a formula for overcoming the deadlock. The solution consisted in having the national congress designate Walter Guevara Arce—a veteran of the MNR—as an interim president, and new elections to be called within a year.

This political pact was rudely overturned on November 1 when Colonel Alberto Natusch Busch, supported by some MNR members of parliament, overthrew Guevara on the pretext that his government was not "legitimate." But Natusch failed to win the support of most of the armed forces, nor did he have much popular support. The first day of the coup, known as the massacre of All Saints' Day, was characterized by violent clashes between pro-Natusch and pro-government soldiers. During the fifteen-day struggle for power approximately five hundred people, civilians and soldiers, were left lying dead in the streets of La Paz.[30] On this occasion the church's mediation proved decisive for putting an end to the coup and reestablishing peace. The two auxiliary bishops of La Paz, Genaro Prata and Adhemar Esquivel, held a series of discussions with Natusch, with different leaders of congress, and with Juan Lechín, the head of the COB.[31] As a result, Natusch backed down and turned power over once again to congress. Congress designated Lydia Gueiler to be president until the next elections.

LUIS ESPINAL: A DICTATORSHIP FORETOLD

On March 22, 1980, the same month as Archbishop Romero's assassination in El Salvador, Luis Espinal, a Jesuit priest, was kidnapped, tortured, and killed outside La Paz. Espinal, a Spaniard, had arrived in Bolivia in 1968. Trained as a journalist and a movie critic, he founded his own weekly newspaper, *Aquí* ("Here"). The newspaper strongly supported the worker's movement, denounced government corruption, and pointed out the ties between certain members of the military and the drug traffickers. Earlier in February dynamite had exploded in the offices of *Aquí*. The general consensus attributed Espinal's death to rightwing paramilitary. His murder was, therefore, a foretaste of the García Meza dictatorship. Around eighty thousand people attended the funeral, including Paz Estenssoro, Juan Lechín, Walter Guevara (then the head of the senate), Hernán Siles Zuazo, Marcelo Quiroga, and Luis Adolfo Siles Salinas.[32] The funeral turned out to be both a homage to the memory of Espinal and a public repudiation of the drug traffickers and their accomplices in the military and the police. In April, Luis García Meza took over the command of the army.

The new elections were held in June. This time Hernán Siles Zuazo and his party, the Popular and Democratic Union, won over Paz Estenssoro and

Banzer. But on July 17, General García Meza seized power and forced President Lydia Gueiler to resign. He declared that he would preside over a government of "national reconstruction."

García Meza (1980-1981)

The violent and cruel nature of the García Meza regime became evident on the very day he seized power. Close to seven hundred people were arrested, and the charismatic socialist leader Marcelo Quiroga was captured and murdered. President Gueiler sought asylum in the papal nunciature and was not allowed to leave the country until October. Purportedly the *golpe* was carried out to save the country from communism. But the *Washington Post* summarized the general consensus when it declared that the real intention of the conspirators was not to stop communism but to protect the drug lords.[33] The close ties between the different drug mafias, García Meza, and his minister of the Interior, Luis Arce Gómez, were so notorious that authors James Malloy and Eduardo Gamarra qualified the regime as a "Kleptocracia."[34]

The day after the *golpe* Manrique energetically denounced the takeover. The government responded by breaking into the homes of religious and closing down the church's radio stations. Many priests and nuns were detained. In August, Bishop Jesús López of Corocoro and a priest were detained for twenty-four hours. In September, the episcopal conference responded with a document entitled "Dignity and Liberty," one of the most eloquent and prophetic documents in the history of the Bolivian church. In it the bishops decried the fact that from the very first moment "persons and works connected with the church became objects of a systematic repression, which frequently meant torture, insults, the breaking in of homes, and censure."[35] Furthermore, the document presented a list of "individual rights" and "social rights," which included the right to "freedom of education . . . the right to work; work security and the right to form unions," as well as the "right of political participation and the right to freedom of political choice."[36] Many priests were warned not to read the document in their Sunday masses.

For a while García Meza tried to build a bridge of reconciliation toward the church. In October he sent the subsecretary of Cult to the episcopal conference. After the meeting the secretary of the conference, Alejandro Mestre, announced—a bit stiffly—that both the state and the church had an "attitude favoring dialogue," and García Meza announced that the relations between the two were "normal." In November Mestre sent a message from the episcopal conference objecting to a proposed law of national security, and especially to an article that restored the death penalty.[37] Within twenty-four hours García Meza announced that the proposal would not be enacted.

In spite of this small rapprochement, the government continued to harass the church. In December 1980 paramilitary forces seized the building that housed the church's newspaper, *Presencia*. In spite of that setback the church's daily was able to come out again in January. After the assassination of Marcelo

Quiroga the regime's most violent and scandalous atrocity was the mass murder of eight leaders of the Movement of the Revolutionary Left (MIR), who had gathered for a meeting in a house in La Paz. On January 15 all were machine-gunned to death by security agents. The church tried to persuade the government to turn the bodies over to the families, but to no avail. In February the episcopal conference criticized the regime once again for torture, assassinations, and human-rights violations of all types. In an attempt to better the government's image García Meza had Arce Gómez, his minister of the Interior, removed. The attempt was in vain because he named Arce head of the army's war college—hardly a demotion. Nevertheless, in a surprise response, the army deposed Arce from his new post—a clear sign that the armed forces were not happy about being linked to a scandalous dictatorship. Aware of that discontent, in May 1981 García Meza announced his decision to leave power in August.

In July masses were celebrated to commemorate the anniversary of the assassination of Marcelo Quiroga and the eight leaders of MIR. In August, in Santa Cruz, Natusch Busch, a perpetual conspirator now holding the rank of general, along with another general, Lucio Añez, demanded the resignation of García Meza. The dictator in fact fulfilled his promise and on August 4 turned power over to a junta of other military leaders in La Paz. Later, in September, a member of that junta, General Celso Torrelio, was designated president. In the meantime, with a long list of accusations ranging from being an accomplice of the drug traffickers to murder hanging over his head, García Meza fled the country and disappeared. Luis Arce Gómez, who had also escaped from justice, was captured in December 1989, and the Bolivian authorities turned him over to American justice. On April 21, 1993, Bolivia's supreme court condemned García Meza in absentia to thirty years in prison. Finally, in March 1995, the former dictator was captured in Brazil and turned over to the Bolivian authorities.[38] The new president, General Torrelio, formally committed himself to restoring democracy; at the same time, the situation of human rights improved considerably, although not completely.

THE STRIKE AT HUANUNI (1981)

The government's new openness was soon put to the test, and the church once again took up its role as mediator. In November 1981 the miners in Huanuni, in the department of Oruro, went on strike. One of their demands was for the government to recognize their right to organize. The government reacted by sending troops to the mines, and many union leaders were arrested. The strike soon spread to mining centers in the rest of the country. The church took the initiative and offered its good offices as mediator between the miners and the government. Both sides accepted, and on November 24 representatives of the workers, the general manager of COMIBOL (the state-controlled mining company), several ministers of state, and representatives of the church met to work out a compromise document. The workers agreed to return to work, and the government recognized their right to strike. It also promised to free the miners held in custody and to pull its soldiers out of the mining areas. At the same time a mixed commission made up of the miners, the government, and representatives of the church was formed.[39] The commission, which began work in December, aimed to deal with the question of salaries, contracts, and the ground rules for the functioning of labor unions. COMIBOL was represented by Armando Urioste and the COB by Guillermo Carrasco. The church's representatives were Alejandro Mestre, the secretary of the episcopal conference, and the two auxiliary bishops of La Paz, Adhemar Esquivel and Julio Terrazas. Several hundred miners marched to La Paz to witness the negotiations. During the discussions, the miners went back on strike. The government responded by taking a harder line. In the middle of this tense situation the church asked both sides to hand over their respective proposals. With the two proposals in hand, the church mediators fleshed out the best parts of both and produced a third proposal, which served as a new basis for negotiation. According to the new agreement the unions would be restored, but gradually. On December 18 the final document was signed by both parties in the presence of the church's representatives.[40]

THE RETURN TO DEMOCRACY
AND THE NATIONAL DIALOGUE

In October 1982 the military left power, and Hernán Siles Zuazo was named president by the congress that had been elected in 1980. But the return to democracy and constitutional order did not resolve the country's major economic and social problems. The political coalition that formed the basis of Siles Zuazo's government was constantly absorbed in internal squabbles. Faced with the COB's incessant demands, the government responded with populist measures, thus provoking more inflation. By 1984 the government was submerged in a deep crisis, and once again the specter of a military *golpe* hung over the country. In the midst of this institutional crisis President Siles, disturbed over accusations from congress that he had drug connections, precipitated another crisis in October by declaring a hunger strike. But the presidential hunger strike seemed merely a desperate measure intended to apply pressure on the opposition parties and the COB to grant the government some relief. Given the lack of clear objectives, his dramatic strike seemed doomed to lead nowhere. Finally, on the third day, the papal nuncio and three bishops (Manrique, Mestre, and Armando Gutiérrez) visited the president and pleaded with him to suspend his hunger strike. At the same time the episcopal conference called upon the political parties and all national leaders to enter into a dialogue in order to resolve the crisis. Siles Zuazo immediately acceded to the bishops' petition and supported the idea of having a national dialogue.[41] Once again the church had come to the rescue by offering a dignified way out of a seemingly impossible situation.

The episcopal conference sent invitations to all political parties that were represented in congress. According to the plan, the church would engage in dialogue, first with the parties, then with the COB, and finally, with the Confederation of Private Business of Bolivia (CEPB). The political stage of the dialogue began on November 14 and lasted until November 21. Eleven groups participated, including Hugo Banzer's National Democratic Action, Siles Zuazo's National Leftist Revolutionary Movement, the original National Revolutionary Movement, Paz Estenssoro's Historical National Revolutionary Movement, the Christian Democratic Party, and even the Bolivian Communist Party. The principal leaders—Paz Estenssoro, Banzer (except for one brief presentation), and Siles Zuazo—did not attend. The church was represented by Luis Rodríguez, the president of the episcopal conference, Alejandro Mestre, the secretary of the conference, Armando Gutiérrez, the former bishop of Cochabamba, and two priests. One of the two, José Gramunt, a Jesuit, acted as the moderator for the meeting. For many politicians and union leaders the solution to the crisis was very simple: have President Siles resign and hold new elections. But the bishops did not want to reduce the dialogue to a mere discussion on what formula to adopt to have a change of government. Their intention was to strengthen democracy by creating a national consensus on certain basic principles and agreements. Siles Zuazo himself resolved the crisis in part by announcing through one of his representatives in the dialogue that he would accept holding new elections a year earlier (in 1985) on the condition that the opposition grant him a "political truce."[42]

The bishops presented the representatives of the parties with a twelve-point document they hoped would serve as a basis for the discussion. The points referred to two principal topics: the economic and the political crises. After several days of intense discussion the politicians signed a document that was to serve as a new basis for a national consensus. At the same time they conceded to President Siles the truce he wanted. In the document the parties all committed themselves to "sustain the democratic system . . . [to] guarantee the peaceful living together of the Bolivian people . . . and to resolve pressing economic and social problems."[43] More concretely, they supported the proposal to hold general elections in 1985.

The second stage of the national dialogue—between the church and the Confederation of Bolivian Workers (COB)—was much less positive. The union leaders present believed that the new political pact and the truce granted to President Siles represented in reality an agreement made against the demands of the workers. The COB's representative, Walter Delgadillo, did not hide his unhappiness with the pact: "We believe that the church has extended its hand to the rich and powerful, but not to the dispossessed of this country."[44] The meeting lasted only two days. This was not merely because of the union leader's disagreement over the new pact, but more poignantly, the COB declared a national strike and all the leaders left to head it.

Finally, the encounter with the representatives of the Confederation of Private Business was conducted in a much more tranquil atmosphere. The business class clearly wished to put an end to the political crisis, but without disturbing the social or economic order.

PAZ ESTENSSORO AND THE STRIKES OF 1986 AND 1987

In the months preceding the July 1985 elections the COB intensified its pressure on the government, and in the midst of strikes and threats of strikes Archbishop Manrique tried in vain to establish a dialogue between Juan Lechín and the government. The election proved that the electorate was beginning to incline toward the right, or what would become a new "center." After the first electoral round Banzer came in first, Paz Estenssoro second, and Jaime Paz Zamora of MIR, third. But the final winner was Paz Estenssoro, who forged a parliamentary alliance that elected him to the presidency, for the fourth time. His government rested on a more solid basis than that of Siles Zuazo. One reason for his success was that the veteran leader of the 1952 revolution realized that times had changed and that the populist style of the revolutionary days was now outdated. From the beginning of his administration Paz Estenssoro announced an austerity plan that included the privatization (in presidential decree number 21060) of many state-owned mines, which were to be converted into worker's cooperatives. The plan also meant that thousands of workers employed by COMIBOL would be laid off. Banzer, who had originally proposed doing just these actions, supported Paz's plan in congress. Given the openly neo-liberal thrust of the government, the COB prepared for a major showdown. During the strikes of 1985, 1986, and 1987 the COB and the Bolivian government engaged in a protracted battle that finally ended in a defeat for the former. The church served as mediator in many of these conflicts.

But times were changing, and the once all-powerful COB, which for decades practically constituted a parallel state with the state, was losing its grip over the workers and the economy. One important factor was the decreasing role mining played in the national economy. Tin and other mining products, which accounted for 80 to 90 percent of Bolivia's exports in the sixties, had fallen to about 50 percent in the seventies.[45] In contrast, oil from the eastern region, as well as certain agricultural products such as cotton, occupied a much more important place in the country's exports. Furthermore, world prices for metals had fallen considerably. Finally, the traffic in cocaine, for better or, more likely, for worse, had now become an important source of income for the country. Given these new realities the government felt itself in a stronger position to face down the miners, who no longer constituted the only basis of the country's economy. Shortly after the government announced its austerity plan the COB called for a strike, and Paz Estenssoro responded by imposing a state of siege in the mines. He also chose not to accept the church's mediation, probably because he wanted to assert the state's authority over the miners.[46]

In the meantime the church's hierarchy was in a process of renovation. In April 1985 Julio Terrazas, the bishop of Oruro, was elected president of the episcopal conference, and Luis Sáinz, one of the auxiliaries of La Paz, was elected general secretary of the conference. These new leaders, with the support of the progressives of the old guard—Manrique and others—believed that the neo-liberal policies of Paz, without any moderation, were destined to provoke an enormous social crisis in the country. For that reason they did not seek to serve merely as mediators but also as advocates for the miners, who were now on the losing side.

In August 1986 the COB called a second major strike in protest over Paz Estenssoro's program. In a "march for life and peace," some ten thousand miners walked from the mining camps toward the capital. The church expressed its solidarity with the miners and organized a collection in all the parishes to help the marchers. Paz responded by imposing another state of siege, and the miners were faced with a military cordon when they reached La Paz. Nevertheless, given the public's sympathy for the miners, the government relented and entered into dialogue with the miners, in the presence of church representatives. Between September 2 and September 13 the miners, government officials, and the church worked out an agreement that put an end to the conflict, at least for the moment. The miners agreed to lay aside their pressure tactics and return to work. The government promised to review its policy with respect to the mines and, concretely, agreed not to close or privatize mines without consulting with the miners first. Furthermore, the government agreed to maintain a minimum of thirteen thousand miners in the state-owned mines and to help relocate another five thousand who had been laid off.[47] The new president of the episcopal conference, Julio Terrazas, expressed his satisfaction with the agreement but also underlined the need for a new, general "social pact."[48]

But the new labor peace lasted only a short time. In March 1987 Juan Lechín called for a new national strike. He accused the government of having laid off thirty-five hundred miners and of not fulfilling other parts of the pact. Some five thousand miners, supported by university students, declared a hunger strike. Lechín asked the church to intercede for the workers before the government. Paz Estenssoro refused to enter into direct negotiations with the workers, but he did accept the church's mediation. In March, Alejandro Mestre, who was now the apostolic administer of the archdiocese of La Paz (Jorge Manrique had resigned), set out to meet with both sides. Praised by Juan Lechín for his "mediating ability," Mestre finally managed to compose a document of six points that both sides accepted. The government promised to donate food to the miners who had been laid off and to create a special fund to help them while they sought work in other sectors.[49] But in reality the strike was a defeat for the miners, who could no longer pressure the government as they had ten or twenty years earlier. In July Juan Lechín retired as executive secretary of the Federation of Miners and of the COB. His leaving coincided with the end of the COB's undisputed control over the economy. Lechín's absence highlighted that shift in power.

THE 1989 ELECTIONS

The church was called upon to mediate in one more political crisis: the presidential elections of 1989. In that election Gonzalo Sánchez de Lozada, one of Paz Esstensoro's ministers, came in first, followed by Hugo Banzer, with Jaime Paz Zamora of MIR in third place. Unfortunately, however, history repeated itself and none of the three managed to obtain the necessary majority to win the presidency. According to law, it was incumbent upon congress to decide in these cases, but the Bolivian congress itself was so divided that it failed to offer a way out of the crisis. The country had to have a president by August 6, Bolivia's independence day, which was also the traditional day for swearing in new presidents. In the midst of the crisis Sánchez de Lozada wrote a letter to Julio Terrazas, the president of the episcopal conference, and proposed that the church convoke all the parties that had won seats in congress in order to reform the electoral laws. The MNR candidate also proposed that the small parties that were not represented in congress be included in the discussions.[50] But the other parties, distrustful of Sánchez de Lozada, warned the church not to let itself be "manipulated by officialism."[51]

In the midst of this rather tense situation the church decided to take the initiative and call the parties together to hold another national dialogue, but in this case, one based on its own proposals, not those of the candidate of MNR. The episcopal conference invited the parties present in congress to make a solemn commitment to support democracy and to work out a document that would outline principles binding on all. The objective of the bishops was to strengthen democracy in the midst of a national crisis and, at the same time, create an atmosphere more favorable for resolving the immediate question of who would be the next president. The agenda did include Sánchez de Lozada's proposal to discuss electoral reforms.

From July 25 to July 27 the three principal candidates, Sánchez de Lozada, Banzer, and Paz Zamora met in the papal nunciature with the papal nuncio, Santos Abril; four Bolivian bishops, Julio Terrazas, René Fernández, Nino Marzoli, and Edmundo Abastoflor; several priests; and lay advisers. At the end of the first day the three candidates announced their intention of reforming the electoral laws, and on July 28 they signed a general agreement that served as the basis for a new national consensus.[52] The agreement included political, social, and economic policies. One point emphasized the need to "modernize and moralize the state," and another underlined the importance of having a common strategy to fight the drug trade.[53] Although it was very general in nature, the document constituted a new consensus that bound the three major political forces to act along the same lines on certain key issues. Following this summit conference the nuncio expressed his satisfaction over the dialogue: "Undoubtedly the three positions have come much closer together, and that was the main objective of the church; on the other hand, there will be some disillusionment for those who expected to hear the name of a new president."[54] Even though the dialogue did not resolve the presidential crisis, it did create an atmosphere favorable for a frank discussion of that issue. Shortly after the dialogue Banzer broke the silence by announcing that he had decided to give his support to Jaime Paz Zamora. On August 6 Bolivia had a new president: Paz Zamora, the youngest of the three candidates. Banzer, the ex-dictator, as in the previous election, realized that the other candidates could not support him, so he did the next best thing, which was to forge an alliance with one of the others and so ensure his share of control over congress.

THE CHURCH AS MEDIATOR: A GENERAL ASSESSMENT

The Bolivian political process from 1952 to the return to democracy in 1982, with twenty different changes of government, including quite a few *golpes de estado*, was anything but a straight line. There was some continuity in the leading personalities who dominated the scene: Víctor Paz Estenssoro, Hernán Siles Zuazo, and Juan Lechín. But democracy cannot rest on a few charismatic individuals. The fundamental problem in Bolivia, as in other Latin American countries, was the absence of stable democratic institutions that enjoyed legitimacy. In this context the church, with its deep historical roots, stood out as the only national institution with the necessary moral authority to call upon all political and social forces to enter into a real dialogue. The church carried out that role with notable success.

Nevertheless, there were criticisms of the church's role. On several occasions the Jesuit director of *Agencia de Noticias Fides*, José Gramunt, who served as moderator during the meetings between the church, political leaders, and union leaders in 1984 and 1989, criticized the tendency to have recourse to the church to solve problems the politicians themselves should have dealt with on their own: "This constant recourse to the church is a sign of relative immaturity in civil society which cannot solve its problems by using the very mechanisms created for that purpose."[55] The church acted as mediator so many times and in so many situations that it was even called upon to resolve an impasse created in 1989 by the municipal elections for mayor of La Paz when the two candidates, Raúl Salmón of MNR and Ronald MacLean of ADN (Banzer's party), tied. The solution in this case was worthy of Solomon: each one would fill half the full term.[56] The critics also noted that the bishops, some more than others, seemed to be guided by an older, paternalistic impulse that led them to move quickly into the thick of a crisis. By so doing they did not allow the politicians and union leaders to resolve their differences in face-to-face confrontation and thereby to grow in maturity and to practice the difficult art of dialogue by themselves. Finally, by intervening so frequently in political conflicts the church ran the risk of losing prestige. In general, the bishops and their advisers were agreed that the church's role as mediator was a special service for emergencies but not for normal times. There can be no doubt, however, that the church played a key role in fostering dialogue in critical moments between 1968 and 1989, when the country was deeply polarized between antagonistic forces. Thus it unquestionably contributed to the institutionalization of civic dialogue in Bolivia and thereby to the consolidation of democracy itself.

8.

Peru (1980-1995)

The Shining Path

The most serious threat to democracy in Peru's recent history was the Shining Path and the violence that terrorist movement produced. Between 1980 and 1992—the year in which Abimael Guzmán was captured—the Shining Path created a reign of terror and came close to breaking the fragile social tissue holding Peru together as a country. During that reign of terror more than twenty-five thousand Peruvians were killed as a consequence of the war between the Shining Path and the forces of order. The violence also led to the destruction of factories, bridges, trains, police stations, electric towers, and so on. The cost of that destruction was calculated to be around twenty-two billion dollars.

In absolute terms Peru did not suffer more than certain other countries of Latin America: during the civil war in El Salvador some 75,000 persons died; in Guatemala there were 100,000 victims of government repression; and some 200,000 persons died during the period of the "Violence" in Colombia. But in terms of sheer fanaticism, cruelty, and violation of the most elemental norms of civilization, the Shining Path constituted a unique case in Latin America, at least in its recent history. In this sense the Shining Path has usually been compared to Pol Pot's Khmer Rouge movement in Cambodia, and less so with Mao in China, even though Abimael Guzmán looked to Mao for inspiration.[1]

Unlike other guerrilla groups in Latin America, the Shining Path did not just attack the rich; it victimized the poor as well. In fact, the vast majority of those killed were peasants in the Andes, natives in the Amazon region, and urban dwellers in the "young towns" surrounding Lima and other coastal cities. The Shining Path set out systematically to kill all leaders of the popular movement as a way of destroying that movement. At the same time, as part of its plan to destroy the state, it murdered mayors, judges, and government officials in cold blood, as well as many hundreds of police, both men and women.

During its reign of terror the Shining Path also stood apart from the rest of the left in Latin America for its antireligiosity. In public trials the Shining Path murdered five priests, two religious women, and hundreds of catechists, who gave their lives to defend their homes and villages. Hundreds of Protestants also were killed. On this point the Shining Path seemed more like the Argentine military or the rightwing death squads in El Salvador. At the height of its power the Shining Path managed to control around 40 percent of Peru. When it was finally defeated, it had already taken over many popular urban areas in Lima. Until Abimael Guzmán was captured, many doubted that democracy in Peru could survive: either society would fall into chaos, or the military would take power.

There was another terrorist group, the Tupac Amaru Revolutionary Movement, known by its initials in Spanish as MRTA. But this group was definitely a lesser threat. To begin with, it was much closer to the model of the other guerrilla movements in Latin America. Founded in 1984, it robbed banks, kidnapped wealthy businessmen, fired mortars at restaurants like Kentucky Fried Chicken, and staged much publicized invasions of towns in the mountains. Nevertheless, the degree of danger that it represented was much less than that posed by the Shining Path. For example, in 1990 the MRTA, which had around twenty-five hundred members, was responsible for only 5 percent of the deaths that occurred as a result of terrorist violence.[2] In fact, MRTA's real enemy was not the state but the Shining Path, which looked down upon its rival as a group of amateurish reformists.

Finally, under President Alberto Fujimori (1990-95; 1995–) the government managed to deal both terrorist groups several telling blows. The capture of Abimael Guzmán was a serious psychological blow; it destroyed the aura of invincibility that surrounded the Shining Path. Furthermore, the government used more sophisticated means of intelligence. It also ceased to use repression against the civilian population as its primary weapon. Furthermore, it put into effect a law of repentance which aimed to encourage less committed followers to desert the cause. These different means were important because they restored the authority of the state, which had lost credibility as a result of corruption and the use of violence against the population.

One important measure that strengthened the state was the institution of judges "without faces"; judges could try accused terrorists without revealing their identity. Before that law was enacted in 1992, civilian judges, frequently acting out of fear, had set free eighty-five hundred persons accused of terrorism. Some of those accused were, in fact, terrorist leaders who returned to their subversive activities. To put an end to that situation, special judges were designated to try the accused without being identified.

However, none of these measures would have been effective were it not for the massive rejection of terrorism by the ordinary people, who chose to cooperate with the state and the forces of order. The initial success of the Shining Path was due in part to the absence of strong social ties in Peruvian society. Lima traditionally lived with its back to the rest of the country, and Lima's upper class was notorious for its disdain toward lower-class Peruvians. And even though most mountain villages lived in relative peace, they had no strong ties to bind them together. When the civilians—peasants, workers, and urban dwellers—started forging ties among themselves, the Shining Path began to experience its first setbacks. Thus the Shining Path was not defeated by the armed forces or the police, who too often repressed the people and sometimes drove them to support the other side, but by the people themselves, who organized and blocked the advance of terrorism.

Given this background, the religious factor and the church played a particularly important role in this story. By conscienticizing the people in Lima and in the mountains the progressive church had already done much to create a sense of solidarity that helped the people organize and defend themselves. For peasants and urban dwellers who had contact with the progressive church *religion* came to be associated with the idea of working for development and building fraternal ties among neighbors. Wherever the church worked to inculcate the ideals of Vatican II and Medellín, the Shining Path usually made relatively little headway. By way of contrast, in those parts of the country where the church had not changed, the Shining Path was more successful. Although of a more conservative mentality, Protestants also sought strength from their faith to resist the terrorists.

In this chapter we will examine the following topics: the social and political background of Peru; the origins and nature of the Shining Path; the official reaction to the Shining Path; the Peruvian church in general; the reaction of the church to the Shining Path, especially in the zones most affected; and the reaction of the Protestants.

FROM VELASCO TO FUJIMORI

Unlike the other military leaders who seized power in Latin America during this period, the Peruvian military leaders who overthrew the government of Fernando Belaúnde Terry (1963-68) were reformists who proposed to foster national capitalism and conscienticize the lower classes. The military regime under General Juan Velasco Alvarado (1968-75, termed the "First Phase") expropriated many American companies and carried out a sweeping land reform that destroyed the old oligarchy. The military also set into motion an educational reform that aimed to create a more socially critical and nationalistic mentality among both teachers and students. Also, under the Peruvian military there were relatively few violations of human rights. Furthermore, the Catholic church supported many of the reforms and even commissioned several priests to act as advisers to the government. The military instilled in the lower classes a new sense of pride and encouraged them to organize themselves. Also, with the approval of the military, the political left grew considerably during those years.

Nevertheless, although some of the goals were met, by and large the great experiment failed. In August 1975 General Francisco Morales Bermúdez removed Velasco from power and inaugurated the "Second Phase" of the revolution (1975-80). The Velasco experiment failed in large part because it never won the support of the middle classes, and after a period of initial enthusiasm, it also lost the support of the lower classes. The very authoritarian nature of the government caused it to lose credibility and support. In 1974 Velasco expropriated the principal newspapers, purportedly in order to make them more representative of the people. But he also did it to silence his critics.

The Morales Bermúdez regime kept some of the basic reforms (the agrarian reform remained) but canceled others, and then prepared the way to return power to the civilians. In 1978 elections were held to elect a constitutional assembly. The big winner was Víctor Raúl Haya de la Torre and the Aprista Party (APRA). The military made a gentleman's agreement with APRA whereby APRA and other political groups would keep their followers under control while the military left power.

In 1980 the country returned to democracy. Fernando Belaúnde of Popular Action was reelected president for a second term. Haya de la Torre had died in 1979, thus depriving APRA of its charismatic leader. The left won 16 percent of the national vote. Belaúnde's second administration could be described as moderately liberal. In 1985, in the midst of an economic crisis and growing terrorism, Alan García, a young protégé of Haya de la Torre, was elected president. García captured the sympathy of many Peruvians with his youthful dynamism and his promise to be the "president of all Peruvians," an allusion to APRA's notoriety for being sectarian. After a few initial successes of a populist nature (government subsidies for food and gasoline, freer circulation of money, and so forth) García's government fell into a deep crisis.

From the beginning García declared a policy of refusing to allot more than 10 percent of what Peru earned from its exports to servicing its foreign debt. As a result, the United States, the International Monetary Fund, and other international organisms suspended aid to Peru. To make matters worse, in 1987 García nationalized the banks and alienated those sectors of the upper and middle classes that had supported him. Finally, hyperinflation (2,775 percent in 1989), caused in large part by García's populist measures, ended up destabilizing the entire economy. In the midst of great insecurity the middle and lower classes lost a good part of their savings and unemployment grew.

The great surprise in the 1990 elections was the victory of Alberto Fujimori, an unknown agronomist and university professor, who defeated Mario Vargas Llosa, the world-renowned novelist. Vargas Llosa, a bitter critic of García, took up the banner of modernization, which for him meant neo-liberalism. But Fujimori won the sympathy of the lower classes, who voted for him in the run-off election. Although Fujimori presented himself as a populist, in reality he shared the same neo-liberal mentality as Vargas Llosa. The son of

Japanese immigrants, he symbolized success achieved by hard work and discipline. These facts alone made him a more acceptable role model for the lower classes than a famous novelist of hispanic-creole background.

Once in power Fujimori applied an economic "shock" and abruptly ushered in the age of neo-liberalism in Peru. After two years of constant battling with parliament he dissolved it by force of arms. This *golpe* against his own parliament was condemned by most countries, the Organization of American States, and the European Union. The United States in particular feared that Fujimori's action would be repeated in other Latin American nations, where democracy was also not faring too well. Foreign journalists were surprised to learn, however, that most Peruvians supported Fujimori. Ironically, the Peruvian president justified his move as necessary to save democracy. Many observers concurred that with or without the closing of parliament the future of democracy in Peru looked very bleak.

The Shining Path, which did not use the usual external symbols of a guerrilla movement, managed to establish many bases in unions, state universities, and popular urban neighborhoods. It even had many sympathizers in high schools. In its advance it organized armed strikes in many provincial cities, and in Lima itself it used those tactics to paralyze public transportation. Finally, it announced that it had achieved "strategic equilibrium" with the armed forces of Peru. While it advanced, parliament, with its endless debates, seemed unaware of the danger. When Fujimori closed parliament, he reflected the generalized public sentiment of insecurity and fear. Most Peruvians supported his move to close parliament because they wanted a more energetic and decisive response against the spread of terrorism.

THE SHINING PATH: ORIGINS AND TRAJECTORY

The Shining Path had its remote origins in the radicalized university student movement of the sixties. It arose in the National University of San Cristóbal of Huamanaga (Ayacucho), which was refounded in May 1959. Ayacucho is one of the poorest and most backward areas of Peru. On the map it seems relatively close to Lima, but in reality it was very isolated geographically, socially, and culturally from the coast. It is located in the middle of the Andean highlands and can be reached only by a long and difficult trip. The land is very poor for cultivating. In colonial times it was a resting post between the southern Andean highlands and Lima, but in the Independence period it was increasingly marginalized from the main commercial centers.[3] For these reasons the newly reopened university represented new hope for the youth of the region.[4]

In 1962 Abimael Guzmán, born in Arequipa in the south, joined the university as a philosophy professor in the faculty of education. He soon became the leader of the Maoist faction among the Marxist groups at the University. He visited China in 1968 during the cultural revolution and returned to Peru to found his own party: the Peruvian Communist Party in the "Shining Path" of José Carlos Mariátegui. Mariátegui (1894-1930) was the original founder of Marxism in Peru. The party's members included Guzmán's fellow teachers and his own students, most of whom came from the countryside and whose cultural horizons were very limited. Furthermore, many of them harbored resentment against the cultural elites of the coast, who looked down on their Andean ways. Guzmán, with his charismatic personality and dogmatic fundamentalism, became a guru for these radicalized youth. However, Guzmán had less success among the poorest of the peasants. His principal power base was the small, rural middle class, especially students in high schools and universities. His movement particularly attracted women of that class.[5] For them, the doors of social mobility in the Westernized world of Peru's middle and upper classes were closed, whereas the Shining Path offered them a chance to be important in life.

In May 1980, just when the rest of the country was going through the process of returning to democracy after twelve years of military rule, the Shining Path initiated its armed campaign to destroy that democracy. According to its ideological tenets, formal democracy, like the reformist military regime, was merely a façade for the oligarchy and foreign imperialism.

Between 1980 and 1982 the Shining Path attacked police stations in Ayacucho, blew down power towers in Lima, and carried out other sporadic terrorist activities. In the beginning it had considerable popular support among the peasants and urban dwellers of Ayacucho. This was evident in 1982 when a mass was celebrated for Edith Lagos, a young leader of the movement who had been killed by the police. The cathedral was filled and thousands accompanied her remains to the cemetery.[6] But this initial popularity soon dissipated when the citizens of Ayacucho and the peasants in the countryside discovered the real totalitarian nature of the Shining Path, which did not hesitate to murder anyone whom it suspected of being a spy or a collaborator with the forces of order.

THE SHINING PATH AND RELIGION

The case of Edith Lagos is an example of the great attraction the Shining Path had for idealistic youth. She had studied at the Salesian high school and, according to her classmates, was a good student and a practicing Catholic. She also studied for a while at a public high school run by progressive Dominican nuns. But when she went to the university, her idealism found its channel of expression not in religion but in the Shining Path, which held to the classical Marxist line that religion is the "opium of the people." For many youth of limited intellectual formation the popular religiosity in which they had been raised was transformed into a sort of popular Marxism, with all the fervor of a new religious movement.[7] Indeed, the Shining Path had many of the characteristics of a fundamentalist sect: it revolved around a cult leader; the followers practiced total submission to the party; they accepted all the dogmas of the party without criticism; finally, they closed off all dialogue with the outside world.

The fundamentalism of the Shining Path explains why it did not approach the Catholic church, as did other Marxist groups in the rest of Latin America. There were two former nuns who joined the movement, but they conformed to the rule: both had already broken all ties with the church before joining Guzmán's movement.[8] Nevertheless, religion was a problem for the Shining Path. In the first years it avoided direct attacks on official representatives of the church, and it did not express disdain for religious symbols. Rather, it attacked civil engineers and other technical experts who worked on development projects such as cooperatives or experimental farms. In reality, attacking the church was not a necessity; in Ayacucho most clergy were so conservative that religion was not attractive for university students. However, as the Shining Path began moving out of the Ayacucho area, it ran into progressive priests and nuns who were attractive role models for the youth. In most areas of the Andes the church remained the only institution capable of maintaining peace and order. Given its fundamentalistic outlook, for the Shining Path, religion, especially progressive religion, constituted a barrier to its plans to achieve total domination over the hearts and minds of the people.

THE OFFICIAL REACTION

The government and the forces of order reacted initially with a mixture of ineptitude and mindless brutality. In 1982 the areas most affected were declared emergency zones and placed under "political-military command." In those areas all constitutional guarantees were suspended. The specialized anti-terrorist police—the Sinchis—and the military occupied those areas as if they were foreign enemy territory. This was a major tactical error because the majority of Andean dwellers were innocent and, indeed, disposed to cooperate with the forces of order. But the police and the military looked upon the Quechua-speaking peasants as potential or actual terrorists. The army and the Peruvian marines detained thousands of peasants and many of them simply disappeared. At the end of the eighties, Peru had one of the highest percentages in the world of cases (3,000) of persons missing for political reasons.[9] During this dirty war the forces of order committed many atrocities in small towns and villages. In one notorious case, in the small town of Accomara in the area of Ayacucho, a company of soldiers killed sixty-nine peasants, including twenty children.[10] In another incident, in May 1988, in revenge for the murder of a captain and three soldiers, the army entered the town of Cayara (in Ayacucho), killed twenty-nine peasants, and later on murdered several of the witnesses to the crime.[11] In other towns from Ayacucho to Puno there were many cases of summary executions, torture, and rape, all of which combined to project the image of Peru as one of the world's worst violators of human rights. Besides the use of clumsy anti-terrorist tactics, corruption in the government and the army also served to justify the armed struggle. In many instances the soldiers and police demanded tribute, or they simply robbed the people of their animals and goods. Peruvians of the lower classes were caught between two fires: the terrorists and the government.

To make matters worse, in 1988 a rightwing death squad—the Rodrigo Franco Democratic Commando—made its debut. It set out to kill lawyers, union leaders, journalists, and politicians associated with the left. This group, which took its name from an Aprista leader who had been assassinated, had close ties to the Aprista Party and the police.

Finally, after several years the government, the army, and the police began to understand what many enlightened military commanders had said from the beginning: terrorism could only be defeated with the cooperation of the civilians. The most important examples of this new policy were the committees of self-defense, made up of the peasants. These committees took as their model the peasant vigilante bands in Cajamarca, in the north, which were created in the seventies to fight banditry. In 1986, after many heated debates, the Law of Peasant Vigilantes—whereby the peasants could legally form armed bands in their own defense—was passed. But there were important differences between the defense committees formed by the government and the original vigilante bands in the north. These latter were not mere armed groups; they also constituted a form of local government. The peasants held court, meted out their own justice, and applied their own laws. By way of contrast, the peasant committees supervised by the government had much less autonomy and in reality functioned as a civilian defense corps under the army. In the beginning the army did not trust the peasant committees. It gave them few arms, and the few that were given out were usually obsolete. Nevertheless, within time the committees proved their effectiveness. In 1991 there were twelve hundred committees throughout the Andes, numbering approximately a hundred thousand armed peasants.[12] The Shining Path attacked many villages in reprisal for arming themselves. But as the villages organized their defenses more efficiently, the Shining Path began losing control of the mountains. When President Gonzalo (Guzmán's party title) decided to concentrate his terrorist activity in Lima, the Shining Path was already being defeated in the countryside.

THE PROTESTANTS

The first religious groups to experience terrorist violence were the small Protestant communities in Ayacucho. According to the 1992 census, the Protestant population of Peru was around 7 percent (compared to 4 percent in 1981). Ayacucho in particular suffered a priest shortage, especially in the countryside. In those remote areas many little Pentecostal churches sprang up, but very soon these communities became victims of the growing violence. The Shining Path systematically murdered technical advisers, but it seemed to have a special onus against the Protestants. The reason was obvious: they represented a rival power over the minds and hearts of the people. Their militant stand against alcoholism and local corruption and their influence in bettering family life made the Protestants an important social force. In 1982 the terrorists murdered two members of the Protestant community of Chuschi, the small town where the Shining Path began its armed struggle. Later, in 1983, they murdered three pastors in small communities in the Ayacucho area, one of whom was hung from a beam in his church.[13]

But the Protestants also became victims of the forces of order. Between 1982 and 1992, 529 Protestants were killed as a result of the war in Peru: 446 by the Shining Path and 49 by the armed forces.[14] In many cases they were forced to flee from their villages. In spite of this persecution, or perhaps because of it, the number of Protestant communities actually grew. In one province of Ayacucho—Leoncio Prado—there were forty-five churches in 1987. By 1990 there were ninety-seven.[15] In May 1991 the long arm of the Shining Path reached Lima, causing the deaths of two prominent Protestants: the director of the Peruvian office of the humanitarian organization World Vision, and the director of the same organization in Colombia, who was visiting Peru. Both were shot to death. As a consequence, World Vision was forced to maintain a very low profile and not until April 1993 did it return to its normal activities.[16]

The Protestants were also victims of counterinsurgency. In August 1984 Peruvian marines invaded the town of Callqui and killed six members of the Presbyterian church. Very often, as in this case, the soldiers or marines, who had little knowledge of the Andes, and even less knowledge of religious distinctions, confused Protestants with terrorists. A pastor who founded a church in Huancavelica, Agripino Quispe, was detained for four years on the charge of being a subversive. He was finally freed in 1989 as a result of a concerted campaign by the National Evangelical Council, Amnesty International, and other human-rights groups.[17] In another case that gained widespread publicity, a taxi driver by the name of Juan Mallea, a member of the Christian Missionary Alliance church, was accused of terrorism. In a clumsy move the police attempted to single him out as the author of a map which revealed the whereabouts of a common grave where several students and teachers had been executed by the police. After a year in prison he was released with the help of Protestant lawyers and human-rights groups.[18]

Concerned over these attacks, a group of Protestants decided to organize in order to offer aid and legal assistance to the Protestants in Callqui. The task of organizing was particularly difficult because many of the Protestants were of a fundamentalist persuasion and did not consider the defense of human rights, much less democracy, proper activities for a Christian. Some of the organizers belonged to the Latin American Theological Fraternity, founded in 1970 with the aim of bringing Latin American Protestantism up to date, especially as regards social problems. In 1984 this group founded the Department of Social Service and Action, which they named Peace and Hope.

In 1986 the Department of Peace and Hope was formally incorporated into the National Evangelical Council.[19] The new department soon became the principal Protestant organization for helping communities under threat in the Andes and for organizing workshops and seminars to conscienticize fellow Protestants on the danger of terrorist violence. In December 1989, for example, a group of Protestant leaders gathered to discuss what political role they should adopt. As a result of that discussion they decided to enter the political arena, and, concretely, to support the candidacy of Alberto Fujimori.

The first three directors of Peace and Hope, Pedro Arana (1984-87), Caleb Mesa (1987-93), and Alfonso Wieland, collaborated closely with human-rights groups and with CEAS, the Episcopal Commission of Social Action of the Catholic bishops. Also, World Vision and OXFAM (United Kingdom), OFASA, and other humanitarian organizations administered by Protestant churches offered aid to the refugees who fled the Ayacucho region.[20] Finally, many Protestants, especially in the city of Huanta, near Ayacucho, joined the peasant self-defense committees.

THE CATHOLIC CHURCH: BACKGROUND

The Catholic church in Peru was considered one of the most progressive in Latin America, before and after the Medellín conference. Cardinal Juan Landázuri Ricketts, the archbishop of Lima (1955-90), performed many different roles in Medellín and later on in Puebla. During the many years that he was president of the Peruvian episcopal conference (1956-88) the Peruvian church was transformed from closed and conservative to very open and modern. Peru was also one of the focal points for liberation theology. Gustavo Gutiérrez, a priest of the diocesan clergy, published his famous work *A Theology of Liberation* in 1971, but even before that he had already influenced the Medellín assembly with his ideas. In 1968 ONIS (National Office of Social Information), a group of socially advanced priests, was founded. Although ONIS usually took stands more to the left than the bishops, it influenced the hierarchy and Catholics in general.

Other important voices of the progressive church were José Dammert, auxiliary bishop of Lima and later bishop of Cajamarca (1962-92); Germán Schmitz, auxiliary bishop of Lima (1970-90); Luis Bambarén, auxiliary bishop of Lima and later bishop of Chimbote. The Jesuit Felipe MacGregor (1963-77) transformed Catholic University into one of the best in the country. Catholic University is the host every year for a summer course run by the theology department, which has become one of the clearest signs of vitality in the church. In the eighties close to fifteen hundred people from all parts of the country and beyond attended the course.[21] Certain areas and regions stood out especially for their pastoral creativity: the Southern Andean region, the Amazon region, and the young towns surrounding Lima. The diocese of Cajamarca under Dammert, and Chimbote under James Burke, an American

Dominican, and Luis Bambarén, his successor, were models of the renovated post–Vatican II church.

On the other hand, the church suffered many weaknesses typical of the
rest of Latin America, such as the shortage of priests. Of the 2,265 priests in
1984, 60 percent were foreign-born.[22] The majority of the foreign clergy belonged to religious orders and congregations, or to missionary associations
such as the Maryknoll priests and brothers, or the Saint Columban Society.
Of the 4,835 women religious, 2,053 were foreigners by birth.[23] The Peruvian church, therefore, had many of the characteristics of a mission land.
Among the fifty-four bishops in 1984 many belonged to religious orders. Six
were Jesuits and five belonged to Opus Dei. More than a third of the bishops
were foreign-born, and most of them worked in prelatures and dioceses in
the jungle or in the southern altiplano.

In 1985, and again in 1988, the pope visited Peru; on both occasions he
was received by enormous, cheering crowds. During the visits liberation theology was in the eye of the storm. The pope balanced his warnings about
"ideologies foreign to the faith" with a stirring call to practice social justice.
Gradually, with new episcopal appointments, the progressive face of the
church began to change. In 1988 Ricardo Durand, the Jesuit bishop of Callao
(and former archbishop of Cuzco), who was an unreserved critic of liberation theology, was elected president of the episcopal conference. In 1990
Cardinal Landázuri retired and was succeeded by Augusto Vargas Alzamora,
a Jesuit, like Durand, and also of a conservative tendency. In 1994 he was
raised to the rank of cardinal. However, these changes occurred too late to
change the entire pastoral orientation of the Council and Medellín. Furthermore, the church personnel that the Shining Path confronted generally
belonged to the progressive sectors committed to the popular movement.
One important exception to this rule was Ayacucho itself. For this reason, it
is important to compare the response of the church in Ayacucho to terrorism
with its response in other parts of the country.

AYACUCHO (1980-1992)

The tourist guides promote visits to Ayacucho especially during Holy
Week. During that week and other religious holidays one can sense the deep
religious fervor of the people. Furthermore, the citizens of Ayacucho point
with pride to the thirty-three churches that go back to colonial Huamanga
(Ayacucho's name then). From a post–Vatican II perspective, however, the
church in the sixties and seventies in Ayacucho, like many other mountain
dioceses, did not appear to have changed much since colonial times. The
diocesan clergy in particular was very conservative and intellectually closed.
Furthermore, the phenomenon of the growing clergy shortage was quite noticeable: of the forty-six parishes in the archdiocese, twenty-three were
vacant.[24] But the situation was actually worse if the age factor is taken into

account. Of the forty-seven priests who belonged to the diocesan clergy, eighteen were more than sixty years of age and seven lived in other dioceses. There were, of course, exceptions to the rule. Among the religious clergy Luis Arroyo, a Franciscan, was very popular among the youth. In general, however, the clergy was just as colonial mentally as the beautiful churches the tourists appreciate. The Salesians ran high schools for the middle classes, but the general atmosphere there was conservative and the religious instruction imparted in the classrooms did not relate much to the social and political problems of the day. For many youth the university stood for everything that the church did not: modernity, creativity, openness, concern for the real world, and so on. The Marxist teachers at the university had as their students young men and women raised in the world of popular Catholicism but with little capacity to relate their faith critically to the modern world.

In order to counterbalance the influence wielded by the national university, in 1967 the archdiocese founded the Víctor Andrés Belaunde University. But, due to lack of money and qualified professors, the new university was unable to compete with the big national university and closed its doors in 1977.[25] In the absence of any competition, the national university, and in particular the more radicalized professors, became a center of attraction for young idealists, who had no alternative place to study. The archbishop since 1979, Federico Richter Fernández-Prada, a peaceable Franciscan, was disconcerted by the terrorist violence and in the beginning did not know how to respond. An example of the church's ambiguous and vacillating response was precisely the funeral of Edith Lagos, the young Shining Path leader killed in 1982. The youth of the city looked upon her as a sort of heroine. During the funeral services—and during most of the period of the Shining Path's reign—the church maintained a discreet silence and avoided taking a stand. Nor did it take a firm stand in defense of the innocent accused of terrorist activities.

The visit of John Paul II to Ayacucho in February 1985 served to console a population that had suffered five years of daily shootings in the streets, car bombs, murders, kidnappings, and so on. In an energetic tone the pope exhorted the terrorists to "Change your ways!" Although the papal exhortation had little impact on the terrorists, the pope's courage and determination stood in contrast to the timidity and silence of the church in Ayacucho. Inspired by the pope's visit, the Conference of Religious in Lima decided in 1985 to organize a Committee to Support the Emergency Zones. Presided over by the Jesuit provincial, Ramón García, the committee announced that its first objective was to "accompany the people who suffer and who need a sign of hope." Finally, in March 1986 a group of twenty religious men and women went to Ayacucho to conduct popular missions in the areas most affected by violence. Between 1986 and 1988 more than a hundred men and women of different congregations participated in these missions.[26] Later, when the violence intensified, the missions had to be suspended. Two of the main promoters of these missions were Father Ernest Ranly of the Precious Blood Fathers, and Sister Julia Yon, of the Missionaries of the Sacred Heart. With his experience in Ayacucho Father Ranly organized workshops, seminars, and retreats to help priests and religious women face the violence with spiritual strength, which was now spreading out of Ayacucho to the rest of the country.

THE JESUITS, OAASA, AND IPAZ

At the same time that the religious went to Ayacucho, the Society of Jesus was invited by the archbishop to establish its presence there. In March 1986 a group of three Jesuits arrived and began attending to the old colonial church that once belonged to the Society before its expulsion in 1767. In 1987 one of the three, Carl Schmidt, took over the direction of OAASA: the Archdiocesan Office of Social Action in Ayacucho. The new office was in reality a continuation of Cáritas, but with a new orientation and new functions. It had a team of twenty-two persons, which included nurses, doctors, social workers, and a Quechua-speaking Dominican sister. OAASA continued to maintain some of the programs of social welfare that Cáritas had conducted before. In addition, it created a social services department, which offered pastoral attention to the prisoners in the four jails in the region and also provided aid to the victims of the violence. Another novelty was the Integral Formation group, which promoted the "values of the Christian faith, justice, respect for life, honesty, truthfulness, trust, and solidarity."[27] OAASA worked closely with other groups with similar objectives such as COTADENA (the Coordinator of the Rights of the Children of Ayacucho). In July 1990, however, the archbishop and the new Opus Dei auxiliary bishop, Luis Cipriani, disbanded OAASA. From Cipriani's perspective OAASA had entered areas that were beyond the competence and the mission of the church. With the end of the popular missions and the closing down of OAASA, the archdiocese ceased to promote new initiatives to face terrorist violence.

But one small beacon of light continued to shine: IPAZ, a center to promote peace and justice, co-founded in 1992 by the Jesuits and certain lay professors at the university. Under the dynamic leadership of Jefrey Gamarra and José Coronel, both social scientists, IPAZ organized workshops, seminars, and talks, frequently inviting speakers from Lima in order to break Ayacucho's isolation.

THE ATTACKS AGAINST THE CHURCH

In the first years the Shining Path was careful not to attack the Catholic church directly. But after a few years of success it decided to throw caution to the wind. In fact, the Shining Path *did* attack the church in the very beginning, but at the moment few were aware of it. In August 1981 forty masked men attacked and destroyed the Institute of Rural Education run by the

Maryknoll Fathers near Juli in southern Peru. A month later a bomb was thrown at the office of the Prelature of Juli. But no one imagined at that time that the Shining Path existed in the southern Andean region. Some attributed the attack to local landowners, who had frequently criticized Maryknoll for its social work.

The first victim of the official church was Víctor Acuña, priest and pastor in the archdiocese of Ayacucho. Father Acuña, who was from the area, had served for years as a chaplain to the police and later as director of Cáritas. On December 3, 1987, a young Shining Path fanatic shot Father Acuña to death while he was celebrating mass in his church near the central market. The Shining Path had previously denounced Father Acuña as a "thief." The real motive for the killing was to test the waters; the Shining Path had decided the time had come to attack the church directly. For a while many believed that Father Acuña's murder was an isolated incident. But it soon became evident that it was part of a deliberate strategy. In June 1989 another priest, Teodoro Santos, was killed when he intervened in a gun battle between the Shining Path and the police in a town near Juaja in the central Andes.

As the Shining Path spread out of Ayacucho clashes with the church increased. In August 1988, in the small town of Jarpa, two hours outside of Huancayo in the central Andes, a band of *Senderistas* (their name in Spanish) attacked and destroyed an educational facility run by the Jesuits for the peasants. In this case the invaders did not touch the religious, but they did kill the governor of the district and two civil engineers in a nearby town. The reaction of the Jesuits was typical of many other religious orders and congregations caught in a similar situation. They decided to abandon their education work for the moment and dedicate themselves exclusively to their sacramental mission. Even that decision was dangerous, because the Shining Path was aware of the fact that the peasants drew strength from their religious faith and the reception of the sacraments. In other areas of the Andes some priests and religious women left altogether. Others remained. As we shall see, that was to be a very costly decision.

The Shining Path continued its rampage throughout the Andes. In May 1989 it destroyed the Institute of Rural Education in the Prelature of Ayaviri. In September 1990, in La Florida in Junín (central jungle area), a band of young *Senderistas* between fifteen and eighteen years of age conducted a public trial that ended with the execution of eight persons. One of the victims was Sister María Agustina Rivas, a seventy-year-old Good Shepherd nun. Sister "Aguchita" worked as a cook and was well loved in the town. She was the first woman religious to fall victim to terrorism. The second was Irene MacCormack, who was killed in a public trial along with four other persons in May 1991 in the town of Huasahuasi, also in Junín. Sister Irene, an Australian by birth, had been threatened previously, but she had refused to leave. Her mission included distributing food to the poor.

On August 9, 1991, a group of *Senderistas* murdered two Polish Franciscans in cold blood. Fathers Miguel Tomaszek and Zbigniew Strzalkowski worked in the town of Pariacoto, located halfway between the northern central city of Huaraz in the mountains and Casma on the coast. The pope himself sent condolences to their families in Poland. On August 25 Father Alessandro Dordi, an Italian missionary, was murdered in the town of Santa, in the diocese of Chimbote. The Shining Path attempted to kill another priest in the same area but failed. The official organ of the movement, *El Diario Internacional*, published in Brussels, announced with satisfaction that the "Maoist forces have executed three priests." The same edition denounced the Polish priests as agents sent by the pope as part of a conspiracy to "manipulate the religious faith of the people in order to consolidate the system of oppression in the country."[28] The *Diario* also denounced Bishop José Gurruchaga of Huaraz for having organized the peasants. Finally, it criticized liberation theology because it aimed to "suffocate the social explosion of the poor and to lead the masses into conditions of abject misery."[29]

The criticism of liberation theology underlines the fact that the real enemy for the Shining Path was the progressive church—precisely because it offered an alternative to idealistic youth. The great majority of the victims of terrorism were not, of course, theologians. Most were practical pastoral agents, men and women who simply aimed to serve the people. But for that very reason their presence constituted an obstacle to the plans of the Shining Path, which demanded total control over the hearts and minds of the people. The importance of the church as a barrier can be seen more clearly in the cases of Cajamarca and Puno.

CAJAMARCA

The Shining Path terrorists had much less success as they expanded outside the region of Ayacucho. One reason was that they had not spent years building up bases of support there as they had in Ayacucho. But there were other important differences. In Cajamarca, for example, the peasants were relatively better off. Also, the system of gross exploitation as practiced in Ayacucho and southern Peru did not exist. Indeed, most peasants were small landowners and therefore characterized by a more independent mentality.[30] One sign of that spirit of independence was the creation of the peasant vigilante bands. The first such band was created in Chota (in Cajamarca) in 1976. Within time many other bands were created throughout the area, and finally, throughout all of northern Peru. According to a study, in 1993 there were peasant defense bands in more than 3,450 villages between the frontier with Ecuador and the southern boundary of Cajamarca.[31] These peasant organizations were originally founded as a defense against banditry and the theft of animals. But they quickly assumed other functions: they settled disputes between towns and even between families, and they applied traditional community norms of justice in the case of practically any type of crime. The bands arose spontaneously, without the intervention of the police and local authorities. In fact, they were created precisely because the police were generally absent in the countryside or too corrupt to be helpful. The specialists who have studied the phenomenon of the peasant bands agree on three points: (1) they were very effective in reducing crime; (2) they constituted the most effective barrier to the advance of terrorism; and (3) the church was very important in their creation. Regarding their efficiency, one witness claims that the peasant bands in Chota and nearby Bambamarca reduced robberies and animal theft to a minimum.[32] Both terrorist groups, the Shining Path and the MRTA, attempted to infiltrate the bands, but in vain. For the peasants in the north, the Shining Path was viewed as a completely outside group that offered nothing positive. In this sense religion played a very important role. According to one researcher: "Terrorist fanaticism found a formidable barrier in the Christian religion, which prevailed in the rural area of Cajamarca."[33]

The influence of the new post–Vatican II trends set into motion in the diocese of Cajamarca by Bishop José Dammert had much to do with this story. When Dammert began as bishop in 1962 he found himself in charge of a very backward and conservative diocese. He set out to convert it into a model according to the orientations of Vatican II.[34] In 1964 he closed the minor seminary, and in its place he founded the Institute of Rural Education. The Institute in Cajamarca soon brought about a radical change in the area. The hundreds of peasants who took courses there received both technical skills and a humanistic formation. Especially after Medellín the Institute fostered the values of community solidarity. As a complement to the Institute, the diocese trained adult catechists with the same mentality. The catechists were prepared to assume the role of religious leadership in each town and village. This was the context in which the peasant vigilante bands arose. Many of the leaders were catechists or former students of the Institute of Rural Education. In the words of Bishop Dammert:

> In Bambamarca, the bands were born of the people, and they were made up of numerous catechists, some of whom were the very leaders of the bands. Under the influence of the conscienticizing work of the church the bands meted out justice in the communities and resolved many internal conflicts.[35]

Dammert observed that the peasant bands that had not received this integral formation frequently fell prey to internal disputes or clashed with other peasant bands. The police, fearing that they were seedbeds of subversives, looked upon the bands with suspicion.

In a similar situation, in Huaraz, in the northern central Andes, the peasants organized themselves as a defense against terrorism and asked the church for help. Bishop José Gurruchaga (the same one who was denounced in *El Diario Internacional*) "baptized" the peasant bands by personally giving to each peasant a *huaraca* (a type of slingshot) as a symbol of their new commitment. For the peasants the *huaraca* was a symbol of peace but obviously also a weapon. Gurruchaga exhorted the peasants not to have recourse to violence like the terrorists. Rather, they should defend themselves by organizing and by practicing greater solidarity in their communities.[36] In Cajamarca, Huaraz, and other Andean cities the church—by means of the bishops' Commission on Social Action or the different local peace and justice commissions—offered legal counsel to the peasants. The church's blessings on the peasant bands had the effect of instilling in them a sense of religious mission. This fusion of civic duty and religious calling can be observed in the words of Víctor Luna, who was elected in 1993 as the first president of the United Front of Peasant Bands of Hualgasyoc, a town in Cajamarca:

> This is the story more or less of the peasant bands which organized themselves to defend their rights as believers in God; the land belongs to God and it is for everyone to use, just as the law is for everyone.[37]

PUNO

The more exact point of comparison with Ayacucho is Puno, in the heart of the southern Andean region. Given its extreme poverty and large Indian population (both Quechua and Ayamara speaking), many believed that Puno was destined to be the "second Ayacucho." Yet, in two aspects Puno was quite different from Ayacucho. First, there was a high degree of social and political consciousness among both peasants and workers—the fruit of years of a struggle to organize them. Second, there was a very active and progressive church, which fully supported the popular movement. Thanks in large part to these differences terrorism failed to take hold in Puno.

Since the decade of the fifties Cuzco and the southern Andean region had been the scene of numerous and intense campaigns to unionize the peasants. The Trotskyite leader Hugo Blanco mobilized the peasants of the Valle de la Convención, near Cuzco; later the agrarian reform under the military (1969) notably fortified the new social consciousness of the peasants. The reform expropriated many haciendas, which were turned into communal centers for the benefit of all the peasants. But, on the negative side, the reform benefited very few peasants because the majority of them did not work on those haciendas. According to one source, of the 1,050 peasant communities in Puno, only 74 received land as a result of the reform.[38] Given that picture, the Peasant Confederation of Peru and PUM (the Unified Mariateguista Party)—the leftist party with the most influence in the region—sought to organize the peasants in order to bring the benefits of the reform to everyone. One of their measures was to invade lands, especially those that had formerly been haciendas and now were peasant cooperatives. In October 1985, fifteen hundred peasants carrying the Peruvian flag invaded the Rural Enterprise of Kunurana, an immense territory of a hundred thousand acres once belonging to five haciendas. The invading party seized twenty-five thousand acres.[39] At the same time many private cooperatives and non-governmental organizations were founded in order to support the peasants and help them to organize.

From the very beginning the church participated in this process. In the sixties the southern Andean regional church, made up of the ecclesiastical jurisdictions of Cuzco, Sicuani, Puno, Juli, Ayaviri, and Chuqibambilla, came into existence. Some of these jurisdictions were *prelaturas nullius* (that is, areas on the way to becoming dioceses) under the pastoral care of a particular congregation or missionary association, such as the Religious of the Sacred Heart in Ayaviri, or the Fathers and Brothers of Maryknoll in Puno. The bishops of these jurisdictions—Luciano Metzinger in Ayaviri, Ricardo Durand, and especially his successor, Luis Vallejos, in Cuzco, and Edward Fedders in Juli—displayed a great sense of regional solidarity in the wake of the Council and Medellín. Together, they created the Andean Pastoral Institute (IPA) in 1969 for the formation of pastoral agents. IPA also aimed to helped the foreign clergy and religious inculturate themselves in the social-religious reality of the altiplano.

This regional church gave priority to the formation of the peasants and the defense of their rights. In this regard the work of Daniel McClellan, a Maryknoll priest, was especially notable. McClellan founded a series of credit cooperatives for the peasants throughout Puno. In 1965 the Institute of Rural Education (called Palermo from the name of an old hacienda where it is located) was founded near Juli. The Institute, like the similar one in Cajamarca, offered specialized courses that emphasized the values of communal work and solidarity as the way to obtain social justice. The church openly supported the peasants in their struggle to rectify the agrarian reform in order to secure real justice. In several of their statements, which had nationwide repercussions, the bishops in the region legitimized the peasants' struggle to obtain their rights, especially "Hearing the Cry of the People" (1978), and "The Land, Gift of God, Right of the People" (1986).[40] In 1982 Luis Vallejos, the archbishop of Cuzco, died in a car accident. His successor, Alcides Mendoza, decided to withdraw from the regional church. In spite of that loss, the other dioceses and prelatures continued to maintain close ties.

As in Cajamarca, the bishops founded centers for the formation of catechists, also known as *pastors* or *animators*. Besides the Andean Pastoral Institute in Cuzco (which moved to Sicuani when Cuzco withdrew from the regional church), there were other centers for the formation of pastoral agents. In Cuzco the Regional Institute for Catechetics and the Evangelization of the Andes was founded. This institute had notable influence in the region but due to internal problems closed down in 1977. In Puno some thousand peasants belonged to the Movement of Christian Animators; in many cases the animators were simultaneously leaders of the popular movement.[41]

This activity of the church in promoting the rights of the peasants brought it many enemies in the area; government officials frequently accused the church of complicity with subversion. In 1983 President Belaúnde publicly accused the non-governmental organizations and the church of being in the service of the subversives.[42] The Aprista government was no better. Alan García and local Aprista leaders frequently accused the church of giving support to the left. In November 1987 the Aprista mayor of Puno accused the church, and especially the foreign clergy in that region, of "protecting and covering up for" the Shining Path.[43] Bishop Calderón of Puno responded by pointing out that terrorism was not growing in the area precisely because of the presence of a "living church."[44] In Puno, as in most of the Andes, the church was caught in the line of fire between the terrorists and officialdom.

The first attack of the Shining Path against the church, as we mentioned earlier, occurred in 1981, when a group of Shining Path terrorists burned down the installations of the Institute of Rural Education in Juli, run by the Maryknoll Fathers, although at that time no one was aware who the authors of the attack were. The attack sparked an immediate and spontaneous response of indignation in the entire region by Lake Titicaca. A march of solidarity was organized in which ten thousand peasants, representing a myriad of popular organizations, participated.[45] During the march the peasants bore slogans that said: "We Are the Church" and "No to Death, Yes to Life!" This demonstration contrasted noticeably with the church in Ayacucho, which maintained a very discreet profile with respect to the violation of human rights during the Shining Path years. In the southern Andean region the church spoke to the people, and the people responded. After that first attack the church used all its resources to unite the peasants and foster solidarity among the popular organizations.

In 1986 the Shining Path increased the level of its activity in the Puno area, principally by attacking communal development projects. In May the church in Puno, Ayaviri, and Juli organized a major march for peace; in August, with the theme "Puno Wants Peace," it invited representatives of all the popular organizations, the police, the military, and the political parties to attend a symposium to discuss ways to combat terrorism and promote peace. The symposium was well attended, although the Aprista Party was noticeably absent.[46] In the final document, for the first time in Peru, the church condemned the Shining Path by name.[47] Besides organizing marches and symposia, the church also founded human-rights offices or "vicariates of solidarity" in every diocese in the area: in Puno and Ayaviri in 1986, and in Juli in 1988. In 1987 a Marian-Eucharistic Congress was held in Puno with five thousand delegates from all over the southern Andean region. The theme of the congress was "To Evangelize Is to Sow Life and Harvest Peace." The congress emphasized the determination of the Christians to stand firm and not respond to the violence of the terrorists or the forces of order with the same tactics. The Shining Path was not slow in reacting; during that period there were numerous bombs thrown against parish halls and educational works run by the church.

In May 1989 the Shining Path attacked and destroyed the Institute of Rural Education in Waqrani, in the prelature of Ayaviri. In the same operation the terrorists also attacked an experimental farm belonging to the National University of the Altiplano.[48] This was, to date, the most violent attack of the Shining Path against the church in the region. The Institute had been founded in 1964, and under the direction of the French-born prelates of the Sacred Hearts missionaries—Luciano Metzinger, Luis Dalle, and Francisco D'Alteroche—emphasized the ideals of liberation theology, group solidarity, and respect for the rights of others. In June, in the midst of these disheartening events, the Institute celebrated its twenty-fifth anniversary. In spite of the circumstances, a celebration was held, among other reasons to send a message to the Shining Path. Hundreds of sympathizers from all over the region showed up for the mass, which the acting prelate, Francisco D'Alteroche, celebrated at the very site of the attack.[49]

Although the church was forced to diminish its educational and pastoral activities in many areas, in others it redoubled its efforts to fortify the people in their struggle. In 1991 the bishops of Puno, Tacna, Juli, and Ayaviri created the Regional Peace Council. More important than the creation of new organizations, however, were the numerous public demonstrations of solidarity—marches, masses, and processions—by which the church animated the people. In September 1992, to cite one example, the prelates of Puno, Ayaviri, and Sicuani walked in procession along with five thousand of the faithful in a pilgrimage to the Sanctuary of the Lord of Huanca, near Cuzco. Andean symbols mixed with symbols of the progressive church. Dressed in festive Indian garb the peasants played traditional mountain music, carried banners of the Inca empire, and waved signs that said "For Life and for Peace."[50] With demonstrations like these the church openly defied the Shining Path, and by doing so it also underlined the latter's essential cowardliness and unpopularity. Even though the Shining Path managed to control many villages, it did so by terror. It offered nothing positive to the peasants, who already knew how to fight for their rights. Furthermore, for most of the peasants religion was a source of consolation and strength in life.

THE JUNGLE

The jungle makes up approximately 63 percent of Peru's territory, although only about 11 percent of the population lives there.[51] Within this immense territory there is a great variety of ecological zones, ranging from higher jungle-mountain terrain to the lower Amazon basin, which Peru shares with Brazil, Bolivia, Colombia, and Ecuador. The terrorists used the jungle as a refuge where they established camps to train themselves, keep prisoners, and indoctrinate youth who had been "recruited" for the cause. The jungle also constituted the principal source of financing for the guerrillas, who forged an uneasy alliance with the drug traffickers. Both the MRTA and the Shining Path demanded tribute from the producers of coca leaves and the mafias that turned the leaves into cocaine. One of the major regions for the production of coca leaves was the Upper Huallaga Valley, located in the departments of Huánuco and San Martín in the center of the country, and a bit to the north of Lima. The isolation of the valley, as well as the lucrative dividends gained by exploiting the coca producers, attracted the terrorists. The two terrorist groups disputed control of the territory.[52] In a report on terrorist violence in the prelature of Moyobamba, which coincides with San Martín, Bishop Venancio Orbe summed up the situation in these words: "The provinces of Tocache and Mariscal Cáceres are controlled by the Shining Path, and the seven remaining provinces in the center and the north are controlled by MRTA."[53] The church was caught between terrorist bands, without even mentioning the drug traffickers, the police, and the military.

In fact, the prelature of Moyobamba was one of the best examples of a positive ecclesial response to the crisis. As in Cajamarca, many peasant vigilante bands, supported by OPSAM (Prelature Office of Social Action), sprang up.[54] Furthermore, OPSAM organized workshops and courses on human rights for the peasants, students, teachers, and catechists. In recognition of its leadership role, in 1991 OPSAM was chosen from among ten other organizations to preside over the Commission to Pacify the Department of San Martín.

In all parts of the central jungle region the church, along with its educational centers, missions, and offices for the promotion of native cultures, such as CAAAP (Amazonic Center of Anthropology and Practical Application), received many threats from the terrorists. Perhaps the most dramatic case of the church's plight concerned the Ashaninkas Indians, who lived along the Ene River in the central eastern jungle. Frequently called Campas (an older, colonial name), the fifty thousand Ashaninkas had already experienced an encounter with guerrillas in 1965 when a column of the Movement of the Revolutionary Left (MIR) invaded their territory. In their attempt to attract the Indians, the guerrillas alluded to older millennarian myths.[55] In 1989 the MRTA attempted to enter the Ashaninkas territory but were expelled by the Indians, who organized themselves in self-defense groups. The Shining Path had better luck. That same year it increased its attacks in the area and by 1990 virtually controlled the Ene River basin.

The Franciscan missionaries who worked among the Ashaninkas had no well-defined strategy for facing the threat. One of them, Father Mariano Gagnon, an American, in charge of the Cutiveri mission along the Ene River, secured arms from the Peruvian army and gave them to the Indians. Gagnon even asked for American military aid. But in November 1989, when Gagnon was absent, a band of *Senderistas* attacked and destroyed the mission at Cutiveri. In desperation Gagnon organized twenty rescue missions by air in order to fly the Indians out of the area to the ecclesiastical territory of the Dominicans some 150 miles away. Finally, he abandoned the area, at least for the time being.[56]

Approximately ten thousand Ashaninkas were captured by the Shining Path and reduced to slavery.[57] Around thirty-five hundred were killed. Long after it was defeated in the rest of the country, the Shining Path remained in the area. In August 1993, in vengeance for helping the peasant self-defense bands, the Shining Path attacked the town of Mazamiri and killed fifty-nine men, women, and children. The vicariate of San Ramón, which includes most of the Ashaninkas within its jurisdiction, in coordination with CAAAP and Cáritas, offered material and spiritual assistance to the Ashaninkas who survived the entire ordeal.[58]

THE EPISCOPAL CONFERENCE, CEAS, AND CAAAP

When the terrorist violence finally became a national problem, the episcopal conference began taking measures to support areas most in need. In Lima certain bishops stood out for their promotion of peace and justice— Germán Schmitz, the auxiliary bishop of the southern cone of Lima; Augusto Beuzeville, who was named a member of the government's Peace Commission (1985); and Luciano Metzinger, former prelate of Ayaviri and a leading promoter in the church of modern means of mass communication. There were other bishops who gave a strong impetus to the peace movement: Cardinal Landázuri, president of the bishops' conference until 1988; José Dammert (Cajamarca), who was vice president of the conference and president for a brief interlude (1991-92); Luis Bambarén, in charge of the bishops' Commission on Social Action (until 1988), and his successor as head of the commission, Miguel Irizar, the coadjutor bishop of Callao. These and other progressive bishops had to face much resistance from the conservative bishops, who tended to view terrorism as a matter purely for the military and the police. The Peruvian episcopate was quite divided, especially in the wake of the official inquiry into liberation theology.

In spite of this internal dissension the conference managed to make several striking statements on peace and violence. The first official statement of the bishops was made in 1983 when the violence was still perceived as a local problem in one area. The pope's speech in Ayacucho in 1985, delivered to all Peruvians, clearly reflected the realization that terrorism was by then a national problem. The first, and the most inspiring, comprehensive statement by the bishops on Peru's crisis was the document "Peru: Choose Life!" published in April 1989. In it, the bishops established their basic thesis that the fundamental cause of the current social-economic crisis was moral. They pointed to public corruption—which reached scandalous proportions in Alan García's government—as one of the principal causes of the crisis. Finally, they called upon the faithful and those who wielded influence to give an example of civic solidarity. In other statements, "We Want Peace" (1991), "Peace on Earth" (Christmas 1991), and "A New Peru: A Task for All" (1992), the conference repeated the same themes in different ways.

The church also participated in the government's emergency program to help the poor in the wake of Fujimori's drastic economic "shock," whereby he removed all subsidies for basic foodstuffs. In fact, Cáritas and a few other church-related humanitarian organizations, were chosen to be the main distributors of food and clothing. But in practice the promised goods never materialized. Nevertheless, the church paid a price for its willingness to be associated with the government's program: the Shining Path singled out churchpeople as government agents.[59]

Even though the influence of the bishops' conference was somewhat weakened as a result of its internal divisions, other organizations dependent on the bishops, such as CEAS and CAAAP, had much more immediate influence. CEAS—the Episcopal Commission of Social Action—was founded in 1965 as a distinct organization in order to inform the bishops about social questions, to coordinate the church's efforts to defend human rights, and to speak for the church on social questions. During the war against terrorism CEAS became one of the most important channels in the country for airing cases of refugees, human-rights violations, and persons accused of terrorism. It also became one of the most reliable sources on what was happening in the emergency zones. Under the two presidents in that period—Luis Bambarén and Miguel Irizar—the commission, with its team of thirty-five lawyers and young professionals, helped pastoral agents throughout the country to organize workshops and seminars on human rights, peace, and violence. Also, beginning in 1985 CEAS organized an annual Day of Fast and Prayer for Peace in all parishes. In 1992 CEAS created the Department of Human Dignity, which aimed to protect the rights of those accused of terrorism and to help refugees who had fled the emergency zones. Although CEAS did not belong formally to the National Coordinating Committee of Human Rights, it did collaborate very closely with all human-rights groups.

For its part, CAAAP (Amazonic Center of Anthropology and Practical Application), with offices in Lima, Iquitos, Tarapoto, and La Merced, was founded in 1974 by the bishops in the jungle as an instrument in the service of their pastoral planning. CAAAP's mission was to do research on the cultural and religious reality of the native peoples, organize efforts to defend their cultures, and train pastoral agents. Like CEAS on a national level, CAAAP organized workshops on human rights and special problems, such as drugs and drug traffickers. In the face of threats from both MRTA and the Shining Path it was forced to reduce its activities in many parts of the jungle. But when the threat receded, CEAS moved back in to help the victims of terrorism, especially the Ashaninkas.

HUMAN RIGHTS AND THE PEACE MOVEMENT

During this entire period the church played a key role in promoting human rights and peace. In fact, it may be affirmed that without the church and the work of committed Christians, the battle for human rights and peace would have been insignificant, and in some parts of Peru, nonexistent. In 1985, in response to the growing violence, and especially after the massacre of eight journalists in the small Andean town of Uchuraccay (1983), several human-rights groups decided to create the National Coordinating Committee of Human Rights. By 1994 the committee had forty-four distinct member groups, as well as seven associate members. The weight of the church can be measured by the fact that twenty of those groups were church-related: CAAAP, the different vicariates of solidarity in the southern Andean region, and other groups such as CEAPAZ (Center of Studies and Action for Peace), which broke off from CEAS in order to have more independence from the official church. Among the associated non-members were CEAS and the Office of Social Action of the prelature of Moyobamba. The National Evangelical Council of Peru also belonged to the group of the associated non-members.[60] The National Coordinating Committee soon became the principal non-governmental organization in defense of human rights in Peru. In general, the international human-rights groups relied on the National Coordinating Committee for information, and not on the government, which frequently vilified the committee with accusations and calumnies.

The first executive secretary of the committee, Pilar Coll (1988-92), a committed Christian, contributed much to giving the committee the public image of a nonpartisan organization dedicated to the service of others. Her successors, Rosa María Mujica and Susana Villarán, continued the same orientation. Rosa María Mujica, a teacher by profession, was also the founder and director of another member group in the national committee: IPEDEHP, the Peruvian Institute on Education in Human Rights. This organization, as its name indicates, specialized in helping teachers to communicate the idea of human rights to their students.

The peace movement, closely tied to the human-rights movement, distinguished itself from the latter by having a more ample agenda, which included social justice and social rights. In the decade of the eighties many different peace groups emerged, each with a slightly different nuance. In May 1985 leading personalities from the academic, ecclesiastical, and political worlds, notably Father Felipe MacGregor, Bishop Metzinger, and Alvaro Rey de Castro, a former attorney general, created CODEPP: Commission for the Defense of Human Rights and the Construction of Peace. In 1989 a group of priests, intellectuals, and artists founded the movement Peru, Life, and Peace.

Both the human-rights and the peace groups worked to mobilize the civilian population to come out and organize against violence, whether from the terrorists or from the forces of law and order. One of their principal activities was to organize solidarity marches, which aimed to break through public passivity and fear. In November 1985 the National Coordinating Committee of Human Rights organized the first of these marches, through downtown Lima. At the end of the march Bishop Beuzeville read a declaration that laid down twenty concrete measures for securing peace and justice in Peru.[61] One of the most important of these civic demonstrations took place on the eve of the municipal elections of 1989 in the face of an armed strike that the Shining Path had imposed on Lima. In response to the strike the candidate of the

United Left, Henry Pease, summoned all the other parties to participate in a great march, which drew close to fifty thousand participants. In every provincial city in Peru similar marches were held, usually as a protest against the Shining Path's armed strikes.

The church cooperated with the government to promote peace, but this relationship was always ambiguous and at times strained, given the fact that many rightwing politicians and the military suspected progressive churchpeople of having ties with the subversives. In 1985 the Alan García administration established an official Peace Commission, made up of leading personalities, including Bishop Beuzeville, who represented the church. But the bishops' conference always feared lurking political manipulation in these government-sponsored commissions. In July 1991, at the end of Fujimori's first year, the government created a Council for Peace and offered the presidency to Bishop Dammert, then the president of the episcopal conference. But Dammert distrusted the promises of the government to respect human rights and declined the invitation. Without a high-profile church presence, the council languished and had little influence.

In the universities, too, a peace movement arose to counter the presence of terrorists. Most of the leaders of the movement were committed Christians, who represented groups such as the National Union of Catholic Students, the Christian Life Communities of the Jesuits, and Protestant student groups. In May 1990 a long-standing anticlerical tradition was broken when the National University of San Marcos invited the new archbishop of Lima, Augusto Vargas Alzamora, to celebrate a mass for peace on the university campus. The archbishop was received by university authorities and the mass was attended by hundreds of students, many of whom prayed for companions who had been killed by the terrorism.[62] As we mentioned earlier, in the National University of Ayacucho, where the Shining Path arose, the peace movement was headed by certain professors with the support of the Jesuits.

LIMA: MARÍA ELENA MOYANO AND MICHEL AZCUETA

The final stage in the war against the Shining Path was especially violent and bloody. As part of its strategy to frustrate the nationwide municipal elections of 1989, the Shining Path murdered 120 candidates and newly elected mayors.[63] From that moment on the Shining Path decided to escalate its attacks in Lima, in part because it was losing control of the mountains in the face of peasant resistance. In 1991, for the first time since the violence began, there were more acts of terrorism in the capital than in the provinces.[64] The year 1992 was marked by a series of brutal attacks: against television stations, police stations, banks, and business establishments. But the attack that most horrified the country occurred on July 16 when a car bomb exploded on a street called Tarata in Miraflores, a fashionable district of Lima. The bomb killed 20 persons and left 130 wounded. Most of the attacks, however, occurred in the poor neighborhoods, and most of the victims were leaders of the popular movement or of unions. The murder of María Elena Moyano, a young leader in the young town of Villa El Salvador on February 15, 1992, was especially shocking because she had become a symbol of resistance against the Shining Path.

María Elena Moyano was born in 1958 in Barranco, a district of Lima, but she also lived part of her youth in Surco, another neighborhood. She participated in a youth group in her parish, which, along with her school, became the center of her life. In an autobiographical note she described her parish group as "youth who were deeply Christian and committed to service of the community."[65] When she was thirteen her family moved to Villa El Salvador, a huge "young town" on the outskirts of Lima. She studied psychology at the university, where she, like thousands of other Peruvian students, was obliged to take a course on dialectical materialism. A Maoist group tried to persuade her to join them. In spite of all these pressures she remained true to her religious convictions. She soon emerged as a leader in her community and participated in the founding of the Women's Federation of Villa El Salvador, of which she was elected president twice. Furthermore, in 1989 she was elected lieutenant mayor of Villa El Salvador, just at the time that the Shining Path began infiltrating popular organizations. With her sparkling charism she galvanized the people to resist the Shining Path's encroachments. In September 1991, with the slogan "Against Hunger and Terrorism" and in spite of many threats against her life, she organized a massive march against the Shining Path. She was killed as she left a communal meeting. Some 300,000 people attended her funeral. Shortly before her death she wrote in her diary:

> As I live, my God, I wish to thank you for giving me everything. Everything! Love, the ability to give of myself and all that I have. Everything. Thank you, God, for allowing me to live.[66]

The other person who came to symbolize popular resistance against terrorism was the mayor of Villa El Salvador, Michel Azcueta. A Spaniard by birth, he came to Peru as a seminarian. He left the seminary, became a teacher, and finally entered politics. He became the first elected mayor of Villa El Salvador when it won autonomy from another district. Under his leadership Villa, as it is popularly known, became a model of community development with the enthusiastic participation of the people themselves. Villa El Salvador, which had 340,000 inhabitants in 1996, became internationally famous. In 1985 John Paul II visited Villa and addressed several hundred thousand fervent pilgrims from other young towns who walked all through the night to be present. In 1987, Azcueta, accompanied by María Elena Moyano, received the prize Prince of Asturias. After completing two periods as mayor he left politics and returned to the classroom and other communal activities. But, like María Elena Moyano, he had received threats from the Shining Path, which resented his efforts to foster popular democracy. On June 16, 1993, as he walked from his pickup truck toward the Faith and Joy School of the Jesuits where he taught, a group of *Senderistas* shot him down. He lived, but only after months of hospitalization was he able to walk again, with the aid of crutches. In November 1995 he was elected mayor of Villa for the third time.

THE END OF A LONG NIGHT

The capture of Abimael Guzmán on February 12, 1992, by General Antonio Ketín Vidal, the head of the National Office against Terrorism, marked the beginning of the end of the Shining Path. With the capture of Guzmán and other leaders, as well as the application of new and more effective measures against terrorism, which included attracting wavering members of the subversives to turn themselves in, the Shining Path's machine of terror was finally stopped. Two years after Guzmán's capture the level of violence and the number of persons who disappeared as a result of the violence decreased dramatically. The church participated in the peace process. Many members of the Shining Path and the MRTA took advantage of the Law of Repentance and turned themselves in to parish churches and from there to the armed forces. This procedure brought with it many problems, one of which involved terrorists who turned themselves in, but in order to show their spirit of cooperation, cynically named innocent people as fellow terrorists. One of the church's most important contributions was to draw attention to those falsely accused and to defend them. Finally, the church, along with the human-rights groups, denounced an amnesty law passed in 1995, which pardoned many police and military who had committed atrocities against civilians.

Unlike other countries in Latin America where the episcopal conferences or certain key bishops assumed a leading role, the Peruvian bishops's conference played a relatively secondary role. In the Peruvian case, the Shining Path's dogmatism and hostility toward the church precluded any possibility of mediating in a dialogue between the forces of order and the subversives. The bishops' conference limited its role to that of consoling and giving moral orientation to the country, or to condemning violence and the abuse of authority by the police or the military. In general, the battle against terrorism in Peru was the work of certain progressive bishops and Christians on the grassroots level: priests, religious women in the Andes and the young towns, peasant catechists, and activists in favor of human rights and peace, such as María Elena Moyano and Michel Azcueta. The Protestants also resisted the onslaught of terrorism and died for their idealism. Most of all, inspired by liberation theology and slogans such as "Solidarity Is the New Name of Peace," committed Christians infused the war against terrorism and violence with a religious mystique. This consoled and strengthened Peruvians of all classes as they struggled to leave behind the long and dark night in which Peru found itself for more than twelve years.

9.

El Salvador (1980-1992)

The Bloodiest Civil War

El Salvador is the smallest of the Central American countries, and one of the most densely populated. It was also the scene of one of the bloodiest civil wars in the history of Latin America. Between the beginning of the war in 1980 and the end in 1992 between 75,000 to 80,000 Salvadorans (out of a population of a little over 5,000,000) were killed. Furthermore, 550,000 were displaced from their homes, and another 500,000 fled the country.[1] Before and during the war the church played a key role, first under the prophetic leadership of Archbishop Oscar Romero, and later under his successor, Archbishop Arturo Rivera y Damas, who acted as mediator between the government and the revolutionary forces. Before looking at the role of the church, it is helpful briefly to review the historical circumstances that led to the war.

The roots of the conflict can be found in the steep social and economic stratification of Salvadoran society. In the nineteenth century the liberal oligarchy usurped the lands of the peasants and Indians and consolidated them to form large coffee-producing estates. Unlike other Latin American countries, which were "banana republics," El Salvador was a coffee republic. In 1932, when President Arturo Araujo, a reformist, was overthrown, a revolution broke out. The army's repression of the revolution cost the lives of thirty thousand peasants. The "massacre" (or *la matanza*) of 1932 made a deep impression on the collective memory of the poor. Between 1932 and 1982 all of El Salvador's rulers were military men who acted as defenders of the oligarchy. Among the many who were killed in the *matanza* of 1932 was Agustín Farabundo Martí, the founder of the Communist Party of El Salvador.

As the twentieth century moved on, a modernizing sector emerged within the traditional landowning oligarchy. The modernizers wanted to foster national industry and to show more respect for the outward forms of civilian democracy. But neither the modernizers nor the conservatives, both of whom depended on coffee exports, were strongly motivated to make real changes.[2] Between 1961 and 1982 the oligarchy and the army expressed their desires through the Party of National Reconciliation.

In the seventies the Christian Democratic Party, representing middle-class professionals, many of whom had ties to the church, was also founded. In 1969 a bizarre clash between El Salvador and Honduras, apparently touched off by a soccer match, in reality was caused by deep social problems that had been building up for a half century. The shortage of land forced many Salvadoran peasants to look for land and work in neighboring Honduras. Honduras passed an agrarian reform law that excluded foreigners. El Salvador responded with displays of martial music and other signs of offended national pride. The 1972 elections created many expectations among reformist groups. But the army manipulated the elections and imposed its own official candidate, Colonel Arturo Molina (1972-77). The candidate of the opposition, José Napoleón Duarte, a Christian Democrat and former mayor of El Salvador, was deported.

In the seventies social tensions deepened and the level of violence grew. New popular peasant movements made their debut, notably FECCAS (Christian Federation of Salvadoran Peasants) and the UTC (the Union of Workers in Rural Areas). But landowners had recourse to their own organizations, especially ANEP (the National Association of Private Business) and FARO (Farmers' Front of the Eastern Region), to impose state terrorism in the rural areas. One such organization created to keep the peasants in their place was a paramilitary force called ORDEN, the National Democratic Organization. Death squads also appeared. The most notorious was the White Warrior Union, linked directly to the police and the army. During this period many union and peasant leaders, as well as priests and laypersons connected to the popular movement, were killed by these groups.

In this increasingly tense atmosphere the different leftist groups coalesced in 1980 to create the Farabundo Martí National Liberation Front (FMLN). They also founded the Revolutionary Democratic Front (FDR), which acted as a legal branch of the FMLN. The National Democratic Front drew together many different political organizations, unions, and popular movements. In October 1979 a reformist military *golpe* overthrew the government of General Carlos Humberto Romero, who had been elected president in 1977. Under General Romero, El Salvador was considered to be one of the worst violators of human rights in Latin America. The new junta that took power, made up of military and civilians, promised to carry out basic social reforms. But the junta experienced several internal crises, and conservative army groups blocked the reforms. By March 1980 all hope of real change had dissipated. The provisional president of the third junta created that month was José Napoleón Duarte, the same man who had been deported by the military in 1972. He tried to carry forward the reformist torch and even managed to proclaim an agrarian reform, which in practice did little for the peasants.[3] But more important than the good intentions of Duarte was the fact that he did not have control over his own forces of order. Official repression of popular organizations grew more severe, and the death squads acted at will. The murder of Archbishop Oscar Romero on March 24, 1980, was the most widely known example of this state of lawlessness and institutionalized violence. In the midst of this anarchical state of affairs, the left decided to take the road of armed revolution. In January 1981 the FMLN carried out its first general offensive, which resulted in the deaths of several hundred persons.

THE ROLE OF THE UNITED STATES

That the civil war in El Salvador was especially long and bloody was due to a large extent to the intervention of outside forces. The FMLN received arms from Nicaragua, Cuba, and the Soviet Union. But the decisive factor was American aid to the government, which enabled it to fight a war far beyond its normal capacity, so much so that the Salvadoran army was practically a mercenary force maintained by the United States. President Carter had responded to the crisis by giving emergency military aid to the Salvadoran government. But his successor, Ronald Reagan, went far beyond that: he converted a regional Central American conflict into a cornerstone of his policy to contain Soviet and communist expansion in Latin America. The Sandinista victory in 1979 was a warning alarm for the new Republican president, who feared that Nicaragua would become a new Cuba and that now El Salvador threatened to go the same way. In spite of his firm ideological convictions, however, President Reagan was greatly limited in what he could or could not do in Central America. The American public still lived in the shadow of Vietnam, and for most ordinary citizens military intervention in Central America, even to save it from communism, was unthinkable. Given this resistance to direct American intervention, Reagan and his advisers had no choice but to rely on the Salvadoran army to stop communism. The hardliners who surrounded Reagan—Secretary of State Alexander Haig; Jeane Kirkpatrick, the ambassador to the United Nations; and William Casey, the director of the Central Intelligence Agency—basically opted for a purely military solution to the problem of revolution in El Salvador. But there were more moderate advisers, who in the long run won out. They supported a policy that combined aggression with economic aid.[4] But neither group doubted that military aid was absolutely necessary to win the war. In 1980 the Salvadoran government received from the United States the rather modest sum of $5,900,000 in military aid. But by 1982 that sum had jumped to $82,000,000.[5] Thanks to this powerful injection of money, the military and other special forces were able to expand rapidly, from seventeen thousand in 1980 to fifty thousand in 1987.[6] Rebel forces numbered around four to five thousand.[7] And thanks to this massive infusion of aid, the Salvadoran armed forces were saved from collapse during the initial stages of the war.

For all practical purposes President Reagan intended to conduct an undeclared war against the Salvadoran revolutionaries. But this policy, and especially the massive human-rights violations by the Salvadoran army and the other forces of order, provoked a strong cry of protest against Reagan's Central American schemes. The American government was forced to defend its policy with the argument that it was fighting to defend "democracy." Within this context the government gave great importance to holding elections during the civil war. In reality, however, the rulers of El Salvador, first Duarte and later Alfredo Cristiani, barely had control over their own army, and they certainly had no control over the paramilitary groups that roamed at will. This was the basis of the FMLN's case that, given the existing state of lawlessness, no real democracy existed in the country. In light of this situation President Reagan was forced to justify—to a congress dominated by Democrats—his call for aid to the Salvadoran military. After the murder of four American women in November 1980, congress demanded that the president "certify" that the government and armed forces of El Salvador were taking the proper steps to safeguard human rights before approving new funds to carry on the war. But Reagan and his successor, George Bush, always seemed to find sufficient grounds to certify that El Salvador was indeed making progress in the area of human rights. In short, the government of the United States followed a most ambiguous, not to say hypocritical policy: on the one hand, it denounced violations of human rights; and on the other, it gave huge sums of money to the very groups that most violated those rights.

The undeclared war of the United States in Central America provoked some of the stormiest debates since the Vietnam war. Those who criticized President Reagan's policies had considerable weight and influence. The episcopal conference of the Catholic church, for example, totally supported Archbishop Rivera y Damas's call for an end to foreign interference in El Salvador. Several times the president of the conference, Cardinal James Hickey, the archbishop of Washington, D.C., appeared before the American congress in order to present recommendations of the Catholic church with respect to the Salvadoran civil war. These recommendations were based on observations gathered from trips some of the American bishops made to El Salvador and from their dialogue with local church leaders.[8] Also, FMLN leaders were aware of the importance of the churches and the human-rights groups. In 1984 both organizations—the FMLN and the FDR—sent a letter to Reverend Jesse Jackson, who had declared his candidacy for the presidency, requesting that he explain the FMLN's position in the Democratic convention that year.[9]

THE CHRONOLOGY OF THE WAR

The Truth Commission, created by the United Nations as part of the peace agreements that were signed in 1992, discerned four stages in the war. During the first stage (1980-83), which the commission entitled "The Institutionalization of the Violence," the FMLN carried out its first offensive and the army responded militarily, frequently committing atrocities. One of the worst atrocities occurred in December 1981 when the Atlacatl Battalion, in search of "terrorists," massacred an entire town, killing more than five hundred men, women, and children.[10] In the political order, under pressure from the United States, elections were held in 1982 for a constitutional assembly. Alvaro Magaña was elected provisional president of the country. Although Duarte's Christian Democratic Party won a majority, the extreme right represented by a new party, ARENA, founded and directed by Roberto D'Aubuisson, a former army major, dominated the assembly. D'Aubuisson was considered to be the mastermind behind the death squads and therefore responsible for the death of Oscar Romero. During the second stage (1983-87), "Armed Confrontation and Human Rights Violations," the fighting intensified and the violence spread. In spite of being in a civil war, new elections were held: in 1984 for the presidency and in 1985 for the legislative assembly. José Napoleón Duarte won the presidential elections in the second round with 53.6 percent of the total vote, and D'Aubuisson came in second with 46.4 percent.[11] Duarte was the first civilian president to come to power in fifty years. During this stage the government established a dialogue with the FMLN, and many face-to-face contacts with the FMLN leadership were carried out in the presence of the church. The kidnapping of the president's daughter in 1985 was the most dramatic occurrence during this stage. During the third stage (1987-91), "Military Conflict as an Obstacle to Peace," Duarte was placed under pressure by the other governments of Central America to enter into a new dialogue with the FMLN. The agreements drawn up in "Esquipulas II" committed the member countries to resolve their internal conflicts without recourse to foreign powers and by engaging in dialogue with the armed opposition. However, the death squads continued to act with impunity. In 1987 they murdered Herbert Anaya Sanabria, the coordinator of the El Salvadoran Commission of Human Rights. ARENA made significant electoral advances, winning the elections for the national assembly and for the municipal boards. Finally, in the last stage (1989-91), the war resumed and the violence reached its maximum level. In the beginning of 1989 Alfredo Cristiani, ARENA's candidate, was elected president. In November the FMLN carried out one of the biggest offensives of the entire civil war and managed to seize sections of the capital city. During this offensive members of the army murdered six Jesuits and two women helpers in the Central American University. Under world pressure, especially from President Bush of the United States and Secretary General Javier Pérez de Cuéllar of the United Nations, both sides renewed dialogue, and after multiple meetings, arrived at a final peace agreement in Chapultepec, Mexico, in February 1992. During this long and complicated process the church was one of the principal protagonists, as we shall see.

THE CHURCH OF OSCAR ROMERO

Oscar Romero, archbishop of San Salvador (1977-80), was assassinated because of his valiant denunciations of the persecution unleashed against the people by the death squads and security forces. He came to symbolize the church, which had radically changed during the sixties. The Salvadoran church is small: in 1991 there were 461 priests altogether, and 1,225 religious women.[12] The majority of the 258 priests who belong to the diocesan clergy are native-born. Around one-fourth of the clergy and one-third of the religious women are located in the archdiocese of San Salvador.[13] The archbishop of San Salvador is, therefore, a key figure in the church. In the nineteenth century the church was treated harshly by the anticlerical liberals, but later it made its peace with the landowning oligarchy, the liberal power base.[14] It was Oscar Romero's predecessor, Luis Chávez y González, archbishop from 1938 to 1977, who made the first important changes in the church. Chávez fostered Catholic Action and Christian unionism, promoted the reforms of Vatican II, and spread the spirit of Medellín. By means of numerous pastoral encounters, the clergy and the religious became conscienticized with respect to both the Council and Medellín.

In the sixties and seventies the base ecclesial communities and other movements appeared in the Salvadoran church. In 1969 FECCAS—the Christian Federation of Salvadoran Peasants—was founded. In the rural areas many priests and religious women offered courses for training catechists and "delegates of the Word." The catechists and the delegates were often the leaders of the peasants' unions. The José Simeón Cañas Central American University, founded by the Jesuits in 1965, contributed much to this process of change. Very soon, however, these efforts provoked hostility on the part of the oligarchy and the established order. In 1970 Father José Inocencio Alas, who worked to conscienticize the peasants, was kidnapped. In the face of the church's protests, he was freed. But the spiral of persecution had begun. In the midst of these changes in the church the different guerrilla movements, FPL (Popular Liberation Forces) and ERP (Revolutionary Army of the People), spread their own revolutionary terror, kidnapping and killing people. Security forces frequently singled out priests, nuns, and lay leaders as targets for their role in organizing the popular movement and for their alleged role in fomenting strikes. In 1972 the Jesuits took charge of a parish in Aguilares and El Paisnal, to the north of the capital. The parish priest, Father Rutilio Grande, trained a team of seminarians and laypersons to conduct popular missions and to offer courses to train delegates of the Word. In 1973 FECCAS organized a general strike among the peasants in that region. The parish offered moral support to the strikers, many of whom participated in the parish's courses.[15] The local landowners, through FARO and ORDEN, centered their attention on the Jesuits and their work in the parish and in the university. In fact, the Jesuits, who aimed to conscienticize the peasants through their pastoral work, drew the line at direct political action. Furthermore, they never approved of the violent methods used by the extreme left. In March 1977, shortly after Oscar Romero became archbishop, Rutilio Grande was murdered. His death moved many, especially the new archbishop. That same year the White Warrior Union threatened to kill all the Jesuits if they did not abandon the country within thirty days.

Progressive groups in the church were initially disillusioned over Romero's being named archbishop. He was known as a conservative and, in fact, had criticized the progressive clergy in the years following Medellín. But when it became apparent that he planned to take a firm stand before the government in defense of human rights, the progressives changed their opinion. Beginning with the single mass (because all other Sunday masses were canceled) for Rutilio Grande, Romero stood out as a prophetic voice in the middle of the violence unleashed by both the guerrillas and the forces of order. His Sunday sermon, as well as his Sunday radio program, became famous within El Salvador and beyond. With a simple but eloquent style he cited cases of disappearances and torture that had been confirmed by the archdiocesan Office of Legal Aid. In the eyes of his admirers among the poor, he came to be, in the words of his biographer James Brockman, the "archbishop of the people."[16] Nevertheless, he was also a solitary figure among the other bishops in the episcopal conference. With the exception of Arturo Rivera y Damas, who had been auxiliary bishop under Archbishop Chávez, the bishops not only disagreed with Romero, but some made their criticisms known to the Vatican. In some cases the criticisms were simply outright calumnies.

After the reformist *golpe* of October 1979 the archbishop offered his conditional support to the new government, especially when the military incorporated two progressive professors from the UCA in the junta. But internal disagreements soon paralyzed the junta. In early January of 1980 Romero was invited to act as a mediator to help work out the differences. His mediating did not produce the fruits desired, and on January 3 the civilians in the junta resigned. From that point on the junta began to move increasingly to the right. Romero in turn began to take a more critical stand before the government and specifically denounced official repression of popular demonstrations. On March 24, 1980, he was assassinated while celebrating mass in the chapel of the hospital where he lived. Years later the Truth Commission of the United Nations singled out Roberto D'Aubuisson as the intellectual author of that crime. After an exhaustive investigation, fully corroborated by some of the participants in the crime, the commission confirmed what was already common knowledge; namely, that D'Aubuisson and his clique of military and former military, who had publicly accused Romero of being a "demagogue" and who incited the people to "adopt terrorism," were those directly responsible for the archbishop's death.[17] Until his death in 1992 D'Aubuisson attributed the murder of Romero to the FMLN. The death of Archbishop Romero was the most dramatic event of 1980; it was also the most poignant harbinger of the coming civil war.

Throughout 1980 the violence unleashed by the death squads grew in intensity. According to one source, between June and August some 2,780 civilians were murdered.[18] In November security forces captured five leaders of the Revolutionary Democratic Front, who met in the Jesuit boarding school of San José in San Salvador. All were summarily executed. The death squads and security forces especially singled out progressive churchpeople. In the course of the year four priests were murdered: Cosme Spesotti (June), Manuel Antonio Reyes (October), Ernesto Abrego, and Mariano Serrano (November). In July a seminarian, Manuel Othmaro Cáceres, was also murdered.[19] In December security forces, clearly acting on orders from above, captured four American women. The four were raped, murdered, and buried. The four—Ita Ford and Maura Clark (sisters of Maryknoll), Dorothy Kazel (an Ursuline), and Jean Donovan (a lay volunteer)—worked with the peasants.[20] The military and police believed that they had ties with the subversives, or, in any case, their efforts to conscienticize the peasants were considered subversive. The murder of these four women had a major impact on public opinion in the United States. President Carter immediately suspended military aid to El Salvador. It was in the wake of this crime that the American congress passed the law requiring the president to certify the progress or lack of progress in the area of human rights before giving new aid to the Salvadoran government. So great was the pressure applied to the government to investigate the case of the four women that the high command of the Salvadoran army decided—for the first time—to cooperate, if only to produce a few sacrificial lambs. In 1984 a judge tried and sentenced four policemen, implicated by the confession of one of them, to thirty years in prison.[21] But those who gave the orders were not touched.

The first major offensive of the FMLN began in January 1981, and the American government responded by restoring military aid to the Salvadoran government. In fact, with so many killings to date, the war actually had begun some time before, and the church had already paid a very high price for its identification with popular organizations and the effort to conscienticize the country politically and socially.

ARTURO RIVERA Y DAMAS: MEDIATOR

If the principal merit of Oscar Romero was to be the "voice of those without a voice," then his successor, Arturo Rivera y Damas, stands out principally as a reconciler and mediator between the parties in conflict. A peaceable and friendly man, he was known as a progressive when he was auxiliary bishop under Archbishop Chávez. But his first years as apostolic administrator after Romero's death were somewhat disappointing for progressives. He did not seem to face the country's problems or make the same kind of prophetic denunciations as his predecessor. He did, of course, continue to speak of concrete cases of human-rights violations in his Sunday sermon and radio program, but he tended to place the excesses and abuses of the armed forces on the same level as those of the FMLN, in spite of the fact that the vast number of violations were committed by the former. The change from Romero to Rivera y Damas was, in part, a question of personality. Rivera y Damas was more prone to follow a softer style in order to minimize confrontations. But there was another factor that conditioned his actions: he was not officially named archbishop until 1983. He could not really act or speak with the same liberty as one who is securely established in a post. Furthermore, he was conscious of the fact that, without Romero, he was even more isolated among the other bishops, who were of a conservative mentality. His principal support came from his auxiliary bishop, Gregorio Rosa Chávez.

In the vacuum created by Romero's death the episcopal conference, headed by José Eduardo Alvarez, attempted to assume leadership of the church. But the conference was dominated by conservatives and did not enjoy an easy rapport with progressives. Barely a month after Romero's murder a small incident brought this internal fissure to light. In May 1980 a group of priests, religious women, and laypersons founded CONIP: the National Coordinating Committee of the Oscar Romero Popular Church. The mere existence of such a group constituted a provocation for the conservative bishops who did not hesitate to condemn it outright.[22] In spite of this lack of support from the other bishops, and the pressure from Rome to maintain the appearance of episcopal unity, Rivera y Damas gradually began to show signs of following an independent course. In September 1981 Mexico and France recognized the FMLN as a "representative political force." This recognition was immediately rejected by the Salvadoran government as well as by the episcopal conference as an example of foreign interference in the country's internal affairs. But Rivera y Damas interpreted the recognition as an international call for dialogue between the government and the FMLN.[23] Finally, on the eve of the papal visit, Rivera y Damas was named archbishop of San Salvador. From that moment on he was able to follow a firmer course with respect to the rest of the hierarchy. For the progressives, he still seemed too moderate. Nevertheless, Rivera y Damas established clear lines of continuity with his predecessor, especially by creating Legal Defense (*Tutela Legal*) and by energetically promoting the idea of arriving at peace through dialogue. This last idea was rejected out of hand by the government, the political right, and conservative groups in the church as "treason." A mysterious group called the Traditional Catholic Movement severely criticized the archbishop for allowing the popular church to exist and for "forcing the country to enter into a sterile dialogue and to negotiate with subversion."[24]

Nonetheless, there were two factors that favored Rivera y Damas as an acceptable mediator for both sides. On the one hand, he was known to be sympathetic to the basic tenets of Christian Democracy, and he was a close friend of many leaders in that party, including President Duarte. On the other hand, the FMLN, which would have preferred Oscar Romero as mediator, recognized that Rivera y Damas defended Romero against the criticisms of the other bishops.

LEGAL DEFENSE

In 1983 Rivera y Damas founded Legal Defense. Like Legal Aid, which functioned under Romero, the new office aimed to investigate cases of disappearances, tortures, and human-rights violations in general. Under the direction of María Julia Hernández, Legal Defense came to be in El Salvador what the Vicariate of Solidarity was in Chile: a secure refuge for victims or relatives of victims of the civil war. It began modestly with three persons, but by 1994 it had twenty-two persons on its staff, including lawyers and social workers who visited jails, prisons, and police stations to guarantee the safety of persons accused of subversion. Legal Defense published detailed reports on all arrests, on the victims of violence, on disappeared persons, and so on. The reports, with names, dates, places, and circumstances, were so complete that they constituted the principal source the archbishop used for his denunciation of human-rights violations. Needless to say, Legal Defense was ignored by the government. On a few occasions the United States embassy publicly criticized the reports in order to ensure the certification of military aid to the government.[25] In spite of these criticisms Legal Defense received numerous international awards. It worked closely with the Red Cross and the United Nations.

THE FMLN AND THE CHURCH

In part the church was accepted as a mediator because of the close ties between the FMLN and progressive sectors in the church. The founders of the FMLN were almost all of Marxist-Leninist origins. By way of exception, some leaders of the ERP came from the ranks of Christian Democracy. With the passage of time, just as it happened in the case of the Sandinistas, Christian militants from the base ecclesial communities or from the popular organizations began to enroll in the ranks of the guerrillas. One guerrilla group—Popular Forces of Liberation—showed its awareness of that fact in 1975 when it published a public letter inviting "progressive Christians" to join the fight.[26] Of singular value in appreciating the religious factor in the history of the FMLN is the testimony of Eduardo Sancho Castañeda, known by his party name as Fermán Cienfuegos. He was a founder of National Resistance, one of the five groups that made up the FMLN. In his memoirs Cienfuegos refers frequently to Oscar Romero and speaks of "Christian revolutionary virtues." For him, Romero was a model of the "ethics of the New Man."[27] Cienfuegos goes on to recognize the role of the "Christian base movement" in awakening the social sensibility of the peasants and others.[28] Finally, he presents several examples of catechists who were models of "Christian revolutionary virtues."

Besides this sympathy toward Romero and the militant Christians, there were FMLN and FDR (Revolutionary Democratic Front) leaders who were practicing Catholics and who consciously identified their political commitment with their Christianity. Two FDR leaders, Guillermo Ungo and Rubén Zamora, were professors at the UCA and felt themselves supported by the Jesuits, especially the rector, Father Ignacio Ellacuría. Zamora, a former seminarian and president of the Commission of Justice and Peace before the beginning of the war, declared that it was his religious faith that led him to politics.[29] The ties between the UCA and the FDR were more than coincidental. The UCA participated in the foundation of the FDR as a "member-observer."[30] During the civil war certain FMLN and FDR leaders, such as *Comandante* Joaquín Villalobos—by invitation from the editors—published articles in *Estudios Centroamericanos*, the bi-monthly journal of the UCA.[31] For both Marxists and Christians the church's presence as a mediator was perfectly normal, although, naturally, the former preferred only progressive Christians.

THE AMBIGUITIES OF DIALOGUE

For the first years of the war the conditions for dialogue did not exist. The government, supported by the hardliners of the Reagan administration, looked for a purely military solution. The FMLN, buoyed up by its initial successes, also was not interested in dialogue. When the episcopal conference offered its good offices to mediate, that offer was not accepted because the FMLN did not trust the impartiality of most of the bishops after Romero's death. It was only after the war reached a stalemate that the first attempts at dialogue were made. In October 1982 Rivera y Damas turned over to the government a letter he had received from the FMLN-FDR. This was the first proposal seeking out dialogue, but nothing came of it. In 1983 President Reagan sent Richard Stone as his representative to meet with the FMLN. In July, Stone conversed with Rubén Zamora and other leaders in Bogotá under the protection of President Betancur.[32] That same month in the Colombian capital Zamora met with delegates of the Peace Commission who had been named by President Magaña. In neither of these meetings were there positive results. But the lack of results was due in large part to the ambiguous attitude of the government of the United States with respect to the very idea of having a dialogue with the FMLN-FDR.

In light of the fact that the massive military aid given to the Salvadoran government had not produced a victory, the moderates in the Reagan administration proposed a change of course. At the same time, the flagrant violations of human rights committed by the Salvadoran army and paramilitary groups only served to provide ammunition for Reagan's opponents in congress. The American president was under pressure not only to maintain the appearance of democracy in El Salvador but even to demonstrate a desire for peace. Herein lay the ambiguities. The American government insisted on elections being held in El Salvador and praised the idea of establishing a dialogue with the enemy. But in practice it did everything possible to place obstacles in the way of the dialogue. At heart, Reagan and his advisers did not really want a dialogue with Marxists, in whose word they did not believe. Neither did the American government seriously consider the demands of the FMLN to reform the El Salvadoran army and security forces. Instead, the Reagan administration increased aid to the Salvadoran government without imposing rigorous conditions on that aid. It was not until the end of the Reagan period that the American government began earnestly to promote the idea of dialogue between the parties in conflict. But there was another ambiguity: the Salvadoran government's lack of control over its own military and police. Although President Duarte went to meetings with the FMLN with the best of intentions, he did not have the power to do what the FMLN most wanted, namely, to impose control over the army and security forces and eliminate the death squads. Given the lack of interest on the part of the United States and the government's lack of control over its own forces, there was a consequent lack of realism in the attempt to promote a dialogue with the enemy.

La Palma and Ayagualo

In spite of these external and internal pressures not to dialogue, President Duarte (1984-89) decided to take the initiative anyway to establish the first formal dialogue with the FMLN. José Napoleón Duarte had been born in poverty, but thanks to the lottery his father won, he was able to graduate as a civil engineer from the University of Notre Dame in the United States. He was one of the principal founders of the Christian Democratic Party and was elected mayor of San Salvador twice. In 1972 he became a candidate for the presidency and won, but as we saw earlier, the army responded by jailing and then deporting him. He possessed qualities many admired; he was idealistic, determined, and generous. His political enemies accused him of being too pro-American, even to the extent of being obsequious. Although Reagan would have preferred someone more to the political right, he discovered in Duarte, who was neither left nor right, the acceptable man for Washington's plans. In May 1984 the two fronts, the FMLN and the FDR, through the mediating offices of the episcopal conference, invited the government to a meeting.[33] After his electoral victory that year Duarte assumed the presidency in June but did not answer the invitation until October. He answered it in a most dramatic fashion—in his inaugural address before the General Assembly of the United Nations, during which he made his own proposal for a dialogue with the guerrillas.[34] His announcement took many, including the American government, by surprise. For a meeting place he chose the small city of La Palma in Chalatenango, and he fixed the date for October 15.

The first meeting between the government and the guerrillas created great expectations. Duarte went to La Palma accompanied by his first vice president, the president of the Supreme Court, the minister of Defense, and several other ministers and advisers. The church was represented by the official mediator, Archbishop Rivera y Damas. He was accompanied by the auxiliary bishop, Gregorio Rosa Chávez, the man in charge of the office of the Holy See in El Salvador, Giacomo Ottonello, and other witnesses. The FDR was represented by Guillermo Ungo and Rubén Zamora, and the FMLN by the guerrilla commanders Fermán Cienfuegos, Facundo Guardado, Lucio Rivera, and Nidia Díaz. The two delegations met in the small parish church of the city; after shaking hands, they entered into an intense four-hour dialogue, interrupted by lunch. In his memoirs, Duarte underlines the cordial atmosphere during the interchange. Ungo and Zamora had been former political allies in the Christian Democratic Party, and Duarte knew the parents of Cienfuegos (Eduardo Sancho Castañeda). In fact, it almost seemed like a family reunion. Rivera y Damas began the meeting with a prayer and read the final communique. Although no substantive proposals were worked out, both sides agreed to form a commission to further the talks.[35] In this sense La Palma was clearly a success.

But the second meeting was less auspicious, and practically sealed an end to the dialogue. The meeting was held on November 29 in a former seminary in Ayagualo, near the capital. In fact, the general atmosphere was not propitious for a meeting. The day after the meeting at La Palma the FMLN launched another offensive, which resulted in the death of Colonel Domingo Monterrosa, the commander of the eastern region. Monterrosa was the man responsible for the massacre at Mozote in 1981 and was one of the most sought after targets of the guerrillas. Duarte himself did not go to Ayagualo but sent instead the minister of the Presidency, Julio Adolfo Rey Prendes. Both the FDR and the FMLN were represented by Rubén Zamora. Rivera y Damas presided over the meeting.

The FMLN produced a document entitled "A Global Proposal for a Negotiated Political Solution toward Peace." The proposal consisted of three stages: during the first stage, all American military aid to El Salvador would be eliminated; during the second, the guerrillas would be reincorporated into civilian life and would participate in the government; during the third stage, the army and the guerrillas would be fused together in a new, reorganized army.[36] For the first time a concrete proposal had been made to end the war. The meeting ended with public declarations by Zamora and Guardado that, in Duarte's opinion, were nothing but propaganda for their cause. In order not to give any more free publicity to the enemy Duarte decided to suspend further talks, at least for the time being.

In April and May of 1985 the FDR-FMLN sent messages through the church urging the government to return to dialogue.[37] But the government refused to dialogue under the conditions suggested by the enemy, such as meeting in territories controlled by the FMLN. In June an urban commando unit of the FMLN murdered four American marines who were unarmed and dressed as civilians, as well as seven civilians, in a restaurant in San Salvador. This brazen terrorist attack virtually put an end to any hopes of dialogue. Furthermore, the FMLN-FDR had lost confidence in the church. In August the episcopal conference published a letter entitled "Reconciliation and

Peace." But the two fronts rejected the letter, noting that it did not make any reference to the role of the United States in the war. Furthermore, it placed the human-rights violations committed by the FMLN on the same level with those of the military.[38]

THE KIDNAPPING OF INÉS GUADALUPE DE DUARTE

The next high-level meeting between the government and the FMLN was precipitated by a totally unexpected incident. On September 10, 1985, the president's thirty-five-year-old daughter, Inés Guadalupe de Duarte, and her friend, Ana Cecilia Villeda, were kidnapped by a FMLN commando unit. Two bodyguards were killed in the assault. Incursions like that into the private lives of politicians and the military were not a normal practice of the FMLN; however, they needed top-level "prisoners" to exchange for their own people. The army had managed to capture a good many of the FMLN's leaders, and the FMLN responded by capturing many Christian Democratic mayors in the zones under its control. Both sides therefore vied with one another in capturing prisoners. Kidnapping the president's daughter was part of this dangerous game. In this case, however, the FMLN's temerity backfired. Within hours thirty-four nations condemned the kidnapping. For his part, President Duarte was caught between two pressures: one, from the United States, the political right, and the armed forces of his own country, which advised against negotiating with the enemy under any pretext; and the other, his instinct as a father to save his daughter, as well as the many mayors who had been captured.[39]

Duarte went to the church for a solution, and the church organized a top-level meeting with the guerrillas. On October 15, in the small town of Guazapa, to the north of the capital, Archbishop Rivera y Damas and Father Ignacio Ellacuría, the rector (president) of the Central American University, were received by six FMLN commanders. This time Rivera y Damas acted as both mediator and representative of the government, with power of decision. The agreement made in Guazapa was the one that was finally adopted after several counter marches. According to the agreement Inés Guadalupe and her friend would be exchanged for twenty-two FMLN prisoners held by the army. Furthermore, as a second step, the mayors who were prisoners would be freed in exchange for ninety-six wounded guerrillas, who would be allowed to leave the country. The FMLN moved their wounded from place to place, and this was an opportunity to place them safely beyond the reach of the Salvadoran army. This idea was Rivera y Damas's.

The meeting in Guazapa was a victory for common sense and moderation. But disillusionment soon followed. Rivera y Damas had no sooner returned from Guazapa when the FMLN, perhaps believing that it could manipulate a father's sentiments for his daughter, added new demands. But world public opinion, including opinion from within the socialist world, was not sympathetic to the guerrillas. As a consequence, a new meeting was held on October 20 in Panama. For three days of intensive discussions, two representatives of the government, accompanied by the president's son, Alejandro Duarte, met with two representatives of the FMLN, in the presence of Rivera y Damas. Thanks to Rivera y Damas's insistence, the meeting, on the point of breaking off several times, continued. Finally, both sides ended up ratifying what had already been agreed upon in Guazapa, although one new point was added: in the future the families of politicians and the military were to be respected.[40]

The Panama agreements were signed on October 22 and executed on October 24. In what turned out to be a complicated logistical operation, Rivera y Damas, accompanied by Alejandro Duarte, a military aid of the president, representatives of the Red Cross, and diplomats from countries that supported the agreements (but not the United States), went to an abandoned town called Tenancingo, to the northeast of the capital. The FMLN arrived and turned over Inés Guadalupe and her friend; simultaneously, the government turned over 22 FMLN prisoners. Later that same day 25 mayors were exchanged for 101 wounded guerrillas, who received a safe conduct to leave the country. The speed and order with which the exchange was carried out surprised and pleased the official observers. When she was set free, Guadalupe Inés said goodbye to her captors with an embrace. In spite of the violence of the war, a civilized and human action had taken place. This was due in large part to the mediation of Rivera y Damas and his policy of "humanizing the war."

HUMANIZING THE WAR

The exchange in Tenancingo was the most dramatic example of a prisoner exchange during the war, but it was not the only one. Earlier, in December 1984, Rivera y Damas had presided over an exchange ceremony in La Joya, in San Vicente. On that occasion several FMLN commanders turned over forty-three army soldiers to Archbishop Rivera y Damas, who was accompanied by his auxiliary bishop and a Red Cross committee. The exchange was preceded by a religious and civil service. Rivera y Damas greeted the FMLN commanders and cited Matthew 25, which refers to prisoners. He ended his address by praising the commanders:

I wish once again to thank you in the name of the church for this gesture and I wish to give witness that these soldiers have been treated with humanity. Let this be an example so that all prisoners be humanly treated; this way we will truly humanize this conflict.[41]

The new meetings between both sides, occasioned by the kidnapping of the president's daughter, had the salutary effect of opening the doors once again to dialogue. Archbishop Rivera y Damas's insistence on humanizing the war, something akin to the rules for a just war in the Middle Ages, reinforced the efforts of both the military and the FMLN to control the extremists among them. However, as later history would show, that call had more effect on the latter than on the former.

FROM SESORI TO THE NUNCIATURE (1987)

The road to dialogue turned out to be quite tortuous and rocky. Throughout 1988 several attempts were made to reestablish contact between the government and the FMLN, but in vain. In May, Archbishop Rivera y Damas went to Panama to meet Ungo and Zamora and other FDR-FMLN leaders, and in July he went to Morazán in the eastern part of El Salvador to hand over a government proposal to the FMLN. Finally, in August the government and the FMLN sent representatives to Mexico to prepare for the third high level meeting (the first having been in La Palma and the second in Ayagualo). Rivera y Damas was also present. After another preparatory meeting in Panama, the eastern Salvadoran city of Sesori was selected for the meeting and the date was set for September 19. Sesori turned out to be a total failure, if not an outright farce. The FDR-FMLN fronts announced that they would not go to Sesori unless the area around the city was demilitarized. But the government, claiming that the FMLN would use the opportunity to seize the area, rejected that condition. In spite of the fact that he knew the FMLN would not show up, Duarte insisted on going anyway, accompanied by the highest officials of his government. The church's representative was Bishop René Revelo, the president of the episcopal conference. Rivera y Damas's absence raised eyebrows.[42] He apparently had more common sense, or less inclination to indulge in expeditions aimed to produce publicity, than the president of the republic. After Sesori the dialogue ceased.

But a year later hope was born again. This time the stimulus to dialogue came from the collective presidents of Central America, who signed the Esquipulas II agreements in Guatemala City on August 7, 1987. According to the agreements, each government in the region with internal conflicts should establish dialogue with the rebels in arms, declare a cease fire, and create a commission of national reconciliation. Duarte himself explained the agreements to the bishops on August 12, with the aim of creating El Salvador's commission. In the meantime, Rivera y Damas was busy acting as intermediary. In September he flew twice to Panama to hand over the government's proposals to the FDR-FMLN for the third high-level meeting. Each time he returned with counter proposals from the FDR-FMLN for the government. Finally, it was agreed to have the third meeting in the papal nunciature in San Salvador on October 4 and 5.

The government was represented by Duarte, several ministers, the secretary general of the Confederation of Workers, and a businessman. The representatives of the FDR-FMLN arrived accompanied by the ambassadors of friendly countries. Some arrived from within El Salvador and others from outside. The FDR was represented by Guillermo Ungo, Rubén Zamora, Jorge Villacorta, and Héctor Oquelí, and the FMLN by Shafik Handal, Leonel González, Jorge Meléndez, and Facundo Guardado. Rivera y Damas acted as moderator at the meeting, and Gregorio Rosa Chávez as his assistant. The host was, of course, the apostolic nuncio, Francesco de Nittis. After the nuncio offered a welcome to all, Rivera y Damas made a religious invocation, and then the representatives went to work. The third major meeting in the civil war began at 1:30 in the afternoon and ended at midnight the next day.

Both sides agreed to create mixed commissions: one to study the possibility of a cease fire; another to examine the other points in Esquipulas II. Rivera y Damas was named president of both commissions. The commissions were formally installed on October 21 in Caracas.[43] Without doubt, the meeting at the nunciature was the most serious and important of the three summit meetings. At La Palma the government and the revolutionaries met face to face. At Ayagualo general proposals were made, but little else. In the nunciature, for the first time, both sides agreed to work on concrete points. FDR-FMLN leaders criticized the agreements made in the nunciature for reducing the problem to technicalities, while obviating the root causes of the war.[44] Nevertheless, they accepted the agreements as a first necessary step. Great expectations had been raised when once again an act of violence jeopardized the entire process. On October 26 Herbert Anaya Sanabria, the director of the non-governmental Commission of Human Rights of El Salvador, was murdered. President Duarte, who denied the existence of the death squads, declared that the murder was probably the work of a lone madman. But this convinced no one; everyone believed that Sanabria had been killed by a death squad tied to the police or to the military.[45] Sanabria's murder destroyed the atmosphere of good will and the dialogue was once again broken off.

There was another motive for suspending dialogue. With the aim of putting Esquipulas II into effect, the national assembly passed an amnesty law. The law granted a pardon to all military and guerrillas, with the exception of those involved in the murders of Archbishop Romero and Herbert Anaya. The leaders of the FDR-FMLN objected that the law, passed without their approval, was an insult to justice. Hundreds of crimes committed by the military, the police, and the death squads would be forgiven.

THE CHURCH AND THE NATIONAL DEBATE (1988)

In the midst of these failures to establish dialogue the church used a new strategy to bring both sides back to the conference table. In June 1988 Rivera y Damas announced a plan to hold a "national debate for peace." One of the principal objectives of the debate was to "achieve a wide consensus on certain minimal points which would be sufficient for a prompt cease fire and the elimination of the causes of the conflict."[46] The archbishop invited 129 educational, cultural, and popular organizations and associations to the debate. Finally, 60 groups—universities, unions, and cultural associations—accepted the invitation. Four non-Catholic churches were present. Among the groups that did not accept the invitation were the Chamber of Commerce and Industry, the Coffee Association, and the Evangelical University of El Salvador. The first two represented the landed oligarchy and the business class, and the last represented the fundamentalist Protestants. The debate, which was held in Holy Family School between September 3 and 4, with Rivera y Damas presiding and Rosa Chávez acting as vice president, was a great success. Part of its success was due to the fact that the most difficult part had been accomplished before the event itself. Each group had previously answered a very detailed survey and sent in its observations. During the debate itself the representatives could see where everyone stood on every important issue. According to the survey results, 82 percent of the participants condemned the war as a solution to the country's problems. Also, 82 percent held that elections "by themselves would not guarantee democracy." There was total unanimity on the proposition that "dialogue constitutes the most rational, just, and Christian method for a solution to the conflict."[47] There was less agreement on other points. Only 39 percent accepted the proposition that the FMLN be recognized as a legitimate insurgent movement.[48]

The political parties themselves did not participate in the debate. Rather, they and their candidates for the 1989 elections made their opinions known in a forum on national reality organized by the Central American University as a follow-up to the National Debate. The left was represented by Guillermo Ungo, the candidate of Democratic Convergence; Rafael Morán Castañeda, of the Party of National Conciliation; and Fidel Chávez Mena, of the Christian Democrats. At first, ARENA, the party of the new right, rejected out of hand dialoguing with the enemy, and as a consequence severely criticized the National Debate. In light of that, the surprise appearance in the forum of Alfredo Cristiani, ARENA's candidate, was well received. Even more surprising was his declaration that he agreed with 85 percent of the resolutions in the final document of the National Debate.[49]

Archbishop Rivera y Damas personally handed the final document over to President Duarte. This was a symbolic gesture, because Duarte was well informed on what had been discussed in the National Debate. More important than the details was the significance of the debate. For the first time during the war an independent public forum—which represented important sectors in society, minus the extreme right—had conducted its own dialogue on the problems of the country, including the war. The debate constituted a sort of national mandate for both the government and the guerrillas to get back to the conference table. Furthermore, the final document, along with the survey, constituted the basis for a new national consensus. In this sense the church had effectively applied pressure on the government and the FMLN to respond to a new agenda no longer established by them alone.

ARENA AND THE FMLN

In 1989 Duarte and his Christian Democrats turned power over to Alfredo Cristiani of ARENA. In elections held on May 19, Cristiani won by 53.8 percent of the total vote, followed by Fidel Chávez, the Christian Democratic candidate, with 36 percent. Given its origins as a party of the extreme right, ARENA's victory was a cause for concern. Founded in 1981, ARENA (National Republican Alliance) was initially built around its founder, Roberto D'Aubuisson. It was anticommunist, anti–social democrat and anti–North American. Further, D'Aubuisson was the mastermind behind the death squads. He kept close contact with officers in the army who shared his ideas. He was declared persona non grata in the United States and was denied permission to enter the country, although he did enter illegally to speak to groups that supported him.

In spite of this sinister history, D'Aubuisson had already begun to lose influence in the party, while Alfredo Cristiani, son of one of the important coffee families and a graduate of Georgetown University, represented a more moderate right that gradually displaced the old rightwing. On the very day that he assumed power—June 1—Cristiani announced his intention of dialoguing with the revolutionaries, a gesture that would have qualified as treason in his own party a few years earlier. This change in power in El Salvador coincided with the change in power in the United States, from Reagan to Bush. Bush, who followed a more pragmatic and less ideological line than his predecessor, would find it comfortable to deal with a man who represented the same tendency in El Salvador. The D'Aubuissons of El Salvador clearly belonged to the Reagan era.

In August, after consulting with Rubén Zamora of Democratic Convergence, Cristiani created a commission to dialogue with the FMLN. The first meeting between the new government and the FMLN was held in Mexico between September 13 and 15. A second meeting in San José, Costa Rica, was agreed upon. ARENA's representatives were new at the dialogue. But those of the FMLN—Joaquín Villalobos, Shafik Handal, and others—were veterans. On the other hand, the absence of Rivera y Damas was quite noticeable. ARENA, which preferred churchmen on the right, designated as the new mediator Bishop Romeo Tovar, president of the episcopal conference and a leading conservative. Tovar was unable to attend the San José meeting, so he sent in his place Marco René Revelo, an old critic of Oscar Romero. As Archbishop Rivera y Damas put it: "The church doesn't have the same closeness with ARENA as it did with the Christian Democrats."[50] Nevertheless, Gregorio Rosa Chávez, who enjoyed Rivera y Damas's confidence, was present at both the Mexico and the San José meetings. Also, Bishop Vicente Juan Segura, the Vatican's representative, was present in San José. President Arias of Costa Rica made a personal plea to both sides to further the peace process.

In San José there was another novelty: for the first time the United Nations and the Organization of American States were present. In the beginning they only participated as observers. But within time the United Nations, through the special representative of Secretary General Javier Pérez de Cuéllar, Alvaro de Soto, assumed a more active role in the dialogue. In spite of this propitious beginning, the dialogue soon ran into a wall of unmovable positions. The critical point was the FMLN's insistence that the armed forces and the police be reorganized as a condition to putting an end to the war. In the words of one of the FMLN's spokesmen: "If they don't cleanse the army of murderers and corrupt officials, there is no possibility of democracy, and without democracy there can be no peace."[51] However, the dialogue was aborted not because of this issue but because of new acts of violence. On October 31 a bomb destroyed the headquarters of the National Federation of Salvadoran Workers and ten union leaders were killed. And on November 11 the FMLN initiated the biggest offensive in the war. Given this violent atmosphere, a third meeting between ARENA and the FMLN, scheduled for Caracas on November 20 and 21, was canceled.

THE MASSACRE OF THE SIX JESUITS

In the early hours of November 16, while FMLN forces seized sections of the capital, a group of soldiers belonging to the Atlacatl Battalion entered the Central American University (UCA) and killed six Jesuit priests along with the cook and her daughter. The victims included Father Ignacio Ellacuría (the rector), Ignacio Martín-Baró (the vice rector), Segundo Montes, Amando López, Joaquín López y López, and Ramón Moreno, all professors at the university. The cook was Julia Elba Ramos; her daughter was Celina Mariceth Ramos. The news of the cold-blooded murder of the Jesuits and the two women went around the world, producing disbelief and universal indignation.

Since the time of Oscar Romero, and even before, the Society of Jesus and the UCA had been favorite targets of the right and the death squads. In 1977—the year that Rutilio Grande was murdered—the White Warrior Union threatened all Jesuits with death if they did not leave the country within thirty days. On several occasions bombs had been exploded within the UCA and near the building where *ECA* (the Central American Studies journal) was published. It was common in the army and the police to refer to the UCA as a "refuge for subversives." But the Jesuit who drew most of the hostility was Ignacio Ellacuría, a Spaniard by birth, who arrived in El Salvador in 1948 as a young Jesuit student. Ellacuría, whose professional specialty included both theology and philosophy, assumed direction of *ECA* in 1976, and in 1979 he became rector of the university. In his writings and addresses he advocated a negotiated solution to the war and rejected any purely military solution. He did not approve of the FMLN's violence. On the contrary, he invited *ECA*'s readers to debate and discuss the political and social causes of the conflict. In his desire to foster dialogue he even invited leaders of the FDR and the FMLN to express their views in the journal. In 1985 he created a "National Reality" chair to promote discussion of the country's problems. He participated with Archbishop Rivera y Damas in the negotiations to liberate President Duarte's daughter. Along with the other Jesuits he disseminated the social doctrine of the church in his theology classes and in other public forums. Although half of the students at the UCA were from the upper classes and did not share the Jesuits' enthusiasm for social change, nevertheless they respected their teachers as men of integrity and as friends. But the extreme rightwing was convinced that Ellacuría and the other Jesuits at the UCA had ties with the FMLN. Some even believed that the Jesuits were the intellectual masterminds of the revolution. As in the case of Oscar Romero, the extreme rightwing and many in the military saw the Jesuits as traitors to the established order.

The army denied any knowledge of the crime and tried to place the blame on the FMLN. Nevertheless, under pressure from the United States, President Cristiani admitted on January 13, 1990, that the murderers were indeed army men. Nine military men were brought before a court, and after two years, two of them, Colonel Alfredo Benavides Moreno, the director of the nearby Military School, from which the soldiers left on their way to the UCA, and Lieutenant Yusshy René Mendoza, were finally sentenced to thirty years in prison. The sentence, which was handed down in September 1991, produced an outcry of protest as it was quite evident that the two officers were but sacrificial lambs served up to protect the real authors of the crime. Three different groups, each one independent of the others, came to the conclusion that the orders to murder the Jesuits had been issued by the high command of the Salvadoran army, which also authorized the subsequent cover-up of the crime. One of those groups was the Special Commission of the House of Representatives of the United States, headed by Congressman Joe Moakley of Boston. Moakley, who took his mission quite seriously, visited El Salvador on many occasions and did not hesitate to voice his opinion that "the high command of the Salvadoran army is involved in a conspiracy to block justice."[52] The second group was the Lawyers Committee for Human Rights based in Washington, D.C. The Lawyers Committee for Human Rights had earlier represented the families of the four American women who were killed in 1980, and during the entire war it followed events in El Salvador very closely. The third group was the Truth Commission of the United Nations, created for the purpose of investigating the violations of human rights, and especially the crimes committed by both sides during the war. All three groups were completely agreed, with concrete names, that many Salvadoran officials of the high command were directly involved in the deaths of the Jesuits.[53]

On November 16, 1992, the third anniversary of the massacre, the provincial of the Society of Jesus in Central America, José María Tojeira, formally requested a pardon for the two officers who had been condemned. He explained that his religious order did not want vengeance but rather justice and the truth. In his opinion, because of the cover-up, neither justice nor truth was being served. In April 1993 Salvadoran justice, following the recommendations of the Truth Commission, which in turn respected the desires of the Jesuits, released the two officers. But the principal authors of the crime never came to trial. In the course of the investigations conducted by Moakley's commission and the Lawyers Committee it was also established that the United States government had participated in the cover-up. A major in the American army, who served as an adviser to the Salvadoran army, was among the first to accuse Salvadoran officials of the killing of the Jesuits. But later on that same official was silenced by his own government.[54] In this case the American government's motive not to investigate the crime too deeply was to prevent a major crisis in the Salvadoran army. Such a crisis would not be compatible with the government's own program to aid the Salvadoran military.

The death of the Jesuits was the most dramatic act in the war since the assassination of Bishop Romero and the four American women. Once again El Salvador came to be synonymous with death squads and savagery. While it is impossible to measure the exact weight the massacre in the UCA had in influencing the events that led to peace in El Salvador, it certainly was important. When the government and the FMLN finally got back to the conference table, world pressure had increased notably to arrive at a negotiated peace. The killing of the Jesuits had a direct impact in the congress of the United States. One year after the massacre, in the light of the slow progress of the investigation, the senate voted, 74 to 24, to cut military aid to El Salvador by 50 percent. The remaining 50 percent depended upon receiving a commitment from the Salvadoran government that it would enter into serious negotiations with the FMLN to bring those responsible for the crime to trial.[55] The lower house had already approved a similar motion. In this sense the massacre of the Jesuits served to bear great pressure on the Bush administration, which in turn applied pressure on President Cristiani to produce results. However, President Bush managed to avoid having the congressional motion put into practice by the simple expedient of advancing money to the Salvadoran government. Furthermore, he justified not cutting off military aid by pointing to human-rights violations committed by the guerrillas. Nevertheless, the alarm had been sounded. It became increasingly clear to the American government that the policy of defending the Salvadoran government and military with closed eyes no longer had much support. Pragmatic political instinct rather than a sense of ethics convinced the administration that a negotiated peace was the only viable way out of the crisis in El Salvador.

THE ROAD TO PEACE

The death of the six Jesuits was one of the worst acts of violence in the war; it also signaled the beginning of the end. Several external and internal factors combined to pressure both sides to arrive at a negotiated peace. The most important external factors were the end of the Reagan administration (January 1989) and the end of the Cold War. In the new post–Cold War world the civil war in El Salvador ceased to have the same importance for the Bush administration as it did for Reagan's. The electoral defeat of the Sandinistas in January 1990 also served to tranquilize the American government. Increasingly, the government came to believe that a negotiated peace was both desirable and possible. As far as internal factors, the political right in El Salvador under Cristiani moderated its positions and came to accept the idea of dialoguing with the FMLN. At the same time, the FMLN, finding itself isolated after the Sandinistas' defeat, and seeing the signs of the times in Europe, moderated many of its Marxist positions.

When the two parties met for the first time since the tragedy in the UCA— in April 1990 in Geneva—there was another novelty: the principal mediator was no longer the church but the United Nations, represented by Alvaro de Soto. In December 1989 the Central American governments had met in San José (Costa Rica) and formally requested Secretary General Javier Pérez de Cuéllar to assume the task of mediating in El Salvador. In January 1990 Alvaro de Soto met with representatives of the FMLN in New York, and shortly after that President Cristiani accepted the mediation of the United Nations. The church ceded its mediating function to the United Nations basically because it had already fulfilled its mission, which was to begin the dialogue and to move it forward. Furthermore, the United Nations emissaries, unlike churchmen, were prepared to discuss technical topics such as restructuring the armed forces, retraining the police, reforming the constitution, and so forth. After the meeting in Geneva many other meetings were held in rapid succession: in Caracas, Oaxtepec, San José (three times), and in 1991 in Chiapas, San José (again), and Mexico. In April 1991 the Mexican Agreements, which constituted a decisive step forward, were signed. In May the Security Council of the United Nations created ONUSAL: the Mission of Observers of the United Nations in El Salvador. The mission of ONUSAL consisted in watching over the process of transition from war to peace. Also, the National Commission for the Consolidation of Peace (COPAZ) was created to help implement the peace agreements. COPAZ was made up of representatives of the government, the political parties, the FMLN, Archbishop Rivera y Damas, and the Lutheran bishop, Medarno Gómez. After other meetings in Mexico two final meetings were held in New York. During these last encounters both President Bush and Secretary General Pérez de Cuéllar applied pressure on President Cristiani to give in on what had been the crucial point in the dialogue since 1984: the reform and reorganization of the armed forces and the police. In the second meeting, in December, conscious that his term was about to end, Pérez de Cuéllar pushed both sides to finish their work. On December 31, with hardly a minute to spare, both parties committed themselves formally to sign a peace agreement.[56] For all practical purposes the war ended at this point. Only a final ceremony was needed.

CHAPULTEPEC: THE FINAL CELEBRATION

On January 16, 1992, in the historic castle of Chapultepec, the principal protagonists—friends and enemies—in the Salvadoran civil war gathered together. Under the presidency of Boutros Ghali, the new secretary general of the United Nations, accompanied by Joâo Baena, the secretary general of the Organization of American States, and in the presence of eight presidents (Mexico, Spain, Colombia, Venezuela, Guatemala, Honduras, Costa Rica, and Nicaragua), Alfredo Cristiani and representatives of the Salvadoran government met face to face with the principal commanders of the FMLN—Shafik Handal, Ana Guadalupe Martínez, Nidia Díaz, Joaquín Villalobos, Eduardo Sancho, and others. Together they signed the peace agreements that put an end to twelve years of civil war. Two former presidents were also present: Daniel Ortega of Nicaragua and Oscar Arias of Costa Rica. Many foreign ministers, as well as U.S. Secretary of State James Baker, observed the ceremony. Among the intellectuals invited were Archbishop Arturo Rivera y Damas and a representative of the papal nunciature. The gesture that drew most attention was Cristiani's initiative to shake hands with Shafik Handal, the principal spokesman for the FMLN.[57] One important person was absent; José Napoleón Duarte had died of cancer in 1990.

The agreements demanded the immediate demobilization of the FMLN and its incorporation into the civil life of El Salvador. The army was given two years in which to reorganize itself; that included reducing its size considerably. The National Guard and the Rural Police—two groups notorious for their human-rights violations—were abolished. The agreements also created the Truth Commission to investigate crimes and acts of violence committed during the war. With these and other agreements the peace process began.

THE TRUTH COMMISSION AND THE AMNESTY LAW

The Truth Commission, created by the United Nations and the agreements of Chapultepec, fulfilled the same mission in El Salvador that the commission presided over by Ernesto Sábato did in Argentina and the Retting Commission did in Chile. Its function was to clarify the truth about hundreds of crimes, murders, and other grave acts of violence committed during the civil war. Unlike the other cases, however, the Truth Commission was not created by the Salvadoran government but rather by the United Nations. The high commissioners appointed to preside over the commission were Belisario Betancur, former president of Colombia; Reinaldo Figueredo Planchart, former minister of Foreign Affairs of Venezuela; and Thomas Buergenthal, an academic and a distinguished jurist of the United States. They were advised by a multinational team of lawyers and human-rights advocates. They decided to investigate thirty cases of "grave acts of violence," based on twenty-two thousand denunciations. When their report was published on March 15, 1993, it provoked a cry of indignation in Cristiani's government and the rightwing media in El Salvador. The report named names of military men and important politicians who were accused of being implicated in the death of Archbishop Romero (Roberto D'Aubuisson), in the massacre of the Jesuits (General René Emilio Ponce, minister of Defense, 1990-93), and in other crimes. Among its most important findings the report concluded that 85 percent of all human-rights violations were committed by "agents of the state," paramilitary groups, and death squads. Only 5 percent were attributed to the FMLN.[58]

It was evident that the commission hoped that its conclusions would prod the government to take the initiative and try the guilty. But in open defiance of the commission, the national assembly, dominated by ARENA, approved a general amnesty for all the military and others who had participated in the war. The Salvador government did what the Argentinean military tried to do: produced a national reconciliation by wiping the slate clean, but with no trials. In the midst of the general rejoicing over the peace that had come, the bitter note of justice denied was interjected. Although there were no trials to judge the guilty, at least there remained the consolation that most of their names were on public record. Finally, during the first months of the Clinton administration, many documents in the State Department, Defense Department, and the Central Intelligence Agency were declassified. These documents confirmed that the government of the United States had treated the death squads with benevolence and had ignored reports about human-rights violations in El Salvador.[59]

THE CHURCH AND THE PEACE

Although justice was denied, peace had arrived, and El Salvador entered a new chapter in its history. The death squads continued to function, especially on the occasion of the 1994 elections. Nevertheless, the atmosphere in the country was noticeably different than it had been when the civil war began. Under the supervision of the United Nations, the Chapultepec agreements and other reforms were put into practice. In January 1992 Arturo Rivera y Damas, the man who, along with President Duarte, helped initiate this entire process, was elected president of the episcopal conference. This was a bit surprising given the fact that the conservative bishops still dominated the conference. Also, in September of 1992, at the request of the FMLN, Rivera y Damas witnessed the oath which the guerrilla commanders took as they converted their army into a political party.[60] This gesture symbolized the role of the church in general during the entire Salvadoran conflict. Through its efforts to mediate, the church sought to reconcile antagonistic forces and to legitimate the new democratic order that arose out of that reconciliation. In 1994, at the age of seventy-two, Rivera y Damas died—a man of peace who fought for peace.

10.

Nicaragua (1979-1990)

Christians and Sandinistas

For progressive Latin American Christians, especially in Central America, the history of Nicaragua, from the overthrow of Somoza in 1979 until the 1990 elections, seemed like a triumphal march that turned into a Greek tragedy. For the first time in contemporary Latin America the possibility existed to forge a Christian-socialist society. Unlike the Cuban revolution, in which the church had little participation, the Christians in Nicaragua participated directly in the Sandinista revolution and worked with enthusiasm to reconstruct the country after that revolution.

But the Sandinista experiment turned out to be a great disillusionment for many Christians who contributed to the process. To begin with, Nicaragua, like El Salvador, was converted into a key piece in President Ronald Reagan's plans to stop the advance of communism in the context of the Cold War. By conducting a war of "low intensity," the American president did all he could to destabilize the Sandinista regime and cripple the country economically. At the same time, unlike in El Salvador, the church was strongly divided. Cardinal Obando, who had supported the revolution against Somoza, openly supported Reagan and the Contras in their opposition to the Sandinistas. Finally, the Sandinistas themselves committed their own quota of errors, which led to their failure. In the 1990 elections, which they lost by a wide margin, the dream of a socialist, Christian democracy, forged by an alliance between Marxists and Christians, faded away.

Nevertheless, with the aid of hindsight, certain positive lessons stand out, especially if we compare Nicaragua's process with that of Cuba. The Cuban revolution was closed to Christians, who in any case did not have a significant presence in it. But in Nicaragua Christians stood out for their presence in the revolution: first in the struggle against Somoza; and later in the Sandinista regime, where they served as a counterweight to the totalitarian tendencies of some of the Sandinistas. In fact, thanks to their presence, Nicaragua did not become "another Cuba." The influence of the Christians can be seen in the educational reform and in the construction of a new popular patriotism. Finally, it is important to note that there were free elections held under the Sandinistas: first in 1984, which the United States did not recognize, and then in 1990, which the Sandinistas lost. The holding of free elections highlights one of the important differences between Nicaragua and Cuba: in the former, thanks to the pragmatism of the Sandinistas and the democratic convictions of the Christians on both sides of the fence, a peaceful transition was made to traditional, multiparty democracy in 1990. Thus the Christian-Sandinista experiment was not, in reality, a tragedy, but rather a painful but instructive step in a long road toward the consolidation of a mature democracy. What is clear is that the tension between the Christians, those who supported the government and those of the middle and upper classes who united around Cardinal Obando, injected in the ideological struggle in Nicaragua a religious element that was absent in the Cuban revolution. At every stage religion was a key element: in the revolution to overthrow Somoza; in the Sandinista experiment; and in the effort to arrive at a viable peace in the transition from the Sandinista to the post-Sandinista period.

In this chapter we will begin by reviewing the political background of the revolution; then we will look at the church during that same period; finally, we will analyze the different stages in the relationship between church and society during the Sandinista regime.

BACKGROUND: LIBERALS, CONSERVATIVES, AND MARINES

Just as in other parts of Latin America, Nicaragua suffered the consequences of a liberal-conservative struggle. The conservatives, whose principal base was Granada, took power in 1857 after overthrowing William Walker, the American filibuster who had been supported by the liberals. But the liberals returned to power in 1893 under General José Santos Zelaya. The liberals, whose principal base was León, represented the modernizing sectors among the coffee producers. As part of this modernizing thrust, Zelaya promulgated several anticlerical laws: he separated church from state, confiscated lands and profits from the confraternities, expelled many religious, and opened the doors to Protestantism. But he was overthrown in 1909 by a conservative revolution aided by a contingent of American marines. The marines left but returned in 1912. This time they stayed until 1933.

The American presence in Nicaragua responded in part to purely economic interests. But it also reflected the designs of a new world power that was establishing its hegemony in the entire Caribbean area.[1] According to the Bryan-Chamorro treaty, signed in 1914, Nicaragua ceded to the United States in perpetuity the exclusive right to build a canal through Nicaragua. Although the canal was never built, a naval base was established there.

The marines were not really an occupying force—they rarely had more than a hundred men—but rather a vanguard to watch over the internal affairs of the country. During the period in which they remained in the country there were elections, almost always favorable to the pro-American conservatives. The country otherwise enjoyed a measure of internal stability. Among the conservative families, one of the most important was the Chamorros, who produced three presidents: two who came to power through elections, and one by means of a revolution. It was during the civil war provoked by General Emilio Chamorro that Augusto César Sandino emerged as a popular hero. Sandino, a liberal military man, demanded that all American troops leave Nicaragua, and he also called for social reforms.

Finally, in 1933, the marines did leave. As a way of guaranteeing the peace, they created a National Guard, which took the place of both the police and the military. The president who had been elected under the supervision of the marines, Dr. Juan Sacasa, invited Sandino to dinner as a peace offering from the government to the rebels. When he left the dinner, Sandino was assassinated by members of the new National Guard, under the command of Anastasio ("Tacho") Somoza García.

The Somoza Dynasty

The Somozas constituted a classic example of a dynasty of dictators.[2] For more than forty years they dominated Nicaragua, which became practically a family fiefdom. The key to their power was control of the National Guard. Anastasio Somoza, head of the National Guard, waited until 1936 before making himself president of the country. He forced President Sacasa to resign and, after a brief intermission, had himself elected president as the Liberal Party candidate. During the Second World War and the Cold War Somoza was openly pro-American, an attitude that won him many economic and military favors from Washington. In 1947 he left power and allowed Leonardo Argüello, of his own party, to succeed him. When Argüello attempted to dismiss Somoza as head of the National Guard, Somoza responded by overthrowing him—twenty-six days after Argüello's inauguration as president. In the following years other figures were elected president of the country, but none of them forgot the lesson learned from the Argüello incident: in Nicaragua, Somoza had the final word. In 1950, after making a pact with the Traditional-Conservative Party, Somoza returned to the presidency. In 1956 Anastasio Somoza was assassinated. The Nicaraguan congress immediately appointed his son, Luis A. Somoza Debayle, as his successor. The second Somoza governed until 1963 when, under pressure from the American government, he handed power over to René Schick Gutiérrez. Schick, who carried out a few limited social reforms, died in 1966 before finishing his term.

In 1967 new presidential elections were held and, in the midst of a massive fraud, the third of the Somozas was elected: Anastasio ("Tachito") Somoza Debayle, the son of the first Somoza and younger brother of Luis Somoza, who died that year. The third Somoza, who graduated from West Point, was promoted to the rank of general at the age of thirty. He was designated head of the National Guard in 1966. In 1971 he left the presidency in the hands of a triumvirate of civilians; but with the legitimization a new constitution gave him, he returned to the presidency in 1972 and was reelected in 1974. Tachito Somoza was as dictatorial and cruel as his father and brother but not as prudent. Under him, official corruption reached scandalous levels, so much so that the middle classes seriously discussed ways of removing him. By that time, also, the government of the United States had begun to question its own policy of unconditional support of the Somozas in the name of anticommunism. Finally, a new threat loomed on the horizon: guerrilla warfare in the hills. Although it had existed for some time, it was not until 1961 that the local guerrilla movement officially adopted the name Sandinista Front for National Liberation (*Frente Sandinista de la Liberación Nacional*, or FSLN).

THE CHURCH: BACKGROUND

The church in Nicaragua is small. In 1988 there was one archdiocese (Managua), four dioceses, two prelatures, and one apostolic vicariate. Altogether, there were 167 priests of the diocesan clergy and 272 belonging to the religious clergy.[3] Close to 60 percent of all priests were foreign-born.[4] In spite of this priest shortage popular Catholicism, which emerged in colonial times, is still quite strong. There are many popular devotions: St. Dominic in Managua, *el Madero* (the cross) in Masaya, the Lord of Esquipulas, and others. At times the bishops have tried to change some of these devotions, but their efforts usually have run into stiff resistance.[5] Religion, with all its devotions and holidays, constituted the heart of popular culture in Nicaragua long before the Sandinistas. In many ways the mystique of the revolution turned out to be a fusion of this deep popular religiosity with the new revolutionary fervor. Some of the popular religious feast days, such as the *Purísima* (the Immaculate Conception), became sources of friction between the church and the Sandinista regime.

The nineteenth-century church was very conservative, but it had not always been that way. There were liberal priests, notably the Indian priest Tomás Ruiz, who fought for independence. Later there were priests who opposed William Walker and his Anglo-Saxon racism, although there were also priests who supported him. Nineteenth-century liberals were quite sectarian and unnecessarily drove many Catholics to the conservative side. Zelaya, as we saw earlier, expelled many religious and expropriated the wealth of the confraternities. Although the bishops had good reasons to fear American Protestant soldiers in their country, they supported them because they restored the conservative oligarchy to power. Finally, when the liberals managed to return to power, they had learned one lesson: the anticlericalism of Zelaya and other liberals had been excessive, and the church could, in fact, be an ally. Under the leadership of José Antonio Lezcano, archbishop of Managua (1913-53), the church managed to regain its social position in society by means of an alliance with both conservatives and liberals. During Sandino's insurrection the bishops exhorted the rebels to put down their arms, and one bishop blessed the arms of the Americans.[6]

The church's relationship with the Somozas until 1972, with a couple of notable exceptions, can be summed up very simply: total legitimization. Archbishop Lezcano, in hopes of receiving protection and favors—which Somoza never denied him—offered unconditional support to his regime. There is no better example of this exchange of support than the ceremony carried out in the national stadium in 1942, during which the archbishop crowned the dictator's daughter "Queen of the Army" with a golden crown taken from the Virgin of Candelaria.[7] One single bishop, Octavio José Calderón Padilla of Matagalpa (1947-70), dared to criticize Somoza and the system of economic exploitation. During this period the Jesuits, expelled in 1881, returned, and many new congregations arrived: the Capuchins, the Josephines, the brothers of LaSalle, the Salesians, and others.

THE CHURCH RENEWS ITSELF

In the decade of the sixties, just as in the rest of Latin America, the Nicaraguan church experimented with a number of important changes that gave it an entirely new orientation. Only in the diocese of Matagalpa in the northern hills was there any continuity between the pre-Vatican and the post-Vatican church. Bishop Calderón Padilla promoted Rural Catholic Action and the base ecclesial communities. In the sixties certain other movements, such as the cursillos of Cristianidad and Charismatic Renewal, had a big impact on the middle and lower-middle classes. In the rural areas the Capuchins in Zelaya founded radio schools, eventually supporting ninety-eight centers for two thousand students.[8] The schools aimed to conscienticize the peasants as well as make them literate. Also, in 1973, the Jesuits founded the Center of Education and Agrarian Promotion (CEPA) to train delegates of the Word. Many of those delegates later participated as leaders in the Sandinista revolution. On the Atlantic coast the Capuchins devoted themselves to the formation of native leaders among the Miskito Indians. In Managua, the Central American University (UCA), founded by the Jesuits in 1961, became an important center for social and political criticism in the seventies. In 1965 Uriel Molina, a Franciscan, founded a university community in a neighborhood called Riguero in the capital. Father Molina was one of the first priests to enter into contact with the Sandinistas. In the parish of St. Paul the Apostle Father José de la Jara founded a Christian community that was a forerunner of the base ecclesial communities. In 1966, in an island in the Solentiname archipelago, Father Ernesto Cardenal, a former Trappist monk trained by Thomas Merton, founded a community based on the ideals of contemplation and solidarity with the peasants. After Medellín the base ecclesial community movement took root, especially in the dioceses of Estelí, Matagalpa, León, Chinandega, and Masaya.

As in the rest of Latin America, the episcopal conference of Medellín inspired many new experiments, but it also created tensions in the church. Most of the progressive priests and nuns were foreign-born. By way of contrast, the more conservative among the clergy tended to be native born. Among women religious the Maryknoll sisters stood out for their conscienticizing efforts in popular parishes. But the hierarchy in general was conservative and slow to accept the reforms of the Council. Finally, with the naming of Miguel Obando y Bravo as archbishop of Managua in 1970, the Nicaraguan episcopal conference finally came around to support the reforms and, at the same time, to distance itself from the Somoza regime.

THE CHRISTIANS IN THE REVOLUTION

Two dramatic events signaled the beginning of the end of the Somoza dynasty: a devastating earthquake in 1972, and the assassination of Pedro Joaquín Chamorro in 1978. The earthquake destroyed the entire center of Managua, killing ten thousand people. The dictator, instead of showing signs of solidarity with the victims, used the opportunity to channel international aid into his own pockets and those of his cronies. Indignation was widespread.

In 1974 several groups of businessmen and professionals founded the Democratic Union for Freedom (UDEL: *Unión Democrática de Liberación*). This was a worrisome portent: the middle classes, tired of a corrupt and scandalous dictatorship, were now beginning to turn against it. The church, too, joined the dissident voices. In 1972 the bishops published a pastoral letter that for the first time demanded an end to the dictatorship. Obando himself played an important role in delegitimizing the regime. In 1974 the Sandinistas managed to kidnap a large number of military, politicians, and diplomats. Obando was called upon to act as a mediator in that crisis; he was successful in having several prisoners exchanged for those who had been kidnapped. One of the prisoners exchanged was Daniel Ortega. On another occasion, in August 1978, Obando once again acted as a mediator, this time because the Sandinistas had seized the national palace. Hundreds of prisoners, including Tomás Borge, were liberated.[9]

The second major dramatic event was the assassination of Pedro Joaquín Chamorro on January 10, 1978. Chamorro was the owner of *La Prensa* and frequently criticized Somoza from the pages of his daily newspaper. Although there was no proof available, public opinion held Somoza responsible for the crime. Chamorro's assassination provoked a wave of indignation and strikes throughout the country. President Carter began looking for an alternative to Somoza, who was no longer seen as an acceptable ally for the United States. But Somoza was not overthrown by the middle classes or the United States but by the Sandinistas, supported by many Christians.

The Sandinista Front for National Liberation (FSLN) was founded in 1961 by Carlos Fonseca, along with Tomás Borge and Silvio Mayorga. In the beginning it copied Fidel Castro's movement. Its principal base of support was the urban middle class. In 1963 the FSLN tried to establish its presence in the countryside but with little success. The pragmatic instincts of some of the leaders, especially Tomás Borge, led the FSLN to see the importance of contacting progressive groups within the church, just at a moment when the church was experimenting with major changes. In fact, the FSLN's instincts proved to be correct: the support of the Christians—students, peasants, priests, and religious—was decisive for the revolution.

In 1968 Tomás Borge invited Father Ernesto Cardenal to discuss common topics. In a second meeting Father Uriel Molina was present, along with Carlos Fonseca.[10] Later, in 1972, Molina went to Chile for a firsthand view of the Christians for Socialism movement. The student community he founded provided many youth leaders for the revolution. After the 1972 earthquake the contacts intensified. Many leaders and militants in the revolution came directly from centers and movements founded by religious. In 1978 the Jesuit-founded Center of Education and Agrarian Promotion directly aligned itself with the FSLN.[11] Likewise, many delegates of the Word trained by the Capuchins in Zelaya joined the ranks of the Sandinistas. During the 1977 offensive many Christians from the Solentiname community participated in the assault on the military base of San Carlos in the south.[12] Everywhere, but especially in the rural areas, progressive church groups helped the revolutionaries by offering them refuge, food, and medicine. Gaspar García Laviana, a Spanish missionary of the Sacred Heart Congregation who had a parish near the border with Costa Rica, became a guerrilla leader and was killed on December 11, 1978, by the National Guard. In October 1977 the Group of Twelve, made up of several intellectuals and two priests, was founded. The two priests were Miguel D'Escoto and Fernando Cardenal. The group elaborated a peace plan, which included the Sandinistas.[13] Furthermore, D'Escoto and Cardenal went to Washington to denounce the Somoza regime before the American congress. Finally, Ernesto Cardenal was sent as a goodwill emissary of the Sandinistas to the outside world.

For his part, Somoza did not hesitate to counterattack the progressive church. In Zelaya, in 1977, the National Guard attacked several churches, and in Estelí in 1978 it murdered a priest, Francisco Luis Espinoza. Although there were obvious differences between Obando's way of thinking and the Christians in the Sandinista movement, the common struggle against the dictatorship covered over the differences. Finally, on July 17, 1979, Somoza fled to Miami, and two days later the FSLN entered the capital. The Sandinista victory came so quickly that it took the other anti-Somoza groups and the American government by surprise. They had no choice but to recognize the Sandinista victory and wait for the next step. A FSLN document, dated October 6, 1980, leaves no room for doubt about the decisive role of the Christians in the movement:

> The patriotic and revolutionary Christians are an integral part of the popular Sandinista revolution, not just now, but for many years. . . .

The Christians have been an integral part of our revolutionary history to a degree not found in any other revolutionary movement in Latin America, and possibly, in the world.[14]

TWO WORLDS IN COLLISION

In the midst of the general jubilation the people of Nicaragua—Sandinistas, base ecclesial community Christians, middle-class Christians—set about reconstructing the country, which had just experienced, in the words of Paul VI, a "prolonged and evident tyranny."[15] The Somoza dictatorship seemed to be a perfect example of the kind of dictatorship the pope described. And, going back to the classic teachings of Juan de Mariana, the participation of Christians in this particular revolution seemed perfectly justified. In fact, in a pastoral letter written on June 2, 1979, the Nicaraguan hierarchy legitimated the armed struggle against Somoza.[16] However, there was much less clarity about what kind of society ought to be constructed after the revolution and who would construct that society. One year after Somoza's defeat the Christians who supported the revolution were strongly divided between those who wanted a society with some socialist orientations and those who favored a Western style, multiparty, and capitalistic system.

Certain authors have distinguished three groups within the church before and after the revolution.[17] One group was the conservatives, who supported Somoza practically without any critical distance. But this group was not popular and ended up supporting the second group, which consisted of middle-class Christians who united around Archbishop Obando y Bravo. This second group feared most of all that Nicaragua would become another Cuba. For this reason they sought direct relations with the Reagan government, in power in January 1981, and gave rise to a counterrevolution. The third group were progressive Christians of the middle and popular classes who looked to the priests in the Sandinista government as their spokesmen. They also did not wish for Nicaragua to become another Cuba. They believed in democracy based on a new popular nationalism. Although they accepted aid from Cuba, they did not approve of the antireligious attitudes of some of the Cuban advisers who collaborated with the literacy campaigns.

In the midst of these political differences ecclesial and theological differences also divided the Christians. The second group—looked upon favorably by the Vatican—believed that *Sandinismo* was simply a Marxist movement and nothing else. The policy Obando adopted was very much like that of the church in Poland vis-à-vis the communist regime: foster internal church unity and close ranks against an external enemy that constitutes a threat to religion and the church. But the Christians who supported the Sandinistas were inspired by liberation theology, and they considered themselves the creators, along with the Sandinistas, of a new society based on Christian (not Marxist) values. The popular cry heard during the revolution—"Sandino, yesterday, today, and forever!"—caught the unique fusion of religious and political sentiment that inspired both Christians and Sandinistas. Although many Christians bore arms during the revolution, they did not believe in violence as a normal way to resolve problems. On the other hand, they exalted the poor and criticized the elitist pretensions of the middle classes. There were certain centers and organizations that openly sympathized with the revolutionary process: the Central American Historical Institute, run by the Jesuits; the Antonio Valdivieso Center, founded in 1979 by Uriel Molina; and the Conference of Religious. In Nicaragua the open support of many Christians for the government made that situation totally unlike that of any Marxist country in Eastern Europe. A survey conducted in 1983 revealed that of the 220 priests who responded, 46 percent supported the Sandinista experiment and the rest were opposed.[18] Given these circumstances, ecclesial unity, much less political unity, was an impossible dream. Furthermore, in the light of the presence of priests in high places in the government, and the sympathy of Christians on the popular level toward the regime, the hierarchy feared losing control of the church. In Nicaragua, political and religious tensions mixed together. Finally, it is instructive to compare Archbishop Obando's conduct with that of Arturo Rivera y Damas in El Salvador. Rivera y Damas did not sympathize with the more radical groups in the Farabundo Martí Liberation Front, but he always opened the doors to dialogue. By way of contrast, Obando y Bravo became strongly biased against the Sandinistas and generally did not foster dialogue. In fact, he himself became a symbol of resistance to the Sandinista government. Although the two situations are different, it is evident that the different episcopal styles greatly influenced the respective churches in El Salvador and Nicaragua. With the exception of a few clashes the Salvadoran church maintained its internal unity during most of the civil war. But the church in Nicaragua was sharply divided.

We can distinguish three stages in the development of relations between the Sandinista government and the church: (1) the hardening of positions (1979-82); (2) the sharpening of tensions (1982-86); and (3) the search for a modus vivendi (1986-90).[19]

FIRST STAGE: THE HARDENING OF POSITIONS (1979-1982)

During the first year after taking power the ruling junta, which termed itself the Government of National Reconstruction, composed of Sandinistas and non-Sandinistas, carried out a number of important reforms. It nationalized the private bank system and the mines, decreed an agrarian reform, and created the Popular Sandinista Army. Nicaragua seemed to be going in the direction of some kind of nationalistic socialism. In fact, however, under the

Sandinistas Nicaragua never went that far. It was really a model of a mixed socialist and capitalist economy. Between 55 percent and 60 percent of the economy remained in private hands.[20] Nevertheless, the business class and the hierarchy feared the totalitarian tendencies of the Sandinistas and very shortly put an end to the honeymoon of the first few months. In April 1980 two leading figures in the junta, Alfonso Robelo and Violeta Barrios de Chamorro, resigned. From that moment on Mrs. Chamorro converted *La Prensa* into the principal organ of criticism of the Sandinista regime. A large block of workers of *La Prensa* left in protest to found their own pro-government newspaper, *El Nuevo Diario*.

At the very moment of the Sandinistas' victory, Archbishop Obando was meeting with anti-Somoza leaders in Caracas who were trying to forge a center-right coalition with minimal Sandinista presence.[21] Other church figures with the same orientation were Pablo A. Vega, the bishop of Juigalpa; Bosco Vivas, the auxiliary bishop of Managua; and Bismarck Carballo, a spokesperson for the archbishop's curia and the director of Catholic Radio. In general the apostolic nuncios and representatives of CELAM also supported Obando. By way of exception, the chargé d'affairs of the papal nunciature, Bishop Pietri Sambi, stood out for his willingness to dialogue. Other moderate bishops included Salvador Schlaefer of Bluefields on the Atlantic coast, Rubén López Ardón of Estelí, Julián Luis Barni of León, and Carlos Santi of Matagalpa. On different critical occasions these bishops did not support Obando in Managua. Nevertheless, the Vatican preferred Obando as its spokesperson.

Soon different areas of conflict brought to the fore the deep fissures in the church and, indeed, in all of society. One critical point of friction was the presence of priests and other religious personnel in the government. The five most widely known priests were Ernesto Cardenal, minister of Culture; Fernando Cardenal, a Jesuit and brother of Ernesto Cardenal, who was minister of Education and in charge of the literacy campaign; Miguel D'Escoto, a Maryknoll priest, who was chancellor, that is, in charge of foreign affairs; Edgar Parrales, minister of Welfare and later ambassador to the Organization of American States; and Alvaro Argüello, a Jesuit who was a delegate of the Association of Nicaraguan Clergy to the State Council. There were also many men and women religious who collaborated with the health and education programs. For example, some three hundred religious participated in the literacy campaign.

In May 1981 the bishops requested that the priests in the government leave their posts. The five, claiming reasons of conscience, insisted on remaining. Finally, in July 1981, after a long and tense dialogue the Vatican grudgingly allowed them to stay but only under certain conditions, one being that they could not exercise their priesthood in public. Archbishop Obando was not pleased with the agreement and in the future avoided all contact with the priests in the government. Later, in 1982, Alvaro Argüello left the State Council and the Association of Nicaraguan Clergy was dissolved under pressure from the archbishop. In 1984, also under pressure from the Vatican, Fernando Cardenal left his religious order, the Society of Jesus, although he continued to maintain close ties with his fellow Jesuits.

Other conflicts served to confirm the fears of the hierarchy about the totalitarian tendencies of the Sandinistas. One such conflict revolved around the literacy campaign. With the aim of teaching the 50 percent of Nicaraguans who did not know how to read or write, the government mobilized thousands of volunteers. The campaign was a notable success: in a very brief period the number of illiterates dropped to 12 percent.[22] Yet the campaign produced friction between the hierarchy and the government. The bishops were concerned over a campaign administered by socialists, which included a good number of Cubans. As a way of allaying those fears, the FSLN published the communiqué of October 1980, cited above. Nevertheless, the conservative bishops considered this and other declarations examples of out-and-out manipulation of religion for ideological purposes.

Another area of conflict was religious feast days and the use of religious symbols. One such conflict arose over the feast of the *Purísima,* which, because of its proximity to Christmas, is celebrated by giving gifts to the children. In 1980 the priest-minister of Welfare, Edgar Parrales, announced that the government would assume the mission of giving gifts to poor children during the feast days. In subsequent years President Ortega, accompanied by other Sandinista commanders, walked through the streets to greet the faithful. The hierarchy protested that the government had no business intervening in religious feast days. In reaction, the bishops organized masses and other activities that excluded government officials.[23]

These tensions between government and church had repercussions within the church, in parishes, and in the ecclesial base communities. In general, Archbishop Obando avoided any pastoral contact with the communities, especially given the fact that many were filled with Christians who enthusiastically supported the Sandinistas. He also removed progressive priests and religious women from parishes and expelled them from the archdioceses. But this in turn provoked hostility from Christians on the base level. In some situations the Sandinistas looked for ways to express their disagreements with the archbishop. The most notorious example of this vindictive attitude concerned Bishop Bismarck Carballo, who was publicly humiliated by some soldiers who allegedly surprised him in flagrante delicto with a woman.[24] Also, in July 1981, the government canceled the archbishop's weekly televised mass. In the midst of this feuding Obando received the support of the Vatican and Cardinal Alfonso López Trujillo, the president of CELAM. In June 1981 López Trujillo visited Nicaragua with the aim of promoting a pastoral program parallel to that of the progressives. In Nicaragua the hierarchy took pains to emphasize the incompatibility between the official church and the so-called popular church.

The Miskitos

A peculiar subchapter within this drama involved the Miskito Indians on the Atlantic coast. Since colonial times the Nicaraguan Mosquitia constituted a special region, which existed on the margin of the rest of society. The main contacts with Western civilization were through missionaries, particularly the Moravians who arrived in the seventeenth century, and then, in 1913, the Capuchins, who were in charge of the vicariate of Bluefields. For lack of experience or prudence the Sandinista government provoked considerable hostility among the Miskitos, especially by trying to impose the literacy campaign on them. Also, in 1982 the government attempted to move the Miskitos away from the border with Honduras, which was where the Contras were operating. The Sandinistas hoped to relocate the Indians in more secure zones, but the Miskitos viewed the attempt with suspicion and reacted with hostility. One of their leaders, Steadman Fagoth, organized a resistance movement but was captured. When he was freed, he fled to Honduras to collaborate with the Contras. The bishops accused the government, with some justification, of violating the rights of the Indians. But the government responded, also with some justification, that it did not intend to violate the rights of the Indians but to protect them.[25] Years later the Sandinistas admitted their heavy-handed treatment of the Miskitos was an error.

Reagan and the Religious Counteroffensive

The new political right, which carried Ronald Reagan to the White House, found these religious tensions excellent material to use in its campaign to liberate Central America from communism. The conservative Nicaraguan bishops and their intellectual apologists formed an alliance with the political and religious right of the United States. A fruit of this alliance was the Institute of Religion and Democracy, founded by Catholic intellectuals such as Michael Novak, Peter Berger, and Humberto Belli. Belli, who had worked as a journalist for *La Prensa* and collaborated with the Sandinistas for a while, accused the latter of manipulating public opinion with a false message of good will toward the Christians. According to Belli, the Sandinistas were not nationalistic revolutionaries but simply old-fashioned dogmatic Marxists with no interest in democracy or religion.[26] These judgments of Belli, fully supported by the hierarchy of the Catholic church of Nicaragua, served to legitimate the plans of President Reagan and his hardline advisers to stop communism in that part of the world. From the beginning Reagan approved of supporting the Contras, who were made up of former Somocistas and real believers in democracy, united in a common front against the Sandinistas. In 1981 American military operations were begun in Honduras with the aim of supporting what President Reagan termed the Freedom Fighters, otherwise known as the Contras or counterrevolutionaries. Under the legitimizing scope this official policy provided, the Pentagon put into practice the new concept of a war of "low intensity."

SECOND STAGE: THE SHARPENING OF TENSIONS (1982-1986)

As the war, financed in large part by the United States, grew in intensity, relations between church and state grew more bitter. According to one estimate, between 1981 and 1990 the American government gave at least 300 million dollars to the Contras.[27] This aid allowed the Contras to expand their forces from forty-five hundred in 1982 to fifteen thousand in 1988.[28] During the worst years of the war close to thirty thousand Nicaraguans were killed. Backed by the military power of the United States, the Contras could enter and leave Nicaragua at will, using Honduras as their base of operations. The United States maintained its own force in Honduras: fifteen thousand soldiers in 1985 and fifty thousand in 1987. As a complement to the operations in Honduras and Nicaragua, Reagan also attempted to impose a military and economic blockade. In 1984 he had mines placed around the principal ports of the country, an action later condemned by the International Court of the Hague. These aggressive actions served to strengthen fears that an imminent invasion was underway. When the United States invaded Grenada in October 1983, this only confirmed those fears.

In November 1984 presidential elections were held. Although three parties refused to participate, six others did. In spite of the fact that the majority of its Western allies recognized these elections, the United States did not. It did, however, recognize the 1984 elections held in El Salvador during a civil war in which the greater part of the population could not vote. In fact, the Reagan administration did not recognize the elections in Nicaragua because to do so would constitute a way of legitimizing the government in Managua. And that would have meant delegitimizing the Contras and the war of low intensity, one of President Reagan's favorite projects.

THE PAPAL VISIT

The papal visit in March 1983 brought inner-church tensions even more to the fore and at the same time deepened tensions between church and state. The Sandinista government went to great lengths to prepare for the visit. It offered free transportation to help people reach the places where the pope would speak. But it also suffered from an excess of optimism—or naivete— with regard to the pope and his accompanying party. Many Sandinistas were convinced that it would be sufficient to show the new Nicaragua to the pope and he would understand what the revolution was all about. They did not realize that the display of banners, slogans, and symbols would only serve to confirm the pope's fears that ideology had supplanted religion in Nicaragua.

One slogan greeted the visitors with the words "Welcome to Free Nicaragua, Thanks to God and the Revolution."[29] In his welcoming speech—which was much too long—Daniel Ortega praised the benefits of the revolution. A bit more discretion would have placed the distinguished visitors more at ease.

On the other hand, the pope was not well advised. Cardinal López Trujillo and his advisers prepared him to visit a Marxist country that harassed the church and manipulated the priests in the government. Most of all, the pope did not seem to appreciate the emotions lower-class Nicaraguans felt about participating in the construction of a new society after overthrowing a long and oppressive dictatorship. The pope constantly condemned "ideologies which are foreign to Christianity," a clear allusion to *Sandinismo*. The incident that most typified the mutual lack of understanding occurred when the pope addressed the people in Managua on March 4. The day before several youths had been killed by the Contras. Many people in the crowd cried out for peace. The pope interpreted the cries as a rude interruption of his speech. He answered by demanding silence from his listeners. Many people were much disillusioned by the papal visit. Finally, the pope, in an effort to strengthen the church, gave full support to Archbishop Obando. Two years later he conferred upon him the rank of cardinal, a sign that he enjoyed approval in Rome.

From that moment on church-state confrontations became even more strained and acerbic. That same year a conflict arose over a new law of obligatory military service. In August the government decided to face the Contra invasion by promulgating the Law of Patriotic Military Service, which was universal and obligatory. Obando and the other conservative bishops objected to the law because it was presumably "totalitarian" in character.[30] On this particular issue, however, other bishops, such as Carlos Santi of Matagalpa and Schlaefer of Bluefields, did not support Obando. In June 1984 Luis Amado Peña, a diocesan priest, was accused of collaborating with the Contras. The government presented a video showing Peña helping to transport arms. In response, Obando accused the government of fabricating the proofs and called for a march to protest Peña's detention. Peña was placed under house arrest in the seminary, and after a year he was pardoned by President Ortega.[31]

In the midst of these tensions the government approached the church with the aim of restoring dialogue. The fruit of this attempt was the creation of the Commission for Church-State Dialogue, made up of bishops Bosco Vivas, Pablo Vega, and Carlos Santi. The government's representatives were René Núñez Téllez, the minister of the Presidency, and Rodrigo Reyes, the minister of Justice. The commission, which met in January 1985, touched upon such topics as the expelled priests, obligatory military service, the Contra war, and other issues. The topic that aroused most tension was the war. The church proposed to establish an official dialogue with the Contras. But the government suspected that the bishops really wanted to legitimize the counterrevolution, or what they called the National Resistance. This would imply, of course, placing the legitimacy of the Sandinista government in question.

In spite of many meetings, not a single agreement was achieved. Finally, in October, the last meeting was held; no new encounter would take place for two more years.

THE CHURCH AND THE COUNTERREVOLUTION

The war of the Contras, or the counterrevolution, was the topic that would provoke the most tension in Nicaragua and the church. Archbishop Obando sympathized with the Contras and hardly concealed his disdain for the Sandinista regime. He maintained a discreet silence in the face of the atrocities committed by the Contras, but he never failed to point out the excesses of the Sandinistas. In July 1983 a husband and wife, Felipe and Mary Barreda, both *cursillistas*, were kidnapped by the Contras and taken to Honduras, where they died after three days of torture. The official church made no public protest whatsoever.[32] But Obando and the other conservative bishops did not limit themselves to maintaining silence; on many occasions they publicly expressed approval of the Contras and even promoted their cause. In a visit to Germany Bishop Pablo Vega declared that the 1984 elections were "fraudulent."[33] In Washington, in June 1986, Vega addressed a meeting of PRODEMCA (For Democracy in Central America), an organization founded to support the Contras. His address was timed to coincide with debates in the American congress on whether or not to give the Contras the sum of 100 million dollars.[34] Also that year Obando made a trip to the United States to ask different conservative groups for aid in supporting the Contras.[35]

But the gesture that most influenced public opinion was Obando's first mass as a cardinal. He was raised to that ecclesiastical rank in April 1985, and on June 13 he celebrated mass not in Managua, but in Miami, surrounded by the most prominent leaders of the counterrevolution: Edén Pastora, Adolfo Calero, and several former Somocistas.[36] By means of these symbolic gestures Obando established himself not as a mere sympathizer but as the principal spokesman for the counterrevolution. The ties between the church and the Contras were so close that *Newsweek* accused certain organizations of the archdiocese of Managua of receiving money from the CIA for the purpose of making anti-government propaganda.[37] Given this close relationship between the church and the counterrevolution, the Sandinista government had grounds for doubting the sincerity of the bishops when they spoke of reconciliation or dialogue.

THE SANDINISTAS RESPOND

In light of the church's open sympathy for the counterrevolution, and prompted by the fear of an American invasion, the government at times overreacted. On the occasion of the incident of Father Amado Peña the government canceled the visas of ten foreign priests, who were accused of carrying out a "systematic campaign" against the laws of the country.[38] In 1989, when the situation was less tense, the ten were allowed back in. In another example, in October 1985 the government closed the offices of CORPROSA (the Archdiocesan Commission of Social Promotion), which received aid from the Adenauer Foundation of West Germany and from the International Agency for Development (AID). The office was accused of using the funds to finance political opposition groups. In January 1986 the Catholic Radio, directed by Bismarck Carballo, was closed down. The radio, with its constant criticisms, had become an irritant for the government. The straw that broke the camel's back occurred when the radio did not transmit the president's end-of-the-year greeting. In June, Carballo, who constantly criticized the government, was denied permission to enter the country when he returned from a trip abroad. And in July Pablo Vega was expelled from the country.

With the aim of calling attention to the campaigns against the country, Father Miguel D'Escoto staged a "gospel insurrection." Between June and August of 1985 he went on a fast for peace in a popular neighborhood of Managua. He was accompanied by Pedro Casaldáliga of São Araguaia in Mato Grosso, Adolfo Pérez Esquivel, and Méndez Arceo of Cuernavaca. Later, in February 1986, Father D'Escoto made the stations of the cross by walking two hundred miles from Jalapa on the frontier with Honduras to the capital. The idea, of course, was to demonstrate that Nicaragua was experiencing the way of the cross. In each little town he was greeted with enthusiasm. The walk ended with a mass concelebrated by seventy-three priests.[39]

THIRD STAGE:
THE SEARCH FOR A MODUS VIVENDI (1986-1990)

Finally, after the war had taken thirty thousand lives, common sense began to take hold. But there was also another factor: the arrival, in July 1986, of a new apostolic nuncio, Paolo Giglio, who persuaded both sides to renew discussions. The government finally accepted the idea of dialoguing with the Contras and even designated Cardinal Obando as the mediator. The Vatican changed its position, in part out of pragmatic considerations. It was evident by then that the policy of de-legitimizing the Sandinista regime had not been very efficacious and, in fact, had divided the church. The new nuncio, though a conservative, believed that concessions could be won only through dialogue, a policy that he had followed when he had mediated between the church and the state in China. Furthermore, the church had seen the favorable results of such a policy in Poland. Finally, it is probable that the Vatican had begun to question the aggressive style of Cardinal Obando, Vega, and the other conservative bishops. During the entire process the episcopal conference of the United States had severely criticized the policy of the American government with respect to Central America and Nicaragua. In fact, the North American bishops did not support Obando. Now, too, the Vatican began to see the wisdom of not identifying itself too closely with the warlike schemes of President Reagan. Particularly after Esquipulas II the Vatican adopted the position of not supporting any armed solution. Once this decision was made, it could not logically continue to support Obando and the other bishops who supported the Contras.

The initiative to seek peace through dialogue came from the Central American presidents in Esquipulas, not from the church. First, President Arias of Costa Rica proposed a global plan for peace. Second, in the general meeting of the five presidents of the region in Esquipulas (Guatemala) in 1987, a general peace plan was agreed upon. According to the agreement, each government was bound to enter into dialogue with whatever revolutionary groups were in its country. Nicaragua led the way by taking the first steps to put the plan into action. In fact, Esquipulas II came as a blessing in disguise, because the Sandinistas could now dialogue with the Contras without giving the appearance of being forced to. Indeed, by then the Sandinista regime had important motives to engage in dialogue with the enemy. One motive was the devastating impact of the war on the country. According to one author, the government assigned 62 percent of the national budget to defense.[40] But the Sandinistas had also committed their own quota of errors. One of them was to have provoked a staggering spiral of inflation, which in 1990 was the highest of all Latin America.[41] As if these factors were not enough, on October 22, 1988, Hurricane Joan arrived, causing great destruction and the deaths of 325 persons.

Finally, there was another factor: the end of the Cold War and the collapse of communism in eastern Europe. These realities had different impacts on the two sides. The Sandinistas were obliged to abandon their Marxist rhetoric and to embrace without ambiguity—at least verbally—the Western democratic system. But the Contras felt the impact even more. Nicaragua was no longer perceived as a threat to the region, especially after President Reagan left office in 1989. Furthermore, the scandal of Irangate, which affected the last two years of Reagan's administration, greatly weakened the American government's case in Central America. After the revelation that there was a connection between Iran and the Contras, the American congress became even less enthusiastic about supporting aggressive warlike actions against a small Central American nation. The options for the Contras were reduced to two: dialogue with the Sandinistas and rejoin society, or keep on fighting, but with increasingly diminished aid from the United States. Each of the four principal actors in the drama—the church, the American government, the Sandinistas, and the Contras—had a motive for dialoguing and ending the war. Nevertheless, it is true that until the 1990 elections the parties least interested in achieving peace were the United States government and the Contras. In fact, Reagan positively disregarded the Esquipulas agreements, but in so doing provoked the Vatican to criticize the American government for the first time in the war for its inflexibility.

ESQUIPULAS II AND THE DIALOGUE OF RECONCILIATION

In September 1986, with the nuncio, Paolo Giglio, acting as host, President Ortega met with Cardinal Obando. The three agreed to set into motion a series of meetings in order to reduce tensions and search for a modus vivendi. Throughout February, April, and May of 1987 the government and the church met and discussed the question of Catholic Radio, the expelled priests, and other topics. They did not reach any substantial conclusions. The decisive factor that changed everything was the meeting of the presidents in Esquipulas. On August 7 the five presidents signed their historic document, which bound each member-nation to reject foreign interference in its internal conflicts and to reject purely military solutions in favor of a negotiated peace. In addition, each nation was to create a national reconciliation commission. Ortega barely returned from Esquipulas when he called together the bishops to explain the agreements and to ask for their cooperation. The episcopal conference and the political parties proposed lists of candidates to make up the commission. Finally, the National Commission of Reconciliation was made up of Cardinal Obando, who acted as its president; Sergio Ramírez, representing the government; Mauricio Díaz and Erick Ramírez, representing the opposition parties; and Gustavo Parajón, a Protestant pastor and director of the Evangelical Committee for Development. Ortega had acted so quickly that he took his critics by surprise, including the American government and the Nicaraguan hierarchy. On a few occasions Obando and the other bishops, suspicious that the Sandinistas might be trying to manipulate them, expressed their lack of trust in the idea of forming the commission. And there were even some observers who considered Ortega's decision to include Obando in the commission a very astute move, because it obliged the cardinal to recognize the Sandinista regime as legitimate. In fact, Ortega's decision was a double-edged blade: Obando, too, was an astute player who could use his new position to advance the cause of the Contras.[42]

At the same time, Ortega gave other signs of promoting an atmosphere of national reconciliation. For a eucharistic congress that was organized in November 1986 the government offered free transportation and lodging for foreign visitors. In August 1987 it authorized the return of Bismarck Carballo and Pablo Vega, and permitted Catholic Radio to function once again. Also, in October, *La Prensa*, closed since June 1986, was allowed to reopen. The National Reconciliation Commission was installed on September 1 in the offices of the episcopal conference, but very soon it was locked in debates over the question of granting amnesty to the Contras, obligatory military service, and dialogue between the government and the opposition. On October 6 Ortega officially designated Obando as mediator between the government and the "resistance" (the Contras). The first meetings were rather low level and of an exploratory nature. In the first days of December in Santo Domingo, Obando, accompanied by auxiliary bishop Bosco Vivas and Carlos Santi, the bishop of Matagalpa, initiated the first dialogue between the

Sandinista regime and the Contras. The government's delegation was headed by Major Richard Wheelock, one of the leading *comandantes* of the revolution. After this first meeting many others followed in rapid succession. In January 1988, Ortega met with the pope and Cardinal Casaroli, the first such high-level meeting since 1983. In February the government and the Contras met in Guatemala, with Obando acting as mediator. Finally, at the beginning of March Ortega designated his brother, General Humberto Ortega, the commander of the army, to head the government's delegation for the first high-level meeting with the Contras. In a very brief amount of time the government and the counterrevolutionaries had gone from total mutual antagonism and open war to the negotiating table.

SAPOÁ (1988)

On March 6, 1988, the government unleashed a major offensive against the Contras, and on March 17 American reinforcements arrived in Honduras. In spite of being engaged in a bloody war, both sides decided to hold the scheduled summit meeting. On March 21 the government initiated a dialogue with the eight legal parties of opposition, and on March 23 it formally met with the armed opposition (the Contras). In the small town of Sapoá, near the frontier with Costa Rica, Contra leaders Adolfo Calero, Alfredo César, and Arístides Sánchez met with General Humberto Ortega in the presence of Cardinal Obando and João Baena Soares, the secretary general of the OAS. World observers were greatly surprised when it was announced that certain fundamental agreements had been reached. One surprise was the announcement of the Contra leaders that they would no longer accept military aid from the United States, only humanitarian aid. But equally surprising was the Sandinistas' promise to offer amnesty to three thousand former members of Somoza's National Guard. Finally, both sides announced a truce of sixty days. During that period they promised to continue the discussions with the objective of achieving a definitive cease fire.[43]

The openness that both sides demonstrated was so surprising that the agreements in Sapoá seemed to have been made in heaven, not on earth. Unfortunately, the ink had barely dried when *realpolitik* set in and practically wiped the agreements away. In the first place, the Reagan administration refused to recognize the agreements and responded by offering more military aid to the Contras. In the second place, the military commander of the Contras, Enrique Bermúdez, also did not recognize the agreements. In effect, Sapoá sharply divided the Contra leaders. Finally, in May a second high-level meeting between the Sandinistas and the Contras was held in Managua. But this time the leaders of the Contras practically disowned Sapoá.

There were other incidents that helped to destroy the spirit of Sapoá. In July the North American ambassador, Richard Melton, and seven functionaries from his embassy were declared persona non grata for their complicity in inciting anti-government demonstrations in the town of Naindaime and other places. The press spoke of the Melton Plan, which, according to the more sensational newspapers, consisted in a conspiracy fabricated in Washington aimed at destabilizing the government in Managua and destroying the fragile peace won in Sapoá. In response, the government closed down Catholic Radio and *La Prensa* once again, although both reopened a short time later.

In spite of all these setbacks, Sapoá did not turn out to be a total failure. After Sapoá the level of intensity of the war diminished considerably—a sign that the Contras were losing strength. In the beginning of 1989 President Ortega announced that the elections for November 1990 would be held in February. He also authorized the return of the ten priests who had been expelled as a result of the incident of Father Peña. Obando, too, seemed to grow more moderate in his declarations concerning the government. In May he surprised many when, through the intervention of Cardinal Darío Castrillón Hoyos of CELAM, he requested the government of the United States to put an end to its economic blockade. Furthermore, unlike 1984, when they practically ignored the elections, the bishops exhorted the faithful to participate in the 1990 ones. Finally, in practice, they had come to recognize the legitimacy of the Sandinista government.

The Evangelicals

Protestants (or *Evangélicos,* as they are more popularly termed) make up about 15 percent of the population. Theirs is a long-standing presence. The Moravians arrived on the Atlantic coast in the seventeenth century, and Anglo-Saxon missionaries at the end of the nineteenth century. Until the sixties their numbers were not significant. But it was precisely during the revolution against Somoza and the Sandinista experiment that their numbers grew rapidly: between 1978 and 1988 by 140 percent.[44] The majority—around 55 percent—belong to different Pentecostal churches, which are traditionally nonpolitical and conservative. But the earthquake of 1972, as well as the revolution, changed the course of things. After the earthquake many Protestants joined together to found CEPAD (Evangelical Committee for Aid to Development). From that point on CEPAD constituted the principal association that drew together the majority of Protestants in the country. In the period right before the revolution small groups of Protestants questioned the conservative orientation of their churches. At the Baptist Theological Seminary the seminarians criticized the pro-Somoza stand of their pastors. In general, however, most Protestants were not prepared for the revolution that shook Nicaragua. As though to catch up, in October 1979 five hundred pastors published a document in which they expressed solidarity with the revolution and condemned the economic blockade around Cuba.[45]

Just as the revolution divided Catholics, so it divided the Protestants. Certain groups, such as CEPRES (the Evangelical Community of Social Promotion) and certain churches, openly supported the government's reforms, and many Protestants participated in the literacy and health campaigns. But the more fundamentalist Protestants—who were the majority—as well as the many new denominations that established themselves in Nicaragua in those years, either had nothing to do with the revolution or openly criticized it.

This attitude provoked hostility on the part of the Sandinistas. In August 1980 several bands of Sandinistas seized thirty temples belonging to the Mormons, the Adventists, and the Jehovah's Witnesses. Through the intercession of CEPAD they were returned to their respective owners. The naming of Gustavo Parajón, a Baptist pastor and president of CEPAD, as a member of the National Reconciliation Commission was a sign of recognition of the Protestant community. Finally, the Sandinistas learned from past mistakes and lost no opportunity to court the Protestants. In March 1987, as part of the campaign of openness and reconciliation, Daniel Ortega visited a Pentecostal assembly to greet Yiye Avila, a well-known Puerto Rican preacher. The visiting pastor placed his hands on Ortega, and the Nicaraguan president asked the assembly for its prayers. In January 1990, during the presidential campaign, Ortega met with a thousand pastors and Protestant leaders. Finally, there were Protestants on the Sandinistas' lists of candidates.[46]

THE ELECTIONS AND AFTERMATH

The Nicaraguan presidential elections, held on February 25, 1990, were among the most closely watched in history. At the government's own invitation close to a thousand observers from the United Nations, the Organization of American States, and other international organizations arrived in the country.[47] Among the more famous observers was former President Jimmy Carter. The two principal electoral forces were the FSLN and the UNO (National Opposing Union). The UNO, whose candidate was Violeta Barrios de Chamorro, consisted of fourteen small parties of the center and the right. In an entirely free contest the candidates used all the typical techniques of the First World, particularly of the United States. Both sides appealed to religion. As we mentioned above, Daniel Ortega visited a meeting of Protestant pastors and leaders, and the FSLN distributed a photo of him next to the cardinal. One day before the elections *La Prensa* published a photo of the cardinal blessing Violeta Chamorro.[48]

The election results were a great surprise for the world and for the Nicaraguans themselves. In contrast to the pre-election surveys, which favored the FSLN, in the election itself the UNO won by 55 percent of the vote against the FSLN's 41 percent.[49] Daniel Ortega recognized the defeat, and Violeta Chamorro assumed the presidency of the country. The analysts who speculated over the reasons for the Sandinistas' defeat suggested several factors: the war; the Sandinistas' own weariness after many years in power; the widespread belief that the United States would come to the aid of Nicaragua if the UNO won, and more. Finally, the Sandinistas recognized that they had been carried away by triumphalism.

In the post-Sandinista period the church continued to play a high-profile role, especially in the efforts to incorporate the Contras back into society. In Tegucigalpa, on March 23, the cardinal acted as mediator between Daniel Ortega and Antonio Lacayo, the new minister of the Presidency, to work out a definitive cease fire between the Sandinistas and the Contras. As a result of that meeting a verification commission was formed. On May 30, in the cardinal's presence, the new president, Violeta Chamorro, and *Comandante* "Franklin" (Israel Galeano), representing the Contras, signed an agreement creating development zones where the Contras could reestablish themselves.[50] In other ceremonies the cardinal blessed Contra soldiers as they turned in their arms.[51] In spite of these public gestures of reconciliation, the rivalry between Sandinistas and Contras did not abate. Even though their leaders signed peace accords, dissident groups continued to roam at will, as though the war had not ended. In reality, many Sandinistas and Contras were disgruntled at the meager spoils they had obtained after so many years of struggle. The government's reconciliation policy soon ran into many obstacles, one of which turned out to be, ironically, the church.

From the beginning Violeta Chamorro set into motion a policy of national reconciliation that included arriving at a modus vivendi with the Sandinistas. Among other high-level agreements President Chamorro decided to keep General Humberto Ortega on as head of the army. This provoked many criticisms from within the UNO. The hardliners, who wanted to exclude the Sandinistas from the government, were led by Virgilio Godoy, the vice president. But the disagreements went beyond official government circles and included the church. In the beginning relations between the church and the UNO government were quite harmonious. In the euphoria that followed in the wake of the elections President Chamorro offered to help build a new cathedral, and the cardinal showed up for every important state occasion, with the obvious intention of legitimizing the new government. But soon the cardinal himself joined the dissident voices with respect to Chamorro's policy of accommodating the Sandinistas. The criticisms centered on Antonio Lacayo, the minister of the Presidency, who was also the president's son-in-law. Lacayo was the principal proponent of the policy of accommodation, while Vice President Godoy was the principal voice of opposition.

The tensions between Sandinistas and former Contras frequently exploded into acts of violence, at times between one another and at other times against the government. In July 1993, near Estelí in the north, a group of Sandinistas engaged government troops in a battle. In August, in another zone in the north, a group of Contras kidnapped thirty-seven government officials. In response, a group of Sandinistas in Managua kidnapped another twenty-eight government officials, including Vice President Virgilio Godoy. Finally, both groups freed their captives. President Chamorro decried such violent attempts at extortion.

A LOOKING BACK

The outstanding characteristic of the recent history of the church in Nicaragua is the extreme polarization and absence of moderating forces. Author John Kirk accuses both sides, at least in the beginning, of demonstrating great "immaturity": Obando for being so partial in favor of the Contras and the Reagan administration; and the Sandinistas for their lack of sensitivity in dealing with the hierarchical church, especially in areas such as education and religious symbols.[52] In fact, the Sandinistas did learn from some of their errors. They went from being a relatively closed revolutionary group to a modern political party. Ideologically, the FSLN ceased to be Marxist and converted itself into a sort of national, social-democratic movement.[53] But similar changes have not occurred in the church. In order to foster church unity the Vatican promoted the figure of Obando, but in so doing it did not listen to the voice of the North American episcopal conference, which called for following a more moderate path. Finally the Vatican, through its nuncio, Paolo Giglio, changed its policy and pressured the hierarchical church to enter into dialogue with the Sandinistas. But in the post-Sandinista period Cardinal Obando seemed determined to follow the old policy of confrontation. In this new period the principal figure promoting national reconciliation was not the head of the Nicaraguan church but rather the president, Violeta Chamorro.

On the level of inner-ecclesial relations the church in Nicaragua continues to be divided. The division is due in part to the fact that the hierarchy does not wish to make its peace with those progressive groups who supported the Sandinistas. But some authors have also noted that the progressive groups, at least in the beginning, identified themselves too much with the regime. Rafael Aragón, a Dominican and historian, observes that many Christians supported the regime so much that they ceased to belong to their base Christian communities, and in some cases ceased to practice their faith.[54] Furthermore, the committed Christians who worked on the popular level did not go out of their way to establish dialogue with middle-class Christians.[55]

Finally, the Nicaraguan church is a clear example of the impact that the conservative changes in the Vatican had on the local church and its relations with the state. In the case of El Salvador, Pope John Paul II supported Archbishop Arturo Rivera y Damas, thus strengthening inner-church unity. But in the case of Nicaragua, the pope's support of Obando y Bravo had the opposite effect: church-state relations grew more tense, and the church became more polarized. The 1990 elections marked the beginning of a new chapter for the political as well as the religious future of Nicaragua. On the positive side, that Central American country ceased to become a Cold War laboratory for experimentation by the big powers, especially the United States. Step by step it has begun to construct its own identity and cure its own internal divisions without constant outside pressure. However, it is evident that full national reconciliation and church unity are still goals for the distant future.

11.

Guatemala (1954-1996)

The Longest Civil War

In many ways Guatemala (9,745,000 inhabitants in 1992), with its social stratification (87 percent live in poverty), military dictatorships, social instability, and violence, is a typical Central American country. But in some other ways, this country, which was the heart of the United Provinces of Central America, distinguishes itself and outdoes the others in certain categories. For example, it is the country with the greatest Indian population: perhaps around 50 to 60 percent, with twenty-two distinct languages belonging to the Maya linguistic family.[1] The rest of the population is made up of whites and "*ladinos*," that is, mestizos. Guatemala was also the scene of the longest guerrilla war in the recent history of Latin America: from the sixties until the end of 1996. Furthermore, it witnessed a more systematic and savage violence than that experienced even by Nicaragua and El Salvador, both of which suffered greatly as a result of internal wars and political repression. In the worst years, which correspond to the military dictatorships of General Lucas García and General Ríos Montt (1978-83), between 100,000 to 150,000 civilians were killed.[2] So grave was the situation in Guatemala that some authors and the Catholic church termed what happened there a genocide, with specific reference to the scorched earth policy of Ríos Montt. Furthermore, death squads systematically eliminated hundreds of leaders of the popular organizations, as well as religious, priests, politicians, teachers, and students. For some special reason there existed what author Susanne Jonas refers to as the "great silence" regarding the violence in Guatemala: the international community in general ignored the plight of Guatemala while paying great attention to what was happening in Nicaragua and El Salvador.

Perhaps this silence is due to the fact that the United States has been more discreet about its presence and influence in Guatemala than in other cases. To be sure, the American government under President Eisenhower planned and executed the overthrow of President Arbenz in 1954. But from that moment on the American army and the Central Intelligence Agency, although they intervened very directly in Guatemala, managed to maintain a relatively low profile. On the other hand, unlike the Sandinista leaders, and to a lesser degree the leaders of the Farabundo Martí Front, the guerrilla leaders in Guatemala did not enjoy a high visibility internationally. Perhaps the fact that the majority of the victims of the violence were Indians may also explain the lack of interest in the drama that occurred there. The decision to grant the Nobel Peace Prize in 1992 to Rigoberta Menchú, a Maya Indian and a victim of the violence in her own country, helped to rectify this obliviousness toward Guatemala. Finally, Guatemala also stands out for another reason: it is the Central American country with the fastest growing Protestant population. According to David Stoll, the percentage of Protestants (or *Evangélicos*) jumped from 2.81 percent in 1960 to 18.92 percent in 1985.[3] In fact, this country has already had two Protestant presidents: General Ríos Montt (1982-83) and Jorge Serrano Elías (1991-93).

Returning to what is common, Guatemala is very similar to the rest of Central America, especially El Salvador and Nicaragua, with respect to the roles played by the Catholic church in its recent history: as a conscienticizing force, as a victim of violence and a voice of protest, and as a mediator in the peace process. We will divide this chapter into three parts: (1) Guatemala's recent political history up until President Cerezo; (2) the church during this same period; and (3) the role of the church as mediator between the government and the guerrilla movement, 1986-95.

POLITICAL BACKGROUND

Guatemala's history in the nineteenth century, as in the rest of Latin America, was characterized by the struggle between liberals and conservatives. In 1871 Justo Rufino Barrios and the liberals, representing the new commercial middle class and the coffee oligarchy, came to power. Guatemalan liberalism unleashed a persecution against the church comparable to that of the Mexican liberals in the twentieth century. In the name of modernization the church lost the major portion of its lands. At the same time the United Fruit Company emerged to become the biggest landowner of all. The last dictator who ruled with the sole backing of United Fruit and the national oligarchy was General Jorge Ubico (1931-44). With the support of the new worker's movement and modernizing sectors in the middle classes and the army, two reformist presidents finally came to power: Juan José Arévalo (1945-50), a teacher; and Jacobo Arbenz (1951-54), a soldier.

Both rulers attempted to carry out numerous reforms. The more radical of the two, Arbenz, decreed an agrarian reform in 1952 and expropriated several thousand acres of the United Fruit Company. However, neither Arévalo nor Arbenz were communists, who were still insignificant numerically. In fact, Arbenz indemnified United Fruit for the expropriations. Yet in 1954 the Eisenhower administration openly supported a CIA-planned invasion to "liberate" Guatemala from communism. Within the context of the Cold War, the United States could not tolerate a reformist government that was supported by communists. Furthermore, it was no secret that the Dulles brothers, John Foster, the secretary of State, and Allen, the director of the CIA, had direct links with the United Fruit Company.[4]

Historians have generally marked the overthrow of Arbenz as the fatal derailment that put the country on the wrong track for the next forty years. It is tempting to speculate what would have happened if Arbenz had been allowed to carry out his reforms. Perhaps the long subsequent history of dictatorships and guerrilla war might have been avoided. The fact is that from 1954 until 1986, with one exception (the government of Julio César Méndez Montenegro, 1966-70), all the country's rulers were military men who defended the landowning oligarchy and the business class by means of repression and violence. Even when they were not directly in power, the military continued to dictate what happened in the country, especially its internal security. Given the control the army had over the state, an American military intervention in Guatemala was not really necessary. Guatemala became a praetorian state in which the civilians had very little room in which to speak or act. Furthermore, Guatemala was characterized by another peculiarity: for years it had no leftist parties, only parties in the center and on the right. Within that context moderate politicians were considered "leftist" by the military and rightwing civilians. In practice, after Arévalo and Arbenz, the vast majority of Guatemalans were simply excluded from political participation. This is the background for understanding the emergence of the armed groups as well as the many popular organizations that initially existed outside the law.

THE GUERRILLA AND THE POPULAR MOVEMENT

Besides longevity, the guerrilla movement in Guatemala distinguished itself by other characteristics. For example, the first guerrillas were ex-military—Captains Augusto Turcios Lima and Marco Antonio Yon Sosa—a fact that partially explains their success in the sixties. These first revolutionary leaders, inspired by the Cuban model, established focal points of resistance in the jungle and the northern altiplano, although they made no effort to comprehend the Indian culture that surrounded them. Between 1969 and 1970 their focal points were wiped out by the army and the first generation of guerrillas disappeared.

In the seventies a new generation, which learned from the errors of the first, emerged to fill the vacuum. For example, the new leaders took much more seriously the Indian culture of Guatemala and tried to attract the Indians to the cause. They also learned to appreciate the religious factor, especially after the changes in the Catholic church. In 1982, after many years of struggle and in spite of their ideological differences, the four principal guerrilla groups coalesced to form one single front: the National Revolutionary Union of

Guatemala (URNG: Unidad Revolucionaria Nacional Guatemalteca). The four founding groups were the ORPA (Organization of the People in Arms); the FAR (Rebel Armed Forces); the EGP (Guerrilla Army of the Poor); and the PGT (Guatemalan Labor Party).[5] Although statistics vary considerably, most authors put the number of guerrillas between six thousand and eight thousand men and women. There were perhaps close to half a million sympathizers.[6] The principal regions where they operated were the most inaccessible areas of the jungle and the altiplano—in Petén, Huehuetenango, San Marcos, and Quetzaltenango. The guerrillas had bases in all twenty-two departments of the country.

At the same time, but especially in the eighties, a popular movement emerged that was not directly connected with the armed groups: teachers, university students, and workers (who reorganized themselves after the first attempt under Arbenz). In 1978 the Committee of Peasant Unity (CUC: Comité de Unidad Campesina), which united all peasant unions in the country, was founded. Finally, the earthquake of 1976, in which twenty-five thousand persons died—the majority very poor—contributed to the political awakening of the country. As a consequence of that natural disaster thousands of peasants were forced to migrate. Also, many Guatemalans were revolted by the venality of many members of the military and the police who made use of the crisis to fill their pockets.

RÍOS MONTT: GENOCIDE IN THE NEW ISRAEL

Repression and political violence were not particularly new phenomena in the eighties. In the two months following Arbenz's overthrow in 1954, some eight thousand peasants were killed under the government of General Armas Castillo.[7] In the sixties the death squads, such as White Hand, selectively murdered student leaders and politicians. In the face of the new guerrilla movement of the eighties, as well as the emergence of the popular movement, the military and the death squads became more systematic and drastic. Furthermore, they counted on the technical expertise of American military advisers who had been in Vietnam. Two acts of repression particularly underlined this new drastic orientation: Panzós and the Spanish embassy. In May 1978, near Panzós, a town in Alta Veracruz, to the north of the capital, the army massacred more than a hundred Kelchis Indians, who had protested over the usurping of their lands.[8] In January 1980 a group of peasants, some of whom were union militants who had founded the Committee of Peasant Unity, seized the Spanish embassy. Their objective was to call world attention to the repression of the military in their villages. The forces of order retook the embassy, killing all the peasants. Among the thirty-nine victims was the father of Rigoberta Menchú.[9]

General Romeo Lucas García (1978-82) inaugurated a policy centering around the concept of "development poles." According to the policy, the peasants—the majority of whom were Indians—were obliged to live in villages or camps controlled by the army or else be considered "subversives." His successor, General Ríos Montt, would go far beyond Lucas in the drastic application of this policy. In March 1982 several hundred young army officials revolted and forced Lucas, whom they accused of corruption and inefficiency in the counterinsurgency war, to resign. They invited Efraín Ríos Montt, then retired from the army, to head the new government. Ríos had been a presidential candidate for the Christian Democratic Party in 1974. He was apparently winning the election when the government perpetrated an electoral fraud. The retired general was known for his honesty and efficiency. But there was a new aspect of his life that was not widely known: after his electoral defeat he became a born-again Christian and joined the Church of the Word (*El Verbo*), a fundamentalist group based in California. What distinguished Ríos Montt was the combination of evangelical fervor and implacable repression of Guatemala's Indian population. Once in power, the born-again president surrounded himself with advisers from his church and every Sunday gave a televised message to the nation on morality and the family. Many missionaries, who enthusiastically envisioned Guatemala under Ríos Montt as the "New Israel" of America, arrived in great numbers.[10] The spokespersons of the new religious right in the United States, particularly Pat Robertson, showered praise on the new experiment.[11]

Under the slogan "Guns and Beans," Ríos Montt declared total war on the population in areas under the guerrillas' control. The statistics accepted by serious observers give an idea of the magnitude of the tragedy that occurred in Guatemala during those years. Between 100,000 and 150,000 civilians were killed or made to disappear. Four hundred and forty villages were simply wiped out. Close to a million people (out of a population of nine million) were forced to flee their homes and live in camps in Mexico.[12] Several thousand peasants formed the Communities of People in Resistance, that is, refugees who refused either to support the guerrillas or to live in the "development poles." The Jesuit anthropologist Ricardo Falla documented the history of the massacres in Huehuetenango and El Quiché by interviewing the survivors. In his book, *Massacres in the Jungle*, he presents long lists of names of victims.[13] It seems that Ríos Montt and the army seriously planned to eliminate the guerrillas by wiping out a major portion of the Indian population of Guatemala—men, women, and children. The use of the word *genocide* is not an exaggeration.

One of the principal mechanisms Ríos Montt used to implement his policy was the Civilian Auto-Defense Patrols (PACs). The army forced rural dwellers to join these army-controlled patrols as a way of defending the villages against the guerrillas. But the patrols also served as a mechanism of control over the population. Those who cooperated received "guns and beans." But there was a price to be paid: those who cooperated (or "cooperated" against their will) lived in the "development poles" and lost their liberty and a good deal of their Indian cultural identity. Finally, rural Guatemala was subjected to total militarization. Close to one-eighth of the entire population of the country was recruited to serve in the patrols.[14] For the Indians, the imposition of this repressive military apparatus constituted a direct attack on their culture. The army, run by whites and *ladinos*, associated the customs and culture of the Indians with subversion. The civilian patrols continued to exist long after the return to democracy, which meant that the army continued to exercise direct control over most of the rural population of the country. Frequently, as Ricardo Falla notes, the patrols, composed of peasants with little discipline, turned into bands of "highway robbers and thieves."[15]

Ríos Montt's fundamentalism also played a role in the application of this policy. At first the army looked with suspicion on all religious activity, Catholic or Protestant, because religion served as a unifying force. But after Ríos Montt came to power the army distinguished between Protestants and Catholics: the former were perceived as allies; the latter, whether they were charismatics or "liberationists," were viewed as potential allies of the subversives.[16] After his fall from power the born-again dictator was hailed in assemblies of American fundamentalists as a "victim" of a conspiracy. But non-fundamentalistic Protestants, aware of the contradictions between the Christian message and Ríos Montt's policies, preferred not to associate themselves with his regime and that type of political-religious fundamentalism.[17]

THE RETURN TO DEMOCRACY: A MILITARIZED SOCIETY

In August 1983 Ríos Montt was overthrown by other military leaders, who put General Oscar Humberto Mejía Víctores in his place. One reason for Ríos Montt's ouster was his moralizing style which irritated many Catholics and some Protestants. But there were other, more weighty factors. In his struggle to moralize the army and rid it of corruption, Ríos Montt provoked hostility among fellow officers. Many military leaders came to the conclusion that they preferred a more "normal" military man to a born-again Christian. Furthermore, the United States had begun to pressure Guatemala to control the excesses that resulted from its counterinsurgency policy, and to return to democracy. In this case, as in others, the pressure to return to democracy was accompanied by promises of economic aid. Finally, many Guatemalans—civilians and military—were conscious of the fact that their country had become an international pariah as a consequence of its human-rights violations.

In 1985 free and relatively honest elections were held. The winner was Vinicio Cerezo of the Christian Democrats. The United States fulfilled its promises and came forth with economic aid, and the Western world received Guatemala back into the fold of democratic nations. Nevertheless, in spite of the good intentions of the new civilian president, it was evident that the army, which continued to battle the guerrillas, had converted itself into a state within the state. Through the counterinsurgency defense patrols, which totalled some 800,000 recruits in 1987, the army controlled the rural areas.[18] Furthermore, it maintained all its privileges. Worse still, the death squads, closely tied to the forces of order, continued their reign of terror. Political assassinations, kidnappings, and human-rights violations continued to be the order of the day.

Among the many crimes committed in that period some were especially scandalous. In November 1989 Diana Ortiz, an American religious, was kidnapped, tortured, and raped. She managed to escape, and her testimony implicated a group of paramilitary.[19] In September 1990 a Guatemalan anthropologist, Myrna Mack, was stabbed to death in the very center of the capital. Mack was a cofounder of AVANCSO (Association for the Advancement of the Social Sciences in Guatemala). As part of her work she offered data on the Indian reality of Guatemala to different church and human-rights groups.[20] Later, a man was accused of the crime and condemned to twenty-five years in prison. But the intellectual authors of the crime, who were protected by persons in power, were never touched. In December of that year the forces of order fired upon a group of unarmed Indians, killing fourteen of them. This incident, which occurred in Santiago Atitlán, provoked a wave of protest throughout the country. What was peculiar in this case was that there were survivors to tell the story.[21]

Finally, there was a murder that directly affected relations between the United States and Guatemala. In 1990 a group of military or paramilitary killed Michael Devine, an American citizen who owned a hotel in El Petén. As a direct consequence of this killing the Bush administration decided to cut off military aid to Guatemala. Later, in 1995, Congressman Robert Torriceli (New Jersey) accused the CIA of having paid Guatemalan officers to commit crimes, which included the murders of Devine and Efraín Bamaca, a guerrilla who had been captured in 1992 and killed while held a prisoner of the army.[22] All of these killings and other crimes committed by paramilitary, frequently in complicity with the CIA, underlined the civilians' lack of control over their own country. Although Guatemala returned to democracy, it did not return to peace.

With this brief overview of political history, we can now examine the role of the church in the same period.

THE CHURCH:
FROM PERSECUTION TO RECONSTRUCTION (1871-1964)

The liberal revolution of 1871 was a disaster for the church. In fact, Guatemala's anticlericalism was the worst in Central America. The archbishop, his auxiliary bishop, the Jesuits, and other religious were all expelled from the country. Church and state were separated, religious schools were suppressed, and church lands were expropriated. President Barrios himself invited a group of Presbyterian missionaries to the country.[23] Archbishop Ricardo Casanova Estrada (1886-1913) assumed the painful task of reconstructing what was left of the church, which in 1912 had only 119 priests in the entire country.[24] In spite of the prevailing anticlerical climate, the archbishop managed to establish a modus vivendi between the church and the new coffee oligarchy, an alliance that remained in force until the 1960s.

The church was able to function again thanks in part to foreign missionaries. In 1943 priests and brothers of the Society of Maryknoll established themselves in Huehuetenango, and in 1955 the Congregation of the Sacred Heart began working in El Quiché. In 1937 the Jesuits reorganized the central seminary for the diocesan clergy. Mariano Rossell y Arellano, the archbishop of Guatemala from 1939 to 1964, gave an important impetus to the rebuilding of the church. Under the banner of anticommunism, Rossell also criticized the reformist government of Arbenz and openly supported his overthrow. From that moment on rightwing groups recognized the church as an important ally and rewarded it. The 1956 and 1966 constitutions eliminated nearly all of the anticlerical restrictions. In the meantime, the signs of reconstruction were encouraging. In 1951 there were 7 dioceses and 1 apostolic administration. By 1991 there were 15 ecclesiastical jurisdictions, with 21 bishops in all. That same year there were 218 diocesan priests, 512 religious priests, and 1,539 women religious.[25]

In spite of the nearly total absence of the official church in the countryside, Catholicism lived on thanks to certain traditional organizations that enjoyed great social prestige: the confraternities and Catholic Action. Unlike most other parts of Latin America, where Catholic Action flourished only among the urban middle classes, in Guatemala Catholic Action was quite successful among the rural peasantry. One author explains this success by observing that the structure of Catholic Action was simply superimposed on traditional local structures. In other words, local community leaders became the leaders of Catholic Action.[26] The traditional community values of solidarity, a "mythical-religious" interpretation of life, and collective work all survived in indigenous Catholicism. Even when certain practices—known as The Custom—existed before Catholicism, they were not necessarily opposed to the latter. Thanks largely to rural Catholic Action and the confraternities, indigenous Catholicism not only survived but became a mainstay of the people during the times of persecution.

TOWARD AN INDIAN CHURCH

As in the rest of Latin America, the Council and Medellín opened up new horizons for the church in Guatemala. This time of change and modernization corresponded to the administration of Mario Casariego, archbishop of Guatemala from 1964 to 1983. The number of foreign missionaries continued to grow. According to Ricardo Bendaña, by 1969 only 19 percent of the clergy were native Guatemalans.[27] In 1961 CONFREGUA—the Guatemalan Conference of Religious—was founded, and in 1964 the episcopal conference of Guatemala came into existence. The cursillos of Cristiandad enjoyed widespread popularity. In 1961 the Rafael Landívar University was founded by the Jesuits. Along with these signs of progress, however, there were also signs of internal fissures in the church, which grew increasingly wider. Casariego, although he was named archbishop during the Council (and elevated to the rank of cardinal in 1969), was essentially a pre–Vatican II man. He took up the banner of anticommunism—with no subtleties—and was known to be a friend of the rich and powerful. He did not encourage lay participation, and by the seventies and eighties he opposed almost all progressive tendencies in the church.

Two dramatic incidents highlighted the ecclesial instability and polarization of those years: the Melville affair, and the kidnapping of the archbishop. In 1967 two Maryknoll priests, Thomas Melville and Blase Bonpane, and a Maryknoll sister, Marian Peter, established contact with the guerrillas; ultimately they attempted to found their own Christian guerrilla organization. Their superiors soon discovered the project, and the three were immediately whisked out of the country.[28] In reality, this incident caused more scandal among church circles in the United States than in Guatemala. Nevertheless, it served to underline the degree of radicalization some foreign missionaries had experienced. Indeed, there were other cases of religious who joined the guerrillas, as we shall see.

The second incident—the kidnapping of the archbishop—was a bit more mystifying. In March 1968 Casariego was kidnapped by MANO, a rightwing paramilitary outfit. Apparently the archbishop was abducted in punishment for supporting President Montenegro's plans to reform the army. However, he was liberated ten days later, safe and sound. The whole affair was viewed with general indifference.

Another sign of internal dissension was the creation of COSDIGUA: the Confederation of Diocesan Priests of Guatemala. Founded and directed by Father José María Ruiz Furlán, popularly known as Father "Chemita," COSDIGUA drew together the more conservative members of the clergy. They leveled their criticisms at both the foreign clergy and Casariego. The organization ceased to exist in 1972.

In spite of Casariego and COSDIGUA, the Council reforms went into effect and the spirit of Medellín inspired base ecclesial communities. Many church groups founded centers to train catechists and delegates of the Word. Catholic Action, built on a pre–Vatican II vertical model, declined. But the base ecclesial communities, more open and flexible, filled the vacuum. A model par excellence of all these changes was the diocese of El Quiché.

The bishops, priests, and religious men and women who worked in El Quiché, converted into a diocese in 1967, expended their energy on creating an Indian church along the lines of Medellín and other church assemblies. In reality, this chapter began with Catholic Action, founded in the diocese in 1942. Catholic Action gave the Maya Indians—and *ladinos* as well—a sense of participation in the church they had not had before. In 1955 missionaries of the Sacred Heart arrived, and along with the Society of Maryknoll in

Huehuetenango, gave notable impetus to this process. In the sixties many cooperatives, frequently founded by Catholic Action, came into being. Also, Indian catechists, imbued with the spirit of Medellín, conscienticized other Indians and promoted literacy programs. Between the two, Catholic Action and the catechists, the church created an impressive network of pastoral agents. In 1968 there were three thousand catechists in the diocese, and eighty thousand members of Catholic Action.[29] The bishops of El Quiché, especially Juan Gerardi Conedera (1974-85), gave full support to the formation of this indigenous church. Also, a group of Jesuits, known as the Jesuits of "Zone 5," a reference to the neighborhood where the Society of Jesus' local CIAS (Center of Investigation and Social Action) functioned in the capital, visited the diocese regularly to offer conscientization cursillos for the youth. One of the Jesuits, Fernando Hoyos, joined the guerrillas in 1980 and was killed in an armed action in 1982.[30] In this same period many institutes and schools for Indian rural teachers were founded.

The fruit of this work could clearly be seen in the seventies and eighties. A new generation of indigenous leaders emerged: some had been formed in the old Catholic Action; others in the cursillos organized by the diocese or the Jesuits; and still others in the new educational institutes for Indians. Inevitably this conscienticizing work had political consequences. In the 1966 elections many Indians, linked to the Christian Democratic Party, ran for mayor in towns throughout the country. This story was repeated in 1974. Finally, this political and social awakening was felt in the new popular movement, which emerged during those years. In 1978 CUC (the Committee of Peasant Unity), the first national peasant union, was founded. Not all new movements, however, grew out of the new orientation of Medellín. In 1973 the Charismatic Renewal, which had considerable impact in many Indian communities in the altiplano, was founded.

RIGOBERTA MENCHÚ

The synthesis between liberationist Christianity and indigenous reaffirmation is personified especially in the life of Rigoberta Menchú, the winner of the Nobel Peace Prize in 1992. Rigoberta was born of Indian parents—"of Quiché ethnic" background, as she relates in her autobiography—in a small town in the Guatemalan altiplano. She was raised in an atmosphere impregnated with pre-Columban and Catholic beliefs. But she rejects the charge that her people are polytheistic. Rather, she points out, what some people think is polytheism is really a reverence for God in nature: "We respect all natural things."[31] But there is no doubting the Catholic influence in her life, which she received by way of her father, who participated in Catholic Action. As she explains, "We felt ourselves to be very Catholic because we believe in Catholicism; at the same time we feel ourselves to be very Indian, and we are proud of our ancestors."[32] As a youth she became a catechist, an experience that helped her later as a militant activist in the CUC. In the CUC she was assigned to be an organizer. She notes that the task was not too difficult because "I learned to organize as a catechist."[33] The Bible was the central book in her life and the life of the community. It was, as she explains in her autobiography, not just a "formational document," but, more poignantly, "our principal weapon." She points with pride to the figures of Judith, Moses, David, and, of course, Jesus, as models of service and self-giving for the good of the community.[34]

In her autobiography Rigoberta does not hesitate to criticize the official church and priests who are insensitive to the Bible message and the injustices the people suffer. In reference to Cardinal Casariego, she accuses the hierarchy of not having "a clear position" on justice and freedom.[35] On the other hand, she praises the priests and religious women who "love the people" and who at different moments helped her personally. She notes that she learned to read and write Spanish in a convent.[36] She began her political career under the influence of her father, Víctor Menchú, who was a militant union organizer and who participated in the founding of the CUC. Víctor Menchú was imprisoned for his activities and, as mentioned above, was killed with other peasants when they captured the Spanish embassy. Earlier her younger brother had been kidnapped, tortured, and killed. Finally, in April 1980, her mother was kidnapped, raped, and left to die among wild animals. In 1979 Rigoberta joined the CUC and devoted herself to traveling around the country to help organize the new union.

During this experience she realized the importance of learning Spanish, which she had not done in her youth. She came to discover a specific Christian vocation within the union struggles. As she puts it: "My task was to contribute to the Christian formation of my companion Christians who were in the organization as a consequence of their faith."[37] She notes that the Guatemalan church is divided in two: "the church of the poor and the church of the hierarchy, which acts like a clique."[38] Of course, she wrote that harsh judgment in 1982, when Casariego was still the head of the church.

A PERSECUTED CHURCH

Given the close ties between the progressive sectors of the church and the popular movement, and in some cases with the guerrillas, the church soon became a target for persecution. Even before the repressive regimes of Lucas and Ríos Montt, churchpeople experienced kidnappings and murders. In 1976 Raisa Girón Arévalo, the director of a Catholic school, was kidnapped, tortured, and left to die. That same year the small aircraft in which William Woods, a Maryknoll priest in charge of the cooperatives in Ixcán Grande, was shot down.[39] In both cases there were threats previous to the attacks. However, systematic persecution began under Lucas and Ríos Montt. According to one summary, "between 1978 and 1985 five diocesan priests, eight religious priests, two religious brothers, of whom four were foreign-born and the other four Guatemalans, were murdered."[40] Furthermore, ninety-one priests and sixty-four religious women were forced to leave the country. Many works of the church were closed: radio stations, schools, and formation centers. In May 1980 a Philippine priest, Conrado de la Cruz, disappeared and was never seen again. That same month Walter Voordeckers, a Belgian priest, was shot down when he left his parish to go to the post office. In June José María Gran, a Sacred Heart priest, and a lay volunteer were shot to death in cold blood.[41] The El Quiché diocese fell under an exceptionally severe sentence. In July Bishop Juan Gerardi barely escaped from an ambush. As a consequence of that incident, as well as several murders in the diocese, he decided to withdraw all church personnel from El Quiché. His decision was made in part to protect the lives of the people under his care, but he also did it as a way of protesting to the government and security forces for being accomplices to the killings. He personally explained his decision to the pope. In November, when he returned to Guatemala, he was detained by the authorities and sent in exile to Costa Rica.[42] One priest, Juan Alonso Fernández, returned to work in the diocese but was murdered in February 1981.

There were a few cases where priests or religious became involved with the guerrillas. An Irish priest, Donald McKenna, who sympathized with the Irish Republican Army, joined the Guerrilla Army of the Poor but left the country shortly afterward.[43] In another case, which was much publicized, a Guatemalan Jesuit, Luis Pellecer, who worked with popular organizations, was kidnapped in June 1981. He appeared three months later, under heavy guard, and gave a press interview in which he admitted having joined the guerrillas. He claimed that he now regretted that action. Furthermore, he denounced liberation theology and progressive Christians. In the opinion of most observers Pellecer was a victim of "brainwashing." He later left the priesthood.

This implacable persecution of the church was extended to include hundreds of catechists and Christians from the base ecclesial communities who fell victim to the death squads or the army during the scorched earth campaigns. The church was relieved when the country returned to democracy in 1985. But, as the case of Diana Ortiz demonstrated, the church continued to be a target of kidnappings and selective murders well after the return to democracy.

THE CHURCH AWAKENS

During Archbishop Casariego's time the church in Guatemala gave the impression of being a silent one.[44] In reality, there were bishops who followed the new orientations of the Council and Medellín, but they belonged to small dioceses and did not attract much attention. In March 1974 the bishops published a collective letter on violence, but Casariego and two other bishops refused to sign it. In 1976 the episcopal conference prepared another letter, "United in Hope," considered by many as one of the best documents of the church. In it the bishops speak of the poverty and injustice in Guatemala and, most of all, of the institutionalized violence. However, once again, Casariego refused to sign it. Finally, in preparation for the 1978 elections, the bishops prepared a letter to orient the faithful. Casariego took the document, eliminated the parts that did not please him, and published it without consulting the other bishops. This action motivated six bishops to write Rome asking for the archbishop to be removed.[45] It was evident that as long as Casariego remained in his post, episcopal unity would be impossible.

In spite of this disarray on the episcopal level, other groups provided leadership for the church. The most important example was CONFREGUA, the Conference of Religious of Guatemala. Founded in 1961, it established a communication network that helped foster a deep sense of unity among the religious who worked in the country. CONFREGUA organized its first national congress in 1973, and a second one in 1980. That year there were 1,021 women and 564 men religious in Guatemala.[46] Long before the bishops spoke out, CONFREGUA assumed the mission of denouncing abuses and human-rights violations. In this context one can appreciate a scroll from the Worker's Union of Guatemala that hangs in a place of honor in the offices of CONFREGUA. The scroll, dated February 1990, praises CONFREGUA "for its dedication and constant defense of the dignity and the rights of the workers and the people." Beginning in 1986 CONFREGUA published *La Carta* ("The Letter"), a bulletin that provides information on concrete cases of human-rights violations. Another important group was the Committee Pro-Justice and Peace, founded in 1977. The Committee, which was established in eleven departments, was ecumenical in nature and not dependent upon the bishops. It also disseminated information on human-rights violations and helped to conscienticize Christians on the base level.[47]

The papal visit in March 1983 revitalized Guatemalan Catholicism. Some authors have underlined the contrast between two events: the one-hundredth anniversary of Protestantism's arrival, celebrated in 1982, and the papal visit a few months later. The first event was characterized by the enthusiastic participation of thousands of Protestants from all over the country. President Ríos Montt and other prominent Protestants, such as Jorge Serrano Elías, watched while Luis Palau preached.[48] The pope arrived in a country where many Catholics felt that the church was in retreat and, given the situation of the episcopal conference, in disarray. Furthermore, the visit was much publicized because the president-dictator refused to pardon the lives of six political prisoners in spite of a personal appeal from the pope. These factors notwithstanding, the visit strengthened the faith of thousands of Guatemalans. The pope also encouraged the bishops and other Catholic leaders to take a more resolute stand against violence and the abuses committed by the government and the forces of order.

Casariego died on June 15, and in January 1984 Próspero Penados del Barrios, the bishop of San Marcos, assumed the mantle of archbishop of Guatemala City. The naming of Penados definitely signified a change in the church. Finally, unity was restored to the episcopal conference. In 1988 the bishops published another letter, "The Cry for Land." The letter was inspired in part by a movement organized by Father Andrés Girón, who in 1986 had led a march to the capital with thousands of peasants demanding land. Guatemala is the only country in Central America that has not had any agrarian reform. In the year of the march 2.25 percent of the population owned 64.52 percent of the land.[49] The bishops refer without ambiguities to the concentration of land in the hands of a few and demand a more just distribution. Unlike previous pastoral letters, this time all the bishops signed. Penados soon stood out as a defender of human rights. In 1989 he founded the Office of Human Rights of the Archdiocese of Guatemala. The office, directed by Ronalth Ochaeta, began with four persons; by 1995 it had a staff of twenty-nine, including lawyers, educators, sociologists, economists, and one theologian. In 1994 the office examined 390 denunciations.[50] Almost all the other dioceses have similar offices. With this new ecclesial unity, and strengthened by the legitimacy it enjoyed on the popular level, the hierarchy was prepared to dedicate itself to the most urgent task of the post–military government era: the construction of democracy and the conquest of peace.

THE DIALOGUE FOR PEACE

Among his first initiatives President Cerezo (1986-91) expressed his desire to enter into dialogue with the guerrillas with the hope of finding the road to peace. The new civilian president's motives were evident: to put an end to an internal conflict that seemed endless; to change Guatemala's poor international image; and to satisfy international pressure, especially from the United States, to put the country's house in order. Furthermore, after Esquipulas II (1987) Cerezo counted on a mandate from the other Central American countries to seek dialogue with the guerrillas. The guerrillas, however, were not sure if they wanted to dialogue. They were aware of the influence of the army and the continued existence of death squads, which acted with impunity. Furthermore, Cerezo's government was far from stable. In fact, it had to withstand three attempts at a *golpe de estado*: in May and August of 1988, and in May 1989. From the guerrillas' point of view only the forms, not the reality, of democracy had been reestablished. On the other hand, they had suffered much and did not have any real hope of winning the war, especially under a civilian government. In the opinion of César Montes, a former guerrilla fighter, unlike the FMLN in El Salvador and the FSLN in Nicaragua, the URNG (Unidad Revolucionaria Nacional Guatemalteca) had not managed to deliver any really decisive or strategic blows: "The Guatemalan movement wasn't able to leave the jungle of Petén or the mountains of Ixcán."[51] In short, the Guatemalan guerrilla movement had lost momentum. There were other factors influencing their decision to negotiate: the collapse of communism in Europe (1989), the electoral defeat of *Sandinismo* in Nicaragua (1990), and the signing of a peace agreement between the Salvadoran government and the FMLN (1992). The guerrillas were caught in a dilemma: negotiate and show their good intentions, or keep on fighting and lose credibility.

The peace process went through four stages: (1) first contact in Madrid in 1987 until the beginning of formal negotiations in Oslo, Norway, in 1990; (2) from Oslo to the fall of Jorge Serrano in 1993; (3) new negotiations under de León Carpio until the moment Bishop Quesada published the documents of the Assembly of Civil Society in 1995; and (4) final negotiations with the United Nations acting as mediator (1995-96). During the first three stages the church, in the person of Bishop Rodolfo Quesada Toruño, played a key role. Quesada was the principal mediator, with the title of conciliator, between the government and the URNG until February 1994, at which point the United Nations assumed the mission to mediate. But Quesada continued to play a key role. Following a mandate of the agreements between the URNG and the government, he founded the Association of Civil Society, which drew together all civilian groups not tied to the government or the guerrillas. Only when the Assembly of Civil Society (which represented the Association) had finished its particular mission did Quesada retire from the peace process.

FIRST STAGE: FROM MADRID TO OSLO (1987-1990)

From the very beginning President Cerezo expressed his desire to engage in dialogue with the guerrillas, and in October 1986 the leaders of the URNG sent him a letter expressing the same sentiment. The first encounter between the government and the URNG took place in October 1987 in Madrid. The government was represented by several deputies from the Guatemalan congress, several observers from the army, and Guatemala's ambassador in Spain. The URNG was represented by Gáspar Llóm and two members of its Political-Diplomatic Commission, Luis Becker Guzmán and Miguel Angel Sandoval. The meeting was described as "low-level," and no particular result was produced.[52] As new meetings were held, the world came to learn more about the mysterious URNG, up until then unknown outside Guatemala. The troika that normally represented the URNG were Pablo Monsanto of the Rebel Armed Forces (FAR), Rolando Morán of the Guerrilla Army of the Poor (EGP), and Rodrigo Asturias of the Organization of the People in Arms (ORPA). Asturias, who had taken the nom de guerre of Gáspar Llóm, turned out to be the son of Miguel Angel Asturias, famed author and winner of the Nobel Prize for literature. Also present at most meetings was Luis Becker, who represented the political commission of the URNG. After Madrid there were no more direct contacts between the government and the guerrillas until April 1991.

Although the meeting in Madrid was important because it was the first, it was evident that something vital was lacking: a mechanism to institutionalize the dialogue. In light of this, and following the recommendations of

Esquipulas II, in August 1987 the National Commission of Reconciliation was created, although it was not installed until October. As a result, it did not participate in the October meeting in Madrid. Afterward, however, it became the key instrument of mediation between the government, the URNG, and Guatemalan society. The commission was composed of Bishop Rodolfo Quesada, who headed it; Roberto Carpio, who acted as vice president; Jorge Serrano Elías, representing the political parties in opposition to the government; and Teresa Zarco, "a notable citizen," who was co-owner of *Prensa Libre*, a daily newspaper. Quesada, the bishop of Zacapa and Esquipulas, Guatemala's national shrine, had been named to the commission by the episcopal conference. He did not, therefore, act on his own, but rather as official representative of the church. As a mediator he proved to have the right qualities: prudence, efficiency, a good sense of humor, and most of all, impartiality. He identified with the church of Medellín, a fact that made him acceptable to the URNG. Several times the rightwing press accused him of "going along" with the guerrillas. But the bishop of Zacapa was no friend of demagoguery, and on a few occasions expressed his irritation with the URNG for supporting irresponsible positions.

The commission finally began its work in 1988 when, at President Cerezo's request, it formally sought contact with the guerrillas. The commission met with the URNG first in March, then in August, in San José, Costa Rica. There were no concrete results from either meeting. On May 11, shortly after the first meeting, a group of army officials attempted to overthrow Cerezo. This attempt at a *golpe de estado*, plus the others that occurred during Cerezo's presidency, greatly limited the capacity of the commission to dialogue with the guerrillas, who would have preferred to deal with a more stable government that exercised control over the army. In this context, more important than these attempts at dialogue was the National Dialogue the commission convoked in February 1989.

The National Dialogue

The dialogue, inspired by the Esquipulas II proposals, drew together eighty-nine delegates from forty-seven different organizations: unions, small businesses, educational centers, peasant federations, human-rights groups, political parties, and the media. The Catholic church was present, as well as the Evangelical Alliance of Guatemala, the Lutheran church, the Episcopal church, the Confederation of Evangelical Churches, and the Jewish community.[53] The delegates were divided into different commissions: health, education, culture, and ethnic groups. The most noticeable absentees were the principal protagonists: the government, the army, and the big businesses which were represented by CACIF (Coordinating Committee of Agricultural, Commercial, Industrial, and Financial Associations) and UNAGRO (National Husbandry Union). Naturally, the guerrillas were not present. Nevertheless, in spite of this lacuna, the National Dialogue had the effect of widening civic participation and pressuring the extremes—right and left—to abandon their rigid positions.

SECOND STAGE: FROM OSLO TO THE FALL OF SERRANO (1990-1993)

Oslo represented the real beginning of the process leading to a negotiated peace. In spite of the signs of weariness which his government displayed, Cerezo exhorted the guerrillas to return to dialogue. For its part, the URNG felt the weight of the events in Europe, as well as the example of the FMLN in El Salvador and the FSLN in Nicaragua, both of which had entered into a process of negotiation with the opposition. The host of the Oslo meeting, held between March 27 and March 29, was the World Lutheran Federation, based in the Norwegian capital. The Commission of National Reconciliation went to the meeting, as well as the Political Commission of the URNG— Luis Becker, Francisco Villagrán Muñoz, and Jorge E. Rosal. Quesada did not attend for reasons of health. Jorge Serrano took his place as head of the commission. The most important result of the Oslo meeting was the acceptance by both sides of the principle that peace must be won by means of negotiation. The delegates signed the first important document of the process: "Basic Agreement on the Search for Peace by Political Means."[54] According to the agreement, the URNG committed itself to a series of meetings with different sectors of Guatemalan society, then to return for direct discussions with the government and the army.

The two major events in Guatemala in 1990 were the meetings between the URNG and the different sectors of society, and the presidential elections, held in November. The first meeting after Oslo, held in Madrid in May, was between the URNG and the political parties. Nine parties, from the extreme right (the National Liberation Movement) to the more centrist ones—the Christian Democrats and the Movement of Solidary Action—sent representatives. The Movement of Solidary Action (MAS) was the party that would bring Jorge Serrano to the presidency that year. This time Bishop Quesada was present as conciliator and president of the National Reconciliation Commission. In the second meeting, in Ottawa in August and September, the URNG came face to face with CACIF, the association of big business. Here, indeed, the two extremes met. The atmosphere was rather tense, and no joint declaration was issued. For the third meeting the guerrilla leaders met in Quito in September with representatives of the different religions and religious associations: the Catholic episcopal conference, CONFREGUA, the different Protestant churches, and the Jewish community. The atmosphere was much more tranquil and productive. In Bishop Quesada's opinion, for the first time the armed conflict was treated in an "integral way."[55] Also, in the words of one URNG official, the churches had "the greatest contact with the population." Finally, in Mexico, in October, two further meetings were held: the first, between the URNG and the unions and other popular organizations; and the second, with academics, educators, and small businesses.

The Election of Jorge Serrano

In November Jorge Serrano Elías came in first, and Jorge Carpio Nicolle (Union of the National Center) second, in the first electoral round. In the second round Serrano won by an ample majority and on January 14, 1992, he assumed the presidency of the country. Serrano had been an adviser to Ríos Montt and, like the general, was also a Protestant converted from Catholicism. His role in the National Reconciliation Commission gained him widespread respect. He began his administration by giving new impetus to the peace negotiations, which were moving very slowly. Unlike Cerezo, who headed a worn-out government leaving power, Serrano represented a new and recently elected government. With his election the expectations of arriving at a negotiated peace were quite high.

In Mexico, on April 24 and 25, for the first time since Madrid in 1987, the major protagonists of the war met: the government, the army, and the URNG. Five top military officials found themselves face to face with the principal guerrilla leaders. Bishop Quesada moderated the sessions. After the meeting in Mexico one meeting after another followed: Cuernavaca (June), Querétaro (July), Mexico City (September), and so on. At each meeting the critical points of difference were clarified. Fundamentally, they came down to four issues: (1) the question of the defense patrols (the PACs) in the countryside; (2) the creation of a truth commission, as in El Salvador or Argentina; (3) the application or not of the Geneva norms relative to civil wars; and (4) the schedule to follow for applying the agreements on the rights of the Indian population. The most critical point referred to the paramilitary defense patrols. From the URNG's perspective, as long as the army exercised absolute control over the countryside—by means of these patrols—democracy simply was not possible in Guatemala. But the army did not want to cede that control, thus leaving the countryside to the guerrillas.

As the discussions advanced, it became evident that the negotiation process was going to be much more difficult and complicated than optimists believed at the beginning. Serrano saw all hopes of gaining an immediate political victory going up in smoke. During 1992 many more meetings were held but with few results. In the meantime both the guerrillas and the army continued to fight, especially in Alta Veracruz and Quiché. There were other unexpected problems that arose: the United Nations observer, Francesco Vendrell, was accused of "excessive protagonism" and asked to leave the process.[56] Vendrell's successor, Jean Arnault, named in July 1992, turned out to be more acceptable to both parties. In January 1993 Serrano and the heads of the army announced suddenly that they had discovered documents captured from the URNG. These documents allegedly confirmed the accusations of the political right that the guerrillas were using the negotiations as a cover while they advanced militarily. Furthermore, the government explicitly singled out the Jesuit anthropologist Ricardo Falla as a subversive who incited the Indians to fight the army.[57]

However, the tendentious character of the documents made them immediately suspect. The whole affair seemed more like a desperate attempt of the hardline military to delegitimize the peace process and progressive sectors of the church than an authentically new revelation. The episcopal conference requested the army to show it the documents. Upon closer scrutiny the documents failed to support the accusations, particularly those leveled against the Jesuit anthropologist.[58]

The Fall of Serrano and the Election of De León Carpio

On May 25, 1993, President Serrano closed congress and assumed extraordinary powers. He was supported by hardliners among the military who did not believe in dialoguing with the enemy. Naturally all peace negotiations were suspended. Many observers compared Serrano's action with that of Alberto Fujimori, who closed his congress in Peru a year earlier. Circumstances favored Fujimori, however, but not Serrano. In Guatemala there was a popular demonstration against the president, and the army, after wavering a bit, withdrew its support and forced Serrano to go into exile. After a few weeks of indecision, congress elected Ramiro de León Carpio, who was in charge of the government's office of human rights, as president. He was to fulfill what remained of Serrano's term, which ended in January 1996. The decision to name as president the defender of human rights in a country characterized by violating those rights was met with universal approval.

De León's election also met with the approval of the URNG. The new president, elected on June 6, acted quickly to set the peace process into motion once again. On July 5 the members of the National Reconciliation Commission handed in their resignations in order to leave De León a free hand. The church also used the occasion to question whether it should be involved in the process. Some bishops, including Quesada, thought the process was much too slow. To be more precise, they did not believe that the two sides were serious about arriving at a negotiated peace.[59] As a result, the church decided to withdraw from the commission, a decision that practically sealed its demise. To fill the vacuum President De León created the Peace Commission, presided over by Héctor Rosales (a layman). Even though he withdrew from the National Reconciliation Commission, Quesada remained on as conciliator until new negotiations began.

In July, De León announced a new peace plan, which the URNG immediately rejected because it did not take into account previous agreements. Then the URNG made its own proposal. Finally Quesada, as conciliator, stepped in and made a third proposal. When both parties met—in January in Mexico—they signed a new agreement ("General Framework for Renewing the Negotiation Process"), which turned out to be a synthesis of the three proposals. Quesada was not present at the meeting in Mexico. From that point on the United Nations, through its representative Jean Arnault, assumed the task of mediating. The most important result of the Mexican meeting was the decision to create the Association of Civil Society.

The Constitutional Reforms and the Church

In the meantime, the church took the initiative to mediate in an internal crisis in the government. De León was elected with the expectation that he would reform the constitution. Nevertheless, the new president, like his predecessor, soon found himself locked in a stalemate with congress over the proposed constitutional reforms. In November, when the crisis seemed unresolvable, the episcopal conference offered its good offices and named three bishops as mediators: Juan Gerardi (the president of the episcopal conference), Gerardo Flores, and Fernando Gamalero. With the help of this church mediation the president and congress broke the impasse and on November 16 signed an agreement that included a list of reforms both parties committed themselves to support.[60] In January 1995 the reforms were submitted to a national referendum. The result was disappointing. Although the electorate favored the reforms, absenteeism (around 84 percent) was so high that it placed the legitimacy of the referendum in doubt. If anything, it served to demonstrate that the majority of citizens of Guatemala did not feel themselves to be a part of legal society.

THIRD STAGE: THE ASSOCIATION OF CIVIL SOCIETY (1994-1995)

The Association of Civil Society (ASC) was a response to the general frustration of the many groups that felt excluded from the structures of formal democracy, and concretely, from the peace process. The bishops also favored the creation of a forum to democratize the process. In fact, President De León made an attempt to do just that when he created the Permanent Forum for Peace. But the forum did not prosper because it was unilateral. In Mexico, however, both parties agreed to create the Association of Civil Society, which would be "open to all non-governmental sectors of Guatemalan society."[61] It also was decided that, although the decisions of the association would not be binding legally, both parties would give them serious consideration. Bishop Quesada, who was now former conciliator and former president of the National Reconciliation Commission, was chosen to found and direct the association. This was a most appropriate choice in light of the fact that many popular organizations considered the church their representative before the government.[62]

The assembly, which represented the members of the Association of Civil Society, was formally inaugurated on May 17. It was made up basically of the same groups that had participated in the National Dialogue in 1988. All assembly members had to be duly accredited before being accepted as a legitimate and representative social group. The assembly was divided into ten different sections: political groups, religious groups, unions, popular organizations, universities, small businesses and cooperatives, the Mayas, women, the media, and research centers and human-rights groups.[63] CACIF (big business) was invited but did not accept. Later on, at the urging of the American ambassador, Marilyn McAfee, CACIF agreed to be present as an observer, and finally participated in the assembly's Peace Commission.[64] For his part, Quesada was not entirely pleased with the idea of admitting only non-governmental groups to the assembly. In his opinion this tended to make the assembly a sort of parallel government.[65]

In spite of its heterogeneous makeup and lack of experience as regards parliamentary procedure, under Quesada's leadership the assembly managed to produce in less than one year five fundamental documents: (1) "The Resettling of Displaced Populations as a Result of Armed Confrontation" (May); (2) "The Identity and the Rights of Indigenous Peoples" (July); (3) "The Social, Economic, and Agrarian Aspects" [of Guatemala] (September); (4) "Civilian Power and the Function of the Army in a Democratic Society" (September); and (5) "Constitutional Reforms and the Electoral System" (October). The speed and efficiency with which the assembly worked stood in stark contrast to the slow and complicated negotiations conducted by the government and the URNG. By that very fact, the assembly stood as a stimulating model. Furthermore, the assembly document had a direct influence on the negotiations. For example, the URNG incorporated into its own proposals the basic ideas in the document on the identity of indigenous peoples.

But the assembly's progress also produced adverse reactions. When the URNG appropriated some of its ideas, the rightwing and the army pointed to that as proof that the assembly was a sounding board for the guerrillas. Somewhat irritated by that reaction, Quesada responded by observing that "coincidences are inevitable; however, we do hope that the documents coincide with the poor and the marginalized in Guatemala."[66] The references to the army in the documents naturally raised a storm among top echelon officers. One article proposed that "all special privileges and legal exemptions for members of the armed forces be suppressed." Another called for the minister of Defense to be a civilian.[67] The minister of Defense, General Mario René Enríquez, accused the assembly of favoring the URNG.[68]

On February 10, 1995, in the large hall of the National University of San Carlos, Bishop Quesada addressed the assembly for the last time. Hundreds of representatives of all the member organizations listened attentively as the bishop of Zacapa made a formal presentation of the assembly's documents, which represented a year's work. With this solemn act the church also concluded its mission to promote peace on an official level. In fact, Quesada had already announced earlier in October that he would retire from the assembly when the documents were finished. The bishops had reached the conclusion that from this moment on the church should work for peace from below, no longer in an official capacity.

THE GOVERNMENT AND THE URNG: A FORCED MARCH

In contrast with the ponderously slow progress made between 1990 and 1993, after the signing of the general agreement in Mexico in January 1994 the negotiations picked up considerable speed. Both parties were under international pressure and the demands of Guatemalan society—tired of endless years of war—to finish their task. Furthermore, the speed and efficiency with which the Assembly of Civil Society worked served as another stimulus. In March the two sides signed a general agreement on human rights. In June they agreed to create a commission "to bring to light human-rights violations and acts of violence" committed during the war. This commission would be the equivalent of the truth commissions that had been created in other Latin American nations. Finally, in November, as a first step toward total peace, the United Nations Mission for Guatemala (MINUGUA) was created and charged with the task of verifying the fulfillment of the agreement on human rights. MINUGUA established an office in the capital and various regional offices. Once again the church was called upon to fulfill an important role. When it was founded, the Archdiocesan Office of Human Rights set about studying systematically all important cases of human-rights violations since the beginning of the conflict thirty-four years earlier. With its store of information it was able to make a major contribution to the new truth commission.

In March 1995 the negotiations once again came to a standstill. But in February 1996 the Sant'Egidio Community, a lay Catholic association dedicated to resolving international conflicts, helped to break the impasse.[69] Finally, in March 1996, under newly inaugurated (January) President Alvaro Arzú, both parties signed a truce. For all practical purposes Guatemala formally put an end to the longest guerrilla war in Latin America's history. The final peace settlement was signed in the National Palace on December 29.

While the government, the church, and the United Nations set about applying concrete measures to consolidate the peace, violence continued to be the order of the day, and the death squads continued to act with impunity. The number of unresolved murders and attempted murders continued to increase. In addition to the case of Diana Ortiz, who survived, and those of Michael Devine and Myrna Mack, who did not, there were many other crimes. In 1991 Moisés Cisneros, a Marist brother, and Julio Quevedo, an agronomist who worked for the social pastoral office of the diocese of El Quiché, were both murdered. In July 1993 Jorge Carpio, who had been a presidential candidate in 1990—and who was President De León Carpio's brother-in-law—was shot down on a highway by a group of armed men. In December 1994 Alfonso Stessel, a Belgian priest who preached in favor of the poor, was murdered. The high percentage of persons tied to the church among these victims is quite striking. It is also evident that the impunity of the death squads still constitutes a major obstacle in the way of consolidating a real democracy in Guatemala.

On April 24, 1998, Bishop Juan Gerardi presented to the public the fourteen-hundred-page document "Guatemala: Never Again!" prepared by the Human Rights Office of the archdiocese. The document was the final report of the "Project to Recover the Historical Memory" (REMHI: "Recuperemos la Memoria Histórica") based on seven thousand interviews of victims or eyewitnesses of the country's violence. Among other conclusions, the report places the blame for 85.43 percent of the violence committed during the thirty-six year civil war on military and paramilitary death squads.[70] Like the different "Never Again" investigations carried out in other countries, REMHI aimed to do more than just present a cold statistical summary of past sufferings. In fact, it also became a therapeutic process by which many communities and individuals were able to face a painful past, overcome it psychologically and spiritually, and reconstruct their identities.

Gerardi not only supervised the project, but he was part of the story. As we mentioned earlier, in 1980 he was forced to abandon his diocese (El Quiché) due to the violence. Forty-eight hours after presenting the report, Bishop Gerardi was savagely murdered when he returned to his home. (At the moment of writing, the assassin or assassins are unknown.) Whatever the circumstances of his death, he will be remembered, along with Oscar Romero, Angelelli, and other bishop-martyrs, as a defender of the poor and marginalized.

In Guatemala the church has not drawn as much attention to itself as the church in El Salvador, the scene of dramatic assassinations such as those of Archbishop Romero, the four American women, and the six Jesuits; or the church in Nicaragua, which attracted attention on account of the high-level conflict between the archbishop and the priests in the government. Nevertheless, the Guatemalan church also played an important role. Certainly, as a consequence of its identification with the poor and especially with the Indian population, the church paid its "share" of blood sacrifice. Likewise, its contribution to the peace process was just as important as in El Salvador and other countries where the church acted as mediator. In this case, however, the person who most symbolizes this story is not a member of the official hierarchy but rather an indigenous woman—Rigoberta Menchú. She also personifies the Guatemalan Indian population, which, without doubt, paid one of the highest prices in terms of suffering and death in the recent history of Latin America.

12.

Mexico

The PRI and Chiapas

The revolution that began in 1910 constituted the basis of a new legitimacy that profoundly influenced Mexican society in the twentieth century. But, as many authors have observed, that revolution remained inconclusive. The party that became the consecrated heir of the revolution—the PRI (Partido Revolucionario Institucional, or the Party of the Institutionalized Revolution)—is a classic example of a bureaucratic-authoritarian party that in reality blocked the consolidation of a real democracy in Mexico. In the decade of the eighties, after governing Mexico for fifty years, the PRI—which at its zenith was a model of independence and stability—began to fall into a deep and prolonged crisis.

In the meantime, the Catholic church, the other great social institution in Mexico, went through the opposite experience. After the revolution it was severely persecuted, especially during the period of Plutarco Calles (1924-28), and later marginalized from public life. Nevertheless, it slowly and gradually recuperated from the crises of those years and managed to convert itself once again into a force to be reckoned with. For years the church accepted the necessity of lending passive support to the state. But with time it abandoned this passivity and began to assume a more assertive role as regards political power. Finally, in the eighties it became one of the most important voices of protest over electoral manipulation and government corruption. At the same time, for different reasons, the state decided to normalize its relations with the church and with other confessions. In 1992 it promulgated a new juridical framework that recognized many rights which had been denied the church for decades. Nevertheless, the new arrangement between state and church produced impassioned debates that left few satisfied. What is important to observe is that the church, historically allied with conservative forces, emerged as a major advocate for redemocratizing Mexico. Like two ships in the night, the PRI and the church passed each other: the former, once so confidently sure of its course but now wandering aimlessly; and the other, once so timid, increasingly sure of itself. The most dramatic example of this reversal of roles is Chiapas. After the Zapatista uprising in January 1994, Bishop Samuel Ruiz, a known critic of the government for its lack of attention to the demands of the Indian population, became the mediator between the government and the Zapatistas.

After briefly reviewing church-state relations from the revolution up until the eighties, we will look at the debate that arose over the new arrangement between the government and the churches in 1992. Then we will return to the case of Chiapas. First, it will help to know more about the PRI's history—its rise and fall—in order to understand the new prophetic role assumed by the church.

THE PRI: A BUREAUCRATIC-AUTHORITARIAN PARTY

Founded in 1928 as the National Revolutionary Party, the PRI was built upon four sectors: the peasants, the workers, middle-class professionals, and the military. Later, after reorganizing itself during the presidency of Miguel Alemán (1946-52), the military sector was eliminated, and the party adopted its current name. The PRI has many characteristics of a colonial institution: it is authoritarian, paternalistic, and corporatist. However, it is not totalitarian. It always permitted the existence of other parties, thus giving the appearance of democracy in Mexico. The other important historical parties are PAN (Party of National Action), PPS (the Popular Socialist Party), and PARM (the Authentic Party of the Revolution). Later, other parties emerged, notably, the Party of the Democratic Revolution (PRD), founded in 1987 by Cuauhtémoc Cárdenas and other dissidents who broke away from the PRI. PAN in particular represented the conservative cause and historically was the party closest to the church. There were also unions, especially the CTM (the National Confederation of Mexican Workers) and the CNC (National Peasants' Confederation), both of which depended on the PRI.

In spite of the limited space that it allowed for the other parties, the PRI always made sure that it alone controlled the state apparatus. In the words of historian Peter Smith: "Since 1917 the government's candidates have completely dominated the presidential campaigns, and they always win more than 70% of the popular vote."[1] In Mexico the elections were really plebiscites. Every six years, in a national ritual, the outgoing president revealed the name of his chosen successor. The PRI dominated all the elections, on both the national and the state levels. Although it was evident that widespread electoral fraud was committed, especially in the north, which was a bastion of PAN, few Mexicans raised an eyebrow. The reason for this complacency was obvious: under the PRI Mexico enjoyed considerable stability and economic growth. In the fifties and sixties a new and prosperous middle class arose which was relatively content with the system.

But the PRI could not avoid the evils that accompany parties that become entrenched in power: corruption and arrogance. The first dramatic sign of a generalized discontent was the massacre of Tlatelolco, or the Plaza of the Three Cultures. This was in October 1968, when several thousand university students clashed with the police. The student demonstration took place on the eve of the Olympic Games, an event designed to show the world Mexico's health and vitality. According to official accounts, twenty-four students were killed, but eyewitnesses spoke of hundreds.[2] For the youth, Tlatelolco symbolized the end of the myth of the institutionalized revolution. At the same time a new left appeared. President Luis Echeverría (1970-76) announced a new policy of openness and at the same time enormously expanded the state apparatus to attend to new social demands. But this expansion also brought with it an increase in the public debt and inflation. Echeverría's successors, López Portillo (1976-82) and Miguel de la Madrid (1982-88), could count on the oil bonanza, which reached its apex in the years 1978-81. The bonanza fed ambitious dreams of unlimited growth. What did grow was the foreign debt, from 4.5 billion dollars in 1969 to 104 billion in 1987.[3] The governments of this period became more and more trapped in a vicious circle: more expansion, more debts, and more inflation. In 1982 President López Portillo was forced to devalue the peso by 55 percent. According to one study, between 1982 and 1988 inflation diminished the buying power of the lower-middle class by 45 percent.[4]

The government under President Carlos Salinas de Gotari (1988-94) tried to reverse this process. Adhering to the norms of neo-liberalism, Salinas privatized many public companies, opened up the economy to foreign investment, and gave industry a new impetus. But the economic crisis was only part of the problem. The PRI, which had grown corrupt and complacent, had increasingly lost public credibility. By the eighties discontent with the PRI had now spread to the middle and lower classes. For the first time in decades the PRI was in serious trouble. In the 1986 race for governors, the electoral fraud committed in certain states was so flagrant that the protests had a national and international impact. In the presidential election of 1988 the great party founded by Calles won barely 50.74 percent of the national vote. Cárdenas's Party of the Democratic Revolution won 31.06 percent, and PAN, 16.81 percent. By the 1994 elections the PRI's power had eroded even more; it won with a minority of 47.41 percent of the vote. In addition, that year the party was rocked by two shockwaves: in March, the official candidate, Luis Donaldo Colosio, was assassinated in Tijuana; and in September, José Francisco Ruiz Massieu, the secretary general of the party, was also assassinated. The new president, Ernesto Zedillo, tried to project a new image for the party. But every time he tried, a new scandal would crumble the party's foundations even more. For most observers it was evident that the party's golden age of monolithic control of state and society had long passed. In the meantime, the church, reborn with a new legitimacy, began to fill in the moral vacuum left by the PRI, now suffering from a grave crisis of credibility.

THE CHURCH: FROM PERSECUTION TO MUTUAL TOLERATION

Four distinct stages in the church's relations with the state can be discerned after the period of open persecution, which culminated in the Cristero uprising (1926-29): (1) marginalization and resistance (1929-40); (2) collaboration and tacit support (1940-68); (3) revitalization and critical support (1968-79); and (4) independence and active leadership (1979–). In 1929 the state and the church formally signed an agreement to coexist in peace. This agreement put an end to the period of open persecution against the church. Nevertheless, during the years in which Calles dominated Mexican politics (1926-34), the church was totally shut out of public affairs. Lázaro Cárdenas (1934-40) tried to implant a laicist educational program, which fostered antireligious criticism in the classroom. The bishops, the clergy, and the faithful resisted this and other anticlerical measures passively. In general, the church confronted anticlerical liberalism with a deeply entrenched integralism, which made no concessions to the state.

This tense coexistence gave way during the Cárdenas years to a new stage of tacit collaboration with the state. Motivated by a certain pragmatism, Cárdenas backed away from the aggressive anticlericalism of his predecessor and dropped his plans to impose a laicist antireligious program on the schools. The church also saw that it was in its own interest to send some signals of good will to the government. One of those signals was sent in 1938, when the bishops supported Cárdenas's decision to nationalize oil. But the public gesture that most captured the public imagination came from Cárdenas's successor, Manuel Avila Camacho, who declared in a press conference in 1940: "I am a believer."[5] That simple statement let it be known that the state was willing to reach a new modus vivendi with the church, naturally without touching the highly anticlerical constitution of 1917. Further, two topics drew the state and the church together in the forties and the fifties: nationalism and anticommunism. The Mexican state in the post–World War II years abandoned any pretense of following a socialist course and openly embraced capitalism. At the same time the leaders of the PRI began marginalizing leftist groups within the party and the unions. In this sense the church was perceived as a tacit ally in the effort to reinforce national values and battle communism.

During this period the church regrouped and worked to consolidate its influence in society. Official anticlerical liberalism, which denied the civil rights of priests and religious women, not only did not diminish the militant spirit of practicing Catholics, it actually invigorated it. In fact, Catholicism— according to pre–Vatican II norms—even flourished. In 1940, for example, there were 4,461 priests. By 1957 that number had risen to 6,000.[6] Further-

more, unlike other parts of Latin America, Mexico did not experience a vocation crisis, at least during that period, and the number of foreign missionaries
was relatively small. In 1963 only 16 percent of the clergy was foreign-born.[7]
Among groups that exercised exceptional influence were the Jesuits, who
came to have 800 members in the sixties. Other groups of a more integralist
nature, such as the Legionnaires of Christ and Opus Dei, also grew noticeably during this period. The situation of religious women was especially
remarkable. In 1945 there were 8,128 religious women; by 1960 there were
19,400.[8] This was also—paradoxically, given official anticlericalism—the
golden age of private religious schools, thanks to the government's noncompliance with the laws. Officially the church could neither own nor administer
educational centers. But the state allowed religious schools to exist as long
as they did not call too much attention to themselves and the church. In the
decade of the eighties, 4.7 percent of all students on the grade-school level
studied in private schools, and 9.8 percent on the high-school level. As a
general rule, around 90 percent of private schools were Catholic.[9]

Politically, the church avoided all signs of activism and rarely spoke out
except to condemn communism. On the other hand, there were movements
and parties that expressed some of the church's teachings. In 1937 the
Sinarquistas—an integralist group—had between 300,000 and 500,000 followers.[10] In 1939 PAN, the Party of National Action, was founded. PAN was
not a confessional party, but because it severely condemned liberal
anticlericalism it seemed to be the party of the church. In Mexico no significant Christian Democratic Party emerged, and therefore PAN filled that
vacuum somewhat. Nevertheless, the Christian Democratic parties of Latin
America never accepted PAN as a member of their political family because
they considered the Mexican party too conservative.[11] In 1955 PAN won six
seats in the national congress, and from that moment on it established itself
as an important opposition party. Before PAN was founded the bishops usually advised Catholics not to participate in politics. But as PAN advanced
and grew the bishops changed their message and began encouraging Catholics to exercise their right to vote.

A NEW AWAKENING (1968-1979)

Vatican II was received by the Mexican church, which still had not felt
the winds of change, as a foreign import. Nor did it march with the rest of the
Latin American church. Nevertheless, there were individuals and certain
groups that foreshadowed the major changes that finally would come. The
diocese of Cuernavaca under Bishop Sergio Méndez Arceo (1952-82) was
an oasis of ecclesial renovation. Among other novelties, Cuernavaca called
attention to itself because of the experiments that Gregory Lemercier, a
Benedictine, conducted in an attempt to apply psychoanalysis to religious
life. Later, Rome called for an end to such experimentation. Still more well-
known was the center founded in 1960 by Ivan Illich to train missionaries to

work in Latin America. In many ways Méndez Arceo was a solitary prophet in the midst of a very conservative hierarchy.

The creation of UMAE—the Union of Mutual Episcopal Help—was probably more significant in the long run. UMAE was founded in 1963 under the guiding leadership of Alfonso Sánchez Tinoco, the bishop of Papantla, in order to coordinate the pastoral activities of seven dioceses in the gulf area. By 1967 UMAE had twenty-five member dioceses. Sánchez Tinoco's death in 1971 essentially ended the organization he had founded. Nonetheless, it had already made its impact. By creating a regional church with a strong sense of self-identity, UMAE broke the dominance of the big archdioceses such as Mexico City, Puebla, and Guadalajara.

At this same time the church was becoming more sensitive to the different Indian cultures in the country. In 1961 the apostolic delegate, Luigi Raymondi, helped to found CENAMI, the National Center of Aid to Indigenous Missions. And in the years after Medellín another center was founded: the National Center for Pastoral Action among the Indians (CENAPI). One of the early directors of CENAPI was Samuel Ruiz, the bishop of San Cristóbal de las Casas, in Chiapas. In May 1968 the bishops wrote a collective letter on development and integration in Mexico. This was the first time since the Cristero rebellion that the Mexican hierarchy spoke out on social and political themes.

But it was especially after the Medellín conference that the Mexican church began to awaken from its long dormancy. In the Medellín conference itself the Mexican bishops formed part of the conservative block. Nevertheless, there were signs of change. After the massacre of Tlatelolco and the student protests—in which many Catholic students participated—the bishops issued a somewhat timid statement encouraging all sides to learn to dialogue. Of a far more assertive nature was the condemnation of the government-induced violence by a group of thirty-seven priests.[12] In August 1969 a commission called the Episcopal Pastoral Reflection sought to conscienticize the bishops with the new mentality of Medellín. Also that year the National Congress of Theology was organized with the participation of seven hundred priests, religious women, and laypersons. By means of this and other meetings the fundamental ideas of Medellín, as well as of liberation theology, were introduced into the Mexican church. As a symbolic gesture of the new confidence the church felt, in 1970, in the town of Anenecuilco, where Emiliano Zapata was born, Bishop Méndez Arceo presented the PRI candidate, Luis Echeverría, with a letter calling for a revision of church-state relations. This was the first time that a prelate of the Catholic church had approached a high-ranking government official (and virtual president) in order to touch a hitherto untouchable topic. In two different letters, "Justice in Mexico" (1971) and "Message on Christian Commitment to Social and Political Issues" (1973), the hierarchy again spoke out on themes that it had not touched in public for decades. Although the bishops' proposals were hardly radical, the very fact that they were taking a position on social and political questions represented a major change.

In those years groups on both ends of the spectrum appeared. In 1969 a group was founded that defined itself in 1972 as Priests for the People and for Socialism. The Jesuits directed the Critical University Center (1969-72), which was recessed after several members joined the urban guerrillas. At the other extreme were groups such as MURO, a rightwing university group, and the Association of Priests of Pius X, which was very close to Lefebvre's movement. Opus Dei found Mexico an especially fertile field; by the seventies and eighties it had around five thousand members, including many academics and economically affluent people.[13] However, none of these integralist groups came to dominate the hierarchy, which tended to be more centrist.

THE CHURCH AS PROTAGONIST, 1979–

Pope John Paul II's visit in January 1979, which inaugurated the Third Episcopal Conference of CELAM in Puebla, may be considered the symbolic beginning of this new stage. For most Mexicans the pope's visit was more important than the episcopal conference in Puebla. The charismatic figure of the pope captivated the people. His unabashed style of speaking out on social justice issues and the rights of the Indians served as an example for the Mexican bishops, most of whom were still reluctant to speak out in the public forum. Although John Paul was not recognized as the head of a state, nevertheless, he was treated as a distinguished visitor, and his relations with President López Portillo and other government authorities were cordial. In fact, the ice had already been broken in 1974 when President Echeverría visited Paul VI, purportedly to gather ideas on development to propose to the United Nations.

The church that received the pope had substantially overcome the trauma of the years of persecution. In general, it was a very healthy church. In 1991 there were 109 bishops in the episcopal conference, including three cardinals, 10,265 priests, of whom 2,047 were religious.[14] The number of women religious was still very high: 24,000.[15] On the other hand, the 1990 census revealed that 90.28 percent of Mexicans considered themselves Catholics (in contrast to the year 1895 when 99.09 percent of the population was Catholic).[16] Another study suggests that the Catholic population was even lower: between 81 percent and 88 percent.[17] The Protestant population was estimated to be around 4.92 percent. As far as political attitudes, studies indicated that the clergy was generally centrist. In a survey conducted in the eighties among 223 parish priests in six states, only 14 percent believed that PAN represented the best interests of the people. In contrast, 29 percent believed that the PRI represented the people best. Finally, 15 percent thought that the left was best for the people. But more than half of those surveyed thought that "no party" represented the interests of the people.[18]

The new role of the church as a protagonist can be understood in light of the crises that afflicted the PRI. While the massacre of Tlatelolco symbolized the loss of the youth, the middle and lower classes were alienated by the combination of economic crisis, inflation, public debt, drug trade, and public corruption. After the pope's visit the bishops in different parts of the country began to capture the general discontent in their pastoral messages. In 1980, in its General Pastoral Plan, the episcopal conference exhorted Catholics to participate actively in public life; it also denounced corruption and criticized the government for allowing the country to become so indebted. But the strongest criticisms were heard in the north, where PAN was making rapid progress, and in the south, where the left was making equally solid progress. In both places the bishops took on the prophetic task of denouncing electoral frauds and exhorting the population to exercise the right to vote. Also, the earthquake of 1985, although it was not a political event, had political repercussions. The church proved to be one of the few institutions that was capable of mobilizing thousands of people to help the victims; by way of contrast, the government stood out for its bureaucratic slowness.[19]

The most dramatic example of the church's new role occurred during the 1986 elections for governors, deputies, and municipal seats in Chihuahua and other states. The PRI's victory—in an area PAN dominated—was singled out by the international press as a clear and evident case of fraud. Archbishop Adalberto Almeida, who had been a member of the bishops' Social Pastoral Commission in the sixties, denounced the apparent fraud and announced his intention to suspend eucharistic services in his archdiocese on July 20. Such a defiant and aggressive response from the church had not occurred since the days of the Cristero uprising. Under pressure from the government the Holy See requested Almeida to call off the suspension, which he did.[20] But the archbishop did not retract his denunciation of electoral fraud. On August 7, along with the bishop of Ciudad Juárez and the apostolic vicar of the mission to the Tarahumara Indians, Almeida issued a statement questioning the legitimacy of the authorities who had just been elected. Almeida was accused of having sympathies for PAN. But in a similar case in the south, Bishop Arturo Lona Reyes of Tehuantepec was accused by the government of sympathizing with the left.[21]

THE BIG DEBATE: WHO LEGITIMATES WHOM?

For their harshness and inflexibility the anticlerical measures in the 1917 constitution of Mexico can only be compared to similar restrictions in Marxist regimes at the height of Stalinism. Article 130 states categorically: "The law does not recognize as juridical persons those religious groups called churches." The same article declares that the "ministers of cult" may never "criticize the fundamental laws nor the authorities of the country." Furthermore, they "will have no right to vote . . . nor may they form political associations." In these terse words the clergy was deprived of all civic rights that citizens normally enjoy in any Western democracy. Article 27 establishes that churches may not "acquire, possess, or administer real estate." The same article stipulates that the church may not run any humanitarian or educational institution. In fact, after the late forties some of these restrictions were not really put into practice. The church *did* administer schools, although they were never registered as "church" schools. By the late eighties public opinion had come to favor Méndez Arceo's proposal made to Echeverría in 1970 to revise church-state relations and, concretely, to eliminate some of the more anti-democratic articles in the constitution.

There were many signs that the social and political atmosphere favored a change. In a survey conducted in 1990 by the government, 80 percent of those surveyed favored changing the constitution to make way for a new church-state agreement.[22] However, very few wanted to go back to a church-state union. But the majority believed that the clergy should have the right to vote and that the church should have the right to give its opinion on political, social, and economic topics. In one survey the majority had more confidence in the church than in the government.[23]

The political moment also favored a change. During Miguel de la Madrid's presidency (1982-88) there was still noticeable friction between state and church. The government proposed to depenalize abortion, a proposal which produced a sharp reaction from the bishops. Also, in 1985 President de la Madrid made a reference to the victims of the Cristeros in his official annual report.[24] Finally, when the church criticized the government for irregularities in the elections, the latter responded by making the electoral code even more rigid, especially with regards to "ministers of cult" who intervene during election campaigns. But these petty attacks stopped abruptly after the 1988 elections, which the PRI nearly lost. In the minds of some leaders it was no longer convenient to be at odds with the church.

Newly elected President Carlos Salinas de Gotari took the first steps to change church-state relations. His first symbolic step was to invite the principal representatives of the episcopal conference to be present at his inauguration in December 1988. Even more significant was his call during his inaugural address to "modernize" church-state relations. By referring directly to the church, Salinas broke a sixty-year-old taboo that prohibited the PRI from recognizing the church's existence in public. Later, in January 1989, the new president invited the president of the episcopal conference, Adolfo Suárez, along with the conference's vice president and the general secretary, and the apostolic delegate, for lunch at his official residence in Los Pinos. This "summit conference" destroyed another taboo, which prohibited direct relations between government and church leaders. By means of these and other public gestures the Mexican president prepared the way for more substantial changes. In June the episcopal conference handed over to Salinas a proposal to modify the legal status of the church. In February 1990 Salinas broke another taboo when he named a personal representative to the Holy See. In May of that year John Paul II visited Mexico for the second time, and in July 1991 Salinas went to the Vatican to return the visit. In both visits

Salinas and the pope touched upon the question of church-state relations in Mexico. After these ceremonial and symbolic exchanges the way was prepared for a legal proposal of change. In the meantime the cordial exchanges among the mighty and the powerful provoked a stormy debate among many Mexicans, who were far less happy about the course of events.

Three different positions emerged during the debate: the position of the Vatican and the bishops; the position of the traditional liberals; and the view of the progressive Christians. In general, the Vatican and the bishops were moved by a sense of pragmatism and a desire to normalize relations between the church and the state. Their objective was to improve the situation of the church in Mexico. In a declaration they formulated to justify the new arrangement with the state, they asked a question: "What would Mexico gain with these changes? Something very important for social harmony: the coinciding of what the law says with the daily conduct of our citizens."[25] But the bishops recognized that they had not gained all that they wanted. As a consequence they exhorted Catholics to continue to seek "reconciliation and harmony." In general, the bishops were satisfied with the fact that church-state relations were vastly improved over what they had been in 1929. But, from the other end of the spectrum, the voice of Mexican liberalism raised a cry of protest and warning. Author Marta Eugenia García Ugarte of the National Autonomous University of Mexico expressed these fears:

> The public and political consequences of this liberty are still unpredictable. Nevertheless, given the integralist vision which the church has of itself and of its function in the world, one can surmise that in direct relation to the weakness of the Mexican state the church will tend to brake the democratizing process in this country.[26]

Finally, the progressives leveled their own criticism at the new church-state arrangement. From their point of view the way affairs had been conducted recalled a pre-Vatican II style, which was elitist and paternalistic. All decisions were made in secret sessions of the PRI and in the Vatican between political and ecclesiastical leaders. The people of God were simply ignored. But the criticism went further. The new church-state pact had the appearances of a mutual legitimization: the PRI finally recognized the church, and the church recognized the PRI. Father Jesus Vergaras, S.J., the director of the Tata Vasco Center, summarized the progressive line of thought: "A large group in the hierarchy is inclined to establish official relationships with the PRI, and that means, endorsing the policies of President Carlos Salinas de Gotari."[27] Nor were all the bishops happy over the intervention of the Vatican, and especially the conduct of the apostolic delegate, Jerónimo Prigione, who assumed the role of mediator between state and church without consulting the local church.

Thanks to the corporative discipline of the PRI, the parliamentary debate on the issue was relatively brief. Salinas had already approved the proposal to change the constitution, and on December 18, 1991, after a twenty-four-hour marathon debate, the congress voted in favor of the constitutional changes, 500 to 36.[28] The no votes came mainly from the Popular Socialist Party, a small party to the left of the PRI. One deputy of that party called the vote a "grave step backward."[29] Also, some members of the Party of the Democratic Revolution voted against the changes, as well as three members of PAN. The PAN representatives criticized the PRI's proposal as deficient because it did not really guarantee religious liberty in Mexico. In any case, in July 1992 the Law of Religious Associations and Public Cult was approved, and in November the General Office of Religious Affairs was created as a dependency of the Secretariat of Government.

THE NEW LAW

The debate did not die down when the new law was enacted. On the contrary, it gave rise to another debate, which revolved around three questions: Was there a real change or not?; Who gained and who lost?; and, What do the changes mean for the future?

The new law is composed of thirty-six articles. In the first few articles the old anticlerical liberal tradition clearly lives on. Although the law is inspired by the concept of church-state separation—a common principle in all modern democracies—in fact, it unnecessarily reproduced articles that only serve to remind Mexicans of their violent, anticlerical past. Article 2, for example, establishes the right to freedom of religion, but the same article also stipulates the right "not to profess a religion."[30] An important advance is found in article 6, which recognizes the rights of the church and other "religious associations" to have a juridical personality. Article 9 recognizes the rights of churches to own property. Article 16 confirms the right to administer "educational and health centers, etc." This was undoubtedly the most advanced of all the articles.

Article 14 repairs a violation of civil rights by declaring that ministers of cult "have the right to vote." But the same article establishes that said ministers may not be elected to public posts. On the other hand, the rule that ministers of cult must be Mexican is dropped. Article 16 declares that churches may not own or administer "means of mass communication" (radio stations or television channels), although article 21 admits of the possibility of transmitting one or another program in the media. With respect to politics, the new law forbids the churches from engaging in any political or partisan activity, such as favoring in any way candidates for public office. Also, a "religious service may not be converted into a political meeting." The same article prohibits the churches from "opposing the laws of the country or its institutions."

Without doubt the new law constitutes an important advance in the process of normalizing church-state relations. The very fact that it allows the

Catholic church to enjoy legal recognition is a positive change. Most criticisms of the law center on the many restrictions, which in reality do not allow much freedom for the churches. Other changes are ambiguous. For example, the recognition of the right of churches to administer their own schools is indeed an advance. But in practice that means that only Mexicans of certain means can receive religious education, which is restricted to private schools.[31]

In the August 1992 assembly of the episcopal conference the bishops and their advisers analyzed the new law. Their conclusion was that the law represented an advance, but that it still had many "imperfections" which would have to be eliminated in the future.[32] The law constituted the most important sign that the historical antagonism between the church and the state in Mexico had ended. But if the objective of the lawmakers was to "domesticate" the church by converting it into a new ally of the state, then they definitely did not succeed. For years a new society and a new church had been emerging in Mexico. In fact, the church had acquired a new moral authority that allowed it to question the state and the PRI. Of course, not all in the church wanted to assume a prophetic role. Many integralists and rightwing Catholics would have preferred to consolidate the church's gains and live in harmony with the state.

But if liberals and bishops thought that a new age of peace and stability had been ushered in, guaranteed by the party and the church, they were soon to be rudely disillusioned. The Zapatista uprising in January 1994, as well as the deep crisis into which the PRI had fallen, put to the test all the basic premises upon which Mexican society and the PRI rested. According to one premise, there could be no further revolutions in Mexico because the PRI had "institutionalized" the revolution. According to another premise, the church, now fairly well neutralized, would never again assume an important public or political role. Those premises collapsed like a house of cards in January 1994.

CHIAPAS: THE BACKGROUND OF AN UPRISING

On January 1, 1994—a date chosen because it coincided with the signing of NAFTA (North American Free Trade Agreement)—close to eight hundred members of the Zapatista Army of National Liberation (EZLN) seized control of the city of San Cristóbal de las Casas in Chiapas. Ten thousand soldiers of the Mexican army promptly were sent to the area, accompanied by an impressive display of tanks, jeeps, and helicopters. One thousand persons were killed in the uprising. From that moment on Chiapas became the center of attention in Mexico, a fact that bothered President Salinas, who no doubt hoped to end his last year as president by leaving the country in peace and relative prosperity. The uprising was also most inconvenient for the candidates of the different political parties in an electoral year; they now had to share the limelight with the mysterious and romantic *Subcomandante* Marcos. Finally, the role of Bishop Samuel Ruiz as mediator was most disconcerting for many groups in the church, and especially for Prigione, the apostolic delegate. Prigione, like other conservatives, would have preferred for the government and the army to deal with the guerrillas in Chiapas, not the church, and certainly not progressive groups known to be somewhat sympathetic toward the Zapatistas' demands.

The state of Chiapas, with its nearly twenty-nine thousand square miles, is bigger than El Salvador (but smaller than Guatemala, with which it shares a common frontier). In fact, given its geography and large Indian population, Chiapas could be an extension of Guatemala. Its population in 1990 was around 3,210,496 inhabitants, of whom 716,000 spoke one or another Indian language.[33] Chiapas was a microcosm of the Indian problem of all Mexico, where 5,000,000 Indians speak their own native language, although 15,000,000 Mexicans have their own distinct Indian culture. Geographically, Chiapas is characterized by a great variety of ecological zones: there are mountains, plains, and valleys. San Cristóbal de Las Casas, the seat of the diocese (although it is not the state capital, which is Tuxtla Gutiérrez), is located on a central elevated plain that ranges between 3,200 and 6,500 feet. The Lacandona jungle—a thickly wooded area—lies between San Cristóbal and the frontier with Guatemala.

Chiapas' economy is based on agriculture (corn, rice, and coffee), animal husbandry, and wood. Tree haciendas are found side by side with cattle haciendas. There are also oil wells and natural gas wells. The local "oligarchy" is made up of cattle farmers, timber interests, and merchants. There are also small property owners. But the goal of the small owners is the same: own land, exploit it, and export. Thanks to this system thousands of peasants lost their lands and became salaried workers. Others looked for land in less desirable areas. The Lacandona jungle quickly filled up with peasants from all kinds of ethnic backgrounds who had been displaced from other areas in the state. In 1972 President Echeverría set into operation a modernization program. Roads were built and hydroelectric plants and dams were constructed. Some land was given to the peasants. Nevertheless, the agrobusiness groups, with the help of local politicians, managed to move in and take over the land. Politically, Chiapas has been under the absolute control of the PRI; all governors since the revolution have belonged to the PRI, and they in turn have always defended those who control the economy.

Chiapas, with its mass of displaced or exploited peasants, seemed like Mexico itself on the eve of the revolution: a powder keg about to explode. Since a major indigenous congress in 1974 many new peasant organizations have emerged. One of the most important of these organizations is OCEZ: the Emiliano Zapata Peasant Organization, created in 1980. Armed with a new consciousness of their rights, the peasants began to invade properties that had once been theirs. But this type of illegal action provoked the government, the police, and the army to retaliate. In July 1980, for example, near the town of Wolonchán, the peasants seized sixty-eight farms. Under the command of General Absalón Castellanos, the army attacked and killed twelve Indians.[34] Later, in 1983, General Castellanos, who was also a major landowner in the area, was elected governor of the state. The average amount of violence in Chiapas was above the "normal" level of violence in the rest of Mexico. According to Amnesty International, "between 1982 and 1985, 525 peasants were killed for political reasons; 70 percent of them in Oaxaca and Chiapas."[35] In 1992 the peasants in the area organized a major march to the capital of the republic: a 620 mile march in fifty days.

The situation, already very tense, was complicated by the introduction of religious conflicts. Fundamentalist groups have grown very rapidly in Chiapas: another sign of social instability and insecurity. The strangest case of a conflict involving religion occurred in San Juan de Chamula. In the beginning of the seventies the local authorities, in complicity with local economic interests, began to expel Evangelicals from the community. By 1994 between twenty-five thousand and thirty thousand had been expelled. According to the "traditional Catholics," as they call themselves, the Evangelicals had broken down the traditional ties that bind the community together. However, this explanation was quite suspect. According to Mardonio Morales, a Jesuit priest who had lived in the area for thirty years, the local power groups have a monopoly over the production and selling of alcohol, and they resented the non-drinking Evangelicals, who refused to buy their products during feast days. The local power groups also resented progressive Catholics, particularly Bishop Samuel Ruiz, who had frequently taken them to task for their heavy-handed conduct.[36]

Finally, to make matters worse, as a consequence of the scorched earth policy of General Lucas and General Ríos Montt in Guatemala in the early eighties, more than 200,000 refugees entered Chiapas.

THE EZLN AND THE CHURCH

The Zapatista Army of National Liberation was probably formed out of another, earlier group, the Forces of National Liberation, which created the Zapatistas as its rural branch. By 1984 the EZLN already had its own structure and ideology. The founders were and are, therefore, survivors of guerrilla warfare and other radical student movements of the seventies. They are Mexicans, of course, but probably not from Chiapas although the great mass of their followers is drawn from the indigenous peasantry of the area. The EZLN built up its organization at the same time that the peasants began organizing themselves. Before their dramatic uprising in January 1994, they had had brushes with the army. In an interview that Father Mardonio Morales gave in September 1993, he warned of the existence of a guerrilla movement in the area. But the authorities, concerned over the public image of Mexico on the eve of signing the NAFTA agreement, qualified the Jesuit's warning as "unfortunate."[37]

In Chiapas, as in Nicaragua, El Salvador, Guatemala, and other parts of Latin America, the church, although it did not intend to, nevertheless facilitated the work of the guerrillas. The First Indigenous Congress of 1974, which was convened by both the government and the church, gave a major boost to the peasants' movement. Furthermore, many catechists in the diocese, imbued with the ideals of liberation theology, became agents for conscienticizing other peasants. It would not be untrue to affirm, as some observers did, that the guerrillas made use of the "religious infrastructure" the church built up in order to convert many catechists to their cause.[38]

In one of the first interviews *Subcomandante* Marcos gave, he referred to religion and the church. He confirmed the existence of certain ties between the church and the guerrilla movement, although he noted that the pastoral work of the church was not intended to produce guerrillas. According to Marcos:

> There are no religious elements taken from the church in the leadership or in the ideology of the Zapatista army. That is the truth. What happened is that the church carried out a very effective social campaign. Our people know that. But the work of the church went in the opposite direction of the armed struggle. . . . People said that . . . there ought to be a peaceful change, with open democratic movements. The entire effort of the church was directed toward that end.[39]

In another interview Marcos (whom the government claimed was a certain Rafael Sebastián Guillén, a former student of the Jesuit high school of Tampico) admitted that the atheism and Marxism of the guerrillas offended the peasants. The guerrillas realized this and accommodated the religious view of the peasants to their ideology.[40] Marcos explained why Samuel Ruiz was their preferred mediator:

> In the Zapatista Army the real leadership—this is not propaganda—is in the hands of the Indians. They recognize Don Samuel as someone who is not their enemy, although he is not one of us. So, they say: who is going to be the spokesman in the middle? It has to be Don Samuel: he's already in the middle.[41]

THE CHURCH IN CHIAPAS AND SAMUEL RUIZ

The church in the southern Pacific region is one of the most dynamic in Mexico. It first acquired its self-identity in the experience of UMAE, and later, in 1976 and 1977, it was formally designated by the episcopal conference as one of the country's fourteen ecclesiastical regions. It is made up of eight jurisdictions: the archdiocese of Oaxaca; the dioceses of Tuxtla Gutiérrez, San Cristóbal de las Casas, Tapachula, Tehuantepec, and Textepec; and the prelatures of Mixes and Huautla. Since the time of UMAE the prelates in these jurisdictions have worked closely together, following a common pastoral plan that gives highest priority to the defense of the Indians' rights and culture. The prelates have also severely criticized local political leaders for their abuse of the Indians. One of the first collective regional letters was published in 1977: "Our Commitment to the Indians and the Peasants of the Southern Pacific." Later, in 1980, in the small town of Puxmetacán, Oaxaca, the bishops issued another collective statement in which they condemned a local political boss for having usurped land from the peasants. At times individual bishops took some very concrete actions. In June 1981 Bishop Arturo Lona Reyes of Tehuantepec excommunicated all those guilty of torturing in his diocese.[42]

Samuel Ruiz was one of the principal architects of this regional church. He was born in Guanajuato in 1924, the son of "wet back" parents (as he describes them, because at one time they crossed the frontier in search of work in the United States).[43] He was raised in a militantly Catholic family during the time of the persecution against the church. He entered the seminary at León at the age of fifteen, and after the Second World War he was sent to complete his studies at the Jesuit-run Gregorian University in Rome. He specialized in Sacred Scripture and received the doctorate in 1952.

Once back in Mexico he joined the teaching staff at the seminary in León and soon became rector. In 1959 he was named bishop of San Cristóbal and was ordained in January 1960. As time passed he grew in his awareness of the historical continuity between his work and that of the first bishop of the diocese, Bartolomé de las Casas (1544-47). The young bishop who began working in 1960 was quite different from the bishop who later distinguished himself for his defense of Indian rights. Initially, like some of the sixteenth-century missionaries, he believed that his task consisted in eradicating paganism from the area and in civilizing (that is, Westernizing) the Indians. Later, after a series of defining experiences, he went through a major conversion that led him to radically question his earlier presumptions.

The first experience was Vatican II. The Council opened horizons and changed his way of conceiving his mission as bishop. In the Council he came to know other prophets of the Latin American church, including Hélder Câmara, Manuel Larraín, and Raúl Silva Henríquez. He collaborated with Bishop Sánchez Tinoco in creating UMAE, and in 1967 he participated in the Episcopal Commission of Social Pastoral Action. Another key experience was his participation in the preparatory meeting for Medellín, held in Melgar, Colombia, in April 1968. At Melgar he was initiated into the world of modern anthropology. He was especially fascinated by the concept of inculturation, which placed traditional methods of evangelizing in a more critical light. One extreme traditional method consisted simply in destroying the local Indian cultures. In Medellín he was in charge of delivering one of the seven principal addresses: "The Evangelization of Latin America." He was elected president of CELAM's Department of Indigenous Missions, and in Mexico he was also elected president of the Episcopal Commission on Indigenous Peoples.

From the very beginning the heart of Ruiz's pastoral planning was the formation of catechists. Following the suggestions of Luigi Raymondi, the apostolic delegate, in 1961 he founded several schools for training catechists and placed them under the direction of the Marist brothers and the Sisters of the Divine Pastor. Gradually he built up a network of catechists in each town, no matter how remote. A few statistics from the Mexican ecclesiastical directory for 1991 reveal that there were only 66 priests (40 diocesan and 26 religious) to serve a diocese with 848,106 Catholics.[44] By way of contrast, there were 8,600 catechists and more than 3,000 little chapels.[45] It is evident from these figures that the church could not attend to the religious needs of the diocese without the catechists. Catechists in Chiapas, as in most other parts of Latin America, are trained to conduct religious services, to teach, and to preach. It was through the catechists that the church acquired an Indian identity.

THE CHURCH AND THE POPULAR STRUGGLE

The First Indigenous Congress was planned jointly by Governor Manuel Velasco Suárez and the bishop. After a year's preparation the congress was held in October 1974. It was an authentic indigenous congress. Four different ethnic groups (the Choles, the Tzeltales, the Tzotziles, and the Tojolabales) sent 2,000 delegates to the congress, in representation of some 400,000 Indians.[46] The delegates discussed—in their native languages—four principal topics: land, commerce, health, and education. The congress marked the beginning of a new sense of self-identity and pride among the Indians. It was also one of the conversion experiences for Samuel Ruiz. For him the congress was an impressive example of indigenous democracy at work. He came to appreciate even more deeply the Indians' culture. From that point on he began to see reality more and more from their point of view.

The ties between the church and the popular peasant movement were very close from the beginning, and this inevitably led to close ties with the guerrilla movement. The existence of these ties was not a discovery of the secular press. For quite some time Bishop Ruiz knew of them and was aware of the dangers that they posed for the church. In an interview that he granted in February 1994, after the Zapatista rebellion had begun, he told the story of the peasant movement and noted that guerrillas "wanted to take over the structure of the catechist movement."[47] He expressed his disagreement with the guerrillas, who in some cases converted his catechists into atheists. But he did not regret his efforts: "I would be the most unhappy of all the bishops of the world if after thirty years of work there were no signs of a political awakening among the laity."[48]

As a consequence of his defense of the rights of the Indians and peasants, Samuel Ruiz, like Bishop Romero in El Salvador, Pedro Casaldáliga in Brazil, and many other church leaders in Latin America, became a target for criticisms and threats. He was among the seventeen prelates who were invited by Bishop Proaño for the fateful meeting in Riobamba, Ecuador, in August 1976. He was detained, along with Bishop Méndez Arceo, and expelled from the country. In 1982 security forces broke into a center run by the Marist brothers in Comitán. Although Mexico was not considered a "national security state," like Brazil or Argentina, in practice it used the arms and methods typical of those rightwing regimes to harass the church.

A dramatic turning point occurred in 1991 when Father Joel Padrón González was arrested and jailed, accused of inciting the peasants to seize land. Previous to that, in 1989, Bishop Ruiz had founded the Bartolomé de las Casas Center for Human Rights. The governor of the state, José Patrocinio González Garrido, singled out the center and Bishop Ruiz as special targets for his verbal attacks, which were usually calumnies. But the governor soon went from words to actions. In 1990 a Belgian priest, Marcelo Rotsaert, was accused of being the intellectual author of peasant land seizures and was deported.[49] When Father Joel, the parish priest of Simajovel, was similarly arrested, Bishop Ruiz and the center mobilized all their resources to defend him. Soon other human-rights groups in Mexico and beyond joined the campaign. Furthermore, Bishop Ruiz had the case taken up to the federal courts. For their part, five hundred Indians marched in protest from Simajovel to the state capital. Along the way others joined them. By the time they reached Tuxtla Gutiérrez they numbered around eighteen thousand. In the face of all this pressure the government backed down, and in November a federal judge threw out the accusation against Father Joel, and he was freed. At the same time the secretary of the government communicated to the apostolic delegate the government's displeasure over the bishop's actions. By fateful coincidence, in 1993 the governor, González Garrido, was named to the powerful post of secretary of government. Given this background, one can see that relations between the church in Chiapas and the government were already quite strained before the Zapatista rebellion.

"IN THIS HOUR OF GRACE"

In August 1993 the pope made his third trip to Mexico. In Izamal, Yucatán, he addressed the "indigenous peoples of America." Samuel Ruiz gave the official greeting and presented the pope with his own pastoral letter, "In This Hour of Grace." Beside being a personal testimony, the letter contains a very accurate description of the social reality of Chiapas. It also criticizes the neoliberal policies of the government, the lack of official protection for the

Indians, and abusive practices by the authorities. Among concrete problems the letter mentions the existence of bad teachers who waste their students' time; the presence of the Guatemalan refugees; the expulsions in Chamulas; alcoholism; and more. Samuel Ruiz narrates the pastoral history of the diocese from the moment he took charge up until the moment of writing. The description leaves no doubt that a potentially explosive situation existed in Chiapas. Five months later the Zapatista rebellion began.

SAMUEL RUIZ AS MEDIATOR

The first reaction of President Salinas after being informed of the rebellion was to send the army to put it down. But it soon became evident that the massive display of troops, tanks, and helicopters would not be sufficient to suppress the rebellion. Furthermore, Salinas also realized that the political cost of a bloody repression in Chiapas would be too high. On January 8 he changed course and created a special commission to look for a peaceful solution, and on January 12 he announced a cease fire. He named Manuel Camacho, the chancellor of the republic and one of the prime candidates to succeed Salinas as president, as head of the Commission of Peace and Reconciliation. The naming of Camacho was a very wise move, because he had a high profile as an important man in the government and showed a real ability to dialogue.

During the rebellion Samuel Ruiz offered his good offices as mediator, but that offer was not immediately accepted by the government. In a very clear attempt to marginalize him, the secretary of government asked two neighboring bishops—Felipe Aguirre of Tuxtla Gutiérrez and Felipe Arizmendi of Tapachula—to be the mediators. But they both declined and in a display of ecclesial unity supported Samuel Ruiz for the mission. In the meantime, Bishop Ruiz interviewed Cardinal Corripio and the members of the permanent council of the episcopal conference in Mexico City. In spite of strong pressures from certain hardline politicians (those who wanted a strictly military solution) and from the apostolic nuncio, Corripio and the episcopal conference decided to support Ruiz. In this context the government-named commissioner, Camacho, took the initiative and interviewed thirty bishops for the purpose of showing his willingness to work with the church. He praised Samuel Ruiz in public as a "friend of peace."[50] When he reached San Cristóbal, he immediately established contact with the bishop and with other important persons in government and society. On January 7 the EZLN had made its own proposal for mediation: Rigoberta Menchú, Samuel Ruiz, or Julio Scherer, the director of the magazine *Proceso*. The logic of the situation finally prevailed; the only person who really understood the situation and who had sufficient international stature to mediate was the bishop of Chiapas. For her part, Rigoberta Menchú, who had sought refuge in the diocese of San Cristóbal in 1980, fully supported Ruiz to be the mediator.[51]

The dialogue began in the sacristy of the cathedral on February 21 and ended on March 3. Nineteen Zapatistas, led by *Subcomandante* Marcos, all wearing ski masks, participated. Camacho arrived with his official committee. Ruiz, the mediator, was accompanied by three other persons. The atmosphere was actually cordial. To break the ice, Bishop Ruiz told stories from his youth. Finally, after ten days of intense work the commissioner, the EZLN, and the mediator presented to the public a document with thirty-four "commitments," signed by both sides. The commitments, or articles, included eleven modifications of current legislation and thirty concrete actions the government should carry out. Some of the articles referred specifically to ways to better the situation of the Indians. Others referred to institutional changes in the government in Chiapas. The dialogue moved along so fast that the government and the guerrillas achieved in ten days what other governments and other guerrilla groups in similar dialogues had achieved only in four or five years. Given this speed, expectations were high that a final agreement could be reached in a few weeks.[52]

A CONTROVERSIAL DIALOGUE

In spite of this auspicious beginning, the dialogue in Chiapas soon became the center of a stormy debate; after a while it bogged down into a hopeless stalemate. In March the "authentic *coletos*" (*coleto* is a local term for an inhabitant of Chiapas), that is, the local power groups, organized a protest against the dialogue and especially against the bishop, whom they accused of being an accomplice of the guerrillas. Calling themselves the Citizen's Front for the Defense of the Dignity of San Cristóbal, they gathered together two thousand persons, who carried out a campaign of aggression and harassment.[53] That same month the Indians organized an assembly made up of five hundred base indigenous organizations to support the bishop.[54]

In the midst of this tense situation, which frequently produced street fights, Luis Donaldo Colosio, the PRI's candidate for the presidency, was assassinated. The murder not only created a major crisis nationwide, but it also put an abrupt end to the dialogue in Chiapas. The EZLN decided that given the atmosphere of violence and insecurity in the country, the conditions for dialogue no longer existed. Camacho tried to keep the dialogue going, but in vain. In June he resigned his post, claiming that he did not enjoy the confidence of Ernesto Zedillo, Colosio's successor as candidate for the presidency. Given the proximity of the elections—August—Zedillo did not wish to take a very clear stand on the question of Chiapas.

The events in Chiapas brought out many pent up hostilities toward church progressives from the political and ecclesiastical right. In April the magazine *Summa*, whose editor also directed a television program, announced that *Subcomandante* Marcos was really Jerónimo Hernández, a Jesuit. The Society of Jesus tried to sue the magazine for defamation, but even when it became evident that the priest in question could not be Marcos, the magazine and other representatives of the mass media persisted in their campaign. In fact, the whole campaign was really a pretext to harass the progressive church in general. During this same period a group of twenty armed men broke into a cultural center run by the Jesuits in Palenque, and the Jesuit provincial received many threatening letters.[55] These actions and threats seemed ominously similar to those that preceded the murder of the six Jesuits in El Salvador.

A CONVENTION IN THE JUNGLE

The Zapatistas used the impasse to organize a National Democratic Convention in the middle of the Lacandona jungle. The convention was widely publicized in universities and popular organizations. Politicians of all parties, intellectuals, students, and progressive spokespersons from the church were all invited. Finally, on August 8 and 9, under a torrential rain, between six thousand and seven thousand people, representing a multitude of academic and popular organizations, attended the convention. Two hundred masked guerrillas of the EZLN acted as hosts.[56] The convention, plus the presence of *Subcomandante* Marcos, captured the imagination of a large sector of the population, all on the eve of national elections. In spite of the circus-like atmosphere surrounding it, the convention served to reveal the existence of a vacuum in Mexico, which reflected a major lack of confidence in the political system.

In the August 21 elections the PRI won with 47.41 percent of the national vote. Though a victory, it was not exactly a vote of confidence. The opposition parties accused the PRI of electoral fraud but finally backed down and accepted the results. In Chiapas there was a general rejection of the PRI candidate, who was finally forced to resign after the army's second offensive in February 1995. In September the country was rocked by another assassination: the murder of José Francisco Massieu, the PRI's secretary general. Given the atmosphere of distrust and uncertainty, Camacho's successor as commissioner, Jorge Madrazo Cuéllar, found it impossible to renew dialogue with the EZLN. In October Samuel Ruiz created CONAI—the National Commission of Mediation—with the aim of restoring the dialogue. The EZLN recognized CONAI as a legitimate instrument of mediation, but the government did not. In his first few days after coming to power President Zedillo proposed creating a congressional commission to deal with the Chiapas question. The obvious but unspoken objective of that proposal was to render CONAI unnecessary. Finally, pressured by a hunger strike that Bishop Ruiz undertook, at the end of December the secretary of government officially recognized CONAI as the only authorized mediating agent in Chiapas.

ZEDILLO: COUNTERMARCHES AND BACK TO DIALOGUE

Zedillo, like his predecessor, hesitated between following the hard line of military action or the soft line of dialogue. First he tried dialogue, then repression, then went back to dialogue. On January 15, 1995, through the mediating offices of CONAI, Zedillo's government established its first contact with the EZLN leadership. Once again hopes were raised, and the EZLN declared a cease fire. But without any previous warning, on February 9, Zedillo, after revealing the identity of Marcos (supposedly Rafael Sebastián Guillén), announced his intention of invading the battle zone to search for Marcos and other Zapatista leaders. Once again the army moved in in force, but this time it took particular pains to submit parishes and centers run by religious to rigorous searches. The media accused Zedillo of acting under pressure from international finance, specifically the Chase Manhattan Bank, which urged the Mexican government to "demonstrate its effective control over the national territory."[57] Other sources expressed their belief that Zedillo, whose public image was that of a gray bureaucrat, was under pressure to demonstrate his capability to be a real leader, and that presumably meant to lead by "blood and iron." Whatever the full reason for Zedillo's impromptu military incursion into Chiapas, he soon drew back. The policy of repression did not produce a single positive result. On the contrary, it was very counterproductive: the search to find the romantic *Subcomandante* Marcos, somewhat like General John Pershing's search for Pancho Villa, only enhanced Marcos's image and underlined the government's ineptitude.

On February 11 Zedillo organized a summit meeting in his residence that brought together his secretary of government; the attorney general of the republic; the cardinal of Mexico City, Ernesto Corripio; the cardinal of Monterrey, Adolfo Suárez; and Samuel Ruiz. The two cardinals defended Bishop Ruiz against the accusation of having prior knowledge of the uprising, and therefore of being indirectly an accomplice to subversion. Zedillo accepted the word of the two cardinals and decided to accept CONAI once again as the official mediating agent. On February 17 CONAI revealed an "emergency initiative" for renewing dialogue.

PRIGIONE VERSUS SAMUEL RUIZ

The crisis in Chiapas not only produced divisions among politicians but among churchpeople as well. The most highly placed critic of Samuel Ruiz was the apostolic nuncio, Jerónimo Prigione, who went to great lengths to tarnish the bishop of San Cristóbal's image, with the evident aim of having him removed from the diocese. Prigione was a career Vatican diplomat who had served in Guatemala, El Salvador, and Africa. In every place he was posted, he was known to be sympathetic toward rightwing military regimes. He was named apostolic delegate to Mexico in 1978 and was one of the principal architects of the new arrangement between church and state in 1992. As a consequence of the new arrangement he was elevated to the rank of apostolic nuncio, a change in status that converted him into the dean of the diplomatic corps in Mexico. His ultraconservative views, as well as his pre–Vatican II diplomatic style, which ignored the views of the local church, did not win him much sympathy among bishops and local clergy. Nor did he hide his antipathy for liberation theology. But Prigione was but a spokesman for many other conservatives in Mexico and in Rome. Among others, Javier Lozano, president of the Episcopal Commission for the Doctrine of the Faith, Luis Reynoso Cervantes, the bishop of Cuernavaca, and Cardinal Juan Sandoval Iñiguez of Guadalajara, usually supported the nuncio.

In the face of much criticism from Mexico and Rome, Bishop Ruiz felt obliged to defend his theological ideas, his pastoral plans, and most of all, his mediation in Chiapas. In May 1994 he went to Rome, where he sought audiences with eight cardinals; he returned to the Eternal City again in June. At the same time some two hundred church and non-church groups expressed their solidarity with him.[58] He was also the recipient of numerous international prizes for his defense of the rights of the Indians.[59] Also, certain key persons in the hierarchy defended him: Sergio Obeso Rivera, the president of the episcopal conference; and the two cardinals, Corripio and Suárez Rivera. The controversy over Ruiz and his mediation became so heated that a senator of the PRI proposed revising the laws on religious activity to impose new sanctions on priests and religious women who get involved in politics.[60]

THE DIALOGUE FALTERS

When the government and the Zapatistas finally returned to the conference table—in April 1995—the crisis in Chiapas was overshadowed by the financial crisis of December, which led the United States to make an emergency loan of twenty billion dollars to the Mexican government. It was this crisis that prompted the Chase Manhattan Bank to make eliminating the guerrillas in Chiapas a condition for further loans.

In February the Mexican congress prepared a proposal to establish a legal framework for resolving the crisis in Chiapas. The proposal included the conditions to be met before conceding amnesty to the guerrillas.[61] Finally, in March, the Law for Dialogue, Reconciliation, and a Just Peace in Chiapas was promulgated. The law reaffirmed CONAI as the normal mediator and granted it the right to make contact with the EZLN. The Zapatistas, however, were less than happy with the law, because it represented a unilateral proposal. They countered by proposing that the discussions be held in the capital. Naturally the government refused. Finally the dialogue began again, on April 9, in the *ejido* (community) of San Miguel in the municipality of Ocosingo. Six EZLN commanders—this time without Marcos—met with government representatives. Both sides agreed to resolve their differences by having recourse to CONAI. A second meeting was held on April 20 in the small town of San Andrés Larráinzar, to the northeast of San Cristóbal de las Casas. That small town continued to be the principal meeting place for many other discussions.

In June three foreign priests who worked in the diocese were accused of "proselytizing" in favor of the guerrillas and were deported. This was interpreted as a sign of government hostility toward Ruiz. In spite of that and many other incidents the dialogue went forward. On February 16, 1996, the government and the Zapatistas signed a forty-page document on Indian culture and civil rights in Mexico. But that "final" document did not really put an end to the struggle. A few months after signing the agreement, the Zapatistas still refused to lay down their arms, claiming that the government had no intention of putting into effect what it had signed.[62] One reason for the government's noncompliance was simply that Chiapas had faded from world interest, undoubtedly a relief to the president and the government.

But Chiapas soon returned to the front pages. In December 1997 a paramilitary death squad massacred forty-five indigenous men, women, and children, and in February 1998 the army broke all previous agreements and occupied the entire area. Tired of the government's constant criticism of his role as mediator, and no doubt convinced that there was little more he could do, on June 25 Bishop Ruiz resigned as mediator.

THE CHURCH AND DEMOCRACY

It is premature to arrive at a final judgment on the crisis in Chiapas. Among some of the safer conclusions, it can be said that Chiapas demonstrated the fact that in spite of living on the margin of politics and public life for years, the church continues to be a preeminent protagonist. Furthermore, Chiapas brought out a great irony: the government, which did everything possible to marginalize the church, was obliged to have recourse to it in order to enter into dialogue with an armed group in its own country. By assuming the mantle of protector of human rights and by becoming the "voice of those without a voice," the church in Chiapas, along with other dioceses in the north and the south, placed its moral authority at the service of democracy. Although not all bishops and groups in Mexico have changed, the church in general has grown in stature and in moral authority. Its role will be key in the coming years as Mexico attempts to forge the basis for a new democracy.

Conclusions

The two most important political phenomena in Latin America in the second half of the twentieth century were, first, the collapse of democracy—yet again—in the majority of the countries; and second, the restoration of that democracy. The causes of the endemic weakness of democracy in Latin America are well known and have been widely studied: the persistence of an authoritarian tradition; the lack of education and civic formation; and the survival of certain colonial habits such as paternalism, elitism, corruption, and so on. The constant *golpes de estado*, as well as the eruption of revolutionary violence, also reflect a profound structural weakness in Latin American society, which is still characterized by enormous social inequalities and vast cultural differences among classes and races. This absence of strong civic ties is conducive to a general lack of confidence in the government and democratic institutions.

Political and social scientists have discussed at length the "governability" of Latin America, but they have rarely touched on a topic so basic as public confidence: the confidence of the citizens in their government and elected authorities, and, even more fundamental, confidence or trust in their fellow citizens. It was precisely this lack of mutual trust that made the mediation of the Catholic church—an institution that is not part of the state apparatus—a necessity.

Given this situation we can appreciate how the church came to play such an important role in the restoration of democracy. The church was the only large national institution with the necessary moral legitimacy to serve as a bridge for dialogue between groups in opposition, which in many cases, were armed. Given its deep roots in Latin American culture and its omnipresence among the popular classes, the church occupied a privileged place that allowed it to serve as an acceptable mediator between different sectors of society.

But the church, traditionally conservative, could not have fulfilled that function if it had not experienced a radical change in its own orientation. The changes that took place in the Second Vatican Council and the 1968 Medellín bishops' conference gave the church new credentials, which restored the legitimacy that it once enjoyed in colonial times as defender of the Indians and other marginalized groups. In this book we have not studied those changes at great length. But it is important to realize that they happened in order to understand why the church was universally accepted as mediator in armed conflicts or as champion of the victims of repression.

The three Central American countries we have seen—Nicaragua, El Salvador, and Guatemala—all shared common characteristics: highly stratified social structures; the absence of a large middle class; the persistence of long dictatorships; and unequal land distribution. Furthermore, all had experienced North American intervention in their internal affairs. Similarly, the church in each of the three had characteristics in common: a very conservative past; a high percentage of foreign church personnel; a great polarization between conservatives and progressives.

Of the three cases Nicaragua is the most ambiguous. There the church played an important role in the three most important processes in that country's recent history: the revolution to overthrow Somoza; the Sandinista experiment; and the return to traditional democracy in 1990. The great novelty of the Sandinista revolution, which distinguished it from the Cuban revolution, was the presence of Christians in the revolution and in the post-revolutionary government. But the church was highly divided, among other reasons because Cardinal Obando y Bravo himself was the principal spokesman for the opposition to the Sandinistas. Given this fact, during the decade of the eighties both society and church experienced deep internal fissures. Each side defended what it considered to be its valid and legitimate interests: the Sandinistas dreamed of creating a just country, and the anti-Sandinistas worked to establish what they believed to be a more authentic democracy. Each side was also guilty of noticeable sectarianism and immaturity.

Finally, after years of war between the Sandinista army and the Contras, as well as interminable mutual recriminations, the official church finally established a modus vivendi with the government. The Sandinista regime was defeated in free elections—another difference from the Cuban process. In the Nicaraguan drama Christians on both sides—those who supported the Sandinistas and those who supported the anti-Sandinistas—played a crucial role in the whole process. Indeed, the relatively peaceful and orderly transition to the post-Sandinista era was due in large part to the presence and influence of the Christians who braked the extremists in both camps.

The case of El Salvador is like that of Nicaragua in many aspects. For example, the FMLN (Farabundo Martí National Liberation Front), like the FSLN, attracted Christians to its cause. On the other hand, El Salvador's internal civil war (thanks largely to the United States) was more violent than the war in Nicaragua, and its political reality was somewhat more complex. According to some simplistic descriptions, a democratic government was confronted with a Marxist guerrilla movement that had some popular support. In reality, the governments of José Napoleón Duarte and Alfredo Cristiani were examples of weak democracies that did not have full control over their own forces of order, which virtually constituted states within the state. In the case of El Salvador the church played a much clearer role than the church in Nicaragua. Thanks to Archbishop Arturo Rivera y Damas's leadership, the church assumed the task of mediating between the two parties in conflict. But mediating also meant reconciling. Rivera y Damas, Oscar Romero's successor, though he did not agree with the ideology or the methods of the FMLN, listened to both sides with sympathy and helped create an atmosphere in which dialogue was possible. The church also promoted grassroots citizen's participation in the National Debate for Peace in 1988.

Guatemala was another example of a formal democracy (after 1986) in which the forces of order frequently functioned with impunity outside the law. Given this fact, especially after the disastrous dictatorships of Lucas García and Ríos Montt, large sectors of the population distrusted the government, and even more, the army. Although no one like Oscar Romero emerged in Guatemala, the church as a whole, especially after Próspero Penados became archbishop, turned out to be quite progressive. In the person of Bishop Rodolfo Quesada the church offered its good offices as a mediator between the government and the guerrillas, a mission it accomplished with notable success. Like the church in El Salvador, the Guatemalan church also sponsored a National Dialogue (1989) in order to fortify democracy. The idea of the dialogue, in which a wide spectrum of society participated, was to open the doors of participation to thousands of Guatemalans who ordinarily considered themselves excluded from the political decision-making process. In both cases the church participated in the peace process, not as a mere neutral spectator but as a protagonist with its own agenda.

It was precisely in order not to limit the dialogue to the government and the guerrillas, who frequently got bogged down in sterile and endless debates, that the bishops and their advisers proposed ways to widen the participation in the dialogue and hence strengthen democracy even more. The public forums that the church promoted, such as the National Dialogue and the Association of Civil Society (1994), achieved the objective of allowing popular sentiment to express itself and to be heard on a national level. The debates in these non-governmental forums were models of constructive dialogue based on mutual respect. They stood in contrast to the slow and ponderous discussions between officialdom and the guerrillas, often carried out in an atmosphere of mutual distrust. The church-organized forums also had the positive effect of stimulating the government and the guerrillas to listen to the rest of the country and move their negotiations along more quickly.

In the Andean region, Bolivia seems somewhat like the Central American countries, especially as regards the mediating role of the church. Between 1968 and 1989 the church intervened as mediator in practically all important nationwide strikes and in every presidential electoral impasse. The labor disputes as well as the electoral impasses put to the test Bolivia's still fragile democratic institutions. The Bolivian church, which renovated itself in the sixties, became a sort of universally acceptable ombudsman. By means of its mediating action it was able to defuse many tensions and create an atmosphere in which dialogue was possible. Of course, during the dictatorships of Hugo Banzer and Luis García Meza the church was perceived as a member of the opposition, and hence not acceptable as a mediator. During those times of persecution the church assumed the role of defender of human rights, a fact that gave it even more credibility during the process of returning to civilian democracy.

Although Peru shares many of the same problems as Bolivia and the rest of Latin America, in other aspects its recent history is not so comparable. Although the government of Alberto Fujimori has committed its share of authoritarian abuses, formally it is a democracy. Therefore Peru has not experienced a real dictatorship since the period of Juan Velasco Alvarado and Francisco Morales Bermúdez (1968-80). And even those were reformist military governments that were relatively respectful—although selectively—of human rights.

The real threat to democracy in Peru's recent history came in the form of terrorism, particularly the Shining Path. By reason of its dogmatism, cruelty, and antireligiosity, it could not be compared with other guerrilla movements in the rest of Latin America. The Shining Path managed to dominate entire neighborhoods in Lima's "young towns" and a major part of the Andes. Every place where it established its reign of terror it practically destroyed the fabric of civic cooperation that held Peru together as a country. Although it cannot be said with certainty that the Shining Path would have come to power, the anarchical situation in which that terrorist organization left the country opened the door for a military takeover.

In this context the church, along with peace and human-rights groups, played a very important role in breaking through the passivity and fear that enervated the civilian population. The official church offered orientation to a country that stumbled from one crisis to the next. But more important than the official voice was the battle carried out by grassroots Christians—catechists, peasant vigilantes, religious women, and priests on the popular level—who helped the people overcome their fear and organize themselves. Certain figures like María Elena Moyano and Michel Azcueta in Villa El Salvador (Lima) symbolized this Christian presence in the popular struggle against the Shining Path.

Brazil and the other southern cone countries, each one according to its own peculiar national characteristics, were all examples of national security states. Although the model par excellence was Brazil, chronologically the dictatorship of Alfredo Stroessner preceded the other cases, and in many ways was a precursor. What was peculiar in the Paraguayan case was the alliance that was forged between the army and the Colorado Party. These were the double columns upon which Stroessner's personalistic dictatorship rested. The democratic opposition had very little space in which to move or breathe. In that situation the church became the only important national institution that could censure the dictatorship. Under the leadership of Archbishop Ismael Rolón, the church fulfilled that role; in the last years of the Stroessner regime, with the silent processions and other religious demonstrations the church effectively de-legitimized the dictatorship to the extent that when Stroessner fell, he had already lost all credibility.

The military regime in Brazil (1964-85) was the prime model of the national security state. In fact, the military governed through a parliament, and political parties were allowed to function. Nevertheless, political participation was closely controlled, and by means of Institutional Act Number 5 (1968) the civil rights of Brazilians were severely restricted. For the first few years the official church supported the military, but when the latter began to institutionalize itself in power, and at the same time to attack progressive churchpeople, the church dramatically changed course. Under the leadership of the progressive bishops—Hélder Câmara, Aloísio Lorscheider, Paulo Arns, Pedro Casaldáliga, and others—the church emerged as the principal voice of protest against the government for violations of human rights. In Brazil, given the absence of any large church-connected political party, the church extended its mantle of legitimacy to cover the entire democratic opposition: parties, unions, the press, and so forth. At the same time the church served as a refuge for thousands of persons from the middle and the popular classes who would otherwise have no special place in which to associate and to find protection: in the base ecclesial communities, mother's clubs, and other popular associations. Finally, when the normal organizations of civil society began to regroup, the church limited its role to that of supporting them and the transition to democracy.

Although the military regime in Chile was an institutional creation of the armed forces, it increasingly turned into a personal dictatorship of General Augusto Pinochet. As in Brazil, the church initially supported the regime but when Pinochet institutionalized the regime, and reinforced state control of the population, the church, under the leadership of Cardinal Raúl Silva Henríquez, became the principal voice of protest against the Chilean dictator. The Vicariate of Solidarity, founded by Silva, came to symbolize the church's defense of human rights. During a second stage of this long dictatorship, Silva's successor, Juan Francisco Fresno, took the initiative to break through the civilians' passivity by calling the parties together to forge a multiparty consensus that became known as the National Accord (1985). This experience served to inject a new vitality into the democratic opposition, which from then on marched in unison and offered a viable alternative to the Chileans. Thus historical ties between the church and the Christian Democratic Party constituted a special nuance in the Chilean case. Unlike Brazil—where Catholic Action was at odds with the bishops, and no large church-connected party existed—in Chile the church intervened directly in the process of returning to democracy by legitimizing the party that became the nucleus around which the other parties clustered.

Although Argentina seems like Chile in many social aspects, its recent ecclesiastical history is quite different. Both the church and the armed forces characterized themselves by a nationalistic integralism that expressed itself in the formula Church–Country–Armed Forces. There was, of course, a valiant minority of progressive bishops who spoke out in favor of human rights during the "dirty war," but their protest had little resonance in the Argentinean episcopal conference, dominated by conservatives. The banner of human rights was taken up by grassroots Christians—priests, religious women, and committed laypersons like Adolfo Pérez Esquivel and the Mothers of Plaza de Mayo. Many of them became victims of state terrorism.

During the transition to democracy, a reality which was forced upon the Argentine military, the bishops offered ethical and moral norms for reconstructing democracy. But relations between the church and the new democratic governments were characterized by certain tensions; a fact that suggests that the Argentine church still had not made its peace with pluralistic democracy. On the other hand, in the midst of a still very conservative church, a progressive church, small but dynamic, has emerged.

In spite of the accentuated secularism that characterizes Uruguayan society, the Catholic church played a significant role during the long civil-military dictatorship which governed the country. The archbishop of Montevideo, Carlos Parteli, representing the progressive tendencies, attempted to steer a critical course with respect to the regime, but his efforts were blocked by the conservative majority in the episcopal conference. As in Argentina, the principal voices of protests arose from below. Certain human-rights groups, such as SERPAJ (Justice and Peace Service) under the leadership of the Jesuit priest Luis Pérez Aguirre, gave an important impetus to the movement to have a national referendum to try the military and others who were guilty of grave human-rights violations. Although the referendum was defeated at the polls (by a relatively small margin), the mobilization to carry it off served to conscienticize Uruguayans on human rights and democracy. As a consequence, the church established itself as an important moral force in a society that before barely recognized its existence.

Finally, Mexico, unlike the majority of the countries in this survey, did not experience a military dictatorship. Nevertheless, the PRI (Party of the Institutionalized Revolution), which has governed the country for seventy years, is an example of Latin America's authoritarian and corporatist tradition, which became incarnated in a civilian party and government. For its part the church, which had receded into a state of conservative passivity as a consequence of its battles with the state, gradually emerged from its dormancy to assume a new leadership role in defense of democracy and human rights. In 1992 the state and the church, along with other confessions, arrived at a new modus vivendi by which the state finally and officially recognized the church. But this new accommodation occurred at the same time that some church groups had begun to censure the PRI and the government for standing in the way of the creation of an authentic democracy in Mexico.

The Zapatista insurrection in Chiapas brought all the ambiguities of the Mexican situation to the fore. In recognition of its social influence, the Zapatistas and the government accepted the church's mediation in the crisis. The Zapatistas saw in Bishop Samuel Ruiz a man who had defended the rights of the Indians. But conservative groups in society and in the church disapproved of Bishop Ruiz's role, in part because it brought into question the new modus vivendi between church and state.

Latin American Protestants (or *Evangélicos*) also experienced many important changes during this period. The historical churches felt the winds of the ecumenical movement and many of them took a strong stand in favor of social change. Among other examples of Catholic-Protestant collaboration, one can mention the Committee of Cooperation for Peace in Chile; the Ecumenical Movement for Human Rights in Argentina; and the Permanent Assembly on Human Rights in Bolivia. In general, these progressive ecumenical Protestants represented a minority within the Protestant community, which tended to be more conservative. In Guatemala and Chile the fundamentalists openly supported the military regimes, and in Nicaragua many supported the Contras.

UTOPIAS AND TOPIAS

Paradoxically, for many Latin Americans, especially the progressive Christians, the return to democracy was a bittersweet experience. For one thing, the return coincided with the rise of a neo-conservativism in the church and with the spread of neo-liberalism, which many of the new democracies had taken up as a new banner. For some observers, neo-liberalism, with its aggressive campaign in favor of the supremacy of the market and its lack of social sensitivity, seemed like a reincarnation of Social Darwinism. In this context some have asked, Was all that struggle and bloodshed worth it?

It may be helpful to bring to mind Karl Mannheim's concepts of "utopia" and "ideology." Briefly, for Mannheim, "utopia" represented not only an ideal place, but a series of ideals which inspires humans to look for that place. "Ideology," on the other hand, represents moments in which men and women have gotten bogged down on the road, or simply lost their way. In this case "ideology" represents a series of ideas and attitudes which undermines idealism and suffocates the human spirit. Without doubt, the period in the Latin American church between the Second Vatican Council and the Fourth Episcopal Conference of CELAM at Santo Domingo (1992) can be described as "utopian": it was a time of great idealism, heroic struggles, and many martyrdoms, which ennobled those struggles.

But there have been other utopian moments in the past. Many authors would consider the beginning of the sixteenth century as the "utopian" phase of the evangelization of Latin America. That was the period when Montesinos, Las Casas, Vasco de Quiroga, and other audacious missionaries defended the Indians and their rights. The second half of the century is more ambiguous. The winds of a neo-orthodoxy emanating from the Council of Trent (1545-63) combined with the strident nationalism of Spain, which reigned after the abdication of Charles V (1556), to put an end to the utopian phase. The campaigns to extirpate idols and to accelerate the hispanization of the

Indians correspond to this new period. The utopian spirit lived on in certain figures or in the Reductions of the Jesuits in Paraguay and other missions located far from the centers of power.

But, as Mannheim suggested, "the road of history leads from one topia over a utopia to the next topia, etc."[1] And history seems to confirm this. The utopian spirit was reborn in the eighteenth century in Tupac Amaru in Peru and in the Creole priests who fought for Latin America's independence. Finally, it was reborn again in the twentieth century: that story was the subject of this book. Perhaps this post-utopian moment is really the beginning of a new road leading to a new utopia.

Notes

1 Church, Power, and Popular Legitimacy

1. Max Weber, *Economy and Society*, ed. Guenther Roth and Claus Wittich (Berkeley and Los Angeles: University of California Press, 1978), vol. 1, pp. 215-245.

2. Peter H. Smith, "Political Legitimacy in Latin America," in *New Approaches to Latin American History*, ed. Richard Graham and Peter H. Smith (Austin, Tex.: University of Texas Press, 1974), pp. 225-255.

3. Claudio Véliz, "Latitudinarian Religious Centralism," *The Centralist Tradition of Latin America* (Princeton, N.J.: Princeton University Press, 1980), pp. 189-217.

4. For examples of the use of religious symbols in political movements, see David Bailey, *¡Viva Cristo Rey!* (Austin, Tex.: University of Texas Press, 1974); Jacques Lafaye, *Quetzalcoatl y Guadalupe* (Mexico, D.F.: Fondo de Cultura Económica, 1977); Jeffrey Klaiber, *Religion and Revolution in Peru, 1824-1976* (Notre Dame, Ind.: University of Notre Dame Press, 1977).

5. See Daniel H. Levine, *Religion and Political Conflict in Latin America* (Chapel Hill: University of North Carolina Press, 1986), pp. 15-16.

6. Charles A. Reilly, "Latin America's Religious Populists," in Levine, *Religion and Political Conflict in Latin America*, pp. 42-57. See also Jeffrey Klaiber, "Prophets and Populists: Liberation Theology, 1968-1988," *The Americas* 46 (July 1989): 1-15.

7. On the church and the national security states see José Comblin, *The Church and the National Security State* (Maryknoll, N.Y.: Orbis Books, 1979).

8. *Latinamerica Press*, June 15, 1989, pp. 1, 8.

9. Juan E. Corradi, Patricia Weiss Fagan, and Antonio Garretón, *Fear at the Edge: State Terror and Resistance in Latin America* (Berkeley and Los Angeles: University of California Press, 1992), pp. 9-18, 121-141.

10. See Carolyn Cook Dipboye, "The Roman Catholic Church and the Political Struggle for Human Rights in Latin America, 1968-1980," *Journal of Church and State* (Autumn 1982): 497-524.

11. See Sonia E. Alvarez's comments on women and the church in Brazil in her essay "Women's Movements and Gender Politics in the Brazilian Transition," in *The Women's Movement in Latin America*, ed. Jane S. Jaquette (Boston: Unwin Hyman, 1989), pp. 21-27.

12. See especially Daniel H. Levine, *Popular Voices in Latin American Catholicism* (Princeton, N.J.: Princeton University Press, 1992).

13. On Latin American Protestantism see David Stoll, *Is Latin America Turning Protestant?* (Berkeley and Los Angeles: University of California Press, 1990); David Martin, *Tongues of Fire* (Cambridge, Mass.: Basil Blackwell, 1990); see also the bibliographical essay by Phillip Berryman, "Is Latin America Turning Pluralist?: Recent Writings on Religion," *Latin American Research Review* 30:2 (1995): 107-122; Edward L. Cleary and Hannah W. Stewart-Gambino, *Power, Politics, and Pentecostals in Latin America* (Boulder, Col.: Westview Press, 1997).

14. Felipe Guamán Poma de Ayala, *Nueva corónica y buen gobierno*, ed. Franklin Pease (Mexico, D.F.: Fondo de Cultura Económica, 1993), vol. 1, p. 3.

15. On church-state relations see J. Lloyd Mecham, *Church and State in Latin America* 2d. ed. (Chapel Hill: University of North Carolina Press, 1966).

16. On the Vatican's Latin American policy, see Eric O. Hanson, *The Catholic Church in World Politics* (Princeton, N.J.: Princeton University Press, 1987), especially pp. 59-74; and Peter Hebblethwaite, "The Vatican's Latin American Policy," in Dermot Keogh, *Church and Politics in Latin America* (New York: St. Martin's Press, 1990), pp. 49-64.

17. On the conservative shift in the church, see Penny Lernoux, "The Catholic Counterreformation," *The People of God* (New York: Viking Penguin, 1989), chap. 3, pp. 28-75.

18. See Hanson, *The Catholic Church in World Politics*, pp. 73-74; Emilio Mignone, *Witness to the Truth: The Complicity of Church and Dictatorship in Argentina, 1976-1983* (Maryknoll, N.Y.: Orbis Books, 1988), pp. 51-54.

19. Hanson, *The Catholic Church in World Politics*, p. 60; Hebblethwaite, "The Vatican's Latin American Policy," p. 55.

20. For a deeper view of the differing ecclesiologies and cosmovisions in the Latin American church, see the classical work by Ivan Vallier, *Catholicism, Social Control, and Modernization in Latin America* (Englewood Cliffs, N.J.: Prentice-Hall, 1970); Brian H. Smith, "Religion and Social Change: Classical Theories and New Formulations in the Context of Recent Developments in Latin America," *Latin American Research Review* 10:2 (Summer 1975): 3-34; Otto Maduro, *Religion and Social Conflicts* (Maryknoll, N.Y.: Orbis Books, 1982). In the eighties and nineties liberation theology became the dividing line between conservatives and progressives. On this topic see Penny Lernoux, "Liberation Theology: Rome versus America," *People of God*, chap. 4, pp. 79-115. See also the chapters by Luis Ugalde, Scott Mainwaring, and Jean-Yves Calvez in *Born of the Poor: The Latin American Church since Medellín*, ed. Edward L. Cleary (Notre Dame, Ind.: University of Notre Dame Press, 1990).

21. Jo Marie Griesgraber analyzes this theme in her paper, "The Role of International Solidarity in the Last 50 Years of the Latin American Church's Struggle for Justice," presented at the annual meeting of the American Society of Ecclesiastical History, Union Theological Seminary, Richmond, Virginia, April 1991. See also Mary M. McGlone, *Sharing Faith across the Hemisphere* (Maryknoll, N.Y.: Orbis Books, 1997).

22. On the last military cycle see especially Corradi, Fagan, and Garretón, *Fear at the Edge*; José Comblin, *The Church and the National Security State*; and Alain Rouquié, *The Military and the State in Latin America* (Berkeley and Los Angeles: University of California Press, 1987). On the "bureaucratic-authoritarian" model of government see James M. Malloy, ed., *Authoritarianism and Corporatism in Latin America* (Pittsburgh: University of Pittsburgh Press, 1977); David Collier, ed., *The New Authoritarianism in Latin America* (Princeton, N.J.: Princeton University Press, 1979).

2 Brazil (1964-1985)

1. Conferência Nacional dos Bispos do Brasil, *Igreja no Brasil 1991: Diretório litúrgico*, p. 126.

2. Ibid., p. 137.

3. Frank McCann, "Vargas and the Destruction of the Brazilian Integralista and Nazi Parties," *The Americas* 26 (July 1969): 15-34.

4. Scott Mainwaring, *The Catholic Church and Politics in Brazil, 1916-1985* (Stanford, Calif.: Stanford University Press, 1986), pp. 41-42.

5. Oscar Lustosa, *A Igreja católica no Brasil República* (São Paulo: Edições Paulinas, 1991), pp. 154-156.

6. Fernando Prandini, Víctor A. Petrucci, Frei Romeu Dale, O.P. (comp. Centro Pastoral Vergueiro), *As Relações Igreja-Estado no Brasil*, vol. 1: *Durante o governo de Marechal Castelo Branco, 1964-1967* (São Paulo: Edições Loyola, 1986), p. 26.

7. Ibid., p. 36.

8. Ibid., p. 27.

9. Ibid., p. 78.

10. Charles Antoine, *Church and Power in Brazil* (Maryknoll, N.Y.: Orbis Books, 1973), pp. 84-85.

11. Prandini, Petrucci, and Dale, *As Relações Igreja-Estado no Brasil*, vol. 1, pp. 93-94.

12. Thomas E. Skidmore, "Brazil's Slow Road to Democratization: 1974-1985," in *Democratizing Brazil*, ed. Alfred Stepan (New York: Oxford University Press, 1989), p. 6.

13. Antoine, *Church and Power in Brazil*, pp. 107-109.

14. Ibid., p. 188; Prandini, Petrucci, and Dale, *As Relações Igreja-Estado no Brasil*, vol. 2: *Durante o governo do Marechal Costa e Silva, 1967-1970* (São Paulo: Edições Loyola, 1986), pp. 97-98.

15. Prandini, Petrucci, and Dale, *As Relações Igreja-Estado no Brasil*, vol. 2, p. 117.

16. Antoine, *Church and Power in Brazil*, p. 250; Marcio Moreira Alves, *A Igreja e a política no Brasil* (São Paulo: Editora Brasiliense, 1979), pp. 216-218.

17. Prandini, Petrucci, and Dale, *As Relações Igreja-Estado no Brasil*, vol. 2, pp. 134-135.

18. Antoine, *Church and Power in Brazil*, p. 148.

19. Moreira Alves, *A Igreja e a política no Brasil*, p. 207.

20. José Oscar Beozzo, *A Igreja do Brasil: de João XXIII a João Paulo II: de Medellín a Santo Domingo* (Petrópolis: Editora Vozes, 1993), pp. 88-89.

21. Prandini, Petrucci, and Dale, *As Relações Igreja-Estado no Brasil*, vol. 2, p. 33.

22. Ibid., pp. 106-108.

23. Ibid., pp. 125-128.

24. Ibid., pp. 125-126.

25. Ibid., p. 126.

26. Ibid., pp. 163-167.

27. Paulo José Krischke, *A Igreja as crises políticas no Brasil* (Petrópolis: Editora Vozes, 1979), p. 76.

28. Arquidiocese de São Paulo, *Brasil: Nunca Mais* (São Paulo: Editora Vozes, 1985), p. 68. The English version appears under the title *Torture in Brazil*, trans. Jaime Wright, ed. with an intro. by Joan Dassin (New York: Vintage Books, 1986).

29. Clara Pope, "Human Rights and the Catholic Church in Brazil, 1970-1983: The Pontifical Justice and Peace Commission of the São Paulo Archdiocese," *Journal of Church and State* 29 (Autumn 1985), p. 433.

30. Ibid., pp. 437-438. On the Herzog case see also Skidmore, "Brazil's Slow Road to Democratization: 1974-1985," in Stepan, *Democratizing Brazil*, pp. 11-12, and Beozzo, *A Igreja do Brasil*, p. 71.

31. Helcion Ribeiro (coordinator), *Paulo Evaristo Arns, Cardenal de esperança e pastor da igreja de São Paulo* (São Paulo: Edições Paulinas, 1989), p. 71.

32. Arquidiocese de São Paulo, *Brasil: Nunca Mais*, pp. 291-293.

33. *Latinamerica Press*, August 31, 1995, p. 1.

34. Prandini, Petrucci, and Dale, *As Relações Igreja-Estado no Brasil*, vol. 6: *Durante o governo do general Geisel, 1978-1979* (São Paulo: Edições Loyola, 1987), p. 90.

35. Prandini, Petrucci, and Dale, *As Relações Igreja-Estado no Brasil*, vol. 3: *Durante o governo do general Médici, 1970-1974* (São Paulo: Edições Loyola, 1987), p. 216.

36. Ibid., pp. 173-174.

37. Prandini, Petrucci, and Dale, *As Relações Igreja-Estado no Brasil*, vol. 6, pp. 34-35.

38. Prandini, Petrucci, and Dale, *As Relações Igreja-Estado no Brasil*, vol. 4: *Durante o governo do general Geisel, 1974-1976* (São Paulo: Edições Loyola, 1987), pp. 219-229.

39. Ibid., pp. 273-274.

40. Ibid., pp. 240-269.

41. Prandini, Petrucci, and Dale, *As Relações Igreja-Estado no Brasil*, vol. 3, pp. 53-54.

42. Ibid., pp. 57-58.

43. Prandini, Petrucci, and Dale, *As Relações Igreja-Estado no Brasil*, vol. 4, pp. 161-171.

44. Mainwaring, *The Catholic Church and Politics in Brazil, 1916-1985*, p. 152.

45. Prandini, Petrucci, and Dale, *As Relações Igreja-Estado no Brasil*, vol. 4, p. 180.

46. Prandini, Petrucci, and Dale, *As Relações Igreja-Estado no Brasil*, vol. 6, p. 78.

47. Ibid., p. 47.

48. Comissão Arquidiocesana de Pastoral dos direitos humanos e marginalizados da Arquidiocese de São Paulo, *Repressão na Igreja no Brasil: reflexo de uma situaçao de opressão (1968/1978)*, p. 11.

49. Prandini, Petrucci, and Dale, *As Relações Igreja-Estado no Brasil*, vol. 5: *Durante o governo do general Geisel, 1977* (São Paulo: Edições Loyola, 1987), p. 231.

50. Ibid., p. 233.

51. Prandini, Petrucci, and Dale, *As Relações Igreja-Estado no Brasil*, vol. 6, p. 73.

52. Ibid., pp. 146-147.

53. Ibid., p. 121.

54. See especially Leonardo Boff, *Ecclesiogenesis: The Base Communities Reinvent the Church* (London: Collins Liturgical Publications, 1986). The original work in Portuguese was published in 1977 (Petrópolis, Editora Vozes).

55. Mainwaring, in *The Progressive Church in Latin America*, ed. Scott Mainwaring and Alexander Wilde (Notre Dame, Ind.: University of Notre Dame Press, 1989), p. 151.

56. *Latinamerica Press*, August 24, 1989, p. 5.

57. Sonia E. Alvarez, "Politicizing Gender and Engendering Democracy," in Stepan, *Democratizing Brazil*, p. 210.

58. Margaret E. Keck, "The New Unionism in the Brazilian Transition," in Stepan, *Democratizing Brazil*, pp. 261-267.

59. Skidmore, "Brazil's Slow Road to Democratization: 1974-1985," in Stepan, *Democratizing Brazil*, p. 21.

60. María Helena Moreira Alves, "Interclass Alliances in the Opposition to the Military in Brazil," in *Power and Popular Protest*, ed. Susan Eckstein (Berkeley and Los Angeles: University of California Press, 1989), pp. 293-294.

61. Skidmore, "Brazil's Slow Road to Democratization: 1974-1985," in Stepan, *Democratizing Brazil*, p. 31.

62. Beozzo, *A Igreja do Brasil*, p. 64.

63. Ibid., pp. 250-251.

64. For a view of the legacy of the progressive church, see Edward L. Cleary, "The Brazilian Church and Church-State Relations: Nation-Building," *Journal of Church and State* 39:2 (Spring 1997): 253-272.

3 Chile (1973-1990)

1. National Institute of Statistics, *Compendio Estadístico 1991* (Santiago), p. 1.

2. *Mensaje*, August 1992, pp. 266-267.

3. Ascanio Cavallo, ed., *Memorias: Cardenal Raúl Silva Henríquez* (Santiago: Ediciones Copygraph, 1991), vol. 2, p. 114.

4. María Antonieta Huerta and Luis Pacheco Pastene, *La Iglesia chilena y los cambios sociopolíticos* (Santiago: CISOC-Bellarmine, 1988), p. 274.

5. Data supplied by the Office of Religious Sociology of the Episcopal Conference of Chile (OSORES), Santiago, 1992.

6. *Mensaje*, August 1992, pp. 283, 285.

7. On the origins of Chilean Christian Democracy see Michael Fleet, *The Rise and Fall of Chilean Christian Democracy* (Princeton, N.J.: Princeton University Press, 1985).

8. On Christian Democracy's centrist role see Timothy R. Scully, *Rethinking the Center: Party Politics in Nineteenth and Twentieth Century Chile* (Stanford: Stanford University Press, 1992).

9. Cavallo, *Memorias*, vol. 2, p. 84.

10. On Alberto Hurtado see the special issue of *Mensaje*, no. 411, August 1992.

11. On Silva Henríquez see Oscar Pinochet de la Barra, *El Cardenal Silva Henríquez: luchador por la justicia* (Santiago: Editorial Salesiana, 1987), and his memoirs, ed. Ascanio Cavallo.

12. Fleet, *The Rise and Fall of Chilean Christian Democracy*, p. 61.

13. Cavallo, *Memorias,* pp. 137-143.

14. Cavallo, *Memorias,* p. 139; Eduardo Araya L., *Relaciones Iglesia-Estado en Chile, 1973-1981* (Santiago: Chilean Institute of Humanistic Studies, 1982), pp. 53-54.

15. Arturo Chacón Herrera and Humberto Lagos Schuffeneger, *Religión y proyecto político autoritario* (Santiago: Ediciones Literatura Americana Reunida y Programa Evangélico de Estudios Socio-Religiosos, 1986), pp. 42-43.

16. Ibid., p. 51.

17. Ibid., pp. 49-50.

18. On the specific role of the army in Pinochet's regime see Augusto Varas, *Los militares en el poder: régimen y gobierno militar en Chile* (Santiago: FLASCO-pehuén, 1987).

19. Eugenio Yáñez, *La Iglesia y el gobierno militar: itinerario de una relación difícil (1973-1988)* (Santiago: Editorial Andante, 1989), p. 2.

20. Ibid., p. 55.

21. Brian Smith, *The Church and Politics in Chile* (Princeton, N.J.: Princeton University Press, 1982), p. 288, n. 10.

22. Yáñez, *La Iglesia y el gobierno militar*, p. 59; Jaime Escobar, *Persecución a la Iglesia en Chile: martirologio (1973-1986)* (Santiago, 1986), p. 76.

23. Cavallo, *Memorias,* vol. 2, pp. 292-294.

24. Smith, *The Church and Politics in Chile*, p. 313.

25. Araya, *Relaciones Iglesia-Estado en Chile, 1973-1981*, p. 98.

26. General Secretariate of the Episcopal Conference of Chile, *Documentos del Episcopado: Chile, 1974-1980* (Santiago: Ediciones Mundo, 1982), p. 16.

27. Ibid., p. 16.

28. Pinochet de la Barra, *El Cardenal Silva Henríquez: luchador por la justicia*, p. 154.

29. Ibid., pp. 157-158.

30. Araya, *Relaciones Iglesia-Estado en Chile, 1973-1981*, p. 105.

31. Pinochet de la Barra, *El Cardenal Silva Henríquez, luchador por la justicia*, p. 159.

32. Ibid., p. 159.

33. General Secretariate of the Episcopal Conference of Chile, *Documentos del Episcopado, 1974-1980*, pp. 99-129.

34. David Stoll, *Is Latin America Turning Protestant?* (Berkeley and Los Angeles: University of California Press, 1990), p. 111.

35. Humberto Lagos Schuffeneger, *Relaciones Iglesias evangélicas-gobierno: Chile, 1973-1976* (Santiago: Instituto Latinoamericano de Doctrina y Estudios Sociales [ILADES], 1977), pp. 42-45.

36. Humberto Lagos Schuffeneger, *La Libertad religiosa en Chile: los evangélicos y el gobierno militar* (Santiago: Vicaría de la Solidaridad, 1978), vol. 1, pp. 53-54.

37. Chacón Herrera and Lagos Schuffeneger, *Religión y proyecto autoritario*, p. 58.

38. Araya, *Relaciones Iglesia-Estado en Chile, 1973-1981*, p. 130.

39. Ibid.

40. General Secretariate of the Episcopal Conference of Chile, *Documentos del Episcopado, 1974-1980*, pp. 159-162.

41. Interview with María Luisa Sepúlveda, executive director of the Vicariate of Solidarity, Santiago, August 17, 1992.

42. *Vicaría de la Solidaridad: undécimo año de labor, 1986* (annual report), p. 155.

43. Araya, *Relaciones Iglesia-Estado en Chile, 1973-1981*, p. 117.

44. *Vicaría de la Solidaridad: duodécimo año de labor, 1987* (annual report), p. 7.

45. Yáñez, *La Iglesia y el gobierno militar*, pp. 99-100.

46. Vicaría de la Solidaridad, *Decimosexto aniversario, Vicaría de la Solidaridad: discurso de S.E. el President de la República Don Patricio Aylwin Azócar; discurso*

de Monseñor Carlos Oviedo Cavada, arzobispo de Santiago, Santiago, October 1991, n.p.

47. Smith, *The Church and Politics in Chile,* pp. 316-317.

48. Araya, *Relaciones Iglesia-Estado en Chile, 1973-1981*, pp. 56-57.

49. Varas, *Los militares en el poder*, p. 155.

50. Carl E. Meacham, "Changing of the Guard: New Relations between Church and State in Chile," *Journal of Church and State* 29 (Fall 1987), p. 414.

51. Episcopal Conference of Chile, *El Renacer de Chile y otros documentos* (Santiago: Centro Nacional de Comunicación Social del Episcopado de Chile, 1984), p. 35.

52. Ibid., pp. 36-37.

53. Ibid., p. 43.

54. Senén Conejeros, *Chile: de la dictadura a la democracia* (Santiago, 1990), p. 252.

55. Meacham, "Changing of the Guard," p. 417.

56. Pinochet de la Barra, *El Cardenal Silva Henríquez: luchador por la justicia*, pp. 234-235.

57. Meacham, "Changing of the Guard," pp. 422-423.

58. *Documentos del Episcopado: Chile, 1984-1987* (Santiago: Episcopal Conference of Chile, 1988), p. 59.

59. Meacham, "Changing of the Guard," p. 427.

60. Tamara Avetikian, "Acuerdo Nacional y transición a la democracia," *Estudios Públicos* 21 (Summer 1986), p. 311.

61. Ibid., p. 364.

62. Meacham, "The Changing of the Guard," p. 427.

63. Cristián Precht, "Del Acuerdo a la reconciliación: la Iglesia chilena y el camino a la democracia," paper presented at the Seventeenth International Congress of LASA, Los Angeles, September 24, 1992, p. 8.

64. Meacham, "Changing of the Guard," p. 430.

65. Precht, "Del Acuerdo a la reconciliación," p. 8.

66. *El Mercurio* (Santiago), August 26, 1992, C-3.

67. Varas, *Los militares en el poder,* pp. 196-197.

68. Precht, "Del Acuerdo a la reconciliación," p. 9.

69. Michael Fleet, "The Role of the Catholic Church in Chile's Transition to Democracy," paper presented at the Seventeenth International Congress of LASA, Los Angeles, September 27, 1992, p. 16.

70. Precht, "Del Acuerdo a la reconciliación," p. 10.

71. Ibid., p. 11.

72. *LASA Forum: Latin American Studies Association*, vol. 19, no. 4 (Winter 1989), p. 20.

73. *Documentos del Episcopado: Chile, 1988-1991* (Santiago: CENCOSEP, Area of Communication, Chilean Episcopal Conference, 1992), p. 41.

74. Ibid., p. 78.

75. *El NO de los cristianos* (Santiago: Instituto para el Nuevo Chile), n.d.

76. Yáñez, *La Iglesia y el gobierno militar*, p. 106.

77. Conejeros, *Chile,* p. 330.

78. *Latinamerican Press*, March 2, 1989, p. 7.

79. Ibid., pp. 329-330.

80. The phrase "authoritarian enclaves" belongs to Manuel Antonio Garretón, in *Partidos, transición y democracia en Chile* (Santiago, FLASCO, working document, April 1990), p. 1.

81. Conejeros, *Chile*, p. 241. The *Informe de la Comisión Nacional de Verdad y Reconciliación*, better known as the "Rettig Report," presented by a special commission created by President Aylwin to investigate cases of human-rights violations during the dictatorship, is more sober and cautious in its conclusions. It speaks of 1,068 dead, 957 "detained and disappeared," and 90 killed by "private groups for political motives" (Santiago, February 1991, vol. 1, 2d. tome, annex II, pp. 883-884).

82. See chapter 5, "La Iglesia Católic: un poder moral con altísima legitimidad," in Carlos Huneeus, *Los chilenos y la política: cambio y continuidad en el autoritarismo* (Santiago: Center of Studies on Contemporary Reality [CERC], 1987).

4 Argentina (1976-1983)

1. CONADEP (The National Commission on the Disappearance of Persons), *Nunca más: Informe de la Comisión Nacional sobre la Desaparición de Personas* 17th ed. (Buenos Aires: EUDEBA, 1992), p. 16.

2. See, for example, Jean-Pierre Bousquet, *Las Locas de la Plaza de Mayo* (Buenos Aires: Fundación para la Democracia en Argentina, 1983), p. 24.

3. Richard Gillespie, *Soldados de Perón: los Montoneros* (Buenos Aires: Grijalbo, 1987), p. 304.

4. On the 1934 eucharistic congress see Jesús Méndez, "Church-State Relations in Argentina in the Twentieth Century: A Case Study of the Thirty-Second International Eucharistic Congress," *Journal of Church and State*, vol. 27, no. 2 (Spring 1985): 223-243; Fortunato Mallimaci, *El catolicismo integral en la Argentina (1930-1946)* (Buenos Aires: Editorial Biblos and Fundación Simón Rodríguez, 1988).

5. Mallimaci, *El catolicismo integral en la Argentina (1930-1946)*, p. 29.

6. See Enrique Ghirardi, *La Democracia Cristiana* (Buenos Aires Centro Editor de América Latina, 1983), pp. 134-137.

7. Mallimaci, *El catolicismo integral en la Argentina (1930-1946)*, p. 44.

8. Fortunato Mallimaci, "El catolicismo argentino desde el liberalismo integral a la hegemonía militar," *500 años de cristianismo en Argentina* (Buenos Aires: CEHILA-Centro Nueva Tierra, 1992), p. 362.

9. Gillespie, *Soldados de Perón*, p. 85.

10. On the Catholic origins of the *Montoneros* see Gillespie, *Soldados de Perón*, pp. 74-99.

11. José Pablo Martín, "El Movimiento de Sacerdotes para el Tercer Mundo," *Nuevo Mundo: Revista de teología latinoamericana* (Buenos Aires: Ediciones Castañeda San Antonio de Padua; Ediciones Guadalupe, 1991), pp. 12-13.

12. Ibid., p. 217.

13. Martín, "El Movimiento de Sacerdotes para el Tercer Mundo," p. 58.

14. Carlos Mugica, *Peronismo y cristianismo* (Buenos Aires: Editorial Merlin, 1973). For other authors who saw a compatibility between Catholicism and *peronismo*, see Carlos Chiesa and Enrique Sosa, *Iglesia y justicialismo, 1943-1955* (Buenos Aires: Centro de Investigación y Orientación Social, 1983), and José Leopoldo Pérez Gaudio, *Catolicismo y peronismo* (Buenos Aires: Ediciones Corregidor, 1985).

15. Martín, "El Movimiento de Sacerdotes para el Tercer Mundo," p. 42.

16. Bousquet, *Las Locas de la Plaza de Mayo*, pp. 33-34.

17. *South America and the Caribbean 1993* (London: Europa Publications, 1992), p. 73.

18. Daniel Frontalini and María Cristina Caiati, *El Mito de la Guerra Sucia* (Buenos Aires: Editorial CELS, 1984), p. 72.

19. Frank Graziano, *Divine Violence: Spectacle, Psychosexuality, and Radical Christianity in the Argentine "Dirty War"* (Boulder, Col.: Westview Press, 1992), pp. 37-38.

20. Frontalini and Caiati, *El Mito de la Guerra Sucia,* p. 24.

21. Ibid., p. 25.

22. CONADEP, *Nunca más*, pp. 70-72.

23. See Jacobo Timerman, *Prisoner without a Name, Cell without a Number* (New York: Knopf [dist. Random House], 1981).

24. Emilio Mignone, *Witness to the Truth: The Complicity of Church and Dictatorship in Argentina* (Maryknoll, N.Y.: Orbis Books, 1986), p. 19. In 1988 there were ninety-four bishops, counting Cardinal Pironio, who resided in Rome, thirteen archbishops and forty-three dioceses, and nine prelatures. See Agencia Informativa Católica Argentina, *Guía eclesiástica argentina [for 1988]* (Buenos Aires), pp. 2-3.

25. Agencia Informativa Católica Argentina, *Guía eclesiástica argentina* (Buenos Aires, August 1988), p. 159.

26. Enrique Amato, *La Iglesia argentina* (Friburgo-Buenos Aires: Centro de Investigaciones Sociales y Religiosas, 1961), p. 219.

27. Arturo Fernández, *Sindicalismo e Iglesia (1976-1987)* (Buenos Aires: Centro Editor de América Latina, 1990), pp. 37-38.

28. Mignone, *Witness to the Truth*, p. 66.

29. Ibid., pp. 135-164.

30. Fernández, *Sindicalismo e Iglesia (1976-1987)*, p. 34.

31. Mignone, *Witness to the Truth*, p. 5.

32. Conferencia Episcopal Argentina, *Documentos del Episcopado Argentino, 1984*, vol. 12 (Buenos Aires, 1989), p. 168.

33. Ibid., pp. 141-142.

34. Ibid., p. 147.

35. Ibid., p. 161.

36. Ibid., p. 174.

37. Bousquet, *Las Locas de la Plaza de Mayo*, p. 107.

38. Mignone, *Witness to the Truth*, pp. 34-35.

39. Eduardo Gabriel Kimel, *La Masacre de San Patricio* (Buenos Aires: Ediciones Dialéctica, 1989), pp. 81-82.

40. Ibid., p. 83.

41. For a brief summary of the church's victims, see CONADEP, *Nunca más*, pp. 347-360.

42. Luis Miguel Barronetto, *Reportajes a Mons: Angelelli* (Córdoba, 1988), p. 143.

43. Ibid., p. 141.

44. CONADEP, *Nunca más*, pp. 359-360.

45. Padre Obispo Miguel E. Heseyne, *Cartas por la vida* (Buenos Aires: Centro Nueva Tierra, 1989), p. 68.

46. Ibid., p. 33.

47. Personal interview with Adolfo Pérez Esquivel, Buenos Aires, February 11, 1993.

48. Bousquet, *Las Locas de la Plaza de Mayo*, p. 43. See also Marysa Navarro, "The Personal Is Political: Las Madres de Plaza de Mayo," in *Power and Popular Protest: Latin American Social Movements*, ed. Susan Eckstein (Berkeley and Los Angeles: University of California Press, 1989), pp. 242-258.

49. *Newsweek*, February 8, 1993, pp. 7-8.

50. Bousquet, *Las Locas de la Plaza de Mayo*, p. 54.

51. See David Stoll, *Is Latin America Turning Protestant?* (Berkeley and Los Angeles: University of California Press, 1990), p. 337; and José Míguez Bonino, "Presencia y ausencia protestante en la Argentina del proceso militar, 1973-1983," *Cristianismo y Sociedad* 83 (1985): 81-85.

52. CONADEP, *Nunca más*, p. 353.

53. Conferencia Episcopal Argentina, *Iglesia y comunidad nacional* (Buenos Aires, 1990), p. 48.

54. Ibid., p. 49.

55. Ibid., p. 47.

56. Ibid., p. 73.

57. Rubén Dri, *Teología y dominación* (Buenos Aires: Roblanco, 1987), p. 113.

58. Graziano, *Divine Violence*, p. 54.

59. Leonardo Pérez Esquivel, "Democracia y dictadura: opciones y compromisos de los cristianos," *500 años de cristianismo en Argentina*, p. 435.

60. Ana María Ezcurra, *Iglesia y transición democrática: ofensiva del neoconservadurismo católico en América Latina* (Buenos Aires: Puntosur, 1988), p. 117.

61. Leonardo Pérez Esquivel, "Democracia y dictadura," p. 430.

62. *Nueva Tierra*, special supplement, January 12, 1991, p. 4.

63. Tito Garabal, *El Viaje comienza ahora: Juan Pablo II en Uruguay, Chile y la Argentina* (Buenos Aires: Ediciones Paulinas, 1987), p. 227.

64. Ibid., p. 254.

65. *Boletín del Centro Nueva Tierra* 6 (March 1990), p. 1.

66. Sergio Ciancaglini and Martín Granovsky, *Nada más que la verdad: el juicio a las juntas* (Buenos Aires: Editorial Planeta, 1995), pp. 328-337.

67. *Latinamerica Press*, April 6, 1995, p. 6.

68. Argentinian Episcopal Conference, *Caminando hacia el tercer milenio* (San Miguel, April 27, 1996), paragraph 20. See also *Latinamerica Press*, May 2, 1996, p. 8.

5 Paraguay (1954-1989)

1. José María Blanch, ed., *El Precio de la paz* (Asunción: CEPAG, 1991), p. 3.

2. Paul H. Lewis, *Paraguay under Stroessner* (Chapel Hill, N.C.: University of North Carolina Press, 1980), p. 18.

3. Ibid., p. 127.

4. Blanch, *El Precio de la paz*, pp. 39-40.

5. Luis Cano, Antonio González Dorado, Ernesto Maeder, et al., *La Evangelización en el Paraguay* (Asunción: Ediciones Loyola, 1979), p. 178.

6. Ibid., p. 201.

7. Miguel Carter, *El Papel de la Iglesia en la caída de Stroessner* (Asunción: RP Ediciones, 1991), p. 46.

8. *Pro Mundi Vita* 38 (1971), p. 21.

9. Paraguayan Episcopal Conference, *Guía eclesiástica del Paraguay* (Asunción, 1989), pp. 80-81.

10. Lewis, *Paraguay under Stroessner*, pp. 186-189; Carter, *El Papel de la Iglesia en la caída de Stroessner*, p. 62.

11. Secretariat of the Paraguayan Episcopal Conference, *Una Iglesia al servicio del hombre: cartas pastorales de la CEP, 1958-1973* (Asunción, 1973), p. 270.

12. Ismael Rolón, *No hay camino . . . ¡Camino se hace al andar! Memorias* (Asunción: Editorial Don Bosco, 1991), p. 64.

13. Ibid., p. 65.

14. Carter, *El Papel de la Iglesia en la caída de Stroessner*, p. 83.

15. Equipo Expa, *En busca de la Tierra sin Mal* (Bogotá: Indo-American Press Service, 1982), p. 39. This book, written in exile, is a summary of the experiences of the founders of the leagues.

16. Ibid., p. 75.

17. J. L. Caravias, *Liberación campesina: Ligas Agrarias del Paraguay* (Madrid: Colección "Lee y Discute," 1975), pp. 103-104.

18. See José María Blanch, ed., *Ko'äga Roñe'ëta (Ahora hablaremos): Misiones, 1976-1978. Testimonio campesino de la represión en Misiones* (Asunción: CEPAG, 1990). This work draws together the testimony of the peasants who belonged to the leagues and who were detained in concentration camps.

19. Equipo Expa, *En busca de la Tierra sin Mal,* p. 158.

20. Carter, *El Papel de la Iglesia en la caída de Stroessner*, p. 78.

21. Rolón, *No hay camino . . . ¡Camino se hace al andar! Memorias*, p. 73.

22. Carter, *El Papel de la Iglesia en la caída de Stroessner*, p. 76.

23. Paraguayan Episcopal Conference, *Entre las persecuciones del mundo y los consuelos de Dios* (Asunción, June 12, 1976), p. 10.

24. Paraguayan Episcopal Conference, *El Saneamiento moral de la nación* (Asunción, June 12, 1979), p. 7.

25. Ibíd., p. 23.

26. Rolón, *No hay camino . . . ¡Camino se hace al andar! Memorias,* pp. 73-74.

27. Blanch, *El Precio de la paz*, p. 227.

28. Aníbal Miranda, cited in Carlos R. Miranda, *Paraguay y la era de Stroessner* (Asunción: RP Ediciones, n.d.), p. 138.

29. Ibid., p. 131.

30. Margarita Durán, *Diálogo nacional: urgencia de nuestro tiempo* (Asunción: Universidad Católica, Biblioteca de Estudios Paraguayos, 1987), p. 13.

31. Edwin Britez, Estéban Caballero, José Nicolás Morínigo, et al., *Paraguay: Transición, diálogo y modernización política* (Asunción: El Lector, 1987), p. 11.

32. Rolón, *No hay camino . . . ¡Camino se hace al andar! Memorias*, p. 79.

33. Durán, *Diálogo nacional*, p. 101.

34. Ibid., pp. 111-112.

35. Ibid., pp. 35-36.

36. Carter, *El Papel de la Iglesia en la caída de Stroessner*, p. 109.

37. Ibid.

38. *Sendero*, October 9, 1987, p. 10.

39. Ibid., October 23, 1987, p. 6.

40. Carter, *El Papel de la Iglesia en la caída de Stroessner*, p. 112.

41. Interview with Archbishop Ismael Rolón, Ipacaraí, March 10, 1992.

42. *Anuario Paraguay 1988* (Asunción: Editora Ñqandutí Vive, 1989), p. 326.

43. Interview with Archbishop Rolón.

44. *Sendero*, May 6, 1988, p. 2.

45. *Discursos y mensajes de su Santidad Juan Pablo II en su visita al Paraguay, 16, 17, 18 de mayo de 1988* (Asunción: Universidad Católica, June 1988), pp. 58-59.

46. *Anuario Paraguay 1988*, p. 321.

47. Carter, *El Papel de la Iglesia en la caída de Stroessner*, p. 122.

48. *Anuario Paraguay 1988*, p. 488.

49. Ibid., p. 511.

50. Rolón, *No hay camino . . . ¡Camino se hace al andar! Memorias,* pp. 107-108.

51. Paraguayan Episcopal Conference, *Teología de la liberación* (Asunción, October 20, 1988), p. 32.

52. Carter, *El Papel de la Iglesia en la caída de Stroessner*, pp. 132-133; Rolón, *No hay camino . . . ¡Camino se hace al andar! Memorias*, p. 112.

53. Rolón, *No hay camino . . . ¡Camino se hace al andar! Memorias*, p. 118.

54. Ibid., p. 121.

55. Carter, *El Papel de la Iglesia en la caída de Stroessner*, p. 139.

56. Víctor Jacinto Flecha, "Historia de una ausencia: notas acerca de la participación electoral en el Paraguay," *Revista Paraguaya de Sociología* 80 (January-April 1991): 79.

57. Paraguayan Episcopal Conference, *El Proceso de transición hacia la democracia* (Asunción, July 25, 1990).

6   Uruguay (1973-1990)

1. Gonzalo Varela, *De la República liberal al estado militar: Uruguay, 1968-1973* (Montevideo: Ediciones del Nuevo Mundo, 1988), p. 24.

2. Ibid., p. 65.

3. Ibid., p. 147.

4. Servicio Paz y Justicia (SERPAJ), *Uruguay: Nunca más*, 3d ed. (Montevideo, 1989), p. 7.

5. Ibid., p. 285.

6. Tribunal Permanente de los Pueblos y SERPAJ, *Tribunal Permanente de los Pueblos: Sesión uruguaya, abril 1990* (Montevideo, 1990), p. 11.

7. Germán Rama, *La Democracia en Uruguay: una perspectiva de interpretación* (Montevideo: ARCA Editorial, 1987), p. 170.

8. Enrique Sobrado, *La Iglesia uruguaya: entre pueblo y oligarquía* (Montevideo: Alfa Editorial, 1969), p. 35.

9. Juan Villegas, *Historia de la Iglesia en el Uruguay en cifras* (Montevideo: Universidad Católica del Uruguay Dámaso A. Larrañaga, 1984), p. 87.

10. Uruguayan Episcopal Conference, *Guía de la Iglesia uruguaya 1981* (Montevideo, 1981), p. 144.

11. Rama, *La Democracia en Uruguay*, p. 157.

12. Varela, *De la República liberal al estado militar*, p. 116.

13. "Declaraciones de la CEU" [CEU: Uruguayan Episcopal Conference], September 15, 1971, p. 2.

14. "Declaración del Consejo Permanente de la Conferencia Episcopal Uruguaya," June 12, 1972, p. 3.

15. Héctor Borrat, *Uruguay 1973-1984: i messaggi e i silenzi* (Bologna, Italy, 1984), p. 109.

16. Román Lezama, S.J., "Una historia de prisión," mimeographed pages, archive of OBSUR (Observatorio del Sur), Montevideo.

17. Carlos Parteli, "A la comunidad católica de Montevideo," November 1, 1973, archive of OBSUR.

18. "Reseña histórica de nuestra pastoral de conjunto (1966-1984)," p. 19, archive of OBSUR.

19. Interview with Father Andrés Alessandri, S.J., director of the Fabve Center during the dictatorship, and interview with Carlos Parteli, archbishop of Montevideo, 1966-85, Montevideo, February 26, 1993.

20. These confidential messages sent to the government were published by Borrat in *Uruguay 1973-1984*.

21. Diego Achard, *La Transición en Uruguay* (Montevideo: Instituto Wilson Ferreira Aldunate, 1992), p. 37.

22. Uruguayan Episcopal Conference, "Ante el próximo plebiscito constitucional," November 12, 1980.

23. Interview with Patricio Rodé, vice-director of OBSUR and director of Social Pastoral Services of the archdiocese of Montevideo, 1983-85, Montevideo, March 3, 1993.

24. Many of the articles published in the magazine *La Plaza* are reproduced in Father Pérez Aguirre's book, *Predicaciones en la plaza* (Montevideo, 1985). Also, interview with Father Luis Pérez Aguirre, S.J., Montevideo, February 26, 1993.

25. Tribunal Permanente de los Pueblos, p. 67.

26. María del Huerto Amarillo and Antonio Serrentino Sabella, "El Movimiento de derechos humanos en el Uruguay," *Cuadernos Paz y Justicia* 4: *La Defensa de los derechos humanos en la transición democrática uruguaya* (July 1988), p. 33.

27. Ibid., p. 34.

28. Tribunal Permanente de los Pueblos, p. 56.

29. Ibid., p. 107.

30. Achard, *La Transición en Uruguay*, p. 53; and interview with former Archbishop Carlos Parteli, February 26, 1993.

31. *Latinamerican Press*, March 1, 1990, p. 2.

7 Bolivia (1952-1989)

1. For a general view of Bolivian history up until the Banzer military regime, see Herbert Klein, *Bolivia, the Evolution of a Multi-Ethnic Society* (New York: Oxford University Press, 1982); for the process since 1952 see James M. Malloy, *Bolivia: The Uncompleted Revolution* (Pittsburgh: University of Pittsburgh Press, 1970); James M. Malloy and Richard S. Thorn, eds., *Beyond the Revolution: Bolivia since 1952* (Pittsburgh: University of Pittsburgh Press, 1971); James M. Malloy and Carl Beck, *Political Elites: A Mode of Analysis* (Pittsburgh: University Center for International Studies, University of Pittsburgh, 1971); and James M. Malloy and Eduardo Gamarra, *Revolution and Reaction: Bolivia, 1964-1985* (New Brunswick, N.J.: Transaction Books, 1988). See also Christopher Mitchell, *The Legacy of Populism in Bolivia: From the MNR to Military Rule* (New York: Praeger Publishers, 1977).

2. This picture of the church is taken in part from a document written by a group of Christian intellectuals entitled *La Iglesia de Bolivia: ¿compromiso o traición? De Medellín a Puebla: Ensayo de análisis histórico* (La Paz, June, 1978). Also see Josep M. Barnadas's chapters on the church in Bolivia in the eighth volume of CEHILA's

general history of the church in Latin America, *Perú, Bolivia y Ecuador* (Salamanca: Ediciones Sígueme, 1987). See also David Maldonado Villagrán, *Resumen histórico: 500 años de evangelización en Bolivia* (La Paz, 1991).

3. Maldonado, *Resumen histórico*, p. 187.

4. *Realidad Nacional*, no. 15 (October 1988), p. 38.

5. *La Iglesia de Bolivia*, p. 43.

6. *Presencia* (La Paz), August 16, 1985. *Presencia*, one of the most prestigous dailies in the country, is owned by the Catholic church and is an excellent source on the church.

7. *Por la senda de S.S. Juan Pablo II en Bolivia* (La Paz: Bolivian Episcopal Conference, 1988), chap. 2, p. 1. On Protestantism in Bolivia, see the chapters by Mortimer Arias in the eighth volume of CEHILA. Carlos Intipampas criticizes fundamentalist groups in his work *Opresión y aculturation: la evangelización de los aymara* (La Paz: HISBOL-CEPITA-ISETRA, 1991).

8. Klein, *Bolivia, the Evolution of a Multi-Ethnic Society*, p. 238.

9. *Presencia*, March 21, 1968, pp. 1, 8.

10. *Presencia*, March 23, 1969, pp. 1, 3.

11. Hugo Assmann, *Teoponte, una experiencia guerrillera* (Oruro, Bolivia: Centro "Desarrollo Integral," 1971), p. 202.

12. *Fedmineros* (Information bulletin of the General Federation of Mining Workers of Bolivia), no. 14, second week of September 1970.

13. Jorge Manrique, *El socialismo y la Iglesia en Bolivia*, La Paz, October 9, 1970, p. 5. See also *Bolivia: 1971-1976: Pueblo, Estado, Iglesia* (Lima: Centro de Estudios y Publicaciones, 1976). This is a collection of documents on the church during that period.

14. "Carta abierta a los obispos de Bolivia: El sentido cristiano de la propiedad en el momento actual: Reflexiones de los sacerdotes mineros," San José Mine, November 19, 1970.

15. Barnadas, in CEHILA, *Perú, Bolivia y Ecuador*, p. 456.

16. Asamblea Permanente de los Derechos Humanos en Bolivia, *La Huelga de Hambre* (La Paz, 1978), p. 13.

17. *La Masacre del Valle de Cochabamba* (La Paz: Cuadernos "Justicia y Paz," 1975).

18. *La Iglesia de Bolivia*, p. 33.

19. Centro de Estudios y Publicaciones, *Bolivia 1971-1976*, pp. 53-54.

20. *El Diario* (La Paz), January 23, 1973, p. 1.

21. *La Iglesia de Bolivia*, pp. 125-126.

22. *Presencia*, July 15, 1978.

23. *Presencia*, November 10, 1976.

24. *Presencia*, June 16, 1976.

25. Centro de Estudios y Publicaciones, *Bolivia 1971-1976*, pp. 180-181.

26. *Paz y Fraternidad* (La Paz: Editorial Don Bosco, 1976), p. 17.

27. La Asamblea Permanente de los Derechos Humanos en Bolivia, *La Huelga de Hambre*, p. 39.

28. Ibid., pp. 189-210.

29. *Presencia*, July 27, 1979, p. 1.

30. Asamblea Permanente de los Derechos Humanos en Bolivia, *La Masacre de Todos los Santos* (La Paz, 1980), p. 14.

31. *El Diario*, November 8, 1979, pp. 1, 14.

32. *En memoria de Luis Espinal, SJ*, special issue of *Diáspora*, newsletter of the Society of Jesus in Bolivia, March-April 1980.

33. PADI, *Bolivia: cronología de una dictadura* (Quito, Ecuador, 1982), p. 57.

34. Malloy and Gamarra, *Revolution and Reaction*, p. 143.

35. *Dignidad y Libertad* (La Paz: Ediciones Paulinas, 1980), p. 7.

36. Ibid., pp. 18-19.

37. *Presencia*, November 18, 1980, p. 1.

38. On violations of human rights during the dictatorships and the trials conducted to condemn the guilty, see Federico Aguiló, *"Nunca más" para Bolivia* (Cochabamba: Permanent Assembly on Human Rights and the Institute of Social and Economic Studies of San Simón National University, 1993).

39. *Ultima Hora*, November 25, 1981, p. 1.

40. *Hoy* (La Paz), December 20, 1981, p. 1.

41. *Presencia*, October 29, 1984, p. 1; October 30, pp. 1, 8.

42. *Presencia*, November 20, 1984, p. 1.

43. Herbert Müller and Flavio Machicado, eds., *El Diálogo para la democracia* (La Paz: Müller y Flavio Machicado Asociados, 1987), pp. 286-287.

44. Ibid., p. 308.

45. Klein, *Bolivia, the Evolution of a Multi-Ethnic Society,* p. 258.

46. *Presencia*, September 14, 1985, p. 1.

47. *Agencia de Noticias Fides*, September 16, 1986, p. 2; *Presencia*, September 14, 1986, pp. 1, 16.

48. *Agencia de Noticias Fides*, September 16, 1986, p. 4.

49. The agreement was not signed until 1989. *Los Tiempos* (Cochabamba), April 28, 1989, p. 1.

50. *Ultima Hora*, May 23, 1989, p. 1.

51. Ibid., p. 3.

52. *Presencia*, July 26, 1989, p. 6.

53. *Presencia*, July 27, 1989, p. 1.

54. *Presencia*, July 28, 1989, p. 5.

55. *Agencia de Noticias Fides*, April 25, 1989, p. 1.

56. *Presencia*, January 1, 1989, p. 1.

8 Peru (1980-1995)

1. See, for example, Iván Hinojosa, "Entre el poder y la ilusión: Pol Pot, Sendero y las utopías campesinas," in *Debate Agrario* 15 (October-December 1992): 69-93.

2. *Newsweek*, August 26, 1991, p. 13.

3. On Ayacucho before the Shining Path see Jefrey Gamarra, "Estado, modernidad y sociedad regional: Ayacucho, 1920-1940," *Apuntes* 31 (second semester 1992): 103-114.

4. On the university origins of the Shining Path see Carlos Iván Degregori, *Ayacucho 1969-1979: el surgimiento de Sendero Luminoso* (Lima: Instituto de Estudios Peruanos, 1990). See also Gustavo Gorriti, *Sendero: historia de la guerra milenaria en el Perú* (Lima: Editorial Apoyo, 1990); David Scott Palmer, *The Shining Path of Peru*, 2d ed. (New York: St. Martin's Press, 1994). On the church's role see chapter six in Simon Strong, *Shining Path: The World's Deadliest Revolutionary Force* (London: HarperCollins Publishers, 1992).

5. On the youth and women in the Shining Path, see Dennis Chávez de Paz, *Juventud y terrorismo* (Lima: Instituto de Estudios Peruanos, 1989); and Robin Kirk,

Grabado en piedras: las mujeres de Sendero Luminoso (Lima: Instituto de Estudios Peruanos, 1993).

6. Cynthia McClintock, "Peru's Sendero Luminoso Rebellion: Origins and Trajectory," in *Power and Popular Protest: Latin American Social Movements*, ed. Susan Eckstein (Berkeley and Los Angeles: University of California Press, 1989), p. 61.

7. In this context see the article by José Luis Idígoras, "Religiosidad popular y marxismo popular," *Revista teológica limense* 10:3 (1976): 289-313; see also Carlos Tapia, "Abimael y la religión," *La República* (Lima), January 1, 1995, p. 21.

8. The two former nuns in the Shining Path were Rosalía Tami Puell, of the Sacred Heart sisters, and Nelly Evans Risco de Alvarez Calderón, of the Immaculate Heart of Mary sisters. On the former see *El Nacional* (Lima), October 31, 1987, p. 19; on the latter, see chapter six in Strong, *Shining Path: The World's Deadliest Revolutionary Force*.

9. *Perú: 1989-1990: Informe de la Coordinadora Nacional de Derechos Humanos* (Lima: August 1991), p. 14.

10. Amnesty International, *"Caught between Two Fires": Peru Briefing* (New York: Amnesty International, 1989), p. 4.

11. Ibid., pp. 4, 6.

12. Oscar Espinoza, *Rondas campesinas y nativas en la Amazonía peruana* (Lima: Amazon Center of Anthropology and Practical Application, 1995), p. 43.

13. *Caminos* (Lima), October 1994, p. 4.

14. *Revista Ideele* (Lima) 58, (November 1993), pp. 16-17.

15. *Caminos*, October 1994, p. 17.

16. *Caminos*, October 1991, p. 2.

17. *Caminos*, November 1989, p. 3.

18. *Sí* (Lima) 334 (July 26 to August 1), pp. 22-31.

19. Tito Paredes, "Peruvian Protestant Missionaries and the Struggle for Human Rights, 1980-1993," paper given at the annual meeting of the American Anthropological Association, November 29 to December 4, 1994, Atlanta, Georgia. Also, interview with Caleb Mesa, former director of the Peace and Hope Department of Action and Social Services, 1987-93, November 30, 1995.

20. Robin Kirk, *The Decade of Chaqwa: Peru's Internal Refugees* (Washington, D.C.: U.S. Committee for Refugees, May 1991), pp. 13-18.

21. Jeffrey Klaiber, *The Catholic Church in Peru, 1821-1985* (Washington, D.C.: The Catholic University of America Press, 1992), pp. 307-308.

22. Ibid., p. 38.

23. Ibid., p. 339.

24. See *Directorio eclesiástico del Perú 1987* (Lima: Secretariate of the Peruvian Episcopate, n.d.), pp. 95-104.

25. Degregori, *Ayacucho 1969-1979*, pp. 46-47.

26. Interview with Ernest Ranly, CPPS, Lima, October 6, 1995.

27. Archdiocesan Office of Social Action (Ayacucho), "Arquidiócesis de Ayacucho: Plan Pastoral social de conjunto: Memoria de 1989 y plan anual de 1990" (Ayacucho, April 16, 1990), p. 8.

28. *El Diario Internacional*, September 1991, p. 3.

29. Ibid., p. 4.

30. John Gitlitz and Telmo Rojas, "Las rondas campesinas en Cajamarca," *Apuntes* 16 (first semester, 1985): 127-128.

31. Orin Starn, ed., *Hablan los ronderos: la búsqueda por la paz en los Andes,* working paper no. 45 (Lima: Instituto de Estudios Peruanos, 1993), p. 6.

32. CEAS (Episcopal Commission of Social Action), *Primer Taller Nacional sobre Rondas Campesinas, Justicia y DDHH: Sumario* (Lima, 1993), p. 53.

33. Oscar Castillo, *Bambamarca: vida cotidiana y seguridad pública,* working paper no. 55 (Lima: Instituto de Estudios Peruanos, 1993), p. 21.

34. On the church in Cajamarca see James Steidel's doctoral dissertation, "Renewal in the Latin American Church: A Study of the Peruvian Dioceses of Cajamarca and Ica," Los Angeles, University of Southern California, 1975.

35. Letter of José Dammert Bellido, bishop of Cajamarca, to Bishop Miguel Irizar, February 25, 1992. In the file entitled "Respuesta a cuestionario enviado a los señores obispos sobre la situación de la violencia," Lima, CEAS. See also Diocese of Cajamarca, Episcopal Commission of Social Action, and Andean Commission of Lawyers, *Primer Taller Nacional sobre Rondas Campesinas, Justicia y Derechos Humanos: Material de Lectura* (Lima, 1992), p. 27.

36. Interview with Bishop José Gurruchaga, Lima, April 24, 1995.

37. In Starn, *Hablan los ronderos,* p. 16.

38. *Sur* (Lima), February 1986, pp. 8-12.

39. Stephen Judd, M.M., "The Emergent Andean Church: Inculturation and Liberation in Southern Peru, 1968-1986," doctoral dissertation, Berkeley, California, Graduate Theological Union, 1987, pp. 102, 237.

40. See *La Señal de cada momento: documentos de los obispos del Sur Andino 1969-1994* (Lima: Centro de Estudios y Publicaciones; Sicuani: Instituto de Pastoral Andina, 1994).

41. Judd, "The Emergent Andean Church," p. 149.

42. Michael L. Smith, *Entre dos fuegos: ONG, desarrollo rural y violencia política* (Lima: Instituto de Estudios Peruanos, 1992), p. 34.

43. *La República* (Lima), February 20, 1988, p. 6.

44. Ibid., p. 7.

45. Judd, "The Emergent Andean Church," pp. 167-168.

46. Ibid., p. 292.

47. *Paz, tarea de todos* (Lima: Centro de Estudios y Acción para la Paz), October-November 1986, pp. 24-25.

48. Smith, *Entre dos fuegos,* p. 105.

49. Ibid., pp. 106-107.

50. *Iglesia en Sicuani,* October 1, 1992, p. 8.

51. Rex Hudson, ed., *Peru: A Country Study* (Washington, D.C.: Federal Research Division, Library of Congress, 1993), p. 70.

52. On terrorism in the Upper Huallaga Valley see the report by José Contreras in *Newsweek,* April 24, 1989, pp. 8-10.

53. Letter of Venancio Orbe, C.P., to Bishop Miguel Irizar, president of the Episcopal Commission of Social Action, April 7, 1992, CEAS Archive, Lima.

54. Diocese of Cajamarca, CEAS, and the Andean Commission of Jurists, *Primer Taller Nacional sobre Rondas Campesinas, Justicia y DDHH,* pp. 27-29.

55. Michael F. Brown and Eduardo Fernández, *War of Shadows: The Struggle for Utopia in the Peruvian Amazon* (Berkeley and Los Angeles: University of California Press, 1991).

56. Gustavo Gorriti, "Terror in the Andes: The Flight of the Asháninkas," *The New York Times Magazine,* December 2, 1990, pp. 40-45, 48, 65-72. With the aid of

William and Marilyn Hoffer, Father Gagnon narrated the history of this war in the jungle in *Warriors in Eden* (New York: William Morrow, 1993).

57. Espinoza, *Rondas campesinas y nativas en la Amazonía peruana*, p. 123.

58. *Expreso* (Lima), August 14, 1994, pp. A30-31; September 25, p. A21.

59. Hudson, *Peru: A Country Study*, p. 234.

60. National Coordinating Committee of Human Rights, *Coordinadora Nacional de Derechos Humanos* (Lima, 1994), pp. 10-11. Also, interview with Miguel Huerta, assistant secretary to the executive secretary of the National Coordinating Committee, Lima, January 5, 1996.

61. Perú, Vida y Paz, *La Paz no es ajena: cronología* (Lima, July, 1994), p. 19.

62. *El Comercio* (Lima), May 13, 1990, p. 1.

63. Hudson, *Peru: A Country Study*, p. 220.

64. Special Commission to Research and Study Violence and Alternatives for Pacification, *Violencia y pacificación en 1991* (Lima: Senate of the Republic, 1992), p. 53.

65. Diana Miloslavich Tupac, ed., *María Elena Moyano: en busca de una esperanza* (Lima: Centro de la Mujer Peruana Flora Tristán, 1993), p. 73.

66. Ibid., p. 90.

9   El Salvador (1980-1992)

1. David Browning, "El Salvador, History," *South America, Central America, and the Caribbean 1993* (London: Europa Publications Limited, 1993), p. 297. For a more complete view of the political aspects of the civil war, see Tommie Sue Montgomery, *Revolution in El Salvador: Origins and Evolution* (Boulder, Col.: Westview Press, 1993), and Saul Landau, "El Salvador," in *The Guerrilla Wars of Central America* (New York: St. Martin's Press, 1993), chap. 3, 66-147.

2. On the Salvadoran oligarchy see Jeffrey M. Paige, "Coffee and Power in El Salvador," *Latin American Research Review*, vol. 28, no. 3 (1993): 7-40.

3. Lawrence Simon and James C. Stephens Jr., "Reforma agraria en El Salvador (1980-1981): su impacto en la sociedad salvadoreña," *Estudios Centroamericanos* (*ECA*) (March 1981), p. 179.

4. Thomas Carothers, "The Reagan Years: The 1980s," in *Exporting Democracy: The United States and Latin America*, ed. Abraham F. Lowenthal (Baltimore: The Johns Hopkins University Press, 1991), chap. 4, 90-122.

5. Ibid., p. 93.

6. A. J. Bacevich, James D. Hallums, et al., *American Military Policy in Small Wars: The Case of El Salvador* (Washington, D.C.: Institute for Foreign Policy Analysis, 1988), p. 5.

7. *Informe de la Comisión de la Verdad para El Salvador: De la Locura a la Esperanza: la guerra de 12 años en El Salvador* (New York: United Nations, 1992-93), p. 24.

8. *Estudios Centroamericanos* (*ECA*) (May-June 1983), pp. 583-586.

9. *Estudios Centroamericanos* (*ECA*) (October-November 1984), pp. 841-842.

10. *Informe de la Comisión de la Verdad para El Salvador*, pp. 118-125; Mark Danner, "The Truth of El Mozote," *The New Yorker*, December 6, 1993, pp. 50-133.

11. *Informe de la Comisión de la Verdad para El Salvador*, pp. 28-29.

12. Secretaria Status Rationarium Generale Ecclesiae, *Annuarium Statisticum Ecclesiae 1991* (Roma: Typis Polyglottis Vaticanis, 1991), pp. 123, 183-184, 197.

13. Data found in the Central Office of Statistics, Archdiocese of San Salvador. In 1992 there were 133 priests in the archdiocese and 875 religious women.

14. See Rodolfo Cardenal, *El Poder eclesiástico en El Salvador (1871-1931)* (San Salvador: UCA Editores, 1980).

15. Rodolfo Cardenal, *Historia de una esperanza: Vida de Rutilio Grande* (San Salvador: UCA Editores, 1985).

16. James R. Brockman, *Romero: A Life* (Maryknoll, N.Y.: Orbis Books, 1989).

17. *Informe de la Comisión de la Verdad para El Salvador*, p. 133.

18. Phillip Berryman, *The Religious Roots of Rebellion: Christians in Central American Revolutions* (Maryknoll, N.Y.: Orbis Books, 1984), p. 158.

19. Scott Mainwaring and Alexander Wilde, eds., *The Progressive Church in Latin America* (Notre Dame, Ind.: University of Notre Dame Press, 1989), pp. 133-134.

20. *Informe de la Comisión de la Verdad para El Salvador*, pp. 60-65. See also Judith Noone, *The Same Fate as the Poor* (Maryknoll, N.Y.: Orbis Books, 1995).

21. Ibid., p. 63.

22. *Estudios Centroamericanos (ECA)* (January-February 1981), pp. 114-115.

23. *Estudios Centroamericanos (ECA)* (September 1981), pp. 919-920.

24. *Estudios Centroamericanos (ECA)* (December 1984), p. 965.

25. *Carta a las Iglesias*, August 16-31, 1984, pp. 4-7. Also, interview with María Julia Hernández, director of Legal Defense, San Salvador, March 1, 1994.

26. Pablo Richard and Guillermo Meléndez, eds., *La Iglesia de los pobres en América Central* (San José, Costa Rica: Ecumenical Research Department, 1982), p. 77.

27. Fermán Cienfuegos, *Veredas de audacia: Historia del FMLN* (San Salvador: Editorial ARCOIRIS, 1993), p. 72.

28. Ibid., p. 117.

29. *Carta a las Iglesias*, December 1, 1987, pp. 7-8.

30. *Estudios Centroamericanos (ECA)* (March-April 1980), pp. 204-205.

31. *Estudios Centroamericanos (ECA)* (March 1986), pp. 169-204.

32. *Estudios Centroamericanos (ECA)* (September 1983), pp. 827-829.

33. *Estudios Centroamericanos (ECA)* (October-November 1984), p. 840.

34. Ibid., pp. 842-847.

35. José Napoleón Duarte, with Diana Page, *Duarte: My Story* (New York: G. P. Putnam's Sons, 1986), chap. 9, "Peace Talks," pp. 208-228.

36. *Estudios Centroamericanos (ECA)* (December 1984), pp. 944-946.

37. *Estudios Centroamericanos (ECA)* (May-June 1985), p. 472.

38. *Estudios Centroamericanos (ECA)* (September-October 1985), pp. 748-750.

39. Duarte, *Duarte*, pp. 241-267.

40. Tomás R. Campos, "Lectura política de los secuestros," *Estudios Centroamericanos (ECA)* (September-October 1985), pp. 684-700.

41. *Carta a las Iglesias*, December 16-31, 1984, pp. 13-14.

42. *Estudios Centroamericanos (ECA)* (August-September 1986), pp. 782-788.

43. For a chronology of the meeting in the nunciature, see *Estudios Centroamericanos (ECA)* (October 1987), pp. 727-732.

44. Ibid., pp. 747-750.

45. Ibid., p. 729.

46. *Estudios Centroamericanos (ECA)* (August-September 1988), p. 771. The August-September 1988 edition of *ECA* is devoted exclusively to the National Debate.

47. Ibid., p. 743.

48. Ibid., p. 764.

49. *Carta a las Iglesias*, October 1-15, 1988, p. 2.

50. *Carta a las Iglesias*, June 16-30, 1989, p. 2.

51. *Estudios Centroamericanos* (*ECA*) (January-February 1992), p. 23.

52. *El Salvador Proceso: Informativo Semanal*, August 15, 1990, p. 18.

53. See *Informe de la Comisión de la Verdad para El Salvador*, pp. 44-50.

54. Martha Doggett, *Death Foretold: The Jesuit Murders in El Salvador* (Washington, D.C.: Lawyers Committee for Human Rights and Georgetown University Press, 1993), pp. 209-236. See also Teresa Whitfield, *Paying the Price: Ignacio Ellacuría and the Murdered Jesuits of El Salvador* (Philadelphia: Temple University Press, 1994).

55. *Carta a las Iglesias*, November 1-30, 1990, p. 2.

56. The long, complicated negotiating process is summed up in the article by Carlos Acevedo, "Balance global del proceso de negociación entre el gobierno y el FMLN," *Estudios Centroamericanos* (*ECA*) (January-February 1992), pp. 15-53. See also Terry Lynn Karl, "La Revolución negociada en El Salvador," *Revista Occidental*, no. 3 (1993): 277-292.

57. *Carta a las Iglesias*, January 1-31, 1992, pp. 10-13.

58. *Informe de la Comisión de la Verdad para El Salvador*, p. 41.

59. *Carta a las Iglesias*, December 16-31, 1993, pp. 15-16.

60. *Carta a las Iglesias*, September 1-15, 1992, p. 6.

10 Nicaragua (1979-1990)

1. See Joseph S. Tulchin, "Nicaragua, The Limits of Intervention," in Abraham F. Lowenthal, ed., *Exporting Democracy: The United States and Latin America* (Baltimore: The Johns Hopkins University Press, 1991), p. 236.

2. On the Somozas see Richard Millett, *Guardians of the Dynasty: A History of the U.S. Created Guardia National of Nicaragua and the Somoza Family* (Maryknoll, N.Y.: Orbis Books, 1977).

3. Angel Arnaiz, *Historia del pueblo de Dios en Nicaragua* (Managua: Centro Ecuménico Antonio Valdivieso, 1990), p. 152.

4. Philip J. Williams, *The Catholic Church and Politics in Nicaragua and Costa Rica* (Pittsburgh: University of Pittsburgh Press, 1989), pp. 192-193.

5. Arnaiz, *Historia del pueblo de Dios en Nicaragua*, pp. 99-100.

6. John Kirk, *Politics and the Catholic Church in Nicaragua* (Gainesville, Fla.: University of Florida Press, 1992), p. 28.

7. Arnaiz, *Historia del pueblo de Dios en Nicaragua*, p. 94.

8. Ibid., p. 117.

9. Irene Selser, *Cardenal Obando* (Mexico City: Centro de Estudios Ecuménicos, 1989), pp. 36-37.

10. Manzar Foroohar, *The Catholic Church and Social Change in Nicaragua* (Albany, N.Y.: State University of New York Press, 1989), p. 118.

11. Michael Dodson and Laura Nuzzi O'Shaughnessy, *Nicaragua's Other Revolution* (Chapel Hill: University of North Carolina Press, 1990), p. 125.

12. Arnaiz, *Historia del pueblo de Dios en Nicaragua*, p. 122.

13. Selser, *Cardenal Obando*, p. 33.

14. Arnaiz, *Historia del pueblo de Dios en Nicaragua*, pp. 123-124.

15. Paul VI, *Populorum Progressio* (1967), par. 31.

16. Kirk, *Politics and the Catholic Church in Nicaragua*, p. 101.

17. On the different groups within the church see Bahman Baktiari, "Revolution and the Church in Nicaragua and El Salvador," *Journal of Church and State*, vol. 28:1 (Winter 1986), p. 20; Ted C. Lewellen, "Holy and Unholy Alliances: The Politics of Catholicism in Revolutionary Nicaragua," *Journal of Church and State*, vol. 31:1 (Winter 1989), pp. 20-21.

18. Joseph Mulligan, *The Nicaraguan Church and the Revolution* (Kansas City, Mo.: Sheed and Ward, 1991), p. 203.

19. Three authors, Rafael Aragón, Luz Beatriz Arellano, and Eberhard Löschke, speak of four stages: "Pacific Co-Existence," 1979-80; "The Crisis: The Road to Confrontation," 1980-83; "Open Confrontation," 1983-87; "Conflictive Collaboration," 1987– . See also Guilio Girardi, et al., *Pueblo revolucionario, pueblo de Dios* (Managua: Centro Ecuménico Antonio Valdivieso, 1989), pp. 45-72. Kirk divides the process into three stages: "From Jubilation to Despair," 1979-1982; "Church-State Relations at Their Nadir," 1983-1985; "In Search of Reconciliation . . . ," 1985-90.

20. Lewellen, *Journal of Church and State*, p. 20.

21. Selser, *Cardenal Obando,* pp. 43-44.

22. Kirk, *Politics and the Catholic Church in Nicaragua,* p. 108.

23. Dodson and Nuzzi O'Shaughnessy, *Nicaragua's Other Revolution,* pp. 151-152; Philip J. Williams, "The Catholic Church in the Nicaraguan Revolution: Differing Responses and New Challenges," in *The Progressive Church in Latin America,* ed. Scott Mainwaring and Alexander Wilde (Notre Dame, Ind.: University of Notre Dame Press, 1989), pp. 86-87. See also Phillip Berryman, *Stubborn Hope: Religion, Politics, and Revolution in Central America* (Maryknoll, N.Y.: Orbis Books, 1994), p. 30.

24. Kirk, *Politics and the Catholic Church in Nicaragua,* pp. 132-133.

25. Selser, *Cardenal Obando,* pp. 63-67; Kirk, *Politics and the Catholic Church in Nicaragua,* pp. 114-116.

26. See Humberto Belli, *Breaking Faith: The Sandinista Revolution and Its Impact on Freedom and Christian Faith in Nicaragua* (Westchester, Ill.: Crossway Books, 1986). See also Ana María Ezcurra, *El Vaticano y la administración Reagan: Convergencias en Centroamérica* (Mexico, D.F.: Ediciones Nuevo Maro y Claves Latinoamericanas, 1984).

27. Kirk, *Politics and the Catholic Church in Nicaragua,* p. 143.

28. Ibid., p. 115.

29. Selser, *Cardenal Obando,* p. 68.

30. *Carta Pastoral*, August 29, 1983.

31. Selser, *Cardenal Obando,* pp. 92-94.

32. Ibid., pp. 72-73; Kirk, *Politics and the Catholic Church in Nicaragua,* pp. 190-191.

33. Selser, *Cardenal Obando,* p. 99.

34. Williams, "The Catholic Church in the Nicaraguan Revolution," in Mainwaring and Wilde, *The Progressive Church in Latin America,* p. 96.

35. Kirk, *Politics and the Catholic Church in Nicaragua,* pp. 163-164.

36. Selser, *Cardenal Obando,* pp. 116-120.

37. *Newsweek*, June 15, 1987, pp. 27-29.

38. Selser, *Cardenal Obando,* pp. 94, 373-374.

39. Girardi, *Pueblo revolucionario, pueblo de Dios*, p. 54.
40. Kirk, *Politics and the Catholic Church in Nicaragua*, p. 180.
41. Ibid., p. 215.
42. Selser, *Cardenal Obando*, pp. 241-248.
43. Ibid., pp. 292-293.
44. Girardi, *Pueblo revolucionario, pueblo de Dios*, p. 118. On the Protestants in the revolution see Benjamín Cortes's chapter in Girardi, *Pueblo revolucionario, pueblo de Dios*, pp. 117-138.
45. Ibid., pp. 124-130.
46. Berryman, *Stubborn Hope*, p. 56.
47. Latin American Studies Association (LASA), *Electoral Democracy under International Pressure: The Report of the Latin American Studies Association Commission to Observe the 1990 Nicaraguan Election* (Pittsburgh: University of Pittsburgh Press, March 15, 1990), p. 31.
48. *Amanecer*, March-April 1990, p. 10.
49. LASA, "Electoral Democracy under International Pressure," p. 35.
50. Mulligan, *The Nicaraguan Church and the Revolution*, pp. 277-278.
51. Ibid., pp. 288-290.
52. Kirk, *Politics and the Catholic Church in Nicaragua*, p. 192.
53. LASA, *Electoral Democracy under International Pressure*, p. 16.
54. Girardi, *Pueblo revolucionario, pueblo de Dios*, p. 101.
55. Ibid., p. 110.

11   Guatemala (1954-1996)

1. Susanne Jonas, *The Battle for Guatemala: Rebels, Death Squads, and U.S. Power* (Boulder, Col.: Westview Press, 1991), p. 103.
2. Ibid., pp. 148-149; Saul Landau, *The Guerrilla Wars of Central America, Nicaragua, El Salvador and Guatemala* (New York: St. Martin's Press, 1993), p. 184.
3. David Stoll, *Is Latin America Turning Protestant?* (Berkeley and Los Angeles: University of California Press, 1990), p. 337.
4. For a more complete history of the role of the United States in the overthrow of Arbenz, see Stephen Schlesinger and Stephen Kinzer, *Bitter Fruit: The Untold Story of the American Coup in Guatemala* (Garden City, N.Y.: Doubleday and Company, 1982).
5. On the guerrilla movement see chapter 4, "Guatemala," in Landau, *The Guerrilla Wars of Central America, Nicaragua, El Salvador and Guatemala*, pp. 148-204.
6. Jonas, *The Battle for Guatemala*, p. 138.
7. Ibid., p. 41.
8. Ibid., pp. 127-128.
9. Ibid., p. 128. See also Rigoberta Menchú and Elizabeth Debray, *Me llamo Rigoberta Menchú* (Havana: Ediciones Casa de las Américas, 1983), p. 294.
10. Stoll, *Is Latin America Turning Protestant?*, p. 181.
11. Pat Robertson wrote the preface to Joseph Anfuso's work, *Efraín Ríos Montt: Servant or Dictator?* (Ventura, Calif.: Vision House, 1983).
12. Jonas, *The Battle for Guatemala*, p. 149. Landau, *The Guerrilla Wars of Central America, Nicaragua, El Salvador and Guatemala*, p. 196.
13. Ricardo Falla, *Massacres in the Jungle: Ixcán, Guatemala, 1975-1982*, trans. Julia Howland (Boulder, Col.: Westview Press, 1994).

14. Jonas, *The Battle for Guatemala,* p. 150.

15. Falla, *Massacres in the Jungle,* p. 154.

16. Ibid., pp. 80-83, 187-188; Stoll, *Is Latin America Turning Protestant?*, pp. 198-203.

17. Stoll, *Is Latin America Turning Protestant?*, pp. 207-210.

18. Jonas, *The Battle for Guatemala,* p. 165.

19. Phillip Berryman, *Stubborn Hope: Religion, Politics, and Revolution in Central America* (Maryknoll, N.Y.: Orbis Books, 1994), pp. 137-138.

20. Landau, *The Guerrilla Wars of Central America, Nicaragua, El Salvador and Guatemala,* pp. 201-202.

21. Berryman, *Stubborn Hope,* p. 143; Landau, *The Guerrilla Wars of Central America, Nicaragua, El Salvador and Guatemala,* pp. 202-203.

22. *Time,* April 10, 1995, p. 14.

23. José Luis Chea, *Guatemala: La Cruz Fragmentada* (San José, Costa Rica: DEI, 1988), p. 60.

24. Ricardo Bendaña, in CEHILA, *Historia general de la Iglesia en América Latina,* vol. 6: *América Central* (Salamanca: Ediciones Sígueme, 1985), p. 301.

25. Secretaria Status Rationarium Generale Ecclesiae, *Annuarium Statisticum Ecclesiae 1991* (Roma: Typis Polyglottis Vaticanis), pp. 110, 122-123, 183-184, 197.

26. Diocese of El Quiché, *El Quiché: el pueblo y su Iglesia, 1960-1980* (Santa Cruz del Quiché, July 1994), pp. 57-58.

27. Bendaña, in CEHILA, *Historia general de la Iglesia en América Latina,* vol. 6, p. 471.

28. Ibid., pp. 468-469; Chea, *Guatemala,* pp. 233-246. See also the testimony of Blase Bonpane, *Guerrillas of Peace: Liberation Theology and the Central American Revolution,* 2d ed. (Boston: South End Press, 1985).

29. Diocese of El Quiché, *El Quiché,* p. 79.

30. Ibid., p. 107.

31. Menchú and Debray, *Me llamo Rigoberta Menchú,* p. 113.

32. Ibid., p. 151.

33. Ibid., p. 208.

34. Ibid., p. 219.

35. Ibid., p. 361.

36. Ibid., p. 263.

37. Ibid., p. 374.

38. Ibid., p. 375.

39. Diocese of El Quiché, *El Quiché,* p. 148.

40. Luis Samandú, Hans Siebers, and Oscar Sierra, *Guatemela: retos de la Iglesia católica en una sociedad en crisis* (San José, Costa Rica: DEI, 1990), pp. 59-60.

41. Berryman, *Stubborn Hope,* pp. 109-111.

42. Diocese of El Quiché, *El Quiché,* chap. 8, "El Cierre de la diócesis del Quiché," pp. 147-158.

43. Berryman, *Stubborn Hope,* p. 113.

44. Bendaña, in CEHILA, *Historia general de la Iglesia en América Latina,* vol. 6, p. 472.

45. Diocese of El Quiché, *El Quiché,* pp. 129-130.

46. Samandú, Siebers, and Sierra, *Guatemala,* p. 44.

47. Ibid., pp. 54-55; Diocese of El Quiché, *El Quiché,* pp. 131-132.

48. Berryman, *Stubborn Hope,* pp. 122-124.

49. Ibid., p. 133.

50. Interview with Mario Martínez, member of the staff of the Office of Human Rights of the Archdiocese of Guatemala, Guatemala City, February 16, 1995.

51. *Crónica* (Guatemala), June 24, 1994, p. 27.

52. Inforpress Centroamericana, *Guatemala, 1986-1994: Compendio del proceso de paz* (Guatemala, 1995), p. 17.

53. Ibid., p. 39.

54. Ibid., pp. 267-269.

55. Ibid., p. 55.

56. Ibid., p. 99.

57. Ibid., p. 113.

58. *Crónica*, July 15, 1994, p. 29.

59. *Crónica*, April 22, 1994, p. 23.

60. *Crónica*, November 12, 1993, pp. 16-20; *Crónica*, March 18, 1994, pp. 17-20.

61. Inforpress Centroamericana, *Guatemala, 1986-1994*, p. 280.

62. *Crónica*, January 14, 1994, p. 21.

63. Assembly of Civil Society, *Documentos de consenso* (February 1995), pp. 7-8.

64. *Crónica*, September 9, 1994, pp. 24-27.

65. Assembly of Civil Society, *Documentos de consenso*, p. 6.

66. Ibid., p. 5.

67. Ibid., p. 86.

68. Inforpress Centroamericana, *Guatemala 1986-1994*, p. 244.

69. *New Catholic Reporter*, February 23, 1996, p. 4.

70. *Latinamerica Press*, April 20, 1998, p. 6.

12 Mexico

1. Peter H. Smith, *Labyrinths of Power: Political Recruitment in Twentieth Century Mexico* (Princeton, N.J.: Princeton University Press, 1979), p. 61.

2. Jesús García, "La Iglesia mexicana desde 1962," in CEHILA, *Historia general de la Iglesia en América Latina*, vol. 5: *México* (Salamanca: Ediciones Sígueme, 1984), p. 387.

3. Peter S. Cleaves, "Businessmen and Economic Policy in Mexico," *Latin American Research Review*, vol. 26:2 (1991), p. 188.

4. Ibid., p. 189.

5. Roberto Blancarte, *Historia de la Iglesia Católica en México* (México, D.F.: El Colegio Mexiquense and El Fondo de Cultura Económica, 1992), p. 74.

6. James W. Wilkie, "Statistical Indicators of the Impact of National Revolution on the Catholic Church in Mexico, 1910-1967," *Journal of Church and State,* vol. 12:1 (Winter 1970), p. 97; Jesús García, "La Iglesia mexicana desde 1962," pp. 368-369.

7. Soledad Loaeza-Lajous, "Continuity and Change in the Mexican Catholic Church," in *Church and Politics in Latin America*, ed. Dermot Keogh (New York: St. Martin's Press, 1990), p. 286.

8. Ibid.

9. Mexican Episcopal Conference, *Iglesia y educación en México* (Mexico, D.F.: Ediciones CEM, 1987), pp. 88-89; Jesús García, "La Iglesia mexicana desde 1962," p. 378.

10. Rubén Aguilar and Guillermo Zermeño, coordinators and compilers, *Religión, política y sociedad: el sinarquismo y la Iglesia en México* (Mexico, D.F.: Universidad Iberoamericana, 1992), p. 23.

11. Robert J. Alexander, *Latin American Political Parties* (New York: Praeger Publishers, 1973), pp. 50-53, 367.

12. Jesús García, "La Iglesia mexicana desde 1962," pp. 472-475.

13. Soledad Loaeza-Lajous, "Continuity and Change in the Mexican Catholic Church," p. 291.

14. Mexican Episcopal Conference, *Directorio eclesiástico de toda la República mexicana, 1991* (Mexico, D.F., 1991), pp. 36, 45.

15. Interview with Father Rubén Cabello, S.J., secretary of the Conference of Mexican Religious Institutes, March 3, 1995.

16. Enrique Luengo González, *La Religión y los jóvenes de México: ¿el desgaste de una relación?* (Mexico, D.F.: Universidad Iberoamericana, 1993), p. 99.

17. Roderic Ai Camp, "The Cross in the Polling Booth: Religion, Politics, and the Laity in Mexico," *Latin American Research Review*, vol. 29:3 (1994), p. 77.

18. Eduardo Sota García and Eduardo Luengo González, *Entre la conciencia y la obediencia: la opinión del clero sobre la política en México* (Mexico, D.F.: Universidad Iberoamericana, 1994), pp. 94-97.

19. Soledad Loaeza-Lajous, "El fin de la ambigüedad: las relaciones entre la Iglesia y el Estado en México, 1982-1989," in Luis J. Molina Piñeiro, coordinator, *La Participación política del clero en México* (Mexico, D.F.: UNAM, 1990), p. 148.

20. José Miguel Romero de Solís, *El Aguijón del espíritu Historia contemporánea de la Iglesia en México (1895-1992)* (México, D.F.: Instituto Mexicano de Doctrina Social Cristiana, 1994), pp. 479-490.

21. Luis Guzmán, "Iglesia y sociedad en la crisis de los años ochenta," in *Hacia una historia mínima de la Iglesia en México*, ed. María Alicia Puente Lutteroth (Mexico, D.F.: Editorial Jus y CEHILA, 1993), p. 222. See also Víctor Gabriel Muro, *Iglesia y movimientos sociales* (Puebla: Programa Editorial Red Nacional de Investigación Urbana DIAU-ICUAP and El Colegio de Michoacán, 1994), chaps. 3 and 4.

22. Ai Camp, "The Cross in the Polling Booth: Religion, Politics, and the Laity in Mexico," p. 86.

23. Ibid., p. 78.

24. Ramón Sánchez Medal, Gerardo López Becerra, et al., *La Presencia en México de Juan Pablo II* (Mexico, D.F.: Grupo Promoval, 1992), p. 47.

25. Ibid., p. 147.

26. Marta Eugenia García Ugarte, *La Nueva relación Iglesia-Estado en México: un análisis de la problemática actual* (Mexico, D.F.: Editorial Patria, 1993), p. 25.

27. *La Jornada*, May 4, 1990, p. 14.

28. Armando Méndez Gutiérrez, *Una ley para la libertad religiosa* (Mexico, D.F.: Editorial Diana, 1992), p. 37.

29. Ibid., p. 154.

30. Secretary of Government, *Ley de asociaciones religiosas y culto público, 1993* (Mexico, D.F.: Dirección General de Asuntos Religiosos y Dirección General de Comunicación Social, 1993), p. 4.

31. See especially the comments by Dr. Jorge Adame Goddard, "Visión histórica," in Secretariate of the Mexican Episcopal Conference, *La Iglesia católica en el nuevo marco jurídico de México* (Mexico, D.F.: Ediciones de la CEM, 1992), pp. 58-59.

32. Ibid., p. 367.

33. *Proceso* (Mexico City), January 10, 1994, p. 46.

34. Carlos Monsiváis and Elena Poniatowska, eds., *EZLN: documentos y comunicados* (Mexico, D.F.: Ediciones Era, 1994), p. 24.

35. Ibid.

36. *Proceso*, October 31, 1994, p. 21. See also *Proceso*, July 11, 1994, pp. 30-33; and Juan Santibañez de Castañón, "Los perseguidos de Chiapas," chap. 15 in Carlos Monsiváis, Roberto Blancarte, et al., *Las Iglesias evangélicas y el Estado mexicana* (Mexico, D.F.: Centro de Comunicación CUPSA, 1992), pp. 135-145.

37. *Proceso*, December 12, 1994, p. 24.

38. *Proceso*, February 28, 1994, pp. 6-11.

39. *Proceso*, February 21, 1994, p. 15.

40. *The New Yorker*, March 13, 1995, p. 42.

41. *Proceso*, February 21, 1994, p. 15.

42. Blancarte, *Historia de la Iglesia Católica en México*, p. 386.

43. Carlos Fazio, *Samuel Ruiz, El Caminante* (Mexico, D.F.: Espasa Calpe Mexicana, 1994), pp. 23-25.

44. Mexican Episcopal Conference, *Directorio eclesiástico de toda la República mexicana, 1991*, p. 38.

45. Fazio, *Samuel Ruiz, El Caminante,* p. 78.

46. Ibid., p. 103.

47. *Proceso*, February 28, 1994, p. 9.

48. Ibid., p. 10.

49. Fazio, *Samuel Ruiz, El Caminante*, pp. 168-185.

50. Ibid., p. 293.

51. *Proceso*, February 28, 1994, p. 10

52. *Proceso*, February 27, 1995, p. 25. This edition of *Proceso* contains the sixteen-page document "Diálogos de San Cristóbal," which is an eyewitness account of the meetings between the Zapatistas, Ruiz, and Camacho.

53. *Proceso*, March 14, 1994, p. 22.

54. *Proceso*, March 21, 1994, p. 36.

55. *Proceso*, July 4, 1994, pp. 18-21.

56. *Proceso*, August 15, 1994, pp. 24-31.

57. *Proceso*, February 13, 1995, p. 9.

58. Fazio, *Samuel Ruiz, El Caminante*, p. 247.

59. *Proceso*, December 13, 1994, p. 27.

60. *Reforma*, February 23, 1995, p. 4A.

61. Ibid., p. 4A.

62. *Latinamerica Press*, March 13, 1997, pp. 1, 8.

Conclusions

1. Karl Mannheim, *Ideology and Utopia* (New York: Harcourt, Brace & World, 1936), p. 198. This is a reprinted version of the 1936 English edition, translated by Louis Wirth and Edward Shills.

Bibliography

This is a bibliography on the Latin American Catholic Church in the twentieth century, with special reference to politics. The first section, which corresponds to chapter 1, includes general works. We will then present all works by countries and areas (the Caribbean), which will appear in alphabetical order. Finally, a section on Protestantism and politics is included at the end.

GENERAL WORKS

Cleary, Edward, ed. *Born of the Poor: The Latin American Church since Medellín.* Notre Dame, Ind.: University of Notre Dame Press, 1990.

——. *Crisis and Change: The Church in Latin America Today.* Maryknoll, N.Y.: Orbis Books, 1985.

Cleary, Edward, and Hannah Stewart-Gambino, eds. *Conflict and Competition: The Latin American Church in a Changing Environment.* Boulder, Col.: Lynne Rienner Publishers, 1992.

Collier, David, ed. *The New Authoritarianism in Latin America.* Princeton, N.J.: Princeton University Press, 1979.

Comblin, José. *The Church and the National Security State.* Maryknoll, N.Y.: Orbis Books, 1979.

Corradi, Juan E., Patricia Weiss Fagan, and Manuel Antonio Garretón. *Fear at the Edge: State Terror and Resistance in Latin America.* Berkeley and Los Angeles: University of California Press, 1992.

Dipboye, Carolyn Cook. "The Roman Catholic Church and the Political Struggle for Human Rights in Latin America, 1968-1980," *Journal of Church and State* (Autumn 1982): 497-524.

Dussel, Enrique, ed. *The Church in Latin America, 1492-1992.* Maryknoll, N.Y.: Orbis Books; Turnbridge Wells: Burns & Oates, 1992.

Graham, Richard, and Peter H. Smith, eds. *New Approaches to Latin American History.* Austin: University of Texas Press, 1974.

Hanson, Eric O. *The Catholic Church in World Politics.* Princeton, N.J.: Princeton University Press, 1987.

Jaquette, Jane, ed. *The Women's Movement in Latin America.* Boston: Unwin Hyman, 1989.

Keogh, Dermot, ed. *Church and Politics in Latin America.* New York: St. Martin's Press, 1990.

Lernoux, Penny. *The People of God: The Struggle for World Catholicism.* New York: Viking Penguin, 1989.

Levine, Daniel. *Popular Voices in Latin American Catholicism.* Princeton, N.J.: Princeton University Press, 1992.

————, ed. *Religion and Political Conflict in Latin America.* Chapel Hill: The University of North Carolina Press, 1986.

McGlone, Mary M. *Sharing Faith across the Hemisphere.* Maryknoll, N.Y.: Orbis Books, 1997.

Maduro, Otto. *Religion and Social Conflicts.* Maryknoll, N.Y.: Orbis Books, 1982.

Mainwaring, Scott, and Alexander Wilde, eds. *The Progressive Church in Latin America.* Notre Dame, Ind.: University of Notre Dame Press, 1989.

Malloy, James, ed. *Authoritarianism and Corporatism in Latin America.* Pittsburgh: University of Pittsburgh Press, 1977.

Mannheim, Karl. *Ideology and Utopia.* New York: Harcourt, Brace & World, 1936.

Mecham, J. Lloyd. *Church and State in Latin America.* 2d ed. Chapel Hill: The University of North Carolina Press, 1966.

Rouquié, Alain. *The Military and the State in Latin America.* Berkeley and Los Angeles: University of California Press, 1987.

Smith, Brian H. "Religion and Social Change: Classical Theories and New Formulations in the Context of Recent Developments in Latin America," *Latin American Research Review* 10:2 (Summer 1975): 3-34.

Swatos, Jr., William H., ed. *Religion and Democracy in Latin America.* New Brunswick, N.J.: Transaction Publishers, 1995.

Vallier, Ivan. *Catholicism, Social Control, and Modernization in Latin America.* Englewood Cliffs, N.J.: Prentice Hall, 1970.

Véliz, Claudio. *The Centralist Tradition of Latin America.* Princeton, N.J.: Princeton University Press, 1980.

Weber, Max. *Economy and Society.* 2 volumes. Edited by Guenther Roth and Claus Wittich. Berkeley and Los Angeles: University of California Press, 1978.

ARGENTINA

Agencia Informativa Católica. *Guía eclesiástica argentina.* Buenos Aires, 1988.

Bousquet, Jean-Pierre. *Las locas de la Plaza de Mayo.* 3d. ed. Buenos Aires: Fundación para la democracia en Argentina, 1983.

Bresci, Domingo. "Panorama de la Iglesia Católica en Argentina, 1958-1984," *Sociedad y Religión* 5 (December 1987): 66-77.

CEHILA (several authors). *500 años de cristianismo en Argentina.* Buenos Aires: Centro Nueva Tierra, 1992.

CELS (Centro de Estudios Legales). *Culpables para la sociedad: impunes por la ley.* Buenos Aires: November, 1988.

Chiesa, Carlos, and Enrique Sosa. *Iglesia y Justicialismo, 1943-1955.* Buenos Aires: Centro de Investigación y Orientación Social, 1983.

Ciancaglini, Sergio, and Martín Granovsky. *Nada más que la verdad: el juicio a las Juntas.* Buenos Aires: Editorial Planeta, 1995.

CONADEP. *Nunca más: Informe de la Comisión Nacional sobre la Desaparición de Personas.* 17th ed. Buenos Aires: EUDEP, 1992.

Conferencia Episcopal Argentina. *Caminando hacia el tercer milenio.* San Miguel, Argentina, April 27, 1996.

————. *Documentos del Episcopado Argentino, 1982-1983.* Vol. 11. Buenos Aires, 1988.

————. *Documentos del Episcopado Argentino, 1984.* Vol. 12. Buenos Aires, 1989.

————. *Evangelio, diálogo y sociedad.* Buenos Aires: Instituto Salesiano de Artes Gráficas, 1980.

————. *Iglesia y comunidad nacional.* Buenos Aires, 1990.

Dodson, Michael. "Priests and Peronismo: Radical Clergy and Argentine Politics," *Latin American Perspectives* 1:3 (Autumn 1974): 58-72.

Dri, Rubén. *La Iglesia de los pobres: para un reencuentro cristiano en Argentina.* Lima: CLADES, 1982.

————. *Teología y dominación.* Buenos Aires: Roblanco, S.R.L., 1987.

Epstein, Edward C., ed. *The New Argentine Democracy.* Westport, Conn.: Praeger, 1992.

Ezcurra, Ana María. *Iglesia y transición democrática: ofensiva del neoconservadurismo católico en América Latina.* Buenos Aires: Puntosur, 1988.

Farrell, Gerardo. *Iglesia y pueblo en Argentina.* 3d. ed. Buenos Aires: Editora Patria Grande, 1988.

Fernández, Arturo. *Sindicalismo e Iglesia (1976-1987):* Buenos Aires: Centro Editor de América Latina, 1990.

Fernández Meeijide, Graciela. "Los derechos humanos en Argentina (1976-1984)," *Cristianismo y Sociedad* 83 (1985): 43-65.

Frontalini, Daniel, and María Cristina Caiati. *El Mito de la guerra sucia.* Buenos Aires: CELS, 1984.

Garabal, Tito. *El Viaje comienza ahora: Juan Pablo II en Uruguay, Chile y la Argentina.* Buenos Aires: Ediciones Paulinas, 1987.

García de Loydi, Ludovico. *La Iglesia frente al Peronismo.* Buenos Aires, 1956.

Ghirardi, Enrique. *La Democracia Cristiana.* Buenos Aires: Centro Editor de América Latina, 1983.

Gillespie, Richard. *Soldados de Perón: los Montoneros.* Buenos Aires: Grijalbo, 1987.

Graziano, Frank. *Divine Violence: Spectacle, Psychosexuality, and Radical Christianity in the Argentine "Dirty War."* Boulder, Col.: Westview Press, 1992.

Gustafson, Lowell S. "Church and State in Argentina." In *The Religious Challenge to the State.* Edited by Matthew C. Moen and Lowell S. Gustafson. Philadelphia: Temple University Press, 1992. Pages 19-50.

Heseyne, Miguel E. *Cartas por la vida.* Buenos Aires: Centro Nueva Tierra, 1989.

Ivereigh, Austen. *Catholicism and Politics in Argentina, 1810-1960.* London: Macmillan Press; New York: St. Martin's Press, 1995.

John Paul II. *Juan Pablo II en la Argentina.* Buenos Aires: Ediciones Paulinas, 1982.

————. *Mensaje a nuestro pueblo y la Jornada Mundial de la Juventud: Juan Pablo II en la Argentina.* Buenos Aires: Ediciones Paulinas, 1987.

Kimel, Eduardo Gabriel. *La Masacre de San Patricio.* Buenos Aires: Ediciones Dialéctica, 1989.

Mallimaci, Fortunato. *El catolicismo integral en la Argentina (1930-1946).* Buenos Aires: Editorial Biblos-Fundación Simón Rodríguez, 1988.

Martín, José Pablo. "El Movimiento de Sacerdotes para el Tercer Mundo." *Nuevo Mundo: Revista de teología latinoamericana.* Buenos Aires: Ediciones Castañeda San Antonio de Padua; Ediciones Guadalupe, 1991.

Mayol, Alejandro, Norberto Habeggere, and Arturo Armada. *Los Católicos postconciliares en la dictadura en la Argentina (1963-1969).* Buenos Aires: Editorial Gaderna, 1970.

Méndez, Jesús. "Church-State Relations in Argentina in the Twentieth Century: A Case Study of the Thirty-Second International Eucharistic Congress," *Journal of Church and State* 27:2 (Spring 1985): 223-243.

Mignone, Emilio F. "The Catholic Church and the Argentine Democratic Transition." In *The New Argentine Democracy.* Edited by Edward C. Epstein (cited above). Pages 157-170.

————. *Witness to the Truth: The Complicity of Church and Dictatorship in Argentina, 1976-1983.* Maryknoll, N.Y.: Orbis Books, 1988.

Míguez Bonino, José. "Presencia y ausencia protestante en la Argentina del proceso militar, 1973-1983," *Cristianismo y Sociedad* 83 (1985): 81-85.

Mugica, Carlos. *Peronismo y cristiano.* Buenos Aires: Editorial Merlin, 1973.

Navarro, Marysa, "The Personal Is Poltical: Las Madres de Plaza de Mayo." In *Power and Popular Protest: Latin American Social Movements.* Edited by Susan Eckstein. Berkeley and Los Angeles: University of California Press, 1989. Pages 242-258.

Onrubia Rebuelta, Javier. *El Movimiento de Sacerdotes para el Tercer Mundo y el origen de la teología de la liberación argentina (1967-1976).* Madrid: Editorial Popular, 1992.

Pérez, Gaudio, and José Leopoldo. *Catolicismo y peronismo.* Buenos Aires: Ediciones Corregidor, 1985.

Rouquié, Alain. *Poder militar y sociedad política en la Argentina.* Vol. 1: Up to 1943; Vol. 2: 1943-1973. Buenos Aires: Emecé Editores, 1981.

SERPAJ (Servicio Paz y Justicia en América Latina). *Mons. Enrique Angelelli, obispo y mártir.* Buenos Aires, n.d.

Timerman, Jacobo. *Preso sin nombre, celda sin número.* New York: Random House, 1981.

Torres, Carlos Alberto. "The Catholic Church in Argentina." In *The Church, Society, and Hegemony: A Critical Sociology of Religion in Latin America.* Edited by Carlos Alberto Torres. Westport, Conn.: Praeger, 1992. Pages 117-197.

BOLIVIA

Agencia de Noticia Fides. La Paz.

Aguiló, Federico. *"Nunca más" para Bolivia.* Cochabamba: Asamblea Permanente de los Derechos Humanos de Bolivia; Instituto de Estudios Sociales y Económicos de la Universidad Mayor de San Simón, 1993.

Anonymous. *La Iglesia de Bolivia: ¿compromiso o tradición? De Medellín a Puebla. Un ensayo de análisis histórico.* La Paz, June, 1978.

Asamblea Permanente de los Derechos Humanos en Bolivia. *La Huelga de hambre.* La Paz, 1978.

————. *La Masacre de Todos los Santos.* La Paz, 1980.

Assmann, Hugo. *Teoponte, una experiencia guerrillera*. Oruro, 1971.
Barnadas, Josep. "La Iglesia boliviana (1962-1975)." In CEHILA, *Historia general de la Iglesia en América Latina*. Vol. 8: *Perú, Bolivia y Ecuador*. Salamanca: Ediciones Sígueme, 1987. Pages 447-457.
Centro de Estudios y Publicaciones. *Bolivia: 1971-1976. Pueblo, Estado, Iglesia*. Lima, 1976.
Compañía de Jesús. *En memoria de Luis Espinal, S.J.* Special number of *Diáspora*, La Paz (March-April, 1980).
Conferencia Episcopal Boliviana. *Por la senda de S.S. Juan Pablo II en Bolivia*. La Paz, 1988.
Gamucio, Mariano Baptista. *Historia contemporánea de Bolivia, 1930-1978*. In *Nueva historia de Bolivia: De Tiwanaku al siglo XX*. Edited by Enrique Finot. La Paz: Gispert & Cía, 1980.
Intipampa, Carlos. *Opresión y aculturación: la evangelización de los aymara*. La Paz: HISBOL-CEPITA-ISETRA, 1991.
Klaiber, Jeffrey. "The Catholic Church's Role as Mediator: Bolivia, 1968-1989," *Journal of Church and State* 35:2 (Spring 1993): 351-365.
Klein, Herbert. *Bolivia, the Evolution of a Multi-Ethnic Society*. New York: Oxford University Press, 1982.
Maldonado Villagrán, David. *Resumen histórico: 500 años de evangelización en Bolivia*. La Paz, 1991.
Malloy, James M., and Eduardo Gamarra. *Revolution and Reaction: Bolivia, 1964-1985*. New Brunswick, N.J.: Transaction Books, 1988.
Mitchell, Christopher. *The Legacy of Populism in Bolivia: From the MNR to Military Rule*. New York: Praeger, 1977.
Müller, Herbert, and Flavio Machicado, eds. *El Diálogo para la democracia*. La Paz: Müller y Flavio Machicado Asociados, 1987.
PADI. *Cronología de una dictadura*. Quito, 1982.
Presencia. La Paz.

BRAZIL

Adriance, Madeleine. *Opting for the Poor: Brazilian Catholicism in Transition*. Kansas City, Mo.: Sheed and Ward, n.d.
Alvarez, Sonia E. "Women's Movements and Gender Politics in the Brazilian Transition." In *The Women's Movement in Latin America*. Edited by Jane S. Jaquette (cited above under *General Works*). Pages 21-27.
Antoine, Charles. *Church and Power in Brazil*. Maryknoll, N.Y.: Orbis Books, 1973. (First edition in French, 1971.)
Archdiocese of São Paulo. *Torture in Brazil*. Translated by Jaime Wright and edited by Joan Dassin. New York: Vintage Books, 1986.
Arquidiocese de São Paulo. *Brasil: Nunca mais*. São Paulo: Editora Vozes, 1985.
Beozzo, José Oscar. *A Igreja do Brasil: De Joâo XXIII a Joâo Paulo II; de Medellín a Santo Domingo*. Petrópolis: Editora Vozes, 1993.
Boff, Leonardo. *Ecclesiogenesis: The Base Communities Reinvent the Church*. London: Collins Liturgical Publications, 1986. (First edition in Portuguese, 1977.)
Bruneau, Thomas C. *The Political Transformation of the Brazilian Church*. New York: Cambridge University Press, 1974.

————. "The Role and Response of the Catholic Church in the Redemocratization of Brazil." In *The Politics of Religion and Social Change: Religion and the Political Order.* Edited by Anson Shupe and Jeffrey K. Hadden. New York: Paragon House, 1988. Vol. 2: 87-109.

Cleary, Edward L. "The Brazilian Catholic Church and Church-State Relations: Nation-Building," *Journal of Church and State* 39:2 (Spring 1997): 253-272.

Comissão Arquidiocesana de Pastoral dos direitos humanos e marginalizados da Arquidiocese de São Paulo. *Repressão na Igreja no Brasil: reflexo de uma situaçao de opressâo*, 1968/1978.

Corradi, Juan E., Patricia Weiss Fagan, and Manuel Antonio Garretón. *Fear at the Edge: State Terror and Resistance in Latin America.* Berkeley and Los Angeles: University of California Press, 1992.

Della Cava, Ralph. "The 'People's Church,' the Vatican, and Abertura." In *Democratizing Brazil: Problems of Transition and Consolidation.* Edited by Alfred Stepan. New York: Oxford University Press, 1989. Pages 143-167.

Ireland, Rowan. *Kingdoms Come: Religion and Politics in Brazil.* Pittsburgh: University of Pittsburgh Press, 1991.

Krischke, Paulo J. *A Igreja as crises políticas no Brasil.* Petrópolis: Editora Vozes, 1979.

————. "The Role of the Church in Political Crisis: Brazil, 1964," *Journal of Church and State* 27:3 (Autumn 1985): 403-427.

Lustosa, Oscar F. *A Igreja católica no Brasil República.* São Paulo: Edições Paulinas, 1991.

————. *Igreja e política no Brasil: Do Partido Católico a L.E.C. (1874-1945).* São Paulo: Edições Loyola/CEPEHIB, 1983.

McCann, Frank. "Vargas and the Destruction of the Brazilian Integralista and Nazi Parties," *The Americas* 26 (July 1969): 15-34.

Mainwaring, Scott. *The Catholic Church and Politics in Brazil, 1916-1985.* Stanford, Calif.: Stanford University Press, 1986.

————. "Grass-Roots Catholic Groups and Politics in Brazil." In *The Progressive Church in Latin America.* Edited by Scott Mainwaring and Alexander Wilde (cited above under *General Works*). Pages 151-192.

Moreira Alves, Márcio. *A Igreja e a política no Brasil.* São Paulo: Editora Brasiliense, 1979.

Moreira Alves, María Helena. "Interclass Alliances in the Opposition to the Military in Brazil: Consequences for the Transition Period." In *Power and Popular Protest: Latin American Social Movement.* Edited by Susan Eckstein. Berkeley and Los Angeles: University of California Press, 1989. Pages 278-298.

Peritore, N. Patricki. *Socialism, Communism, and Liberation Theology in Brazil.* Athens, Ohio: Center for International Studies, Ohio University, 1990.

Pope, Clara Amanda. "Human Rights and the Catholic Church in Brazil, 1970-1983: The Pontifical Justice and Peace Commission of the São Paulo Archdiocese," *Journal of Church and State* 27:3 (Spring 1985): 429-452.

Pradini, Fernando, Víctor Petrucci, and Romeu Dale. *As relações Igreja-Estado no Brasil.* 6 volumes. São Paulo: Centro Pastoral Vergueiro; Edições Loyola, 1986-1987.

Regan, David. *Church for Liberation: A Pastoral Portrait of the Church in Brazil.* Dublin: Dominican Publications, 1987.

Ribeiro, Helcion, ed. *Paulo Evaristo Arns, Cardenal de esperança e pastor de igreja da São Paulo.* São Paulo: Edições Paulinas, 1989.

Ribeiro de Oliveira, Pedro A. *Religião e dominação de clase: Génese, estructura e função do catolicismo romanizado de Brasil.* Petrópolis: Editora Vozes, 1985.

Skidmore, Thomas. "Brazil's Slow Road to Democratization: 1974-1985." In *Democratizing Brazil: Problems of Transition and Consolidation.* Edited by Alfred Stepan (cited above under Della). Pages 5-42.

Todaro Williams, Margaret. "Church and State in Vargas's Brazil: The Politics of Cooperation," *Journal of Church and State* 18 (Autumn 1976): 443-462.

THE CARIBBEAN

Aristide, Jean-Bertrand, with Christophe Wargny. *Jean-Bertrand Aristide: An Autobiography.* Maryknoll, N.Y.: Orbis Books, 1992. (First edition in French, 1992.)

Desmangles, Leslie G. *The Face of the Gods: Vodou and Roman Catholicism in Haiti.* Chapel Hill: The University of North Carolina Press, 1992.

Fernández, J. Damián. "Revolution and Political Religion in Cuba." In *The Religious Challenge to the State.* Edited by Matthew C. Moen and Lowell S. Gustafson. Philadelphia: Temple University Press, 1992. Pages 51-71.

Gómez Treto, Raúl. *The Church and Socialism in Cuba.* Maryknoll, N.Y.: Orbis Books, 1988.

Kirk, John M. *Between God and the Party: Religion and Politics in Revolutionary Cuba.* Tampa: University of South Florida Press, 1989.

————. "(Still) Waiting for John Paul II: The Church in Cuba." In *Conflict and Competition: The Latin American Church in a Changing Environment.* Edited by Edward L. Cleary and Hannah Stewart-Gambino (cited above under *General Works*). Pages 147-165.

CHILE

Araya L., Eduardo. *Relaciones Iglesia-Estado en Chile, 1973-1981.* Santiago: Instituto Chileno de Estudios Humanísticos, 1982.

Avetikian, Tamara, ed. "Acuerdo Nacional y transición a la democracia," *Estudios Públicos* 21 (Summer 1986): 309-396.

Centro Ecuménico Diego de Medellín. *Los cristianos en el proceso chileno, 1963-1983: Encuentro de teólogos y cientistas sociales.* Santiago, 1984.

Chacón Herrera, Arturo, and Humberto Lagos Schuffeneger. *Religión y proyecto político autoritario.* Santiago: Ediciones Literatura Americana Reunida/ Programa Evangélico de Estudios Socio-Religiosos, 1986.

Conejeros, Senén. *Chile: de la dictadura a la democracia.* Santiago, 1990.

Correa, Enrique, and José Antonio Viera-Gallo. *Iglesia y dictadura.* Santiago: Ediciones Chiel y América-CESOC (Centro de Estudios Sociales), n.d.

Escobar M. Jaime. *Persecución a la Iglesia en Chile: martirologio, 1973-1986.* Santiago, 1986.

Etcheberry, Blanca, and Grace Gibson. "El Hombre del Papa en Chile." *Qué Pasa,* August 3, 1992, 12-15.

Fernández, David. *La Iglesia que resistió a Pinochet.* Madrid: IEPALA Editorial, 1996.

Fleet, Michael. "The Role of the Catholic Church in Chile's Transition to Democracy." Paper presented at the 17th Annual LASA (Latin American Studies Association) Congress, Los Angeles, 1992.

————. *The Rise and Fall of Chilean Christian Democracy.* Princeton, N.J.: Princeton University Press, 1985.

Fleet, Michael, and Brian H. Smith. *The Catholic Church and Democracy in Chile and Peru.* Notre Dame, Ind.: University of Notre Dame Press, 1997.

Garretón, Manuel Antonio. *Partidos, transición y democracia en Chile.* Santiago: FLACSO, April 1990.

Hevia, Renato. *Camino a la democracia.* Santiago: Ediciones Chile América, CESOC, 1989.

Hourton, Jorge. *Combate cristiano por la democracia, 1973-1987.* Santiago: Ediciones Chiel y América-CESOC, 1987.

Huerta, María Antonieta, and Luis Pacheco Pestens. *La Iglesia chilena y los cambios sociopolíticos.* Santiago: CISOC-Bellarmino, 1988.

Huneeus, Carlos. *Los chilenos y la política: cambio y continuidad en el autoritarismo.* Santiago, 1987.

Hurtado, Alberto. *¿Es Chile un país católico?* Santiago: Edición Splendor, 1941.

"La Iglesia chilena cambia de piel." *APSI,* July 13-16, 1992, 19-22.

Instituto Nacional de Estadísticas. *Compendio estadístico 1991.* Santiago: October 1991.

Instituto Para el Nuevo Chile. *El NO de los cristianos sin lugar.* 1988.

Lagos Schuffeneger, Humberto. *La Libertad religiosa en Chile: Los evangélicos y el gobierno militar.* 3 volumes. Santiago: Vicaría de la Solidaridad, 1978.

————. *Relaciones Iglesias evangélicas-gobierno: Chile, 1973-1976.* Santiago: ILADES (Instituto Latinoamericano de Doctrina y Estudios Sociales), 1977.

Martínez, Carlos. *Aproximación de la Iglesia con los movimientos políticos en Chile, 1973-1980.* Santiago: Instituto Chileno de Estudios Humanísticos, 1982.

Meacham, Carl E. "Changing of the Guard: New Relations between Church and State in Chile," *Journal of Church and State* 29 (Autumn 1987): 411-433.

Meneses C., Aldo. *El Poder del discurso: La Iglesia Católica chilena y el gobierno militar.* Santiago: ILADES-CISOC, 1989.

OSORE (Oficina de Sociología Religiosa de la Conferencia Episcopal de Chile). *Datos estadísticos 1991: Clero secular; congregaciones religiosas; sacramentación en Chile.* Santiago, January 1992.

"El Padre Hurtado. ¿Quién fue? ¿Qué haría hoy?" *Mensaje* (August 1989). Special edition.

Pinochet de la Barra, Oscar. *El Cardenal Silva Henríquez: luchador por la justicia.* Santiago: Editorial Salesiana, 1987.

Precht, Cristián. "Del Acuerdo a la reconciliación: la Iglesia chilena y el camino a la democracia." Paper presented at the 17th Annual LASA (Latin American Studies Association) Congress, Los Angeles, 1992.

"Recordaron Séptimo Aniversario de Firma del Acuerdo Nacional." *El Mercurio*, August 26, 1992, C3.
Rettig Guissen, Raúl (Presidente de la Comisión). *Informe de la Comisión Nacional de Verdad y Reconciliación*. 3 volumes. Santiago, 1991.
Salinas, Maximiliano. *Historia del Pueblo de Dios en Chile*. Santiago: Ediciones Rehue, 1987.
Scully, Timothy R. *Rethinking the Center: Party Politics in Nineteenth and Twentieth Century Chile*. Stanford, Calif.: Stanford University Press, 1992.
Secretario General del Episcopado de Chile. *Documentos del episcopado. Chile, 1974-1980*. Santiago: Ediciones Mundo, 1982.
———. *Documentos del episcopado. Chile, 1984-1987*. Santiago, 1988.
———. *Documentos del episcopado. Chile, 1988-1991*. Santiago, 1992.
Silva Henríquez, Raúl, with Ascanio Cavallo. *Memorias cardenal Raúl Silva Henríquez*. 3 volumes. Santiago: Ediciones Copygraph, 1991-1994.
Smith, Brian. "The Catholic Church and Politics in Chile." In *Church and Politics in Latin America*. Edited by Dermot Keogh (cited above under *General Works*). Pages 321-343.
———. *The Church and Politics in Chile*. Princeton, N.J.: Princeton University Press, 1982.
Stewart-Gambino, Hannah. "Redefining the Changes and Politics in Chile." In *Conflict and Competition: The Latin American Church in a Changing Environment*. Edited by Edward L. Cleary and Hannah Stewart-Gambino (cited above under *General Works*). Pages 21-44.
Valenzuela, Arturo, and Pamela Constable. *A Nation of Enemies: Chile under Pinochet*. New York: W. W. Norton, 1991.
Valenzuela, J. Samuel, and Arturo Valenzuela. *Military Rule in Chile: Dictatorships and Oppositions*. Baltimore: The Johns Hopkins University Press, 1986.
Varas, Augusto. *Los Militares en el poder: Régimen y gobierno militar en Chile, 1973-1986*. Santiago: FLACSO-pehuén, 1987.
Vergara, Pilar. *Auge y caída del neoliberalismo en Chile*. Santiago: FLACSO, 1985.
Vicaría de la Solidaridad. *Decimosexto aniversario, Vicaría de la Solidaridad: Discurso de S.E. el Presidente de la República don Patricio Aylwin Azócar; discurso de Monseñor Carlos Oviedo Cavada, arzobispo de Santiago*. Santiago, October 1991.
———. *Vicaría de la Solidaridad: Undécimo año de labor 1986*.
———. *Vicaría de la Solidaridad: Duodécimo año de labor 1987*.
———. *Vicaría de la Solidaridad: Decimotercer año de labor 1988*.
Yáñez, Eugenio. *La Iglesia y el gobierno militar: itinerario de una relación difícil (1973-1988)*. Santiago: Editorial Andante, 1989.

EL SALVADOR

ECA: *Estudios Centroamericanos* (Universidad Centroamericana José Simeón Cañas).
DEI: Departamento Ecuménico de Investigaciones (San José, Costa Rica).

Acevedo, Carlos. "Balance global del proceso de negociación entre el gobierno y el FMLN." *ECA* (January-February 1992): 15-53.

Bacevich, A. J., James D. Hallums, Richard H. White, and Thomas F. Young. *American Military Policy in Small Wars: The Case of El Salvador.* Washington, D.C.: Institute for Foreign Policy Analysis, 1988.

Berryman, Phillip. *The Religious Roots of Rebellion: Christians in Central American Revolutions.* Maryknoll, N.Y.: Orbis Books, 1984.

———. *Stubborn Hope: Religion, Politics, and Revolution in Central America.* Maryknoll, N.Y.: Orbis Books, 1994.

Bonner, Raymond. *Weakness and Deceit: U.S. Policy and El Salvador.* New York: New York Times Books, 1984.

Brockman, James R. *Romero: A Life.* Maryknoll, N.Y.: Orbis Books, 1989. (First edition in Spanish, 1985.)

Cáceres Prendes, Jorge. "Political Radicalization and Popular Pastoral Practices in El Salvador, 1969-1985." In *The Progressive Church in Latin America.* Edited by Scott Mainwaring and Alexander Wilde (cited above under *General Works*). Pages 103-148.

Campos, Tomás R. "Lectura política de los secuestros." *ECA* (September-October 1985): 684-700.

Cardenal, Rodolfo. *Historia de una esperanza: Vida de Rutilio Grande.* San Salvador: UCA Editores, 1985.

———. "The Martyrdom of the Salvadorean Church." In *Church and Politics in Latin America.* Edited by Dermot Keogh (cited above under *General Works*). Pages 225-246.

———. *El Poder eclesiástico en El Salvador (1871-1931).* San Salvador: UCA Editores, 1980.

Central Pastoral de la UCA. *Carta a las Iglesias desde el Salvador.* San Salvador: Servicio Informativo del Centro Pastoral de la UCA, 1981-92.

Cienfuegos, Fermán. *Veredas de audacia: Historia del FMLN.* San Salvador: Editorial Arcoiris y Corporación CIAZO, 1993.

Danner, Mark. "The Truth of El Mozote." *The New Yorker* (December 6, 1993). Pages 50-133.

Dogget, Martha. *Death Foretold: The Jesuit Murders in El Salvador.* Washington, D.C.: Lawyers Committee for Human Rights and Georgetown University Press, 1993.

Duarte, José Napoleón, and Diana Page. *Duarte: My Story.* New York: G. P. Putnam's Sons, 1986.

Ellacuría, Ignacio. *Veinte años de historia en El Salvador (1969-1989) Escritos políticos.* 3 volumes. San Salvador: UCA Editores, 1993.

El Salvador Proceso: Informativo Semanal. San Salvador: UCA/ECA.

Gettleman, Marvin, Patrick Lacefield, Louis Menashe, David Mermelstein, and Ronald Radosh, eds. *El Salvador: Central America in the New Cold War.* New York: Grove Press, 1981.

Henríquez, Pedro. *El Salvador: Iglesia profética y cambio social.* San José, Costa Rica: DEI, 1988.

Karl, Terry Lynn. "La Revolución negociada," *Revista Occidental: Estudios Latinoamericanos* 28:3 (1993): 227-292.

Landau, Saul. *The Guerrilla Wars of Central America*. New York: St. Martin's Press, 1993.

López Vallecillos, Talo. "Trayectoria y crisis del Estado salvadoreño (1918-1981)," *ECA* (June 1981): 499-528.

Martín-Baró, Ignacio. "La guerra civil en El Salvador," *ECA* (January-February 1981): 17-32.

Montgomery, Tommie Sue. "El Salvador: De la guerra civil a la 'revolución negociada,'" *Norte Sur: La Revista de las Américas* (April-May 1993): 22-25.

Noone, Judith. *The Same Fate as the Poor*. Maryknoll, N.Y.: Orbis Books, 1995.

Organización de las Naciones Unidas. *De la locura a la esperanza: La guerra de 12 años en El Salvador: Informe de la Comisión de la Verdad para El Salvador*. San Salvador and New York, 1992-93.

Paige, Jeffrey M. "Coffee and Power in El Salvador," *Latin American Research Review* 28:1 (1993): 7-40.

Richard, Pablo, and Guillermo Meléndez, eds. *La Iglesia de los pobres en América Central: Un análisis socio-político y teológico de la Iglesia centro–americana (1960-1982)*. San José, Costa Rica: DEI, 1982.

Secretariado Social Interdiocesano. *Persecución de la Iglesia en El Salvador*, 1977.

Simon, Lawrence, and James C. Stephens Jr., "Reforma agraria en El Salvador (1980-1981): su impacto en la sociedad salvadoreña," *ECA* (March 1981): 173-180.

Sobrino, Jon, et al. *Companions of Jesus: The Jesuit Martyrs of El Salvador*. Maryknoll, N.Y.: Orbis Books, 1990.

Whitfield, Teresa. *Paying the Price: Ignacio Ellacuría and the Murdered Jesuits of El Salvador*. Philadelphia: Temple University Press, 1994.

Wickham-Crowley, Timothy. *Guerrillas and Revolutions in Latin America*. Princeton, N.J.: Princeton University Press, 1993.

GUATEMALA

Adams, Richard Newbold. *Crucifixion by Power: Essays on Guatemalan National Social Structure, 1944-1966*. Austin: University of Texas Press, 1970.

Anfuso, Joseph, and David Sczepanski. *Efraín Ríos Montt: Servant or Dictator?* Ventura, Calif.: Vision House, 1983.

Arquidiócesis de Guatemala. *Directorio* 1994.

Asamblea de la Sociedad Civil. *Documentos de consenso*. Guatemala, February 1995.

Bendaña, Ricardo. "Guatemala" (several chapters). In *Historia general de la Iglesia en América Latina*. Edited by Enrique Dussel. Vol. 6: *América Central*. Salamanca: Ediciones Sígueme, 1985.

Bermúdez, Fernando. *Cristo muere y resucita en Guatemala*. México, D.F.: Casa Unida de Publicaciones, 1985.

Berryman, Phillip. *Stubborn Hope: Religion, Politics, and Revolution in Central America*. Maryknoll, N.Y.: Orbis Books, 1994.

Bonpane, Blase. *Guerrillas of Peace: Liberation Theology and the Central American Revolution*. Boston: South End Press, 1985.

Calder, Bruce. *Crecimiento y cambio de la Iglesia católica guatemalteca, 1944-1966*. Guatemala: Seminario de Integración Social Guatemalteca, 1970.

Cardenal, Rodolfo. "Radical Conservatism and the Challenge of the Gospel in Guatemala." In *Church and Politics in Latin America*. Edited by Dermot Keogh (cited above under *General Works*). Pages 205-224.

Chea, José Luis. *Guatemala: La cruz fragmentada*. San José, Costa Rica: DEI, 1989.

Diócesis del Quiché. *El Quiché: el pueblo y su Iglesia, 1960-1980*. Santa Cruz del Quiché, Guatemala, 1994.

Falla, Ricardo. *Massacres in the Jungle: Ixcán, Guatemala, 1975-1982*. Boulder, Col.: Westview Press, 1994.

Inforpress Centroamericana. *Guatemala, 1986-1994: Compendio del proceso de paz*. Guatemala: Inforpress Centroamericana, 1995.

Jonas, Susanne. *The Battle for Guatemala: Rebels, Death Squads, and U.S. Power*. Boulder, Col.: Westview Press, 1991.

Menchú, Rigoberta, and Elizabeth Burgos Debray. *Me llamo Rigoberta Menchú*. Habana, Cuba: Casa de las Américas, 1983.

Samandú, Luis, Hans Siebers, and Oscar Sierra. *Guatemala: retos de la Iglesia Católica en una sociedad en crisis*. San José, Costa Rica: DEI, 1990.

Schlesinger, Stephen, and Stephen Kinzer. *Bitter Fruit: The Untold Story of the American Coup in Guatemala*. Garden City, N.Y.: Doubleday and Company, 1982.

MEXICO

Aguilar, Rubén, and Guillermo Zermeño. *Religión, política y sociedad: el sinarquismo y la Iglesia en México*. Mexico, D.F.: Universidad Ibero-americana, 1992.

Blancarte, Roberto. *Historia de la Iglesia católica en México*. Mexico, D.F.: Fondo de Cultura Económica, 1992.

Camp, Roderic Ai. "The Cross in the Polling Booth: Religion, Politics, and the Laity in Mexico," *Latin American Research Review* 29:3 (1994): 69-100.

Conferencia del Episcopado Mexicano. *Documentos colectivos del episcopado mexicano: A diez años del Concilio Vaticano II, 1965-1975*. 2d ed. Mexico, D.F.: Comisión Episcopal de Medios de Comunicación Social, 1985.

———. *Documentos colectivos del episcopado mexicano*. Vol. 2: 1976-86. México, D.F., 1994.

———. *Iglesia y educación en México*. Mexico, D.F.: Ediciones Conferencia Episcopal Mexicana, 1987.

Fazio, Carlos. *Samuel Ruiz, El Caminante*. Mexico, D.F.: Espasa Calpe Mexicana, 1994.

García, Jesús. "La Iglesia mexicana desde 1962." In CEHILA, *Historia general de la Iglesia en América Latina*. Vol. 5: *México*. Salamanca: Ediciones Sígueme, 1984. Pages 361-493.

García de León, Antonio. *Resistencia y utopía: Memorial de agravios y crónicas de revueltas y profecías acaecidas en la Provincia de Chiapas durante los últimos quinientos años de historia.* 2 volumes. Mexico, D.F.: Ediciones ERA, 1985.

García Ugarte, Marta Eugenia. *La Nueva relación Iglesia-Estado en México. Un análisis de la problemática actual.* Mexico, D.F.: Editorial Patria, 1993.

Grayson, George, and Allan Metz. *The Church in Contemporary México.* Washington, D.C.: Center for Strategic and International Studies, 1981.

Loaeza-Lajous, Soledad. "Continuity and Change in the Mexican Catholic Church." In *Church and Politics in Latin America.* Edited by Dermot Keogh (cited above under *General Works*). Pages 272-298.

————. "El fin de la ambigüedad: las relaciones entre la Iglesia y el Estado en México, 1982-1989." In *La Participación política del clero en México.* Edited by Luis J. Molina Piñeiro. Mexico, D.F.: Universidad Nacional Autónoma de México (UNAM), 1990. Pages 145-153.

Luengo González, Enrique. *La Religión y los jóvenes de México: ¿el desgaste de una relación?* Mexico, D.F.: Universidad Iberoamericana, 1993.

Méndez Gutiérrez, Armando, ed. *Una Ley para la libertad religiosa.* Mexico, D.F.: Editorial Diana, 1992.

Metz, Allan. "Church-State Relations in Contemporary Mexico, 1968-1988." In *The Religious Challenge to the State.* Edited by Matthew C. Moen and Lowell S. Gustafson. Philadelphia: Temple University Press, 1992. Pages 102-128.

Molina Piñeiro, Luis J., ed. *La Participación política del clero en México.* Mexico, D.F.: Universidad Nacional Autónoma de México (UNAM), 1990.

Monsiváis, Carlos, Roberto Blancarte, et al. *Las Iglesias evangélicas y el Estado mexicano.* Mexico, D.F.: Centro de Comunicación Cultural CUPSA, 1992.

Monsiváis, Carlos, and Elena Poniatowska, eds. *EZLN: documentos y comunicados.* Mexico, D.F.: Ediciones Era, 1994.

Mora, Raúl. "Religión y vida en Chiapas," *Nueva Sociedad* (March-April 1995). Pages 142-155.

Muro, Víctor Gabriel. *Iglesia y movimientos sociales en México, 1972-1987: Los casos de Ciudad Juárez y el Istmo de Tehuantepec.* Mexico: Programa Editorial Red Nacional de Investigación Urbana; El Colegio de Michoacán, 1994.

Negrete, Martaelena. *Relaciones entre la Iglesia y el Estado en México, 1930-1940.* Mexico, D.F.: El Colegio de México and la Universidad Iberoamericana, 1988.

Olimón Nolasco, Manuel. *Tensiones y acercamientos. La Iglesia y el Estado en la historia del pueblo mexicano.* México, D.F.: Instituto Mexicano de Doctrina Social Cristina, 1990.

Pomerlau, Claude. "The Changing Church in Mexico and Its Challenge to the State," *The Review of Politics* 43:4 (October 1981): 540-559.

Proceso: Semanario de Información y Análisis, 1994-95.

Puente Lutteroth, María Alicia, ed. *Hacia una historia mínima de la Iglesia en México.* Mexico, D.F.: CEHILA and Editorial Jus, 1993.

Romero de Solís, José Miguel. *El Aguijón del espíritu. Historia contemporánea de la Iglesia en México (1895-1992).* Mexico, D.F.: Instituto Mexicano de Doctrina Social Cristiana, 1994.

Ruiz García, Samuel. *En esta hora de gracia*. Mexico, D.F.: Ediciones Dabar, October 1993.

Sánchez Medal, Ramón, Gerardo López Becerra, et al. *La Presencia en México de Juan Pablo II*. Mexico, D.F.: Grupo Promoval, 1992.

Schmitt, Karl. "Church and State in Mexico: A Corporatist Relationship," *The Americas* 40:3 (January 1984): 349-376.

Secretaría de Gobernación. *Ley de Asociaciones Religiosas y Culto Público 1993*. Mexico, D.F.: Dirección General de Asuntos Religiosos y Dirección General de Comunicación Social, 1993.

Secretario general de la CEM. *La Iglesia Católica en el nuevo marco jurídico de México*. Mexico, D.F.: Ediciones de la CEM (Conferencia Episcopal Mexicana), 1992.

Smith, Peter H. *Labyrinths of Power: Political Recruitment in Twentieth Century Mexico*. Princeton, N.J.: Princeton University Press, 1979.

Sota García, Eduardo, and Eduardo Luengo González. *Entre la conciencia de la obediencia: la opinión del clero sobre la política en México*. Mexico, D.F.: Universidad Iberoamericana, 1994.

Tangeman, Michael. *Mexico at the Crossroads*. Maryknoll, N.Y.: Orbis Books, 1995.

Trinidad González, José, ed. *Relaciones Iglesia-Estado en México. Sugerencias y aportaciones de la Universidad Pontificia de México*. Mexico, D.F.: Librería Parroquial de Clavería, n.d.

Vergara, Jesús. *¿Un México nuevo? Análisis de la realidad nacional*. Mexico, D.F.: Centro Tata Vasco, 1994.

———. *La Vuelta al hombre: Análisis de la realidad nacional: Año de 1992*. Mexico, D.F.: Centro Tata Vasco, 1993.

Vergara, Jesús, and Leonardo Méndez. *Democracia solidaria o caída del sistema (Análisis de la realidad nacional, 1994)*. Mexico, D.F.: Centro Tata Vasco, 1995.

Wilkie, James W. "Statistical Indicators of the Impact of National Revolution on the Catholic Church in Mexico, 1910-1967," *Journal of Church and State* 12:1 (Winter 1970): 89-106.

NICARAGUA

Amanecer: Revista del Centro Ecuménico Antonio Valdivieso.

Aragón, Rafael, and Eberhard Löschcke. *La Iglesia de los pobres en Nicaragua: historia y perspectivas*. Managua, 1991.

Arnaiz Quintana, Angel. *Historia del pueblo de Dios en Nicaragua*. Managua: Centro Ecuménico Antonio Valdivieso, 1990.

Baktiari, Bahman. "Revolution and the Church in Nicaragua and El Salvador," *Journal of Church and State* 28:1 (Winter 1986): 15-42.

Belli, Humberto. *Breaking Faith: The Sandinista Revolution and Its Impact on Freedom and Christian Faith in Nicaragua*. Westchester, Ill.: Crossway Books, 1985.

Berryman, Phillip. *The Religious Roots of Rebellion: Christians in Central American Revolutions*. Maryknoll, N.Y.: Orbis Books, 1984.

————. *Stubborn Hope: Religion, Politics, and Revolution in Central America.* Maryknoll, N.Y.: Orbis Books, 1994.

Bonpane, Blase. *Guerrillas of Peace: Liberation Theology and the Central American Revolution.* Boston: South End Press, 1985.

Bradstock, Andrew. *Saints and Sandinistas: The Catholic Church in Nicaragua and Its Response to the Revolution.* London: Epworth Press, 1987.

Crahan, Margaret E. "Religion and Politics in Revolutionary Nicaragua." In *The Progressive Church in Latin America.* Edited by Scott Mainwaring and Alexander Wilde (cited above under *General Works*). Pages 41-63.

Dodson, Michael, and Laura Nuzzi O'Shaughnessy. *Nicaragua's Other Revolution: Religious Faith and Political Struggle.* Chapel Hill: The University of North Carolina Press, 1990.

Ezcurra, Ana María. *Ideological Aggression against the Sandinista Revolution: The Political Opposition Church in Nicaragua.* New York: Circus Publications, 1984.

————. *El Vaticano y la administración Reagan: convergencias en Centro-américa.* Mexico, D.F.: Ediciones Nuevo Maro y Claves Latinoamericanas, 1984.

Foroohar, Manzar. *The Catholic Church and Social Change in Nicaragua.* Albany, N.Y.: State University of New York Press, 1989.

Girardi, Guilio. *Faith and Revolution in Nicaragua.* Maryknoll, N.Y.: Orbis Books, 1989.

————, ed. *Pueblo revolucionario, pueblo de Dios.* Managua: Centro Ecuménico Antonio Valdivieso, 1989.

González Gary, Oscar. *Iglesia católica y revolución en Nicaragua.* Mexico, D.F., 1986.

Jerez, César. *The Church and the Nicaraguan Revolution.* London: Catholic Institute for International Relations, 1984.

Kirk, John M. *Politics and the Catholic Church in Nicaragua.* Gainesville, Fla.: University of Florida Press, 1992.

Lancaster, Roger N. *Thanks to God and the Revolution.* New York: Columbia University Press, 1988.

Latin American Studies Association. *Electoral Democracy under International Pressure: The Report of the Latin American Studies Association Commission to Observe the 1990 Nicaraguan Election.* Pittsburgh: University of Pittsburgh, March 15, 1990.

Lewellen, Ted C. "Holy and Unholy Alliances: The Politics of Catholicism in Revolutionary Nicaragua," *Journal of Church and State* 31:1 (Winter 1989): 15-33.

Millet, Richard. *Guardians of the Dynasty: A History of the U.S. Created Guardia Nacional of Nicaragua and the Somoza Family.* Maryknoll, N.Y.: Orbis Books, 1977.

Mulligan, Joseph. *The Nicaraguan Church and the Revolution.* Kansas City, Mo.: Sheed and Ward, 1991.

Nuzzi O'Shaughnessy, Laura, and Luis H. Serra. *The Church and Revolution in Nicaragua.* Athens, Ohio: Ohio University Center for International Studies, 1986.

Oquist, Paul. *Dinámica socio-política de las elecciones nicaragüenses de 1990.* 2d. ed. Managua: Friedrich Ebert Stiftung, 1991.

Pochet, Rosa María, and Abelino Martínez. *Iglesia: ¿manipulación o profecía?* San Jose, Costa Rica: Editorial DEI, 1987.

Selser, Irene. *Cardenal Obando.* Mexico, D.F.: Centro de Estudios Ecuménicos, 1989.

Tulchin, Joseph S. "Nicaragua: The Limits of Intervention." In *Exporting Democracy: The United States and Latin America.* Edited by Abraham F. Lowenthal. Baltimore and London: The Johns Hopkins University Press, 1991. Pages 233-263.

Williams, Philip. "The Catholic Church in the Nicaraguan Revolution: Differing Responses and New Challanges." In *The Progressive Church in Latin America.* Edited by Scott Mainwaring and Alexander Wilde (cited above under *General Works*). Pages 64-102.

————. *The Catholic Church and Politics in Nicaragua and Costa Rica.* Pittsburgh: University of Pittsburgh Press, 1989.

PARAGUAY

CEPAG=Centro de Estudios Paraguayos Antonio Guasch

Blanch, José María. *Ko'aga Roñe'ëta (Ahora hablaremos): Misiones 1976-1978: Testimonio campesino de la represión en Misiones.* Asunción: CEPAG, 1990.

————, ed. *El Precio de la paz.* Asunción: CEPAG, 1991.

Britez, Edwin, Estéban Caballero, José Nicolás Morínigo, et al. *Paraguay: transición, diálogo y modernización política.* Asunción: El Lector, 1987.

Cano, Luis, Antonio González Dorado, Ernesto Maeder, et al. *La Evangelización en el Paraguay.* Asunción: Ediciones Loyola, 1979.

Caravias, J. L. *Liberación campesina: Ligas agrarias del Paraguay.* Madrid: Colección Lee y Discute, 1975.

Carter, Miguel. *El Papel de la Iglesia en la caída de Stroessner.* Asunción: RP Ediciones, 1991.

Chartrain, François. *L'Eglise et les partis dans la vie politique du Paraguay depuis d'independance.* Doctoral dissertation. Paris: Université de Paris, 1972.

Conferencia Episcopal Paraguaya. *Guía eclesiástica del Paraguay.* Asunción, 1989.

————. *El Proceso de transición hacia la democracia.* Asunción, 1990.

————. *Una Iglesia al servicio del hombre.* Asunción, 1973.

Durán Estragó, Margarita, ed. *Diálogo nacional.* Asunción: Biblioteca de Estudios Paraguayos; Universidad Católica, 1987.

————. *La Iglesia en el Paraguay: una historia mínima.* Asunción: RP Ediciones, 1990.

Equipo Expra. *En busca de la Tierra sin Mal.* Bogotá: Indo-American Press Service, 1982.

Galeano, Luis A. "Las Transformaciones agrarias, las luchas y los movimientos campesinos en el Paraguay," *Revista Paraguaya de Sociología* Year 28:80 (January-April 1991): 39-62.

Jacinto Flecha, Víctor. "Historia de una ausencia: notas acerca de la participación electoral en el Paraguay," *Revista Paraguaya de Sociología* Year 28:80 (January-April 1991): 63-87.

Lewis, Paul H. *Paraguay under Stroessner*. Chapel Hill: The University of North Carolina Press, 1980.
Meliá, Bartomeu. *Una nación, dos culturas*. Asunción: RP Ediciones and CEPAG, 1990.
Miranda, Carlos. *Paraguay y la era de Stroessner*. Asunción: RP Ediciones, n.d.
O'Brien, Andrea. "The Catholic Church and State Tension in Paraguay." In *Church and Politics in Latin America*. Edited by Dermot Keogh (cited above under *General Works*). Pages 344-351.
"Paraguay: la Iglesia frente a los problemas de un país en evolución." *Pro Mundi Vita* 38 (1971).
Rolón, Ismael. *No hay camino . . . ¡Camino se hace al andar! Memorias*. Asunción: Editorial Don Bosco, 1991.
Sendero. Organo de la Conferencia Episcopal Paraguaya.
Simón, José Luis, ed. *La Dictadura de Stroessner y los derechos humanos*. Asunción: Comité de Iglesias, 1990.

PERU

IEP=Instituto de Estudios Peruanos
Amnesty International. *"Caught between Two Fires": Peru Briefing*. New York, 1989.
Berg, Ronald H. "Sendero Luminoso and the Peasantry of Andahualas," *Journal of Interamerican Studies and World Affairs* 28:4 (Winter 1986-1987): 165-196.
Brown, Michael F., and Eduardo Fernández. *War of Shadows: The Struggle for Utopia in the Peruvian Amazon*. Berkeley and Los Angeles: University of California Press, 1991.
Castillo, Oscar. *Bambamarca: Vida cotidiana y seguridad pública*. Lima: IEP, documento de trabajo no. 55, 1993.
CEAS (Comisión Episcopal de Acción Social). *Evangelización y pastoral social: avances y perspectivas: Simposio por los XXV años de la Comisión Episcopal de Acción Social*. Lima, 1991.
Centro de Estudios y Publicaciones; Instituto de Pastoral Andina. *La Señal de cada momento: documentos de los obispos del Sur Andino, 1969-1994*. Lima, 1994.
Chávez de Paz, Dennis. *Juventud y terrorismo*. Lima: IEP, 1989.
(Comisión Especial del Senado). *Violencia y pacificación: Comisión Especial del Senado sobre las Causas de la Violencia y Alternativas de Pacificación en el Perú*. Lima: DESCO; Comisión Andina de Juristas, 1989.
Conferencia Episcopal Peruana. *Paz en la tierra*. Lima, December 1991.
————. *¡Perú, escoge la vida!* Lima, April 1989.
Coordinadora Nacional de Derechos Humanos. *Informe sobre la situación de los derechos humanos en el Perú en 1994*. Lima, 1995.
Degregori, Carlos Iván. "Jóvenes y campesinos ante la violencia política: Ayacucho 1980-1983." In *Poder y violencia en los Andes*. Compiled by Henrique Urbano. Cuzco: Centro de Estudios Regionales Andinos Bartolomé de las Casas, 1991. Pages 395-417.

————. *Qué difícil es ser Dios: Ideología y violencia política en Sendero Luminoso.* 2d. ed. Lima: el Zorro de Abajo Ediciones, 1990.

————. *El Surgimiento de Sendero Luminoso: Ayacucho, 1969-1979.* Lima: IEP, 1990.

————, and Romeo Grompone. *Elecciones 1990: Demonios y redentores en el Nuevo Perú.* Lima: IEP, 1991.

Espinoza, Oscar. *Rondas campesinas y nativas en la Amazonía peruana.* Lima: Centro Amazónico de Antropología y Aplicación Práctica, 1995.

Figueroa Anaya, Nelson, and Asunta Montoya Rojas. *De voces y sueños y osadías: mujeres ejemplares del Perú.* Lima: Centro de Producción y Documentación Radiofónica "El Día del Pueblo," 1995.

Fleet, Michael, and Brian H. Smith. *The Catholic Church and Democracy in Chile and Peru.* Notre Dame, Ind.: University of Notre Dame Press, 1997.

Gagnon, Mariano, and William and Marilyn Hoffer. *Warriors in Eden.* New York: William Morrow, 1993.

Gamarra, Jefrey. "Estado, modernidad y sociedad regional: Ayacucho, 1920-1940." *Apuntes* (Universidad del Pacífico) 31 (Second Semester, 1992): 103-114.

Gitlitz, John, and Telmo Rojas. "Las Rondas campesinas en Cajamarca," *Apuntes* 16 (First Semester, 1985): 115-141.

Gorriti, Gustavo. *Sendero: historia de la guerra milenaria en el Perú.* Lima: Editorial Apoyo, 1990.

————, "Terror in the Andes: The Flight of the Asháninkas." *The New York Times Magazine*, December 2, 1990, 40-45, 48, 65-72.

Hinojosa, Iván. "Entre el poder y la ilusión: Pol Pot, Sendero y las utopías campesinas," *Debate Agrario* 15 (October-December 1992): 69-93.

Idígoras, José Luis. "Religiosidad popular y marxismo popular," *Revista Teológica Limense* 10 (1976): 289-313.

Judd, Stephen. "The Emergent Andean Church: Inculturation and Liberation in Southern Peru, 1968-1986." Doctoral dissertation. Berkeley, Calif.: Graduate Theological Union, 1987.

Kirk, Robin. *The Decade of Chaqwa: Peru's Internal Refugees.* Washington, D.C.: U.S. Committee for Refugees, May 1991.

————. *Grabado en piedras: las mujeres de Sendero Luminoso.* Lima: IEP, 1993.

Klaiber, Jeffrey. *The Catholic Church in Peru, 1821-1985: A Social History.* Washington, D.C.: The Catholic University of America Press, 1992.

————. "The Church in Peru: Between Terrorism and Conservative Restraints." In *Conflict and Competition: The Latin American Church in a Changing Environment.* Edited by Edward L. Cleary and Hannah Stewart-Gambino (cited above under *General Works*). Pages 87-103.

————, ed. *Violencia y crisis de valores en el Perú.* 3d. ed. Lima: Pontificia Universidad Católica; Fundación Tinker, 1988.

McClintock, Cynthia. "Peru's Sendero Luminoso Rebellion: Origins and Trajectory." In *Power and Popular Protest: Latin American Social Movements.* Edited by Susan Eckstein. Berkeley and Los Angeles: University of California Press, 1989. Pages 61-101.

MacGregor, Felipe, and José Rouillon. *Siete ensayos sobre la violencia en el Perú.* Lima: Fundación Ebert; Asociación Peruana de Estudios e Investigaciones para la Paz, 1985.

Miloslavich Tupac, Diana. *María Elena Moyano: en busca de una esperanza.* Lima: Ediciones Flora Tristán, 1993.

Obispado de Cajamarca, Comisión Episcopal de Acción Social, and Comisión Andina de Juristas, *Primer taller nacional sobre rondas campesinas.* Lima, 1992.

Palmer, David Scott, ed. *The Shining Path of Peru.* 2d. ed. New York: St. Martin's Press, 1994.

Paredes, Tito. "Peruvian Protestant Missionaries and the Struggle for Human Rights, 1980-1993." Paper presented at the annual meeting of the American Anthropological Association. Atlanta, Georgia. November 29–December 4, 1994.

Perú, Vida y Paz. *La Paz no es ajena: cronología.* Lima, 1994.

Prelatura de Ayaviri. *Plan pastoral, Prelatura de Ayaviri, 1988.* Ayaviri, Peru: 1988.

Smith, Michael L. *Entre dos fuegos: ONG, desarrollo rural y violencia política.* Lima: IEP, 1992.

Starn, Orin, ed. *Hablan los ronderos: la búsqueda por la paz en los Andes.* Lima: IEP, documento de trabajo no. 45, 1993.

Steidel, James. "Renewal in the Latin American Church: A Study of the Peruvian Diocese of Cajamarca and Ica." Doctoral dissertation. Los Angeles: University of Southern California, 1975.

Strong, Simon. *Shining Path: The World's Deadliest Revolutionary Force.* London: HarperCollins, 1992.

URUGUAY

Achard, Diego. *La Transición en Uruguay.* Montevideo: Instituto Wilson Ferreira Aldunate, 1992.

Borrat, Héctor. *Uruguay 1973-1984: i messaggi e i silenzi.* Bologna, Italy, 1984.

Caetano, Gerardo, and José Pedro Rilla. *Vale la pena: 10 años por la paz y los DDHH.* Montevideo: Servicio Paz y Justicia, 1991.

Centro de Documentación y Biblioteca (SERPAJ). "La Defensa de los derechos humanos en la transición democrática uruguaya." *Cuadernos Paz y Justicia 4.* Montevideo: Servicio Paz y Justicia, 1988.

Conferencia Episcopal Uruguaya. *Guía de la Iglesia uruguaya 1981.*

———. *Sacerdocio y política.* Montevideo: Departamento de Opinión Pública, 1971.

Delgado, Martha. "Respuestas de las organizaciones sociales a la represión." *Cuadernos Paz y Justicia 4: la Defensa de los derechos humanos en la transición democrática uruguaya.* Montevideo: SERPAJ, 1988: 11-19.

Del Huerto Amarillo, María, and Antonio Serrentino Sabella, "El Movimiento de derechos humanos en el Uruguay." *Cuadernos Paz y Justicia 4: la Defensa de los derechos humanos en la transición democrática uruguaya.* Montevideo: SERPAJ, 1988: 20-40.

Gilbert, Daniel. "Uruguay 1971: la Iglesia en una situación prerevolucionaria." Montevideo: OBSUR (Observatorio del Sur). December 2, 1971.

Lezama, Ramón. "Una historia de prisión." Mimeographed, 30 pages. Montevideo: OBSUR.

Parteli, Carlos. "Mons. Carlos Parteli: mis memorias," *Jaque* (Montevideo) (December 1985 and January 1986).
Pérez Aguirre, Luis. *Predicaciones en la Plaza*. Montevideo, 1985.
Rama, Germán. *La Democracia en Uruguay: una perspectiva de interpretación*. Montevideo: ARCA Editorial, 1987.
Servicio Paz y Justicia (SERPAJ). *Uruguay: Nunca más*. 3d. ed. Montevideo, 1989.
Sobrado, Enrique. *La Iglesia uruguaya: entre pueblo y oligarquía*. Montevideo: Alfa Editorial, 1969.
Tribunal Permanente de los Pueblos, and SERPAJ. *Tribunal Permanente de los pueblos: Sesión uruguaya, Abril 1990*. Montevideo, 1990.
Varela, Gonzalo. *De la República liberal al estado militar: Uruguay, 1968-1973*. Montevideo: Ediciones del Nuevo Mundo, 1988.
Villegas, Juan. *Historia de la Iglesia en el Uruguay en cifras*. Montevideo: Universidad Católica del Uruguay Dámaso A. Larrañaga, 1984.
———, María Luisa Coolighan, and Juan José Arteaga. *La Iglesia en el Uruguay*. Montevideo: Instituto Teológico del Uruguay, 1978.

PROTESTANTISM

In each chapter there are references to works on Protestantism in that particular country.
Alves, Rubem. *Protestantism and Repression: A Brazilian Case Study*. Translated by John Drury. Maryknoll, N.Y.: Orbis Books, 1979.
Bastián, Jean Pierre. *Breve historia del protestantismo en América Latina*. Mexico, D.F.: Casas Unida de Publicaciones, 1986.
———, ed. *Protestantes, liberales y francmasones: sociedades de ideas y modernidad en América Latina, siglo XIX*. Mexico, D.F.: CEHILA and Fondo de Cultura Económica, 1990.
Berryman, Phillip. "Is Latin America Turning Pluralist?: Recent Writings on Religion," *Latin American Research Review* 30:2 (1995): 107-122.
Burnett, Virginia Garrand, and David Stoll. *Rethinking Protestantism in Latin America*. Philadelphia: Temple University Press, 1993.
Cleary, Edward, and Hannah Stewart-Gambino, eds. *Power, Politics, and Pentecostals in Latin America*. Boulder, Col.: Westview Press, 1997.
Diamond, Sara. *Spiritual Warfare: The Politics of the Christian Right*. Boston: South End Press, 1989.
Gutiérrez, Tomás, ed. *Protestantismo y política en América Latina y El Caribe*. Lima: CEHILA, 1996.
Kapsoli, Wilfredo. *Guerreros de la oración: las nuevas iglesias en el Perú*. Lima: SEPEC (Servicio Ecuménico de Pastoral y Estudio de la Comunicación), 1994.
Kirk, J. Andrew. *Liberation Theology: An Evangelical View from the Third World*. Atlanta: John Knox Press, 1979.
Klaiber, Jeffrey. "New Religious Phenomena in Latin America and among the Hispanics in the United States." Chapter 5.5 in Volume 1 of *Nord und Süd in Amerika: Gegensätze, Gemeinsamkeiten, Europäischer Hintergrund*. Freiburg im Breisgau: Rombach Verlag, 1992. Pages 546-559.

Lalive D'Epinay, Christian. *Haven of the Masses: A Study of the Pentecostal Movement in Chile*. London: Lutterworth, 1969.

Martin, David. *Tongues of Fire: The Explosion of Protestantism in Latin America*. Cambridge, Mass.: Basil Blackwell, 1990.

Marzal, Manuel. *Los Caminos religiosos de los inmigrantes en la Gran Lima*. Lima: Pontificia Universidad Católica, 1988.

Miller, Daniel R., ed. *Coming of Age: Protestantism in Contemporary Latin America*. Lanham, Md.: University Press of America, 1994.

Nuñez C., Emilio A., and William O. Taylor. *Crisis in Latin America: An Evangelical Perspective*. Chicago: Moody Bible Institute; Moody Press, 1989.

Padilla, Washington. *La Iglesia de los dioses modernos: Historia del protestantismo en el Ecuador*. Quito: Corporación Editora Veintemilla y 12 de Octubre, n.d.

Prien, Hans-Jürgen. *La Historia del cristianismo en América Latina*. Salamanca: Ediciones Sígueme, 1985. (First edition in German, 1978.)

Protestantismo y liberalismo en América Latina. San José, Costa Rica: DEI, 1983.

Schäfer, Heinrich. *Protestantismo y crisis social en América Central*. San José, Costa Rica: DEI, 1992.

Stoll, David. *Fishers of Men or Founders of Empire? The Wycliffe Bible Translators in Latin America*. London: Zed Press, 1982.

———. *Is Latin America Turning Protestant? The Politics of Evangelical Growth*. Berkeley and Los Angeles: University of California Press, 1990.

Willens, Emilio. *Followers of the New Faith: Culture, Change, and the Rise of Protestantism in Brazil and Chile*. Nashville, Tenn.: Vanderbilt University Press, 1967.

Index

ABC Color, 101-2
Action for National Liberation (Brazil), 28
Acuña, Víctor, 154
agrarian reform, 45, 157-58, 168-69
Alfonsín, Raúl, 66, 76, 83, 87-89
Allende, Salvador, 43, 46-48
Alesandri, Jorge, 46, 47
Almeida, Adalberto, 246
Alvarez, Gregorio, 115
Angelelli, Enrique, 77, 82-83
Aquí, 131
Aramburu, Juan Carlos, 77, 78, 81
Araujo Sales, Eugênio de, 30, 31
Arbenz, Jacobo, 216-18, 219
Arce, Mariano José de, 4
Arce Gómez, Luis, 132-33
ARENA (National Renovating Alliance), 23, 172, 185-87, 192
Argentina: anti-Semitism in, 75, 76; Catholic nationalism in, 67-70, 75; church support for military government, 66, 69-70, 75-81, 90-91; church role in human rights, 66, 72-75, 83-85, 87-91; "Dirty War," 66, 75-91; "Final Report," 87-91; guerrilla movements, 72-75; history, 66-75; Malvinas War, 87-88; *peronismo*, 70-75
Arias, Oscar, 191, 209
Arnault, Jean, 233, 234
Arns, Paulo Evaristo, 16, 20, 30-32, 35-36, 39-40
Arzú, Alvaro, 237-38
Association of Civil Society, 234-37
Asturias, Rodrigo (*See*, Llóm, Gáspar)
authority, types of, 3
Aylwin, Patricio, 48, 56, 61-65
Azcueta, Michel, 166-67

Baggio, Sebastiano, 14

Bamaca, Efraín, 222
Banzer, Hugo, 121, 126-31, 135-39
"Barbie," Klaus (Klaus Altmann), 129
Barrientos, René, 121, 123-24
Barrios de Chamorro, Violeta, 202, 213-15
Bartolomé de las Casas Center for Human Rights, 256
base ecclesial communities, 10, 36-38, 173, 197
Base Educational Movement, 22, 26
Becker Guzmán, Luis, 230, 232
Belaúnde Terry, Fernando, 143, 144, 158
Belli, Humberto, 204
Benavides Moreno, Alfredo, 188
Berryman, Phillip, 1
Bigó, Pierre, 57
Boff, Leonardo, 37, 40
Bogarín, Juan Sinforiano, 94, 95, 97, 99
Bolivia: Banzer era, 126-29; church role in democratization, 134-40; church role under military regime, 121-31; Cochabamba Valley massacre, 126; Guevara in, 124-25; Justice and Peace Commission, 127-29; miners' union, 123-24, 133-34, 136; revolution of 1952, 121-23; strikes, 129-30, 133-34, 136-38; unstable period, 130-34
Bonamín, Victorio, 77, 79
Bonpane, Blase, 224
Bordaberry, Juan María, 111-12, 114, 115
Borge, Tomás, 198-99
Branco, Castelo, 23, 26
Brazil: *Abertura*, the, 36; coup of 1964, 20, 31; guerrilla movement in, 27-30; history of, 20-25; political parties, 20-24, 38-39; role of church, 20-40, 267; strikes in, 38-39
Burnier, João Bosco Penido, 33-35

Bush administration, 171, 172, 186, 190-91

CAAAP (Amazonic Center of Anthropology and Practical Applications), 161-64
Calero, Adolfo, 207, 211
Camacho, Manuel, 257, 258
Câmara, Hélder, 20-22, 25-26, 28, 29, 254, 267
Cámpora, Héctor, 74
Carballo, Bismarck, 208, 210
Cardenal, Ernesto, 199
Cárdenas, Cuauhtémoc, 240
Cárdenas, Lázaro, 242
Cáritas, 162-63
Carter, Jimmy, 99, 100, 129, 170, 175, 213
Carter, Michael, 1
Casaldáliga, Pedro, 20, 30, 33, 34
Casanova Estrada, Ricardo, 222-23
Casariego, Mario, 223-24, 226-28
Castro, Fidel, 47, 74
catechists, 10, 255
Catholic Action, 5, 10, 21-22, 26, 37, 44-45, 68, 71, 72, 73, 94, 223-25
Catholic symbols and dictatorship, 7-8, 49
Catholic University of Asunción, 94-97
CEAS (Episcopal Commission of Social Action), 9, 150, 163, 164
CELAM (Latin American Episcopal Conference), 13, 14-15, 203, 212, 245, 255
CENAMI (National Center for Aid to Indigenous Missions), 244
CENAPI (Center for Pastoral Action among the Indians), 244
Central Intelligence Agency (CIA), 50, 216-18, 222
CEPA (Center of Education and Agrarian Promotion), 197, 199
CEPAD (Evangelical Committee for Aid to Development), 212-13
Cerezo, Vinicio, 221, 229-31
Chase Manhattan Bank, 261
Chávez y Gonzalez, Luis, 173
Chile: Allende government, 47-48; "Chicago boys," the, 48-49; church

background, 43-44; church in democratization, 45-65; Democratic Alliance, 59; history of, 42-45; National Accord, 50, 60-65; National Phalanx, 44-45; Padahuel airport incident, 54; Pinochet regime, 48-63; Socialist Party, 42, 60
Christian Agrarian Leagues, 93, 95, 97-98, 109
Christian Democratic Party: in Argentina, 70, 79; in Brazil, 22-23; in Chile, 44-47, 50, 59, 60, 63, 64, 69; in El Salvador, 179, 186; in Guatemala, 220; in Latin America, 17-18, 243; in Uruguay, 113-14
church, the, in Latin America: colonial, 3-5; defense of human rights, 8-9; and democracy, 6-19; divisions in, 15-16; as mediator, 263-70; modern, 5-7; present conditions, 11-19
"Church and National Community," 86-87
Church of Silence in Chile, The (TFP), 57
Cienfuegos, Fermán, 177, 180
CIMI (Native Missionary Council), 33, 35, 37
CLAR (Latin American Conference of Religious), 13, 14
Clark, Maura, 75
CNBB (Brazilian episcopal conference), 20-40
COB (Bolivian workers' confederation), 121, 123-24, 134-38
Colorado Party: in Paraguay 92-95, 100-103, 107-8; in Uruguay, 111, 113-14, 116
Colosio, Luis Donaldo, 258
Comblin, Joseph, 28, 57
COMIBOL (Bolivian state mining company), 124, 133-34, 136
Commission of Peace and Justice, 31
Committee of Cooperation for Peace, 51, 52, 54, 55
CONADEP (National Assembly on the Disappearance of Persons), 83, 85-86, 88-91
CONAI (National Commission of Mediation), 259-62

CONFREGUA (Guatemalan Conference of Religious), 223-24, 228, 232
conscientization, 10-11, 55, 173
Contreras, Manuel, 54
Copello, Santiago Luis, 69-70
corporatism, Catholic, 71
Corzo, Antonio, 113, 115
Corripio, Ernesto, 260, 261
Costa e Silva, Arthur da, 24, 26-27
Cristiani, Alfredo, 185, 186, 188-92
Cristeros uprising, 8, 242, 246, 247
CUC (Committee of Peasant Unity), 219, 225-26

Dammert, José, 150, 155, 162, 165
D'Aubuisson, Roberto, 172, 174, 186, 192
De León Carpio, Ramiro, 234-36
DESAL (Center for Latin American Social Development), 46
D'Escoto, Miguel, 208
Devine, Michael, 222
DINA (Directorate for National Intelligence), 51, 53-54
"Dirty War," the, 66, 75-91
disappearances, 53-54, 66, 81-82, 112, 117, 147
Dominicans in Bolivia, 122-23, 127, 128
Donovan, Jean, 175
DOPS (Department of Political and Social Order), 23, 27, 29
Duarte, Alejandro, 182
Duarte, Inés Guadalupe de, 181-82
Duarte, José Napoleón, 169-70, 172, 176, 179-80, 182-85, 191, 192, 264
Dulles brothers, the, 218

Echeverría, Luis, 241, 244-45, 247, 251
Ecuador, lack of church role in, 2
Ecumenical Movement for Human Rights, 83, 85, 269
Ellacuría, Ignacio, 187-88
El Salvador: Chapultepec peace agreement, 172, 191-92; church role as mediator, 175-92, 264-65; FMLN, 169, 174-92; history, 168-70; murder of American marines, 180-81; murder of Jesuits, 13, 172, 187-89;

negotiations in, 179-92; paramilitary groups, 169-72, 174-75, 178, 184, 186; U.N. role, 171, 172, 174, 188-92; U.S. role, 170-71, 175, 178-81
ERP (Revolutionary Army of the People), 173, 177
Espinal, Luis, 131-32
Espinoza, Pedro, 54
Esquipulas II agreements, 183-84, 201
Eucharistic Conference of 1934, Buenos Aires, 69-70
EZLN (Zapatista Army of National Liberation), 250, 252-53

Falange (See, National Phalanx)
Falla, Ricardo, 220, 233
FDR (Revolutionary Democratic Group), 169, 177-78, 180-84
FECCAS (Christian Federation of Peasants), 173-74
Figueiredo, Jackson de, 21
Figueiredo, João Baptista, 24, 35, 36, 38
FMLN (Farabundo Martí National Liberation Front), 18, 169, 174-92, 264
Ford, Ita, 175
Franceschi, Gustavo, 68, 69
Francia, José Gaspar Rodríguez de, 92, 109
Frei Montalva, Eduardo, 44, 45-47
Freire, Paulo, 10, 22, 97
Fresno, Juan Francisco, 9, 14, 17, 42, 50, 58-65, 267
Friedman, Milton, 48
FSLN (*See,* Sandinistas)
Fujimori, Alberto, 142, 144-45, 162
FUNAI (National Foundation for the Indian), 33-34
fundamentalists, Protestant: and dictators, 7; expelled from Chiapas, 252; Pinochet and, 52-53; Ríos Montt and, 7, 220-21, 225

Gagnon, Mariano, 161
García, Lucas, 216
García Meza, Luis, 121, 132-33
Geisel, Ernesto, 24, 29-30, 36
Gerardi, Juan, 235, 237-38
Giglio, Paolo, 208, 210, 215
Godoy, Virgilio, 214

González, Carlos, 63
González Garrido, José Patrocinio, 256
"Gospel and Violence" manifesto, 127
Goulart, João, 22, 23, 25, 27
Gramunt, José, 139
Guatemala: Association of Civil
    Society, 234-37, 265; CACIF
    activities, 231-32, 235-36; church
    role, 226-38; coup of 1954, 216-18;
    guerrillas in, 218-19, 229-34, 236-
    39; history, recent, 217-22; National
    Dialogue, 231-32, 235, 265; Panzós
    massacre, 219-20; persecution of
    church, 227-28; Protestants in, 217,
    220-21, 225; revolution of 1871,
    217, 222; U.N. role, 233, 234, 237;
    U.S. role, 216-19, 221-22
"Guatemala: Never Again!" 237-38
Guevara, Che, 124-25
Gurruchaga, José, 155, 156-57
Gutiérrez, Gustavo, 150
Guzmán, Abimael, 141-42, 145, 167

Handal, Shafik, 184, 186, 191
Hernández, Jerónimo, 258-59
Herzog, Wladimir, 31
Heseyne, Miguel, 83, 89
Hickey, James, 171
human rights, church centers for
    defense of, 8-9
Hurtado, Alberto, 43, 45, 65

"ideology," concept of, 269-70
"I Have Heard the Cry of My People,"
    32
Illich, Ivan, 243-44
Indians: in the Amazon, 32-35; in the
    Chaco, 105-6; in El Salvador, 168; in
    Guatemala, 216-38; in Mexico, 244,
    246, 251-62; in Nicaragua, 196, 197,
    204; in Peru, 151-62
Institutes of Rural Education, 153-54,
    156, 158-59
integralism: in Argentina, 67-70, 72-73,
    75-77, 89; in Bolivia, 128-29; in
    Brazil 21; in Chile, 46, 57; in
    Mexico, 243
Interamerican Commission on Human
    Rights, 84-85

internal wars, 1
IPAZ (peace and justice center), 153
ISAL (Church and Society in Latin
    America), 123, 125-26
Is Chile a Catholic Country? (Hurtado),
    43

Jarpa, Sergio, 59-64
Jentel, François, 33
Jesuits: assassination of, in El Salvador,
    13, 172, 187-89; in Bolivia, 123,
    139; and Christian Agrarian
    Leagues, 93, 95, 96-98; in Guate-
    mala, 225; in Mexico, 243, 245, 258-
    59; in Nicaragua, 197; in Peru, 150-
    51, 153-55, 166-67
John XXIII, 13, 45
John Paul II: role in Argentina, 86, 87;
    in Brazil, 39-40; in Chile, 62; in El
    Salvador, 215; in Guatemala, 228; in
    Latin America, 9, 13-14; in Mexico,
    245-48, 256-57; in Nicaragua, 205-
    7, 215; in Paraguay, 104-6; in Peru,
    151, 156, 162; in Uruguay, 119
"Justice in Mexico," 244
Justicialismo, 71, 74
Justo, Agustín, 68, 69

Kazel, Dorothy, 175
Kelly, Alfredo, 77
Kennedy, Edward, 61

Lacalle, Luis Alberto, 119-20
Lacayo, Antonio, 214
Laghi, Pío, 14, 77, 81
Lagos, Edith, 146, 152
Landázuri Ricketts, Juan, 150, 151, 162
Larraín, Manuel, 44-45, 254
Las Casas, Bartolomé de, 254, 269
Latin American Theological Fraternity,
    149-50
Lawyers Committee for Human Rights,
    188-89
Lechín, Juan, 121, 130-31, 135-38
legitimacy: of the church, 6, 246-49;
    church and removal of, 100-109;
    church as source of, 6-11, 25-26, 60-
    65, 197, 246-49; in South America,
    3-6; types of, 3

Leme, Sebastião, 21
Letelier, Orlando, 54
Lezama, Román, 114
Lezcano, José Antonio, 196-97
liberalism vs. Catholicism, 5
liberation theology, 15, 40, 64, 150, 154, 244
Lima, Alceu Amoroso, 21
Livieres Banks, Jorge, 102
Llóm, Gáspar, 230
Lona Reyes, Arturo, 254
López, Amando, 187
López, Carlos Antonio, 92, 94
López, Francisco Solano, 92, 94
López Portillo, José, 241, 245
López Rega, José, 74-75
López Trujillo, Alfonso, 14-15, 203-4, 206
López y López, Joaquin, 187
Lorscheider, Aloísio, 20, 30, 34-35, 39-40, 267
Lorscheiter, Ivo, 35, 39, 40
Lucas García, Romeo, 219-20
Lula da Silva, Luis Inacio, 38
Lunkenbein, Rodolfo, 33-35

MacCormack, Irene, 154
MacGrath, Marcos, 8
Mack, Myrna, 222
Madrid, Miguel de la, 241, 247
Mallea, Juan, 149
"Manifest of Eighteen Bishops of the Third World," 72
Mannheim, Karl, 269-70
Manrique, Jorge, 123, 124-26, 129-30, 132, 136
Manuel Rodriguez Patriotic Front, 59, 62
Marcos, *Subcomandante*, 253, 258-61
Mariátegui, José Carlos, 146
Maritain, Jacques, 68, 70
Martí Farabundo, Agustín, 168
Marxism, 145-47
Maryknoll, Society of: in Bolivia, 122-23; in El Salvador, 175; in Guatemala, 223, 224; in Nicaragua, 198; in Peru, 151, 153-54, 158, 159
Massacres in the Jungle (Falla), 220
Maurer, Clement, 122, 124-26, 128-30

Medellín conference 1968, 5-6, 10, 11, 13, 15, 30, 45, 150, 244, 254
mediator, church role as: in Bolivia, 122, 131, 136-40; in Brazil, 42; in El Salvador, 175-92; in Guatemala, 229-38; in Latin America, 9, 263-70; in Mexico, 240, 257-62
Médici, Emilio Garrastazú, 24, 26-27
Melton, Richard, 211
Melville, Thomas, 224
Mena Portal, Juan José, 94-96
Menchú, Rigoberta, 10, 217, 219, 225-26, 238, 257
Menchú, Victor, 226
Méndez Arceo, Sergio, 243-44, 247, 256
Mendiharat, Marcelo, 114
Menem, Carlos, 89
Mensaje, 45, 56
Mestre, Alejandro, 128, 130, 132, 134, 135, 137
Mexico: anticlerical constitution, 242-43, 246-49; church in Chiapas, 253-62; Cristeros uprising, 8, 242, 246, 247; First Indigenous Congress of 1974, 253, 255-56; history of, 239-46; Law of Religious Associations and Public Cult, 249-50; PAN Party, 240, 241, 243, 246, 249; peace talks, 257-62; PRI Party, 239-61, 268; Tlatelolco massacre, 241, 244; Vatican relations, 247-48; Zapatista uprising, 240, 250-62, 268-69
Meyer, Marshall, 86
Mignone, Emilio, 1, 80, 82
Mignone, Mónica, 82
MNR (National Revolutionary Movement), 121, 123-24
Moffit, Ronnie, 54
Monterrosa, Domingo, 180
Montoneros, the, 72-74
Monzón, Uberfil, 97
"Moral Cleansing of the Nation, The," 99-101
Morales, Mardonio, 252-53
Moreno, Ramón, 187
Mothers and Relatives of the Disappeared in Uruguay, 117, 118
mothers' clubs, 10-11, 37

Mothers of Plaza de Mayo, 66, 80-82, 84-85, 268
Moyano, Mariá Elena, 166-67
MRTA (Tupac Amaru Revolutionary Movement), 142, 160-61, 163, 167
Mugica, Carlos, 73, 74, 81
Mujica, Rosa María, 164
Mullin, Carlos, 113, 115

National Accord (Paraguay), 101-9
National Accord for the Transition to Full Democracy (Chile), 60-65, 267
nationalism: Catholic, 67-70; Christian vs. chauvinistic, 52
National Phalanx (Chile), 44-45
national security regimes, 1, 6, 23-24, 48-64, 75-91, 111-12
Natusch Bush, Alberto, 131
neo-Cristendom model, 21-22
neo-liberalism, 48-49, 269
Nevares, Jaime de, 83, 86, 89
Nicaragua: Bryan-Chamorro treaty, 194; Christian presence in revolution, 193-94, 198-201; Church/Sandinista relations, 201-13; Contras, 193, 200, 204-7, 209-12, 214-15; history, 193-95; National Commission of Reconciliation, 210-12; Sandinistas, 18, 194, 198-215; Sapoá agreements, 211-12; U.S. role, 194-95, 200, 204-5, 211-12, 215
Noriega, Manuel, 8
nuncios, papal, 14, 59, 77, 81, 208-10, 215, 260-61

OAASA (Archdiocesan Office of Social Action in Ayacucho), 153
OAB (Organization of Brazilian Lawyers), 36, 39
Obando y Bravo, Miguel, 7, 14, 16, 18, 193, 198-204, 206, 211-12, 215, 264
OCEZ (Emiliano Zapata Peasant Organization), 251-52
Onganía, Juan Carlos, 70-72
Opus Dei, 151, 153, 243, 245
Ortega, Daniel, 198, 203, 206, 210, 213-14
Ortega, Humberto, 211, 214
Ortiz, Diana, 222

Ovando, Alfredo, 121, 124
Oviedo, Carlos, 65

Pacelli, Eugenio (See, Pius XII)
Pacheco Areco, Jorge, 111
Padrón González, Joel, 256
PAN (Party of National Action), 240, 241, 243, 246, 249
papacy, the, 11-15, 245, 247-48
Paraguay: Chaco War, 92; church role in democratization, 94-109; Colorado Party, 92-95, 100-103, 107-8; concentration camps, 93, 98; history, 92-95; Itaipú power plant, 99, 100; National Accord, 101-9; processions of silence, 104, 107; Stroessner regime, 92-109
paramilitary groups, rightwing, 53-54, 73-76, 148, 169-72, 174-75, 178, 186, 262
Parteli, Carlos, 110, 113, 114, 115, 117, 119, 268
participatory spaces, 10-11
"Pastoral Message to the People of God," 35
Paul VI, 13, 115, 245
Paz, Néstor, 126
Paz Estenssoro, Víctor, 121, 123, 130-31
Paz Zamora, Jaime, 121, 136, 138-40
Peace and Hope, 149-50
Pellecer, Luis, 227
Peña, Luis Amado, 206-8, 212
Penados del Barrios, Próspero, 228-29
Pérez Aguirre, Luis, 116-18, 268
Pérez de Cuéllar, Javier, 190
Pérez Esquivel, Adolfo, 66, 83-85, 116, 208, 268
Pérez García, Alan, 144, 159, 162, 164
Periera, Antõnio Henrique, 29
Perón, Eva, 5, 70-71
Perón, Isabel, 75-76
Perón, Juan Domingo, 70-75
Peru: Ayacucho region, 147-49, 151-55; church and human rights in, 151-67; coca traffic, 160-61; history, recent, 143-46; judges "without faces," 142; Law of Repentence, 167; peasant vigilantes, 148, 155-57, 161-62;

Shining Path, 141, 145-48; terrorism in, 143-46, 161-62
"Peru: Choose Life!" 162
Peter, Marian, 224
Pinochet, Augusto, 7, 9, 42, 43, 48-65, 267
Pironio, Eduardo, 14-15, 77
Pius IX, 12
Pius X, 245
Pius XI, 12-13
Pius XII, 12-13, 69
Plaza, Antonio J., 77-78
PMBD (Party of the Brazilian Democratic Movement), 38-39
Ponce de León, Carlos, 82, 83
Popular Unity, 47-48
Porres, Martin of, 4
Precht, Cristián, 51, 55, 62
Prensa, La, 202, 204, 210
PRI (Party of the Institutionalized Revolution) 239-61, 268
priests as guerrillas, 28, 199-201, 224, 225, 227, 245
Priests for the Third World, 72-74
Prigione, Jerónimo, 248, 251, 260-61
Primatesta, Raúl, 77-79
Protestants: fundamentalist, 7, 52-53, 220-21, 225, 252; in Guatemala, 217, 220, 228; and human rights, 19, 85-86, 269; and legitimization, 7, 52-53; and Sandinistas, 212-13; and Shining Path, 148-50

Quarracino, Antonio, 77, 78, 81
Quesada Toruño, Rodolfo, 230-36, 265

Radical Civic Union Party, 67, 87
Ramos, Celina Mariceth, 187
Ramos, Julia Elba, 187
Ratzinger, Joseph, 40
Raymondi, Luigi, 244, 255
Reagan administration, 57, 100, 170-71, 178-79, 193, 200, 204-5, 211-12
"Rebirth of Chile, The," 58
"Reconciliation in Chile," 51
redemocratization, 6-11
Ríos Montt, Efraín, 7, 216-17, 219-21, 265
Rivas, Maria Agustina, 154

Rivera y Damas, Arturo, 16, 18, 168, 170, 171, 175-92, 264-65
Roderigo Franco Democratic Commando, 148
Rodríguez, Andrés, 107-8
Rolón, Ismael, 8, 16, 96-97, 100-102, 104, 106-8
Romanization, 12, 21
Romero, Oscar, 16, 168, 170, 173-75, 178, 184, 192
Rosa Chávez, Gregorio, 176, 180, 184-86
Rossell y Arellano, Mariano, 223
Rossi, Agnelo, 25, 26, 29
Ruiz, Samuel, 240, 244, 251-62, 268-69

Sábato, Ernesto, 87, 89
Salinas de Gotari, Carlos, 241, 247-48, 250, 257
Sánchez de Lozada, Gonzalo, 138
Sandinistas, the, 18, 194, 198-215, 264
Sandino, Augusto César, 195
Sanguinetti, Julio María, 116, 119
Santi, Carlos, 206, 210-11
Schmitz, Germán, 150, 162
Second Vatican Council (*See*, Vatican II)
SERPAJ (Justice and Peace Service), 84, 110, 112, 116-19, 268
Serrano Elías, Jorge, 217, 231-34
Shining Path, the: 1, 141, 266; activity in various regions, 151-67; origins, 145-46; reaction to, 147-48; and religion, 146-47
Siles Salinas, Luis Adolfo, 127
Siles Zauzo, Hernán, 121, 129-32, 134-36
Silva Henríquez, Raúl, 14, 18, 42, 50-56, 58, 65, 267
Smith, Brian, 1
Social Christianity movement, 44-45, 56
Sodano, Angel, 58
Somoza, Anastasio, 195-96
Somoza Debayle, Anastasio, 195-200
Spanish Bourbons, 4
state terrorism, 75, 87
Stroessner, Alfredo, 8, 9, 92-109, 266
Suárez, Adolfo, 247, 260
Superior Academy of National Security (Chile), 49

Swaggert, Jimmy, 52

Tacuara, the, 72
Tagle Covarrubias, Emilio, 50, 51
Talavera, Ramón, 95
Terrazas, Julio, 134, 137, 138
Theology and Liberation collection
(Editorial Vozes), 40
Theology of Liberation (Gutiérrez), 150
Third Latin American Episcopal
Conference of Puebla (1979), 57,
86-87
Timerman, Jacobo, 76, 86
Torres, Juan José, 121, 124-26
Torriceli, Robert, 222
Tortolo, Adolfo, 77, 78, 79
Torture in Brazil (Arns/Wright), 32
Tradition, Family, and Property, 25, 46,
57
Trent, Council of, 269-70
Triple A (Argentinean Anti-Communist
Alliance), 73, 75-76
Tupac Amaru, 270
Tupamaro Movement for National
Liberation, 111-12
Tutela Legal (Legal Defense), 176-77

UCA (Central American University),
187-88
UMAE (Union of Mutual Episcopal
Help), 244, 253-54
Ungo, Guillermo, 178, 186
United Fruit Company, 217-18
United Nations, 171, 187-92, 233-34, 237
URNG (National Revolutionary Union
of Guatemala), 18, 218-19, 229-34,
236-39
Uruguay: Argentine regime and, 112;
church limits, 110, 112-14; church
relation to dictatorship, 110, 114-15;

church role in democratization, 110,
115-20; civilian-military regime,
111-16; Colorado Party, 111, 113-
14, 116; guerrillas in, 111-12;
National Referendum, 118-19; Naval
Club Pact, 116; United Front, 113-14
Uruguay: Never Again (SERPAJ), 119
U.S. episcopal conference, 171
"utopia," concept of, 269-70

Vargas Llosa, Mario, 144
Vatican II, 5, 10, 13, 15, 26, 30, 78, 243,
254
Vega, Jaun Antonio de la, 106-7
Vega, Pablo, 207, 208, 210
Vekemans, Roger, 46, 57
Velasco Alvarado, Juan, 143-44
Vicariate of Pastoral Work among
Workers, 56
Vicariate of Solidarity, 19, 42, 50-51,
54-57, 58, 61, 66, 267
Videla, Jorge, 68-69, 75-76, 79-82, 87,
88
Villalobos, Joaquín, 186, 191

Walking toward the Third Millennium
(Argentine bishops), 91
Weber, Max, 3
White Warrior Union, 169, 187
Woods, William, 225
World Vision, 149, 150
Wright, James, 32

Yrigoyen, Hipólito, 67, 78

Zamora, Rubén, 178, 180, 183, 184
Zapatista uprising, 240, 250-62, 268-69
Zedillo, Ernesto, 258-60
Zelaya Santos, José, 194, 196
Zuviría, Gustavo Martínez, 69